THE HORSE

ERIC

THAT LEAPS

ENNO

THROUGH

TAMM

CLOUDS

COUNTERPOINT
BERKELEY

Copyright © 2011 by Eric Enno Tamm.
All rights reserved under International and Pan-American Copyright Conventions.

Library of Congress Cataloging-in-Publication Data

Tamm, Eric Enno.
The horse that leaps through clouds : a tale of espionage, the Silk Road,
and the rise of modern China / Eric Enno Tamm.
p. cm.
Includes bibliographical references and index.
ISBN 978-1-58243-734-7
1. China—Description and travel. 2. Silk Road—Description and travel. 3. Tamm, Eric
Enno—Travel—China. 4. Tamm, Eric Enno—Travel--Silk Road. 5. Mannerheim, Carl
Gustaf Emil, friherre, 1867-1951—Travel. 6. Spies—Russia—Biography. 7. China—
Politics and government. 8. China—Social policy. 9. Social change—China. I. Title.
DS712.T3546 2011
951'.035—dc22
2011002820

Printed in the United States of America

COUNTERPOINT
1919 Fifth Street
Berkeley, CA 94710

www.counterpointpress.com

Distributed by Publishers Group West

10 9 8 7 6 5 4 3 2 1

For Mom and Dad

CONTENTS

NORTHERN CHINA

THE HORSE THAT LEAPS THROUGH CLOUDS

NOTES

HORSETHATLEAPS.COM
An interactive multimedia website has been launched to engage readers and to complement this book, which chronicles two epic journeys, past and present, along the Silk Road—and offers a cautionary tale about the breathtaking rise of China.

From 1906 to 1908, Baron Gustaf Mannerheim, a Russian spy, trekked from St. Petersburg to Peking as part of a secret intelligence mission to gauge the growing power of China. Along the way, he sketched twenty Chinese garrison towns, took 1,370 photographs and mapped 3,087 kilometres of his route. A century later, with a sketchbook and digital SLR camera in hand, I retraced his journey, taking more than three thousand photographs.

At Horsethatleaps.com, you'll find interactive Google maps, historical photographs and slideshows for each chapter. The website also includes videos, graphs, drawings, reviews, news, events, resources and a blog where readers are welcome to post comments and discuss issues raised in the book.

You can also follow me on various social media:
Blog: horesethatleaps.com/blog
Facebook: facebook.com/horsethatleaps
Twitter: twitter.com/ericennotamm
Flickr: flickr.com/ericennotamm
YouTube: youtube.com/ericennotamm

NAMES AND SPELLINGS

Living in central Asia and China's borderlands is far more dangerous than just travelling through as a foreigner. That's especially
true if you are a pious Muslim, belong to an ethnic minority or hold
views counter to the lunatics, thugs and autocrats who rule this restive region. Accordingly, I have disguised the identities of some of
my local guides and helpers, especially those who spoke candidly
about their political views. Those identified with both a given name
and surname have not been altered.

Personal and geographical names present another challenge.
During his trek through China a century ago, Baron Gustaf Mannerheim transliterated Chinese names in his diary using Swedish
spellings, which occasionally correspond to the Wade (later Wade-
Giles) system of Romanization in use at the time. For other local
languages such as Turki, he phonetically spelled names using a mix
of French, English, Swedish, Russian and even German, creating a
mind-boggling variety of name forms. Finnish philologist Harry
Halén has deciphered this morass in an indispensable guide, *An
Analytical Index to C.G. Mannerheim's Across Asia from West to East
in 1906–1908: Places, Persons and General Terms.*

Nowadays, the pinyin system, which offers more accurate transliteration, is widely and officially used in China and throughout the
world. As a result, many spellings have changed, and some place
names have changed entirely since Mannerheim's trek. The confusion doesn't stop there: many places go by two names, one Chinese
and the other in the language of the local ethnic minority. To reduce
confusion, I have elected to use modern pinyin spellings or ethnic
minority names, such as Kashgar and Ordos, that are well established. In order to be pedantically precise, I've kept bygone spellings when directly quoting historical sources. In a few cases, I have
used Wade-Giles or Cantonese for proper names such as Tsingtao
beer or Sun Yat-sen.

PROLOGUE

Crossing the Mannerheim Line

*To know Mannerheim strengthens one's belief in mankind, for he is
in fact the* chevalier sans peur et sans reproche.—former Colonel
PAUL RODZIANKO, Imperial Russian Army (1940)[1]

O N JUNE 4, 1942, Adolf Hitler's private plane, a Focke-Wulf Fw
200 Condor, dropped out of a stormy sky on its descent to an
airstrip in Imatra, a picturesque Finnish town about two hundred kilometres from Leningrad, where Nazi troops were laying
siege to the beleaguered Soviet city. It was a rare outing for the
Reich Chancellor. He had been to Rome, had met his victorious
troops in Paris and had made inspection tours in Poland and Russia. But this visit was truly extraordinary and took everyone by surprise: the Führer was flying to Finland for a birthday party.

Baron Gustaf Mannerheim, Commander-in-Chief and Marshal of Finland, was turning seventy-five. He had written his sister insisting that any sort of celebration would be in "bad taste"
given the war casualties being suffered by Finns fighting alongside
German soldiers.[2] He planned to tour the front lines instead. But
at 8 o'clock the night before his birthday, Hitler's aide-de-camp,

General Rudolf Schmundt, called to say that the Reich Chancellor would be at Mannerheim's party the next day. And, the General politely added, he would need to be served a special diet.

Mannerheim greeted Hitler and his entourage in front of a railway dining car hidden in a forest near the airstrip. Inside, the partygoers feasted on a hastily organized luncheon of cabbage pasties, cold salmon with mayonnaise and goose stuffed with apples and baked in cream.[3] "While the rest of us enjoyed the good but simple dishes," Mannerheim later recalled, "[Hitler] ate his vegetarian meal washed down with tea and water."[4]

After birthday congratulations, Hitler said how he, "an unknown soldier from the First World War," appreciated meeting Mannerheim, a decorated First World War general and Finland's liberator. (In 1918, Mannerheim led Finland's meagre army to defeat socialist insurgents in a civil war and became founding regent of the independent republic.) Hitler then turned to current events. In a low-pitched and somewhat hoarse voice, the Reich Chancellor rambled, repeated himself and frequently paused to collect his thoughts. (Some eleven minutes of this bizarre birthday were secretly taped, the only recording of Adolf Hitler in private conversation.[5]) The war wasn't going well; his attack on Moscow had turned into a debacle. The number of Soviet tanks they had encountered, Hitler sighed, was a "surprise of a most unpleasant nature."

Mannerheim knew well the unpleasantness of Soviet might. Only a few years earlier he had become known around the world for leading Finland's defence against Soviet invasion. For 105 days during the Winter War of 1939–40, the free world held its breath— and stood idly by—as one of the world's smallest and poorest democracies defended itself against the largest and most heavily industrialized empire the Earth had ever seen. Stalin unleashed a quarter of his armed divisions against the Finns, who had no tanks, few planes and many cannons dating from the nineteenth century. "History affords few examples of a conflict so overwhelmingly one-sided," writes one historian.[6]

Finland eventually sacrificed its eastern province of Karelia but miraculously saved itself. Soviet propagandists and foreign correspondents quickly attributed Finland's success to a defensive line of concrete bunkers and ramparts made of earth and timber stretching eighty kilometres across the Karelian Isthmus. They dubbed it the Mannerheim Line. In reality, as its namesake knew, the hastily reinforced line was too old and too thin to withstand modern artillery. It was the bravery, wits and *sisu* (guts) of Finnish soldiers that held the line—and halted Communism's advance.

Mannerheim became an instant celebrity for outwitting the Red Army, although some in the West expressed unease about this "generalissimo" who could have made himself Finland's dictator but did not.[7] The Marshal certainly looked the part: he paraded around in riding boots and an impeccable uniform with a swastika embedded in an iron cross around his neck. During Finland's civil war, some of his own countrymen called him "The Butcher." One North American newspaper said he was "as pro-German as his name denotes" and had "a record for ruthless treatment of his political opponents which could only be matched by Hitler himself."[8] He was, the newspaper concluded near the end of the war, a "natural-born Fascist."[9]

Yet Mannerheim wasn't a Nazi, pro-German or even an ethnic German. His name was of Dutch ancestry and he was born a baron into a Swedish-speaking noble family in Finland. His swastika had nothing to do with Nazism either: the Finnish air force had adopted the swastika in 1918 as a lucky symbol, a popular motif at the time. Mannerheim had been decidedly anti-German throughout his military career. He fought *against* Germany in the First World War and would do the same by the end of the Second World War,[10] his secret lunch with the Führer notwithstanding. In fact, a German military attaché noted the jarring contrast between Mannerheim, "a man of the world, a tall and slender apparition, with the unaffected movements of a grand seigneur" and "Hitler, thick-set, with lively, definite movements and an imperious expression."[11]

The two seemed to have nothing in common besides fighting the Soviets. Yet the Führer and the Marshal had a mutual Swedish friend, a link that suggests at least one other shared interest.

Sven Hedin mesmerized a generation with his stories of adventure in the unknown world of Inner Asia. As a boy, Hitler had read the legendary Swedish explorer's books and befriended him later in life. In 1936, Hedin gave the opening address at the Berlin Olympics and published a book the next year with the inopportune title of *Germany and World Peace*, in which he praised Hitler for his "humanity" and "unswerving desire for peace."[12] Part Jewish, Hedin was ridiculed and ostracized for his naïveté toward the Nazis.

Hedin even secretly intervened to seek Hitler's help in defending Finland against Soviet attack in 1939. Yet at one meeting in Hitler's new Empire-style chancellery in Berlin, the Führer seemed more interested in the Oriental diet of the plucky seventy-five-year-old: "Give me the key to your secret and tell me what you do to keep so healthy and alert at your age!"

Hedin told Hitler about the dry, alpine air of Inner Asia and his Tibetan diet of "thick yellow sour milk, and also the delicious sweet milk of the yak cows."

"Yes, yoghurt, sour milk is the best of all foods," Hitler agreed, "healthy and good to eat . . . But a people that lives at such a terrific height and in such a hard, cold climate must surely eat a great deal of meat and fat?" History's most fanatical vegetarian wondered whether Tibetans were "not liable to certain diseases brought on by their constant meat diet?"

As the conversation wore on, Hedin began "to fear that the reason [Hitler] was digging his teeth so firmly into the Tibetan diet was to keep me off the subject of Finland." By the end of their meeting, Hitler had acquiesced to none of Hedin's pleas to help Finland.

An interest in Inner Asia also forged Mannerheim's lifelong friendship with Hedin. In 1906, both men were conducting clandestine expeditions into the heart of Asia. Hedin snuck into Tibet—a land forbidden to foreigners—disguised as a monk. A brilliant cartographer with an ego the size of the peaks that he scaled, the Swede mapped this uncharted world and met the Panchen Lama, the second-holiest pontiff of Tibetan Buddhism. Mannerheim was a thirty-nine-year-old colonel in the Imperial Russian army (Finland was, at the time, a grand duchy of the Russian Empire), but masqueraded as an ethnographic collector. He was on a two-year secret mission for Tsar Nicholas 11 to collect intelligence for a possible invasion of China. Mannerheim was the last Tsarist agent in the so-called Great Game, the struggle for empire between Britain and Russia in Asia.

For much of the twentieth century, little was known about Mannerheim's expedition. He published only one ethnographic paper in 1911 on two obscure nomadic tribes living on the margins of the Gobi Desert. Only a few copies of Mannerheim's Russian military intelligence report on China—marked "Not to Be Made Public" on the cover—had been distributed to select friends and scholars in Finland: it was largely unknown in the West. And, oddly, he only instigated the editing of his travel journal at the start of the Second World War—thirty years after his epic trek. When the two-volume *Across Asia from West to East* was finally published in 1940, Hedin praised it fawningly. The travelogue with maps and photographs, he told Mannerheim in a personal letter, had forever earned "its honorary position in the history of Asian discoveries."

"For hours," Hedin added, "I dug deep into the rich and extensive observations."[13]

I GREW UP on a hardy staple of war stories. "Marshal Mannerheim was a great hero," my father would often say. In 1942, as Hitler was eating asparagus soup with Mannerheim, my father was a sixteen-year-old farm boy across the Gulf of Finland in Estonia. He remembers a rousing radio speech Mannerheim once made calling on Finns and Estonians, whose language and culture are closely related, to overthrow their Soviet occupiers: "Finland shall become

great, Estonia shall become free and the Russians shall be crushed!"
For my father's generation, Mannerheim is a national hero beyond
reproach. His reputation, like an Arthurian legend, has only grown
with time. He's even been called "the last Knight of Europe."[14]

In 2000, while I was studying Nordic politics at Lund University in Sweden, a Finnish friend, Anssi Kullberg, told me about
Mannerheim's trek across Asia. We talked about one day retracing
the Marshal's footsteps. Several years later, and back in Canada, I
ordered a copy of *Across Asia* through my public library. Only five
hundred copies were originally printed in 1940, and even a 1960s
reprint is an antiquarian find today.

As a result, the book is virtually unknown among scholars.[15]
What little has been written about Mannerheim's ride along the
Silk Road, I came to realize, is largely ethnographic in nature. Yet
the most remarkable aspect of his journal—and what distinguishes
Mannerheim from most other Silk Road explorers of the time—is
the detailed military, geopolitical, economic and social observations
he made during the last years of the Qing Dynasty.

It was a heady time in the Middle Kingdom. Secret societies and
revolutionaries were provoking mass uprisings. The Imperial Court,
in response, was implementing extensive reforms to strengthen its
rule. In his intelligence report and travelogue, Mannerheim chronicles almost every facet of Chinese modernization, including reform
of the military, foreign investment, coal mining and industry, railways, education, local administration and the colonization of Muslim and Mongolian borderlands. Near the end of his trip, he even
met the exiled Thirteenth Dalai Lama, who was campaigning to
free Tibet from Peking's repressive rule.

At the turn of the nineteenth century, bookshelves were chocka-
block with titles such as *Changing China, The Awakening of China,
The New China, The Rebirth of China* and so on. Western technology
and imported consumer goods—along with radical political ideas,
democracy and Christianity—were spreading to every corner of

the Chinese Empire. The country was rapidly opening itself to the modern world after four hundred years of self-imposed isolation. Western businessmen fantasized about a market of 460 million new customers. Others saw a vast workforce. "The Chinaman fulfils in the highest degree the ideal of an intelligent human machine," wrote one American in 1899. "The people themselves may lack the initiative, but foreign capital will utilize the opportunity for flooding the markets of the world with the products of cheap Chinese labor."[16]

The Far East was rising—economically and militarily. In 1905, Japan defeated Russia in a war in Manchuria, a victory that shocked the world. In Europe and the United States, talk turned to the "Yellow Peril," a growing menace in the East. Hawkish scribes were busily writing books of their own: *The Coming Struggle in Eastern Asia, The Orient Versus the Occident* and, most ominously, *The War of the Civilisations.*

The world of a century ago seems strangely familiar.

"HISTORY DOES NOT repeat itself, but it rhymes," Mark Twain once quipped. A century after Mannerheim's trek, bookstores are being inundated with dozens of similar titles, such as *China Shakes the World, The Chinese Century, The New Asian Hemisphere, China Rising, China Wakes* and more. "China in the first decade of the twenty-first century stands on the edge of something very big, something very different from anything that has gone before," writes one author.[17] Yet the same thing was said about China at the beginning of the last century.

Is China really shaking the world, I wondered, or is the world shaking up China? Could the Communist Party truly open the country to the outside world yet keep Western ideas such as democracy and freedom at bay, as Qing officials mistakenly believed a century ago? What could reform during the late Qing Dynasty teach me about China's current breathtaking rise? "Chinese leaders began the adoption of Western arms and machines," writes historian John Fairbank about the Qing Dynasty, "only to find themselves sucked into an inexorable process in which one borrowing led to another, from machinery to technology, from science to all learning, from acceptance of new ideas to change of institutions, eventually from constitutional reform to republican revolution."[18] Could the very reforms meant to strengthen the Communist Party's grip on power be their undoing?

These questions gnawed at me. And the answers were nowhere to be found in recent books or newspaper stories with hyperbolic headlines warning about a ravenous industrial dragon gobbling up the world's resources and markets.

History, carefully studied, does have much to teach us. Nobody knows this better than the Chinese. Their scholars, writes historian Margaret MacMillan in *The Uses and Abuses of History,* frame history not as a linear process but in terms of "dynastic cycles," where dynasties come and go "in an unending repetition, following the unchanging pattern of birth, maturity, and death, all under the aegis of heaven."[19] Could Mannerheim's century-old journal, I began to wonder, be a cautionary tale about China's breathtaking rise today? "Study the past if you would divine the future," to quote a popular Confucius aphorism.[20]

And so, on the centennial of his expedition, I set out in the footsteps of Baron Mannerheim. Armed with his travel diary and maps, a notebook, sketch pad and camera, I boarded a train at the Helsinki railway station one brilliant summer's morning. Finland marked, Mannerheim believed, "one of the farthest outposts of Western civilization."[21] Beyond Finland, beyond one of the most democratic, prosperous, open societies in the world, beyond the shattered remnants of the Mannerheim Line, lies Eurasia, a vast continent ruled by a bizarre patchwork of oil-soaked autocrats, one outlandishly ruthless crackpot and the world's last major Communist regime and rising superpower. Before me stood a gauntlet of political and geographic extremes, including some of the world's hottest deserts, highest mountain ranges and cruellest dictatorships. My overland route—much of it tracing the famed Silk Road—stretched seventeen thousand kilometres to Beijing.

It was a vast region I knew virtually nothing about. Reading Mannerheim's journal only piqued my curiosity. His descriptions of sweeping oceans of broiling sand, velvety alpine pastures dotted with yurts and buried Buddhist ruins seemed fantastical. Many of the ethnic groups he encountered sounded like alien beings from episodes of *Star Trek:* Abdal, Torgut, Yugur, Shiksho, Pakhpo, Dolan, Xibo. Had these mysterious races living in China's outer reaches survived to the twenty-first century?

One of Mannerheim's photographs, in particular, captivated me. It shows a "zigzag path" winding through a treacherous alpine pass dusted with fresh snow. His small horse caravan was attempting to cross the Tian Shan range, or "Heavenly Mountains," in winter. The soaring massif separates China from Central Asia. A charcoal-coloured crag loomed in front of him, its top shrouded in clouds. Somewhere, beyond those clouds, I hoped to find the answers to my questions.

However, before even departing my hometown of Vancouver— a hotbed of refugees and ex-patriots from the People's Republic— the Chinese consulate, through its network of spies and informants, caught wind of my plans to venture into China's restive and rugged borderlands. I was repeatedly denied a visa. Trekking through China would be trickier than I imagined. Like Mannerheim, I would need a cover.

EURASIA

---◆---

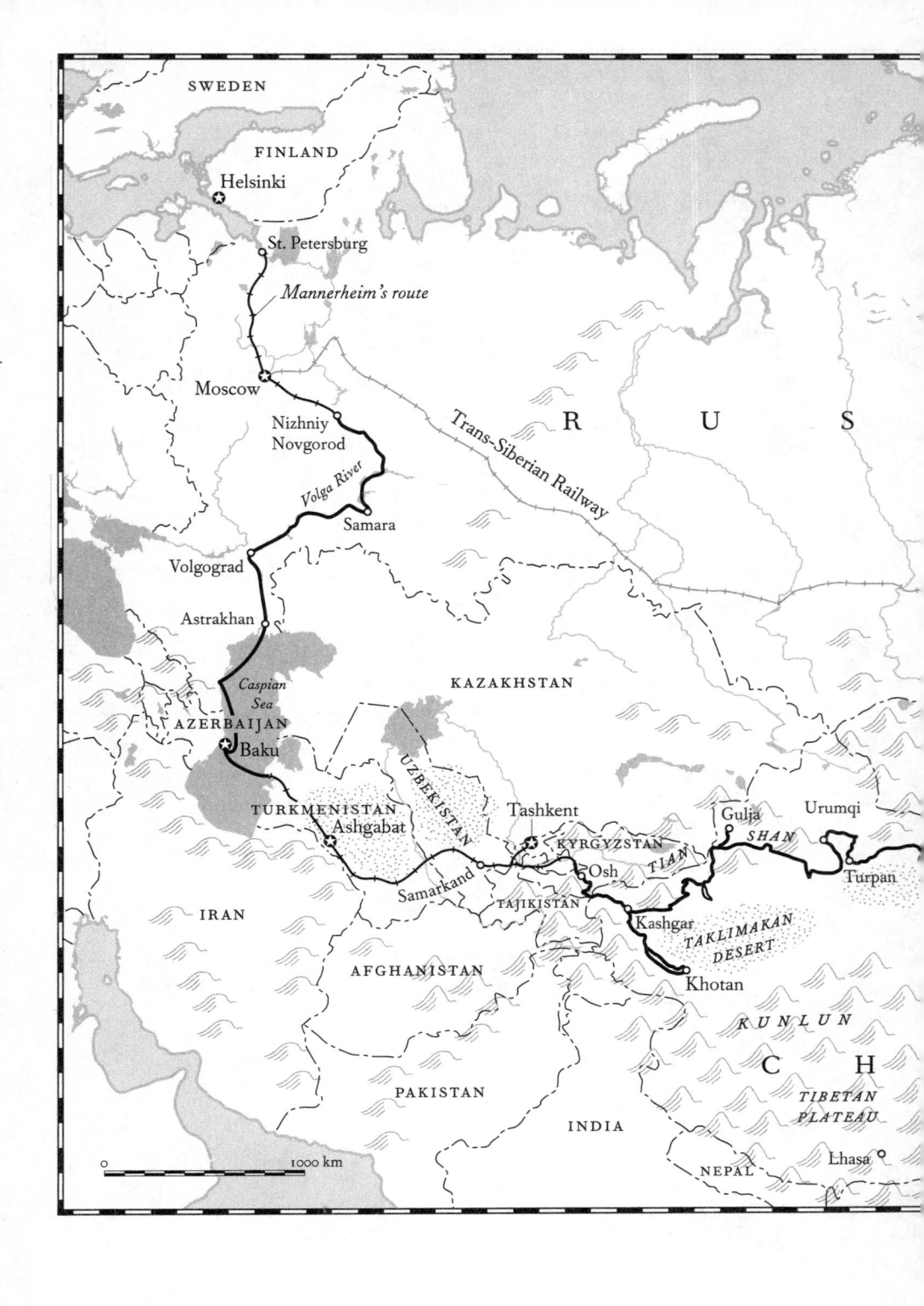

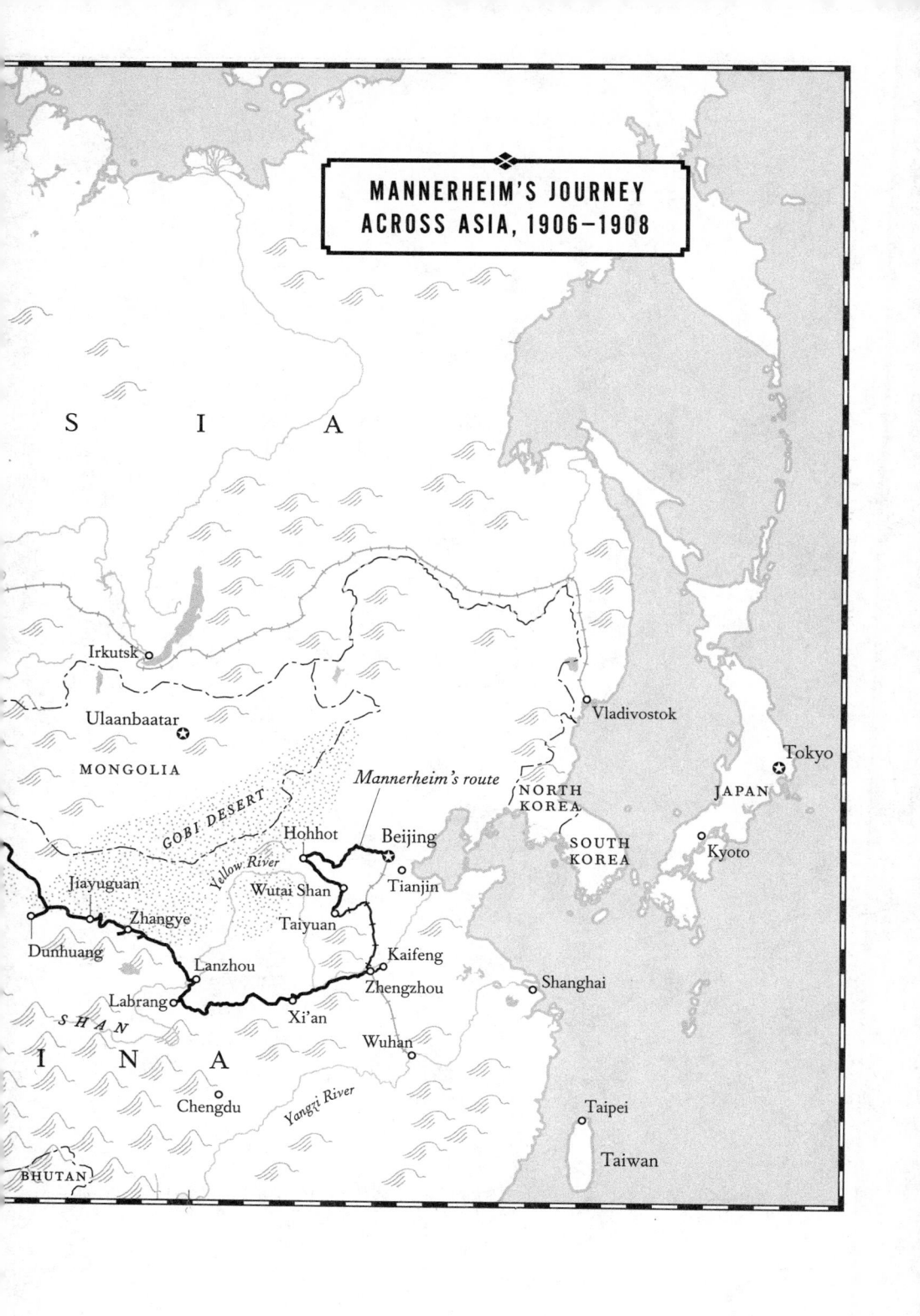

MANNERHEIM'S JOURNEY
ACROSS ASIA, 1906–1908

S   I   A

Irkutsk

Ulaanbaatar

MONGOLIA

GOBI DESERT

Hohhot   Beijing   *Mannerheim's route*   NORTH
                                                         KOREA
Yellow River   Wutai Shan   Tianjin
Jiayuguan   SOUTH
                Taiyuan   KOREA
Zhangye
Dunhuang   Lanzhou   Kaifeng
                                Zhengzhou   Shanghai
Labrang   Xi'an
SHAN   Wuhan
I   N   A

Chengdu   Yangzi River

BHUTAN

Vladivostok

Tokyo

JAPAN

Kyoto

Taipei

Taiwan

ST. PETERSBURG

The Secret Agent

*So delicate and so secretive is espionage that there is nowhere
you cannot put it to good use.*—SUN TZU, *The Art of War*

IN THE SPRING of 1906, Joseph Conrad began writing *The Secret
Agent*. The darkly comedic novel describes the menace of fanaticism in the world and a terrorist bombing in London. In the
novel, Conrad captures the angst of the turn of the century—a time,
it seems, very much like our own. "But what is one to say to an act
of destructive ferocity so absurd as to be incomprehensible, inexpli-
cable, almost unthinkable; in fact, mad?" Conrad asks.[1]

A rash of bombings and assassinations—"propaganda by deed"
was the newly minted phrase—was terrifying the real world.[2] In
Russia alone, terrorists shot to death or blew to bits thousands of
government officials in 1906.[3] The terrorism soon spread, grip-
ping the entire world. By 1913, four kings, six prime ministers,
three presidents and dozens of diplomats and politicians had been
assassinated.[4]

St. Petersburg was, in one respect, modern terrorism's hometown. In 1862, a young Swedish inventor named Alfred Nobel,
whose father was a well-known armaments manufacturer in Russia,

detonated an underwater explosion using nitro-glycerine in a canal near his family's St. Petersburg factory. Two years later, he invented dynamite. Relatively safe and easy to use, dynamite levelled the playing field in more ways than one: its destructive ferocity could blow apart royal carriages and palaces and create widespread hysteria thanks to new mass-market newspapers and the telegraph. In one shockingly destructive act, a lone fanatic could create mass terror.

Narodnaya Volya, a Russian terrorist group, did just that. In 1881, members detonated a bomb inside the Winter Palace, and the next year a grenade blew the legs off Alexander II, ending his enlightened reign. Faced with spiralling violence, reactionary authorities became brutally repressive toward dissident workers, students and the intelligentsia, who called for social and economic reforms. Soon even Liberals willingly financed and blessed terrorism.[5] It all culminated in a general strike and attempted revolution in October 1905.

That autumn, returning from the Russo-Japanese War in Manchuria, Baron Gustaf Mannerheim, an officer in the fifty-second Nezhinskii Dragoon Regiment, found St. Petersburg "charged with fear and dissension."[6] Only thirty-eight, he had recently been promoted to colonel for his battlefield valour and looked forward to a promising commission. Early the following March, he was summoned to the General Staff Building in St. Petersburg. It is a colossal neoclassical structure crowned by the "Chariot of Victory" statue. A central archway links the building's two curved wings of snow-white colonnades and gilt balustrades. Inside to greet him was General Fyodor Fyodorovich Palitsyn, Chief of the General Staff, who asked if he'd be willing to return to Asia to undertake a secret intelligence mission.

Russia's humiliating defeat at the hands of the Japanese in 1905 exposed serious intelligence failures in the Imperial army at every level: tactical, operational and strategic.[7] Russia had woefully underestimated its rival. Palitsyn created independent intelligence sections and directed his attention to Asia's "young, warlike, energetic powers, thirsting for action and conquest."[8] Japan's modernization and growing military strength had proven deadly for Russia. Now, Palitsyn began worrying about China's rise.

For close to a century, Russia and Britain had been locked in the so-called Great Game, the struggle for empire in the East. In its thirst for trade and territories, Russia pushed her armies through the steppes of Central Asia, reaching the Pamir Mountains bordering India in the 1890s. The British were petrified at the idea of a Russian invasion of their crown colony, though Russia—badly defeated by Japan and weakened by internal rebellion—could not realistically afford a showdown against Britain there.

China, however, was another matter. The Middle Kingdom had badly atrophied under the Manchus, the ruling ethnic caste of the Qing Dynasty. Two-and-a-half centuries of decadent living, internecine feuds and imperviousness to a changing world had weakened the Empire. China's weaponry and military tactics were outdated, even medieval. Modern factories, steel bridges, railways and telegraphs were almost nonexistent in most regions. Natural disasters, famine and internal rebellions had further enfeebled China. In the late nineteenth century, Japan and the Great Powers easily carved out trade and territorial concessions. These were humiliating submissions for the once all-powerful Manchus.

Still, the central lesson of the war with Japan was not lost on the Russian General Staff: an Asian country using Western technology and industrial production methods could defeat a great European power. Palitsyn knew a reformed China with modern railways and armaments factories could become dangerously strong. Indeed, emboldened by Japan's example, China began implementing sweeping reforms of its own. Yet he also realized that China's territory bordering Russian Turkestan was militarily weak. Its most western province of Xinjiang, or "New Dominion," was rife with Muslim unrest and thus vulnerable to Russian conquest. The Great Game was shifting eastward and the General needed accurate, on-the-ground intelligence. Specifically, the objectives for this secret mission would be to:

> collect information and military-statistical material, especially on the Chinese provinces beyond the Great Wall;
> establish to what extent recent reforms by the Chinese government could be observed in different regions;
> investigate defensive preparations, military reforms and troop training;
> study the rate of ethnic Chinese colonization of the provinces and reforms of local government implemented by Peking;
> assess general conditions and local attitudes toward Chinese policies, the political movements in regions or in local tribes toward self-government, the role of the Dalai Lama in such movements, local opinion concerning Russia and Japan as well as the scope of Japanese influence in all activities undertaken by the Chinese government; and
> survey the route to Kashgar, and from there to Lanzhou and Peking, primarily to establish whether Russian cavalry and separate military units could be sent to Lanzhou.[9]

The epic two-year assignment caught Mannerheim off guard. "It was, however, not so easy to decide, almost on the spur of the moment, to leave civilization for so long just after I had returned from a war full of hardships," he wrote.[10] He asked for time to consider the offer.

I CAUGHT THE *Sibelius Express* at the Helsinki Station on a warm summer morning. The train lumbered through birch and pine forests then crossed the Finnish border into another world. The ruins of the Mannerheim Line lie hidden in the Karelian forests about a hundred kilometres inside the Russian frontier. The border region is a netherworld of corruption, gangster capitalism, alcoholism, dire poverty and post-Soviet industrial decline. The train passed through impoverished towns of peeling paint, dilapidated clapboard dachas and rustic Orthodox churches. Karelia is the kind of place where ruby-cheeked babushkas sell salted fish and unpasteurized cow's milk in reused pop bottles, while younger women sell themselves. "When Finns came there sixty years ago they said 'Hands up!' to the Russians," a Finnish friend told me. "Now when Finns come to Karelia they say 'Legs up!'" Abandoned roadside checkpoints and watchtowers reminded me of "the cruelest despotism the world has ever known," as Mannerheim described.[11]

After five hours, the verdure and poverty of the Russian countryside gave way to the suburban blight of modern St. Petersburg: massive power plants, smokestacks, transmission towers, idle factories, oil terminals and prefab concrete blocks. I stepped off the train at Ladozhsky Station into the muggy air of the Neva River delta. Alexey Shkvarov, a retired navy captain, greeted me with a cautious handshake and no smile.

"A gift," I said, handing him a bottle of Marskin Ryyppy, or "The Marshal's Drink," a famous schnapps sold in Finland. The recipe consists of aquavit spiced with gin and vermouth. It was a favourite of Marshal Mannerheim and a perfect gift, I figured, for a Russian sailor.

"I don't drink," he said bluntly.

The Finnish Institute of St. Petersburg had put me in contact with Shkvarov to guide me around the city. Shkvarov, age forty-six, had a trimmed salt-and-pepper beard and neatly parted hair. His casual attire—loafers, polo shirt and Moschino sunglasses—belied an earnest, at times severe, demeanour. He grew up in St. Petersburg and served twenty-one years as a naval engineer before going into business. He now owned a construction company, newspaper, restaurant, TV studio, small museum and publishing house—a modest tycoon of the New Russia. In his spare time, he was completing a master's degree in history at St. Petersburg State University. "It was my childhood dream," he told me. His research topic was Mannerheim's service in the Russian Imperial army.

"Mannerheim was Russian for fifty-one years, almost his whole life," Shkvarov said, smoking a Marlboro and weaving his shiny black Nissan suv through St. Petersburg's chaotic traffic. "His time in the Russian army explains much about his later life, but Finns don't like to talk about it."

"Russians don't like to talk about it either," I interjected. "Mannerheim was persona non grata in St. Petersburg for most of the twentieth century. He was vilified. The Communists called him a fascist, 'The Butcher.'"

"It was part of our history," Shkvarov intoned pensively. "Part of our tragedy."

We crossed the Alexander Nevsky Bridge into downtown. Shkvarov pointed to a statue of the bridge's namesake, boasting how the Russian prince crushed the Swedes on this very spot in 1240. A beautiful monastery now stands in his honour. The boulevard, broad and commanding, also bears his name. "Few of the world's capitals," Mannerheim once wrote, "possess such a fine thoroughfare as the Nevskij Prospekt."[12] I then spotted, on our left, Moskovsky Station, where travellers catch trains to the Russian capital. "I don't like Moscow," Shkvarov said. "It's full of money and criminals. St. Petersburg is the imperial and military capital."

Peter the Great never liked Moscow either. In 1703, he turned his back on ancient Moscovy with its superstitious boyars and medieval traditions. He founded St. Petersburg as Russia's "window to the West." Raising a modern European metropolis from the fever-ridden marshland of the Neva River would be proof of Russia's modernization. The Tsar brought in architects from continental Europe to build its boulevards and bridges, embankments and edifices. By the end of Catherine the Great's reign, the city's architecture oozed the power and glory of ancient Rome. Shkvarov pointed out the city library housed in a neoclassical palace, Anichkov Bridge with its stone arches and galloping bronze horses and the Kazan Cathedral inspired by St. Peter's Basilica in Rome. At the end of the thoroughfare, in the dazzling sunlight, I saw the Admiralty. Its gilded steeple and weather vane punctuated the naval headquarters like an exclamation point.

We hung a right on Bolshaya Morskaya Street. It had been a tony address in Mannerheim's day. Fine restaurants, palaces, banks and the Fabergé goldsmith shop once lined the prestigious street.[13] Now, an inexpensive hostel occupies one of its neoclassical townhouses; chipped yellow paint and crumbling stucco blight its exterior. After checking in, we walked a block toward the General Staff Building. Its central archway over Bolshaya Morskaya frames a magnificent view: the baby blue Baroque facade of the Winter Palace and towering Alexander I column made of pink Finnish granite. We were standing at the heart of an empire. I took out my camera. Shkvarov grinned approvingly.

From here, we began a two-day tour of Mannerheim's St. Petersburg. On Lermontovsky Prospekt, a ten-minute drive from the hostel, we stopped at our first historic site. Shkvarov parked in a leafy square fronting an elegant U-shaped building recently painted custard yellow. "This is the former home of the Nicholas Cavalry School," Shkvarov said. The building, which still belongs to the Russian army, was the first place where Mannerheim lived and studied in St. Petersburg. Shkvarov dug out a black leather briefcase from the back of the SUV and produced a 680-page tome, written in Russian. He'd spent years researching and writing *Lieutenant-General Mannerheim: Born for Imperial Service*.

Carl Gustaf Emil Mannerheim was born on June 4, 1867, to Count Carl Robert Mannerheim and his wife, Hélène (née Hedvig von Julin), at Louhisaari Manor. It was one of the finest nobleman's estates in Western Finland. One of seven children, Gustaf grew up in a cosmopolitan household, speaking Swedish (his native language), French, German, English and a little Finnish. He was a rambunctious child. "I have a lot of cause to worry about Gustaf whose unruly and wild nature just won't change," his mother once complained.

In 1880, his father, a liberal-minded *bon vivant,* went bankrupt and sold the manor to pay off his gambling debts. Abandoning his family, the Count escaped to Paris with his mistress. Hélène fell painfully ill and died of a heart attack the next year. Albert von Julin, an uncle, took responsibility for Gustaf. The youngster enrolled in the Finnish Cadet Corps, a boarding school in Hamina on the opposite side of the country. But the young Baron detested the provincial atmosphere of the small town. "I look forward with joy to the moment when I can turn my back on Finland for ever and go my own way," he wrote to his sister Sophie.[14] One evening he took "French leave," sneaking off to stay at a friend's in the countryside. He was caught and expelled immediately.

His family worried about the restive youth, who now wanted to enrol in the Nicholas Cavalry School in St. Petersburg. At the time, the Tsar—pressed by Russian nationalists—was becoming increasingly repressive toward Finnish culture and the grand duchy's autonomous status. Mannerheim's family frowned on Imperial service. But the allure of St. Petersburg, a grand European metropolis, was too great. Mannerheim enrolled as a *junker,* or officer cadet. He was twenty years old.

The Nicholas Cavalry School "had the worst reputation in Russia," Shkvarov said. The older *junkers* notoriously picked on younger classmates, he explained. One cadet remembered how "hot-headed Gustaf was always ready to dash into a fight." He once slashed the head of a classmate and nearly cut off his ear in a sword fight.[15] But the unruly Finn matured over his two years, learned to control his temper and graduated near the top of his class. "Long before he commanded a regiment Gustaf Mannerheim learnt to command himself," the cadet remembered.[16]

From the school building, we sped down cobblestone canal streets, past the onion-shaped domes of the Church of Our Saviour on Spilled Blood, along Mars Field and the embankment to another custard-coloured neoclassical building. This one had stately columns and was a military engineering college. Shkvarov attended this school for five years. A century ago, he explained, it was the barracks of the Chevalier Guards, a crack regiment assigned to the Tsar's Court and Winter Palace. Uncle Albert wanted his nephew Gustaf to join "a cheap regiment and make your way up by hard work and diligent studies."[17] But Mannerheim had a different view: "I have neither influence nor means. A Guards uniform is therefore especially important."[18]

Shkvarov pointed to Mannerheim's first apartment across the street and then took me next door to the Marshal Hotel. It was named after Marshal Mannerheim and housed a curious exhibit. The walls were plastered with cut-and-paste displays of photographs and text depicting Mannerheim's entire life. Leonid Vlasov, a self-professed "professor" (his academic credentials are still unclear to me), mounted the exhibition. He has authored several books in Russian on Mannerheim. This retrospective seemed based on Vlasov's racy *Women in the Life of Mannerheim,* a book Shkvarov helped to publish. Most biographies are oddly—perhaps suspiciously—mute on the Baron's love life. But according to Shkvarov, Mannerheim was a ruthless womanizer who used women for "his pleasure or his career." By all accounts, he was strappingly handsome. Standing six foot four, well proportioned and in full regalia, he was nicknamed "the Knight."[19] "Many pairs of eyes brightened if he appeared in the drawing-rooms of St. Petersburg," recalled one fellow officer. Mannerheim dated princesses, actresses and ballerinas. Some of them, Shkvarov said, accused him of having "pieces of Finnish ice in his heart."

In 1892, Mannerheim, appointed to the Chevalier Guards, married Anastasia Arapova, the daughter of a Russian general and former Chevalier Guard himself. He had died some years earlier, leaving her a considerable fortune. It's been said that she was not particularly attractive, suggesting Mannerheim married for money and status. Whatever the case, it didn't last: Anastasia moved to France with their two daughters in 1902, effectively ending the marriage.

"Vlasov likes the private life of Mannerheim, but the private life of such a man is very dark," conceded Shkvarov, eyeing the portraits. "Who really knows about the relationships with all these women?"

We ate lunch in the hotel's Café Marshal. I ordered pike-perch à la Mannerheim, a favourite of its namesake still served in some Helsinki restaurants. The fish is baked in an omelette shell with royal shrimp and white wine sauce. Carving into a pork cutlet, Shkvarov expounded on the key factor, as he saw it, that had made Russia into a vast empire and Great Power. "For the whole of our history, one thousand years, we lived with a Tsar," he said. "If we have Putin until the end of his life, it will be better than having changes. We don't live with laws, but with the orders of the Tsar."

"Most European countries successfully transitioned from monarchies to democracies. Why can't Russia?" I asked.

"We need a Tsar," Shkvarov repeated. "Russia is different from all European countries. We need a strong hand. The years of democracy have been a nightmare." Russia, he explained, only needs three things to regain its strength and stature as a Great Power: "the Tsar, love of the Motherland and Orthodoxy."

As he described his formula for Russia's revival, I couldn't help thinking how utterly at odds his views are with those of his countrymen a century ago. Back then, an oil boom in Russia was spurring industrialization. It produced enormous wealth but left most workers in a squalid state. Half a million people lived in overcrowded slums festering with alcoholism, untreated sewage and disease. (In his first year in St. Petersburg, Mannerheim caught typhoid and a gastric malady.) Trade unions were outlawed, which drove workers into the revolutionary underground.[20] On January 22, 1905, Imperial troops slaughtered thousands during a peaceful protest. In the streets, people began chanting, "There is no Tsar!" Bloody Sunday ushered in a nightmarish year: the Grand Duke was assassinated, Russia was defeated in Manchuria and revolution broke out all over the empire.²¹ On October 17, Tsar Nicholas 11 was forced to sign a manifesto granting civil liberties and the election of a Duma to stave off revolution. It appeared Russia was on the path to democratic reform. Yet for Shkvarov, this was the beginning of "The Tragedy." He saw democracy as bringing only chaos and decline to Russia—then and now.

"Look at the past, step into the future" is the motto of Shkvarov's publishing company, Russian Military Encyclopaedia. Its mission is to revive the belief in Russia's "unshakable force and power." He publishes military histories, biographies of famed commanders and historical novels. All reflect his longing for the past and for tsardom. His interest in imperial glory wasn't restricted to historical revisionism, but included reconstruction too. He wanted to physically restore the past. He had already constructed or rebuilt four Orthodox churches and chapels around St. Petersburg. After lunch, he took me forty kilometres west of the city, through a leafy suburb of Imperial summer palaces, to a quaint building set on a forested lot.

It was built in 1891 and had formerly been the bathhouse of the Volynskiy Infantry Regiment. Shkvarov had recently renovated it into a restaurant and small military museum of curios he had collected. Shkvarov had plans to turn the weedy back lot into a hotel, pond and war monument. His fledgling military-themed resort is called Volynskiy Outpost.

We sat at a comfortable corner table in the empty restaurant elegantly styled after a nineteenth-century officers' club, adorned with oil paintings and historical maps. Shkvarov motioned for music—a military waltz—to be played. A waiter set marinated mushrooms and pickled herring on the table, followed by borscht and lamb kebabs on large iron skewers. Shkvarov insisted on ordering vodka for me. A few shots emboldened me to challenge Shkvarov's absurd notion that a Tsar could make Russia strong again. It had proven disastrous in the past, I pointed out. Nicholas 11, by all accounts, was an imbecile: petty-minded, reactionary, distrustful, militarily incompetent. "And let's not forget the mad monk Rasputin who hijacked the palace court," I insisted. Under his reign, in the words of one historian, Russia became "an autocracy without an autocrat."[22]

Shkvarov dragged on a Marlboro, mulling over a response. "He was a family man," he said. "He was a kind Tsar. He wasn't interested in politics; that was his struggle." On the wall behind him hung a touching portrait of the Tsar and his young son Aleksey, a peachy cheeked but sickly hemophiliac whom Rasputin claimed he could heal. Somewhat defensively, Shkvarov then added: "Mannerheim wanted to restore the monarchy in Russia." The Baron was indeed deeply loyal to Nicholas II. At his coronation, Mannerheim had the honour of being the Tsar's personal bodyguard. He even kept an autographed photograph of Nicholas II in his home, now a museum, in Helsinki. When surprised visitors would ask about it, Mannerheim would simply say: "He was my Emperor."[23] Yet Mannerheim, like Shkvarov, seemed blind to the outlandishly inept ruler who actually stymied the very reforms that could have modernized—and stabilized—Russian society.

"What about democracy?" I asked. "Don't you think democracy could now help stabilize Russia?"

"If we'll have democracy, we'll have a revolution," Shkvarov said. "We can't live without a strong hand."

The phrase "strong hand" (or *silnaya ruka*) has become a common refrain in Russia since the end of the boozy Boris Yeltsin years. Many Russians hail Putin as the "stabilizer" who restored order and prestige to Russia. He jailed dissident oligarchs, muzzled the independent media, rigged elections, harassed opposition parties and dissidents. The Kremlin effectively nationalized the petroleum industry and is aggressively reasserting itself in Central Asia in an attempt to control oil and gas flows—the prize in the New Great Game. Under Putin's presidency, Russia became a democracy without a democrat. Shkvarov welcomed this change.

Shkvarov's New Russia was beginning to look a lot like the old one. Now, however, Russia's rulers are no longer recruited from the blue-blooded aristocracy, but rather the cold-blooded secret police. Putin rose through the ranks of the KGB and its successor, the Federal Security Bureau, or FSB. By the end of his first term as President, former KGB agents made up a quarter of senior government officials.[24] Shkvarov, who has friends in the FSB, also welcomed this new elite.

"The KGB has very clever men in its organization," he said. "Most of them are the real patriots of Russia."

THE STATE HERMITAGE has one of the world's largest and oldest collections of art and cultural artefacts. It is housed in six buildings, the largest being the former Winter Palace. At a back door along the embankment, I navigated through metal detectors and past several security guards into the museum's stately sanctum. Anna Galakhova, a blond, middle-aged press officer, greeted me. We sat on dark antique furniture in a long, plush corridor outside the museum director's office.

"Mannerheim is a very difficult figure for Russia," she said in halting English. "Not everyone sees him in a positive way." One publication, she said, criticized the Hermitage for doing an exhibit on a man whom many war veterans think is a fascist.

"But he was also a great Imperial officer," I offered.

"He was a very beautiful man," she gushed, placing her hand over her breast, "and he loved women."

The Hermitage's exhibition, held in the Imperial Guards Museum the previous year, had showcased some four hundred items including the famous photograph of Mannerheim guarding Nicholas II at his coronation, his Chevalier Guards sword, personal letters, a notebook from the Russo-Japanese War, and artefacts and photographs from his Asia expedition. It also included Soviet propaganda describing Mannerheim as a "blood drunkard," "The Executioner" and Hitler's "humble servant."[25]

At the appointed time, I stepped through massive oak doors into a grandiose office with double-height ceilings. Huge eighteenth-century tapestries of idyllic country life adorned the red walls. An oil painting of Catherine the Great, who dubbed her personal art collection her "hermitage," hung on the wall. Just below it was a desk heaped a half-metre high with papers, books and various knick-knacks.

Barricaded behind this mountainous jumble sat Mikhail B. Piotrovsky, director of The Hermitage and heir to a curatorial dynasty. His father was an eminent archaeologist and the museum's director from 1964 to 1990. Like a prince, he had grown up in the Winter Palace and succeeded his father as director in 1992. Piotrovsky is an intense, quick-witted man with wavy grey hair and glasses.

"Why would the museum mount an exhibit about a man who is so controversial in Russia?" I asked. "He led an army that killed a quarter-million Russian soldiers."

"Everything is a controversy in Russia," Piotrovsky said dismissively. One of the priorities of The Hermitage, he explained, was to revisit Russia's history in a thought-provoking way. The Hermitage could help to dispel the public's confusion about Russia's past resulting from decades of Soviet propaganda. In this way, Piotrovsky wanted to present Mannerheim as a truly "Russian figure," a view that would have been heretical during Soviet times. In fact, the exhibit is part of a revival: in recent years, he explained, there have been a number of books, TV documentaries and exhibitions in Russia about the former Imperial guardsman. A "mythology of Mannerheim," as Piotrovsky called it, has even taken shape around the Baron's many romantic affairs, gallantry and loyalty to St. Petersburg. Despite pressure from Hitler, Mannerheim refused to order Finnish troops to invade the city during the war. Many Russians believe his love of St. Petersburg prevented an attack, although Piotrovsky knew it was actually part of his "clever thinking" on military strategy. In any case, Piotrovsky said, "Mannerheim is very fashionable in St. Petersburg right now."

The director praised Mannerheim's contribution to the ethnography and geography of Asia and wished me luck on my adventures. I was led back into the opulent corridor to a large wooden door. It opened onto a marble staircase and into the Winter Palace. Thousands of tourists in large guided groups pushed their way through the magnificent halls caked in gold and hung with glittering crystal chandeliers. The opulence of the palace's some thousand rooms, decorated with the greatest artistic treasures known to civilization, was disorienting.

TWICE A MONTH, Mannerheim took his guard duty in the Winter Palace. He marched five kilometres along the quay of the Neva River to the palace, where he would slip into his lavish uniform: a white tunic with silver collar and chevrons, tight buckskin breeches (which were put on wet over bare skin), jackboots, scarlet vest and helmet crowned by the Imperial emblem, the double-headed eagle, which guardsmen dubbed "the pigeon." He would march up the Field Marshal's Hall to the Tsar's study. At night, he guarded his sleeping chambers while Ethiopian servants brought coffee at regular intervals.

Mannerheim's life resembled that of an aristocratic playboy. "Up until now, it has been lavish feasting: balls and other functions every single day," he wrote his uncle. "If one wishes to gain social status here in St. Petersburg, to make acquaintances, and useful contacts etc., there's no other choice but to attend all possible dance balls and parties of high society."[26] He could often be found at the polo club on Krestovsky Island and took a special interest in food. Louis Sparre, the husband of Mannerheim's sister Eva, remembered Mannerheim taking him to dinner at the palace of the Grand Duke, where they ate caviar and ice cream.[27] "I am beginning to get quite exhausted of this millionaire lifestyle," Sparre complained to his wife.

Yet the aristocracy's conspicuous consumption belied the misery and violence of turn-of-the-century Russia. From October 1905 to April 1906, the army and police executed fifteen thousand people, wounded twenty thousand and quashed a breakaway peasant republic on the Volga River.[28] The Tsar's brutal repression hit uncomfortably close to home for Gustaf Mannerheim.

In 1903, his brother Carl, an outspoken lawyer, was exiled from Finland for his political views. Every day, he wrote Carl, it becomes "more and more distasteful to remain in the [Imperial] service."[29] Mannerheim even thought about resigning his commission.[30] With his marriage over and nothing keeping him in St. Petersburg, he instead accepted Palitsyn's secret mission. "[A] trip in peaceful and civilized China," he later wrote to his father during the trek, "is considerably less dangerous than to currently command a regiment in Russia."[31]

Mannerheim had come to the General Staff's attention the previous year when he proposed a reconnaissance mission across Mongolia. He was well suited for secret intelligence work: he was an excellent horseman, spoke several languages, had performed courageously in battle and could travel on a Finnish passport. "I had orders to conceal the fact that I was an officer," he wrote, "and to travel in the guise of a private Finn, who is a member of various scientific societies."

At the time, a lost Buddhist civilization was rumoured to be buried under the desert sands of Inner Asia. The Great Powers all sent archaeological expeditions there. Scholarship was occasionally entangled with spying: the British cloaked their espionage as "geographical surveys," while the Russians preferred "scientific expeditions" and the Japanese sent dubious "monks" in search of their Buddhist origins. In order to disguise his mission as a scientific expedition, Mannerheim contacted Senator Otto Donner, a prominent Finnish scholar and president of the Finno-Ugrian Society. Donner duly commissioned Mannerheim to collect archaeological and ethnographic materials for a new museum in Helsinki.

With no scientific training, the career soldier had to depend on two English textbooks, *Hints to Travellers* and *Notes and Queries on Anthropology*, to learn "the practical knowledge necessary for an explorer."[32] He also read the first-hand accounts of Marco Polo, Nikolai Przhevalsky, Sven Hedin and Aurel Stein, and spent long hours studying the archives of the General Staff. While visiting his brother Carl in Sweden, he bought an Ernemann Klapp, a state-of-the-art camera, and a spare, and ordered five hundred photographic plates and cheap gifts from Paris, including small music boxes, stereoscopes *à images pornographiques* and photographs of coloured women. The gifts, Mannerheim figured, would be "much appreciated by the natives."[33]

Two weeks before departing, the Baron visited Björnholmen, outside Helsinki, to bid farewell to his father and sister. "Gustaf photographed everything and everyone; he is so eager to learn enough," Sophie recalled.[34] On July 6, 1906, he gathered his sixteen travel trunks and bordered the midnight train for Moscow.

I ATE MY last supper in St. Petersburg at Chopstick, a Chinese restaurant in the Grand Hotel Europe on Nevsky Prospekt. The hotel opened its doors in 1875 as Hôtel de l'Europe with a Baroque facade and luxurious Art Nouveau interiors. Mannerheim often stayed here when he didn't have a permanent residence in the city. In Soviet times, it served as a hospital, orphanage and government building and then reopened as a hotel in 1991. An extensive restoration recently brought back to life its aristocratic ambience. It was now the posh refuge of Russia's fabulously wealthy; a fleet of black Mercedes was parked out front.

Around the corner is the Mikhailovsky Theatre, once the centre of French culture in St. Petersburg. French was in vogue in court and Mannerheim spoke the language at home with his wife. (His Russian was reportedly poor.) I saw a delightful performance of *Swan Lake* in the beautifully restored theatre. At 10 PM, I rushed out of the crowded, muggy theatre into a refreshingly cool evening.

I hastily collected my luggage from the hostel and made my way to Moskovsky Station.

The date was July 6—the hundredth anniversary of Mannerheim's departure from St. Petersburg. I nervously made my way past a police SWAT team patrolling the entrance to the railway station and boarded the night train. I settled into a stuffy compartment with two plump Russian businessmen and a woman with flaming auburn hair. Dreary suburbs and then boreal forests rolled by in the oyster-coloured light of a midsummer's night. At midnight, Russia's rousing national anthem—a revision of the old Soviet hymn—crackled over loudspeakers and then the wagon fell silent.

I closed my eyes and tried to imagine St. Petersburg on the brink of violent revolution a century ago and the relief Mannerheim must have felt escaping his troubles. An unsettling thought then occurred to me: my own troubles still lay ahead.

TWO

AZERBAIJAN

The Nobels' Prize

From well to wick it was all Nobel.
—ROBERT W. TOLF, *The Russian Rockefellers*[1]

MANNERHEIM LEFT MOSCOW by train to Nizhniy Novgorod, a bustling river port clogged with steam launches, cargo ships, timber rafts and oil tankers. He had just enough time to visit the imposing red-brick Kremlin before boarding a passenger steamer. It took five days to make the 2,200-kilometre trip down the Volga River to the Caspian Sea. "The journey is thoroughly enjoyable. Brief halts. Rapid progress," Mannerheim wrote. "One lovely scene succeeds another, the landscape presenting a series of characteristic and beautiful pictures as it changes slowly from hilly woodland to a flat, yellow, sandy steppe." The scattered provincial towns, in contrast, consisted of shabby wooden houses with unkempt gardens "connected by dusty streets, badly paved or not paved at all." Even the bigger ports—Kazan, Simbirsk, Samara, Saratov and Tsaritsyn (now Volgograd)—were unimpressive. "The larger towns boast squalid horse-trams, drawn by pathetic-looking beasts."

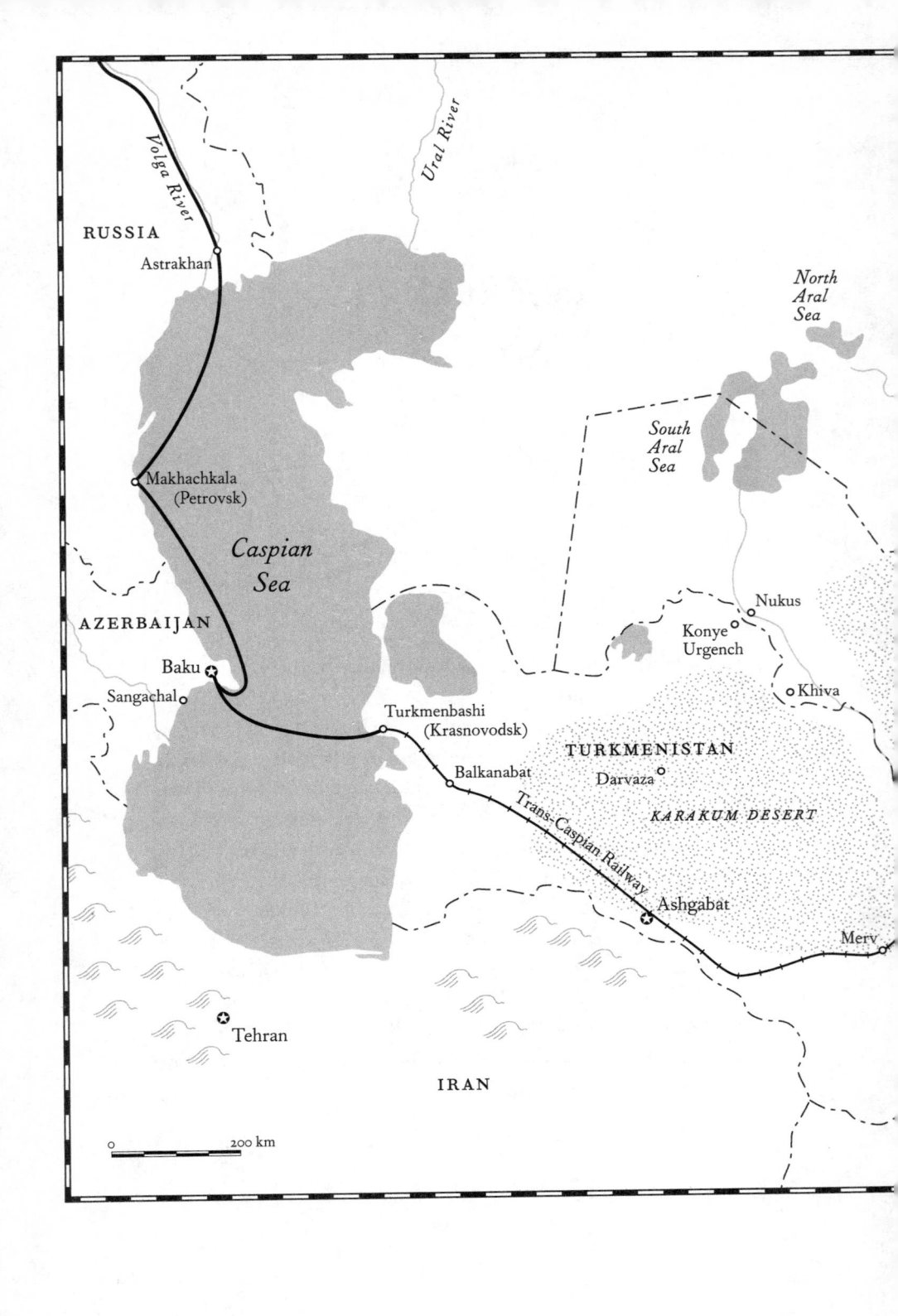

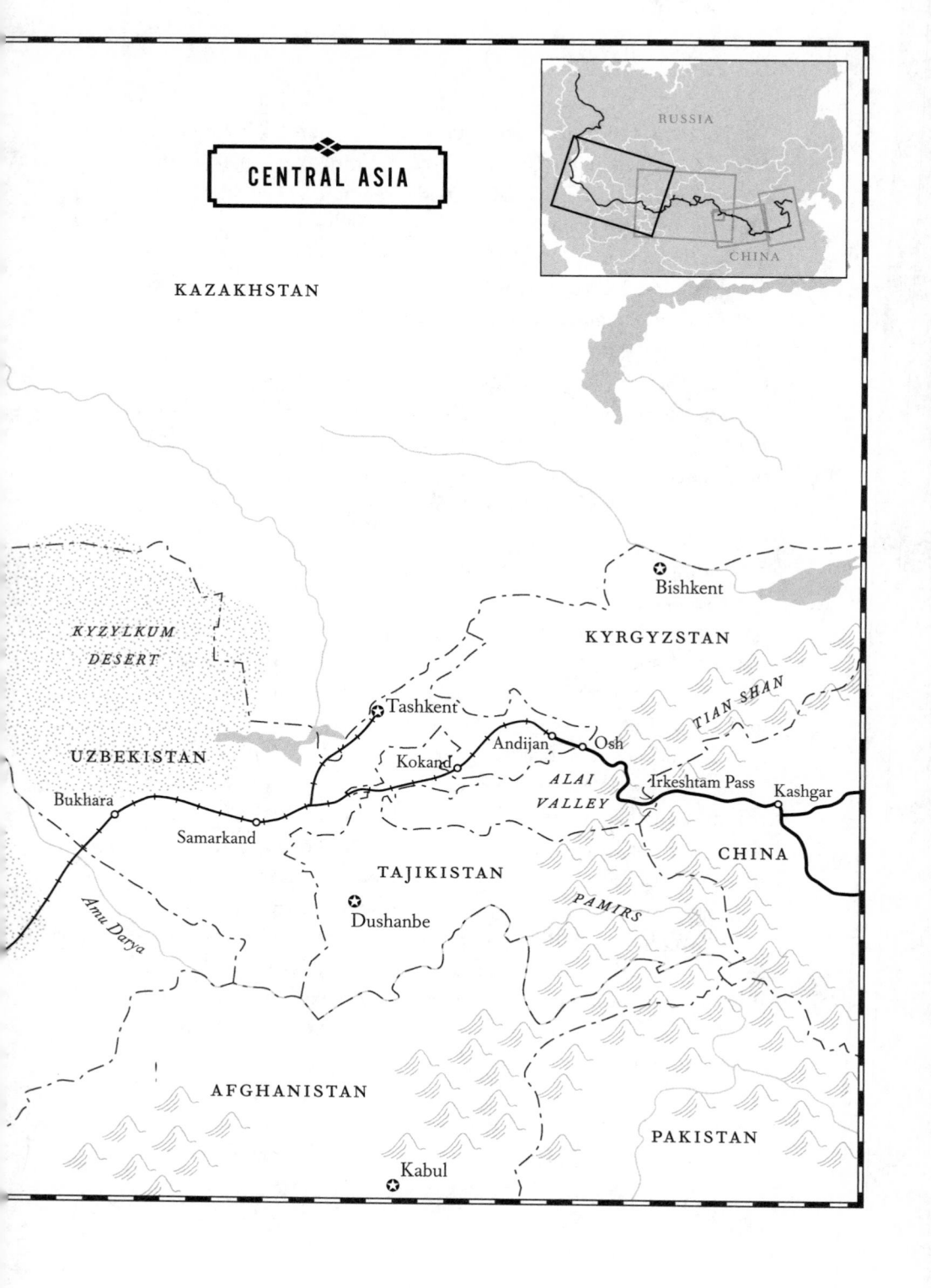

Onboard, the Baron met a tall young Roman Catholic priest from Saxony heading to Saratov, a town on the Volga where, in the 1760s, German colonists had settled. The political situation was the topic of conversation. The rolling agricultural lands between Samara and Saratov were the poorest and most violently rebellious in the empire. A peasant army destroyed more of the gentry's property in Saratov than anywhere else during the attempted revolution that autumn. So many estates were razed that, according to one witness, "the steppe [was] lit up at night by the burning manor houses."[2]

"The only hope for Russia is the formation of a party similar to the Catholic Centre in Germany," the priest told the Baron. Yet political centrism was nowhere to be found in an empire riven by class hatred and brutalized by an authoritarian regime. In his diary, Mannerheim was conspicuously mum on the charred estates and marauding peasants. He just snobbishly remarked that his fellow passengers were "very second-rate."

At Astrakhan, at the mouth of the Volga, Mannerheim met an old friend and her "insignificant" husband from St. Petersburg. Together they continued on an old paddle wheeler to Baku, about 940 kilometres across the Caspian. After a rough passage, they stopped midway in Petrovsk the next day.

Petrovsk was, Mannerheim described, "a little, white bathing resort shut in between the mountains of the Caucasus and the Caspian. Poor and empty." It had a lovely beach, though, with coarse sand and large combers. Mannerheim went for a "refreshing bathe in the sea, the waves tumbling me over and massaging me pleasantly." With his St. Petersburg friends, he enjoyed drinks in a seaside café and snapped a photograph of their *"strandparti."* One disconcerting detail in the photograph of the dainty couple suggests that all was not well in the Caucasus: out of the husband's jacket poked the butt of a revolver.

I HAD WANTED to cruise down the Volga in the Baron's wake. Several companies offered weeklong trips from Moscow or Nizhniy

Novgorod on fancy cruise ships, but there was no ferry or flight from Astrakhan to Baku, the capital of Azerbaijan. An overland trip also appeared impossible. The railway and highway both ran through war-ravaged Chechnya. Mannerheim's "bathing resort" had become a bloodbath too. Petrovsk (now Makhachkala), the capital of the Russian Republic of Dagestan, routinely experienced terrorist bombings, kidnappings and running gun battles between security forces and separatist rebels. "Sadly," one travel website advised, "the authorities may pose an even greater threat to travelers than rebels, bandits, and gangs."

And so I found myself on Aeroflot Flight 147, a three-hour journey from Moscow to Baku. On board, I read a guidebook and the *Moscow Times*. Near the end of the flight, a bit of tawny-coloured land caught my eye. I peered out the window. A hazy film hung over the Apsheron Peninsula. Shaped like a dagger, it thrusts seventy kilometres out into the Caspian Sea. The jut of land is smeared with oily ponds and briny lakes whose shores are crusted white. The Bay of Baku, ringed in green, is notched into the peninsula's southern edge. Like a swarm of mosquitoes, thousands of black oil derricks dot the landscape, sucking up the earth's black blood. I was about to descend into the greatest oil town of all time. "If oil is king," one traveller wrote in 1906, "Baku is its throne."[3]

The former Soviet republic sits on 7 to 13 billion barrels of proven oil reserves. Production has more than tripled in a decade, and 2006 was a gusher, with oil output jumping by 50 percent and GDP by more than 30 percent.[4] Despite the oil riches, Azeris are shockingly poor: the average monthly salary is $125, and half of the population of 8 million lives below the poverty line. The stocky middle-aged woman sitting beside me was one of the thousands of migrants who go to Russia for work. Just before our descent, she went to the washroom and returned in a new blouse and freshly coiffed hair. She began caking on makeup and then unfolded a thick wad of American hundred-dollar bills. Licking her thumb, she counted out three thousand dollars.

Stepping out of the air-conditioned terminal, I almost choked on my first breath in Baku. The air was dry and stifling. I blinked uncontrollably in the blinding sunlight. I had arranged for a driver and car to take me into town. A short distance from the airport, I spotted a suburb of new villas overlooking a toxic green lake and forest of oil derricks. It gave new meaning to the phrase "industrial park." At a bend in the road stood a billboard portraying a man with a large hooked nose and bushy moustache, like Groucho Marx. "Our president," the driver said.

Through rigged elections, Ilham Aliyev took over Azerbaijan's presidency from his ailing father, Heydar, a former KGB officer and Politburo member—the first dynastic succession in post-Soviet Central Asia. Like the stench of oil, images of the two men are ubiquitous in Baku.

We arrived at a "Stalin project," a drab concrete monstrosity a block from Baku's seaside promenade. The filthy lobby smelled like a sewer. The elevator creaked and rattled as we made our way to the sixth floor. I was pleasantly surprised by the clean, spacious apartment that I had rented from a Russian-speaking Tartar. The rooms were light, airy and air-conditioned. I noticed liquor glasses and a decanter next to a clock depicting the sacred mosque of Mecca. In Baku, Happy Hour and the Hajj peacefully coexist.

I spent the afternoon wandering around Baku's Old Town. Set on a sloping hill on the west side of the bay, the ancient, walled quarter is a warren of flat-roofed homes, forgotten mosques, Tartar palaces and tourist shops. Cats and kids ran along its narrow passages. To the southeast stands "Boomtown," the picturesque European quarter that grew up after the first oil boom in the 1870s. It has neatly arranged streets, parks, theatres and lavish mansions built by oil barons a century ago. Nowadays, the quarter—an exuberant blend of architectural styles from Art Nouveau to Ottoman—is the centre of expat life in Baku, with dozens of overpriced bars, apartments, restaurants and hotels for foreign oil executives.

In the evening, on the city's seaside promenade, crowds gathered to enjoy the cool Caspian breeze, amusement rides and buskers. I sat on the seawall soaking up the carnival atmosphere. Ahmed, a twenty-three-year-old Pakistani, greeted me in English. He was short and dark-skinned with a broad, innocent smile. He bought me a soda and wanted to be friends.

A trader from Jalalabad, he had been in Baku for seven months importing sporting goods destined for Eastern Europe. However, he disliked Baku and its residents. "Azeris are not good Muslims," he complained. Ahmed was Pashtun and a Sunni Muslim with "strong traditions," as he repeatedly told me. He was appalled at the vodka drinking and scantily clad Azeri girls. "Is she Muslim?" he said, pointing to a busty girl in a spaghetti-strap top. "In Pakistan she would be killed!" There wasn't even a mosque in his neighbourhood, he complained.

"I'm a good Muslim," he said. "I don't drink. I don't smoke. I don't fuck."

"Me too," I said, groping for something in common. "I don't smoke either."

THE *ADMIRAL KORNILOFF* sailed into Baku Bay in the late evening of July 15, 1906. "The town forms an amphitheatre on the eastern slope of hills," Mannerheim wrote. "Lights peep out from far and near, surrounded by the mysterious shapes of the hills, and illuminate endless rows of oil derricks that appear out of the dark earth like an army of ghostly creatures."

The previous year, two-thirds of Baku's oilfields were set ablaze during a gruesome wave of ethnic violence. "The flames from the burning derricks and oil wells leaped up into the awful pall of smoke which hung over the inferno," remembered one survivor. "I realized for the first time in my life all that can possibly be meant by the words 'Hell let loose.'"[5] Tension between Muslims and Christians, Azeris and Armenians, had been festering for some time. Russian officials stoked the racial fires by arming the majority Azeris in the hope of crushing Armenian nationalists. Azeris resented the wealth and status of the many educated Armenians who profited greatly from the booming oil industry. The oil magnates a century ago were, with only a few notable exceptions, a nasty lot. The son of one Azeri oilman called them "a caste which left nothing to be desired in the way of barbaric luxury, debauchery, despotism, and extravagance."[6] Bolsheviks too were busy turning Baku into a revolutionary cauldron.

In May 1905, a general strike and ethnic bloodshed paralyzed the city. Azeris attacked the villas of rich Armenians, who responded with equal vengeance. One oil tycoon held out for three days and shot some forty Muslims with his Winchester repeater before a wild mob set fire to his mansion and massacred his family. "The odor of the corpses stifled us," ran one account. "Everywhere women with mad eyes were seeking their children, and husbands were moving the heaps of rotting flesh."[7] Cossack soldiers rode through the streets wantonly shooting citizens to restore order. Baku became known as the "greatest blood spot on the mysterious, rebellious and blood stained Caucasus."[8] By summer's end, a thousand oil wells were destroyed and some two thousand people lay dead. Baku's first oil boom was at its end.

"THE OIL INDUSTRY has certainly created a building boom in the city," I said. "High-rises appear to be sprouting up like mushrooms."

Steinar Gil smiled, amused by my naïve observation. "There's some legitimate real estate development, but most of it [the construction] is money laundering," he said.

The plucky Norwegian ambassador had become famous for his bluntness. Corruption, rigged elections, political persecution, assassination of journalists, ethnic hatred—he covered it all while digging into an Italian buffet lunch at the swanky SAS Radisson on my second day in Baku.

"There are two catastrophically weak sectors of society," he explained. "Health care and education. It's not only underfunded and disorganized, but bribery and corruption are rampant. You can't get anything done without paying a bribe. You never know when a student gets a diploma whether he's qualified or not. You can just buy a diploma."

Vast sums of money—probably in the hundreds of millions of dollars, but no one really knows—were being laundered every year, draining the government's coffers. "This is an oil-producing country with some history, a hundred thirty years, but it has not developed any kind of technology or industry," Gil said. Little of the oil wealth, he went on, was trickling down to the people or being put to productive use creating industries.

That evening I went for a drink at the Ocean Deck Bar and Grill, an expat watering hole in Malakonsky Park. Situated over a pond and connected by a causeway, the bar is a veritable island unto itself. Two hardy Scottish oilmen sat with a forty-something American. They were all ruby-faced and middle-aged, and chatted about their stints in Saudi Arabia. Scott, the American, lived alone in a former oil baron's mansion just around the corner. The *Baku Post* advertised apartments in the area for as much as four thousand dollars per month. Scott described his oversized Jacuzzi surrounded in white marble as a Roman bath. His huge living room had vaulted ceilings and gilded cornices. "It's over the top with no sense of style," Scott said nursing a beer. "I live in a whorehouse." Some things never change: in 1906, one visitor to Boomtown bemoaned that "everything bespeaks the comfortless vulgarity of the *nouveau riche*."[9]

The next morning a turquoise-coloured minibus took me to the source of Azerbaijan's riches—and woes, some say. Operated by British Petroleum (BP), the minibus climbed the western hills overlooking the spent oilfields of Bibi Eibat. In 1900, this oilfield exploded with gushers. One "fountain" spurted oil seventy-five metres skyward, causing a black mist to rain on Baku ten kilometres away.[10] The world had never seen such a spectacle. The same could be said of the carnage left behind: Bibi Eibat is now industrial bad-lands; rusted black derricks stand like tombstones over parched earth and electric-lime-coloured lagoons.

At the top of the hill, a hairpin swung us around the southern headland of the bay below. Immediately, three massive offshore oil-rigs came into view. With land-based oilfields largely sucked dry, the most lucrative drilling is now offshore. The minivan continued southward, passing fawning billboards of Heydar Aliyev, derelict oilrigs hugging the shore and dozens of cranes busily building a 150-metre-tall steel tower for a new oil platform. Forty-five kilome-tres from Baku, we arrived at Sangachal, the largest oil terminal in the world. The 256-hectare facility consists of three massive white tanks each holding 800,000 barrels of oil plus four smaller tanks connected by a labyrinth of pipelines, oil heaters and gas separa-tors. A sole gas flare stands twenty storeys over the site. Against the dramatic backdrop of Garadag, or "Black Mountain," the thin stack and orange flame look like a Zoroastrian totem.

Vasif, a young Azeri engineer, guided me around the recently opened Caspian Energy Centre, a modern education facility in the shape of a ship's bow. "We are working with children to inspire them about the oil and gas industry," he said, showing me a small tortoise refuge and classrooms. I was then offered cookies and a perfunctory PowerPoint presentation chronicling the oil history of Baku, whose second boom came in 1994. That year Heydar Aliyev signed the $10-billion "contract of the century" with a BP-led con-sortium to develop the Azeri-Chirag-Gunashli oilfields. Located 120 kilometres offshore, the fields contain 5.4 billion barrels of recoverable oil. The first oil flowed into Sangachal three years later.

I wanted to see the terminal itself, but security was prohibitively tight. An army garrison protected the facility and a military obser-vation post atop Garadag kept a watchful eye over Azerbaijan's prized industry. Instead, another young Azeri named Alasker drove me in a Land Rover around the terminal. It was under expansion, with crews constructing a natural gas plant. At one point, Alasker pointed to a white pipeline coming out of a building and into the ground. It was the start of the Baku-Tbilisi-Ceyhan pipeline, a $2.9-billion project to unlock the Caspian's crude and deliver it to thirsty Western markets. It can pump 1 million barrels per day, and today was its inauguration, with the first drop of crude reaching the Turkish port of Ceyhan on the Mediterranean Sea.

The pipeline is as much about politics as economics. By pumping oil 1,760 kilometres overland through Georgia to Turkey (both American allies), the pipeline bypasses both Russia and Iran, ensuring a steady supply of oil for the West. Petroleum is the prize in the New Great Game. The United States, Russia and China are all aggressively pushing energy and security alliances in Central Asia. "Everyone wants our oil," Alasker said.

That evening I met Ahmed, and we wandered down to the seaside park for a (non-alcoholic) drink. Thousands of partygoers crowded the cafés, amusement rides and a plaza where an Azeri pop concert was in full swing. The stage stood below a massive white derrick decorated with lights like a Christmas tree. Illuminated letters, spelling out "BAKU TBILISI CEYHAN," stretched across the backdrop. It was a party celebrating the pipeline's inauguration. An Azeri pop singer crooned as pyrotechnics lit up the stage, which faced an enormous billboard of Heydar Aliyev. At 11 PM, the sky exploded in fireworks, showering the city in a fiery kaleidoscope of colourful light and plumes of smoke. Oil was setting Baku ablaze once again.

MANNERHEIM'S ARRIVAL IN Baku in 1906 also coincided with the completion of the largest pipeline yet constructed. The builder, Emanuel Nobel, was president of the Nobel Brothers Petroleum Production Company and a personal friend of the Baron.

Emanuel's grandfather had emigrated from Sweden to Finland and then to St. Petersburg, where he invented mines for the Russian military and manufactured armaments and industrial machinery.

He had three sons: Robert, Ludvig and Alfred. Emanuel's father, Ludvig, transformed the Nobel Factory into the largest manufacturer of gun carriages in Russia and produced the first modern rifles. In March 1873, Robert travelled to Baku to source local walnut for rifle stocks. He bought an oil refinery instead.

Baku had long been known for its oil. In places, the black syrup literally bubbled up from the bowels of the earth. In ancient times, Zoroastrians worshipped at fire temples just outside the city. In the thirteenth century, Marco Polo mentioned Baku's oil in his chronicles. Early production simply entailed hand-dug pits. It wasn't until the arrival of the Nobels that modern oil production took off.

In 1877, the Nobel brothers built Baku's first oil pipeline between the Balakhani oilfield and Black Town, a bayside district of some two hundred refineries fifteen kilometres away.[11] Volumes of smoke vomited from chimneys, covering streets and buildings in soot, and gave Black Town its name. The refined kerosene was originally shipped to St. Petersburg in expensive wooden barrels, but a year later the Nobels built the world's first oil tanker, the *Zoroaster*. Thanks to the tankers, by 1890 Baku became the busiest port in the world, a global centre for innovation. Ludvig was declared "Oil King of Baku."[12]

Rugged geography unfortunately locked Baku's oil inside the Russian Empire. So the Nobels' next step was to build a railway to Batumi, transforming the Black Sea port into a refining and distribution hub. Yet the mountain route was so steep that it took two engines to haul eight tanker cars at a time, so, using four hundred tons of Alfred's dynamite, Emanuel, who took over the company after his father's death, blasted a tunnel through the mountains. By 1906, he had constructed the world's longest pipeline, some 880 kilometres long and costing $12 million.[13]

Most of the crude was refined into kerosene, heralding the Age of Illumination in the Russian Empire. Then another Nobel innovation revolutionized its use: the Swedes began to use waste oil instead of coal to fuel their bulk tankers. Oil was cheaper, cleaner and more reliable than coal and by the turn of the century, the world's navies and merchant fleets were converting to its use. Securing oil became of military and strategic importance. The United States with its booming oil industry controlled more than 60 percent of the global supply.[14] With their new pipeline, the Nobels hoped to challenge American dominance of world markets.

But the horrific destruction of 1905 ended Baku's pipe dreams. Mannerheim himself stayed only two hours. The situation was still dangerously volatile. That summer Baku was at the height of more labour strikes. Any nobleman risked murder and robbery by revolutionary bandits.

That was almost Mannerheim's fate a decade later. The Baron and Emanuel Nobel were together in St. Petersburg when revolutionaries overthrew the Tsar in March 1917. Bread riots broke out and soldiers began to mutiny en masse. With the empire on the brink of collapse, Mannerheim did what any self-respecting aristocrat would. "I achieved the almost impossible feat," he wrote, "of securing a ticket for a ballet performance at the Imperial Opera." After the performance, the streets were mysteriously quiet. Nobel suggested they stroll over to a nearby club frequented by Duma deputies. Not a soul had visited the club that evening, a sleepy porter told them. The next morning an angry mob spotted Mannerheim wearing his Imperial officers' uniform in Hôtel de l'Europe. He fled to Nobel's office. His pursuers, the Baron recalled, "were filled with revolutionary fervour and in a dangerous mood."[15] Disguised in an overcoat, Mannerheim outsmarted some revolutionary guards and eventually made his way to the safety of the Nobel mansion on the other side of the Neva River.

Their privileged lives, as aristocrat and industrialist, were over. The Bolsheviks eventually expropriated Nobel's entire oil empire, and Mannerheim was forced to flee to Finland, where he would spend the rest of his life battling Bolshevism.

NOBEL PROSPEKT IS nowadays the main thoroughfare running through Black Town. During Soviet times, it was called Workers' Prospekt, but was renamed after independence.

"The face of the city is changing," said Ibrahim, pointing out construction cranes. "They are building high-rises all over the city. Nobody likes it." I nodded, recalling Steinar Gil's bleak assessment.

Ibrahim, my guide for the day, was charmingly cynical. Bearded, bespectacled and balding, he was a stocky man in his thirties. He had grown up in Soviet times, experienced the euphoria of Communism's collapse, but became grimly mocking as he watched the country morph into a dynastic kleptocracy. His friend Alam, a quiet, thick-necked fellow in dark sunglass, agreed to tour us around in his Lada Samara.

A Soviet workers' statue stands at the entrance of Nobel Prospekt, which swings eastward along the harbour. Black Town is still a working industrial zone. Railway cars, dozens of storage tanks, refineries and tailing ponds blight the neighbourhood, along with an oily stench. Yet in the heart of this otherwise horrendous 'hood sits a walled oasis. We navigated up a winding side street and into the gated compound, parking in front of a miniature castle. It was the famed House of Nobel.

Despite enormous wealth, the Nobels had rather modest taste in architecture. Their home was a two-storey villa whose only flourish is a crenellated turret on one corner. Around it, they built a ten-hectare complex of bungalows and apartment buildings for their oil executives. Soil, plants, trees, even water were imported to create the lush gardens. The Nobels called their verdant refuge Villa Petrolea. Sadly, the gardens had become weedy, overgrown and parched. Many of the buildings looked neglected too: peeling paint, cracked stucco. But the castle-like villa was being restored. A Turkish mason said that Michael Nobel, a nephew of Alfred, had donated money to renovate it into a conference centre, museum and the Baku Nobel Oil Club, an exclusive private club for executives. It would be completed in two months.

We continued along Nobel Prospekt, climbing the hill overlooking the bay. A cool breeze refreshed us as we crested the hilltop. On the other side, we descended onto a scorching inland plateau of spent oilfields. The desolate plain was an ecological apocalypse: broken-down derricks, leaky pipelines, teetering power poles, rusted tanks and burning rubbish heaps littered the sandy landscape. Sheep grazed on the meagre vegetation hardy enough to sprout from the oil-caked earth.

"Can you imagine kids growing up here?" asked Ibrahim, aghast at the ramshackle huts built around a well pump and toxic tailings pond. "This water is very dangerous. It's radioactive."

We looped back inland to the suburb of Sabunchi. Here, we found the headquarters of the Balakhani Oil Company. The stately architecture looked familiar. A courteous old man with a prickly moustache and clumsy gait told us that the Nobels built the neighbourhood for their oil workers. "This one too was built by Nobel," he said pointing to a squalid apartment building as we strolled through the residential complex.

A nearby shopkeeper overheard us talking. "Nobel built everything here, but now we don't have water," she complained bitterly, pressing her clenched fists into her hips. "We've been without water for three months."

"It used to be quite beautiful here," the old man quietly added. "It's 100 percent bad now." Everything looked rundown and overcrowded. "The house of Nobel did a lot for Azerbaijan," he said. "Of course, they made a lot of money but they also built things for the people."

Another man, who ran a kiosk, was quick to add his voice. "I only have good things to say. When the Nobels started to explore for oil here they built all these buildings for workers," Hussein said, waving his hands at the grey brick facades. The neighbourhood consisted of twenty-one buildings with four hundred apartments, plus a library and school for girls. Sabunchi, he explained, was one of the first neighbourhoods in Baku to get modern water and sewer infrastructure. In their day, the apartments provided some of the finest worker housing in Baku. The Nobels also pioneered medical care, technical training, the abolition of child labour and elementary education for workers' children. For that reason, rebellious workers left the Nobel oilfields largely untouched during the mayhem of 1905. "The Nobels have amassed their fortune by an honesty and broadness of principle rare even in England today," wrote a British visitor in 1884. "Their generosity towards their employés is remarkable."[16]

I later met the chairwoman of the Committee for Oil Workers' Rights. Mirvari Gahramanli, a stocky, affable woman, spoke nostalgically about the past, about the stronger labour laws during Soviet times and the charitable works, including public parks, theatres and schools, of the early oil barons. "The Nobel brothers were very generous to oil workers," she said. "They are considered good people in Azerbaijan history. They were always involved in philanthropic activities." She heaped scorn on Azerbaijan's current oil industry, especially foreign companies that bankroll the country's venal regime. The tenacious activist had been fired from her job for trying to unionize fellow workers and was beaten unconscious during a protest against fraudulent elections. "Unlike the current corrupt government, the Nobel brothers helped poor people," she concluded.

The Nobel apartments were in better shape a century ago, but despite being run down they still looked like Bel Air compared to the shanties lining the roadway to Sabunchi. We stopped at one cluster of shacks built of brick, clay, corrugated metal and clapboard. Leaky pipelines crisscrossed alleyways, and well pumps buttressed backyards. Garbage, tires and oil filled a huge pit. The smell was horrific.

"Hey!" Ibrahim yelled. "Take a photo of that."

He was pointing to a sparkling white BMW parked next to a grimy hovel. "That's part of the mentality here," he said, chuckling. "You have the best car but live in a shack."

The Balakhani oilfield lay a kilometre away, a jungle of electrical lines, derricks and slimy ponds. The Nobels began modern deep-well drilling here, hitting gusher after gusher, some of which spouted for days. By 1900, however, Balakhani's production had begun to sag. Nowadays it only dribbles oil, the wells mostly spent. We stopped at one spectacularly fluorescent pond. I crouched down to take a photograph of the slick surface. The vapours were so noxious that I stumbled with dizziness on my way back to the car.

We quickly retreated for lunch to a downtown café shaded by mulberry trees. We ate a salty goat cheese called *motal*, tomato salad and hardy lamb kebabs, washed down with fresh plum juice.

"There was an incredible party in the seaside park last night celebrating the opening of the Baku-Tbilisi-Ceyhan pipeline. The entire city seemed to be there," I said. "Did you attend?"

Ibrahim rolled his eyes. "It's just hypocrisy," he groaned. "The money isn't going to go to the people. It's going to go to the government. There are many such ridiculous amusements sponsored by the government."

After lunch, he took me to the homes of the country's super rich on Teymur Aliyev Street. There was little to see. The mansions, like fortified compounds, were hidden behind high walls. The temperature in the car was almost forty degrees. Ibrahim's shirt was sopped in sweat. To escape the midday heat, we sought refuge at a seaside café, where Ibrahim pursued his argument that oil is Azerbaijan's greatest curse—corrupting public life, distorting the economy, bankrolling a ruthless despot. Even the harbour, he pointed out, was polluted with oil. We sat at a table far from the seawall to avoid the whiff of oil slicks. Like many Azeris I spoke to, he also blamed the West for putting its oil interests before human rights in Azerbaijan. "My main dream is that maybe one day the oil wells will go dry," he said. "Then maybe, just maybe, we'll have a chance to be a democracy."

The previous month, Thomas L. Friedman, the *New York Times* columnist, had written an article in *Foreign Policy* on "The First Law of Petropolitics." As Friedman explained: "The price of oil and the pace of freedom always move in opposite directions in oil-rich petrolist states . . . [T]he higher the average global crude oil price rises, the more free speech, free press, free and fair elections, an independent judiciary, the rule of law, and independent political parties are eroded." Unfortunately for Ibrahim, oil prices had just hit a historic high.

"The forecast is oil for the next fifty years," he lamented. "Since life expectancy here is sixty years old, I'll probably never see democracy in Azerbaijan."

ON MY LAST night in Baku, I went for dinner with Fikrin, a thick-set young lawyer with Transparency Azerbaijan, an affiliate of an international organization leading the fight against corruption. He had helped to arrange my visit to Baku, so I treated him to dinner at a rooftop restaurant overlooking the Bay of Baku. Digging into a sturgeon kebab, Fikrin lamented how Azeris' traditional lands have been carved up by neighbouring countries: some 16 million Azeris live in Iran; 300,000 live in Georgia; most recently Armenia, with Russia's help, took the ethnic enclave of Nagorno-Karabakh after a protracted war in the 1990s. "Azerbaijan's fate is tied to geography and geology, land and oil," Fikrin said. "It's a transit country separating the East and West."

With Fikrin's assistance, I bought a ticket for a ferry to Turkmenistan the next morning. I paid sixty American dollars, a ridiculous sum. The chief of the port police asked to be paid in small bills, presumably to distribute the largesse among his sticky-fingered colleagues. Only four other foreign travellers—a rough-looking Australian, a handsome Dane, a bookish Englishman and an American college student—were on board the old Soviet-era freighter. The shirtless crew looked like shipwreck survivors. A man in an officer's shirt appeared briefly; otherwise, the ship seemed to be under the command of twenty-year-old sea cadets.

Before I left Baku, I bought a book to read on the sea crossing. Rena Safaraliyev, executive director of Transparency Azerbaijan, recommended *Ali and Nino* by Kurban Said, a mysterious writer born as Lev Nussimbaum who spent his childhood in Baku in the 1910s. "Although the book deals with the previous oil boom, it is basically the same," she told me. "It's about the transformation of Baku from a sleepy Muslim town to the centre of the oil industry."

I tried to read in my filthy stateroom, but the heat and humidity were oppressive. My skin was buttery with sweat. I climbed to the top deck and found Martin, the Dane, sunning himself. The setting sun was as red as a maraschino cherry, and the sky was awash in streaks of pink, lemon and tangerine like a tropical cocktail. "Polluted skies make the most beautiful sunsets," Martin mused. Black oil derricks also jutted up from the shallow bay, adding to the surrealism.

I sat in the lee of the wind, which was enormously refreshing, and read *Ali and Nino*. Set at the time of the Russian Revolution, the novel chronicles the life of a young Tartar prince who falls in love with a Georgian princess. Their life—a metaphor for Baku—is torn between Islam and Orthodoxy, East and West, tradition and modernity. Throughout the novel, oil is depicted as a curse to everything and everyone that it touches. Baku suffers "perpetual torture by the oil derricks," Said wrote.[17] Near the end, the young lovers flee Baku by ferry as revolution breaks out. Their last vision of Baku, like mine, was a haunting one: "The town disappeared in the dark. The black oil derricks looked like grim prison guards."[18]

THREE

TURKMENISTAN

Fear and Loathing

*He who makes a beast of himself gets rid of the pain
of being a man.* —SAMUEL JOHNSON

LANDING ON THE Caspian's southeastern shore from Baku, Mannerheim happened upon a restless and backward outpost on
the margins of the Russian Empire. "On Monday morning we
reached Krasnovodsk, a small prettily situated town on the barren,
rocky shore," he wrote on July 16. "The harbour was deserted, the
houses small, one-storeyed with flat roofs. No trees, no bushes—
tropical heat and enormous masses of dust. The town is surrounded
by high, barren hills. After about 7 months in Europe I was on Asi-
atic soil once more."

From the ship's passenger deck a few kilometres from shore, I
spotted Krasnovodsk. It looked pretty much as Mannerheim
described: a cluster of low-slung buildings dwarfed by a jagged
massif. The harbour was lifeless. A few rusted Soviet-era freighters
and a grey patrol boat were moored next to idle loading cranes and
empty warehouses. Not a soul stirred. One ship had been scuttled
at the dock, its corroded superstructure eerily poking out of the

turquoise sea. "We are definitely in Asia now," said my Australian companion.

The five of us were ordered up to a medical room. I felt feverish and dehydrated, my throat swollen and lips cracked. The night voyage had been insufferably hot. The ship's galley had run out of bottled water, leaving me parched. I had barely slept three hours. A Turkmen official doused a thermometer in alcohol and stuck it in my dripping armpit. I waited nervously.

This perfunctory medical exam was my last hurdle to entering one of the strangest and most secretive dictatorships on Earth. Foreign journalists, lawyers, human-rights activists and even schoolteachers were banned from Turkmenistan. Stories trickling out of the country described a land ruled by a tyrant with the flair of Liberace and the savagery of Stalin.

Of all the Central Asian crackpots—and there are a lot of them—Saparmurat Niyazov is the wackiest. He proclaimed himself President for life and Turkmenbashi, "Leader of All the Turkmens." He built statues, palaces, mosques and monuments all over the country exalting his reign—a vainglorious orgy of kitsch. He even renamed Krasnovodsk "Turkmenbashi." He abolished the opera and ballet, banned beards, declared gold teeth unhygienic, closed libraries and rural hospitals and orchestrated Stalinist show-trials against his enemies, both real and imagined. The first time I'd ever heard of him was in a *New York Times Magazine* article headlined: "When a Kleptocratic, Megalomaniacal Dictator Goes Bad." Revenues from one of the world's largest gas reserves bankrolled this lunacy.[1]

To my surprise, the thermometer showed a normal reading. I was told to go down to the cargo deck, packed with railway oil tankers, for departure. My arrival was timely. I was one of the last foreign travellers to witness the final, demented days of this "one-man Stan."[2] A few months later, Niyazov died of an apparent heart attack.

A feeling of otherworldliness overcame me as I disembarked. A portrait of Niyazov hung on the nondescript customs building. He had thick jet-black hair with a widow's peak, a furrowed brow and plump jowls. A gold bust of him stood by the entrance.

"He looks like an ape," one of my fellow travellers said.

"Planet of the apes," another blurted out from behind.

It was a fitting comparison. My arrival certainly had the suspense of landing on a strange planet. The environment was Martian: oppressive heat, blinding sunlight, dust, a disquieting calm. The surrounding mountains were devoid of vegetation, an otherworldly range of pinkish rock. Niyazov too seemed alien and his architectural tastes space-aged; a stadium in the capital, caked in gold, no less, looked like a gigantic flying saucer.

My Central Asian travel agent had warned me, via email, not to leave the port without my official government guide. Tatyana turned out to be a steely bombshell in her thirties. She had creamy skin, blond hair and blazing red lipstick. A surly Belorussian—at one point, she told a policeman to "fuck off"—she was one of the few Russian speakers who stayed behind after the collapse of the Soviet Union. My fellow travellers threw me suggestive smiles and winks as she led me away. An Armenian driver with white hair and gold teeth was waiting for us in a Nissan Pathfinder.

We entered the town on a road lined with nineteenth-century wooden colonial buildings. The downtown, however, was a mass of hideous Soviet-era concrete blocks and postmodernism. Historic Krasnovodsk was vanishing: authorities were razing its colonial architecture, including an Armenian Apostolic Church and a mosque. At the central bazaar, I exchanged money from a dark, lanky Turkmen who held several shopping bags full of *manat,* the local currency. (The black-market rate was five times better than the official exchange rate.) I stuffed 470,000 *manat*—about twenty dollars—into my bag. We then made our way to a Constructivist behemoth called Hotel Hazar, although Hazard would have been a more fitting name. It was decrepit and dirty. Two prostitutes beckoned from a balcony. In the second-floor foyer, an old woman boiled water for tea in a bucket over an open flame. Water only ran from 7 to 10 o'clock each evening. My room was small, with a lumpy bed and a toilet that oozed an eye-watering odour.

"I'm really sorry about the hotel," Tatyana said. "It's the only thing I could get."

"This is like paradise compared to that ship," I said, relieved at the sight of an air conditioner.

Mannerheim's crossing was "comfortable and quick" with "good cuisine" served in a spacious dining saloon—quite the opposite of my experience. Yet even the Baron was in need of beach therapy. "A refreshing bathe in the clear green waters of the Caspian," he wrote, "gave me strength to bear the heat that at first seemed overpowering." After my hellish sea voyage, I felt the need to follow his example.

The beach was located on a sandspit three kilometres north of the city. Plastic water bottles, melon peels and cigarette packs littered the sand. I spotted two dead fish. The cool turquoise water was nonetheless clean and invigorating. I floated on my back, gazing at the brilliant blue sky. Later, tickling my toes in the hot sand, I finished *Ali and Nino*. Tatyana went for a brief dip too, but spent the rest of the time hiding in the SUV, smoking cigarettes. (Niyazov had banned smoking in public.) There were only a few other beachgoers: nearby a Turkmen family snapped photos and frolicked with an inflatable orca. For a brief spell, life in Turkmenistan seemed abnormally normal.

That night we ate at Deniz Patisserie Café, which my guidebook says "makes for a good escape if you are staying at the Hazar." We sat outside in the cool evening breeze. Over a plate of *shashlik* and refreshing yoghurt, I asked Tatyana about life here.

"I'd never leave Turkmenistan for Georgia, Armenia or Russia," she said. Seventy-five litres of fuel cost a dollar, three years of home electricity cost twenty dollars and her telephone was free. "Turkmenistan is like paradise," Tatyana said, mouthing a tightly scripted official line. "It's like how Communism should have been."

IN 1869, A small Russian force sailed from Petrovsk to the southeast coast of the Caspian Sea. It was a clandestine operation. The Russians didn't want to alarm the British, who controlled Afghanistan to the south. The Russians built the garrison town of Krasnovodsk as a bridgehead for their conquest of Central Asia. They initially failed to sack the fortress of Geok-Tepe, which lies hundreds of kilometres south across the Karakum Desert. After that first defeat, they deployed a special railway battalion to build a track to the edge of the desert and beyond. The Trans-Caspian Railway eventually pierced the heart of Inner Asia. Russian Cossacks slaughtered and pacified local Turkmen tribes and besieged khanates. Sabre-wielding Turkmens, no matter their valour and horsemanship, were no match for dynamite, heavy artillery and modern rifles—all easily and quickly transported on rails. By the late 1890s, the railway had almost reached the border of the Chinese empire. This iron thread forcibly stitched the Silk Road into Russia's Imperial tapestry.

I had been warned that the railway's standards had not risen since Mannerheim's journey. "A filthy kitchen, an improvised, shaky dining-car on 4 wheels, carriages broiling in the sun, dirty and tattered seats, ill-fitting doors, everything gave one an impression of disorder and lack of organisation," wrote the Baron. Thankfully, I would be making the desert crossing to Turkmenistan's capital, Ashgabat, in Tatyana's air-conditioned SUV.

Life in Turkmenistan is marginal. About 80 percent of the country, which is slightly larger than California, is inhospitable desert. The sparse population of 5 million ekes out life mostly on its edges. Their freedom to roam is severely constrained by security forces. Just outside Turkmenbashi, we were stopped at the first of five military checkpoints during our six-hundred-kilometre drive. The highway shadowed the railway up a plateau and across a desolate saltpan all the way to the capital. Camels wandered along the roadside and sheep kicked up clouds of dust. We stopped at a bazaar in Balkanabat, a depressing Soviet-era town, to buy snacks and water before the desert crossing. Stepping out of the SUV felt like walking into an oven. In the Karakum Desert, the temperature hit fifty-five degrees Celsius. Without stopping, we raced southward toward the Kopet Dag range, which runs along the Iranian border. At one point, I spotted a shimmering body of water, perhaps a lake, in the distance. Tatyana saw it too. "A mirage," she said.

Mannerheim also saw nothing but an "endless plain." Aboard the sweltering train, he looked in vain for any trace of life. "Here and there," he wrote, "you catch a glimpse of Turkomans riding their tall beautiful horses, reminiscent of English thoroughbreds, or swaying on their camels, whose rolling gait is distressingly uncomfortable." Traditionally, Turkmens were nomadic horse breeders. Agriculture was nonexistent and, in fact, impossible in the desert. "Some insignificant flocks of sheep, a few camels with saddles on their backs, grazing on ground where there is scarcely a blade of grass to be seen, are the only signs of life visible," the Baron wrote. At the foot of the Kopet Dag range, however, the desert now turned miraculously green.

The Soviets had built the Karakum Canal to tap the Amu Darya, 1,375 kilometres to the east. It now irrigates Turkmenistan's cotton industry. Highway, railway and canal form a lifeline for dozens of agricultural settlements. "Everyone, except school children, must go to the fields to pick cotton, even the elderly, until 7 o'clock in the evening," Tatyana explained matter-of-factly. "The cities are cleared and people are sent to the countryside." From September to November, the country becomes a forced labour camp. Tatyana, a professional cellist with delicate hands, had been exempted. "I thanked God that I didn't have to go to the fields."

Not far from the capital, we reached Geok-Tepe, the former Turkmen stronghold. The Russian army, Tatyana explained, dug a tunnel under the fortress wall and blew it up with explosives in 1881. The wanton slaughter and rape outraged Europe. "The whole country was covered with corpses," recalled one witness. "I myself saw babies bayoneted or slashed to pieces. Many women were ravished before being killed."[3] The Russians were settling old scores: Turkmen bandits and slave traders had been attacking their caravans and expeditions for centuries. Near the historic ruins, President Niyazov built a massive futuristic mosque, eponymously named Saparmurat Hajji. It boasts Italian marble and a Bohemian chandelier weighing two tonnes, Tatyana explained. We skipped it in light of what lay just down the road.

In Kipchak (also Gypjak) stands the largest mosque in Central Asia. A vast marble concourse and spurting fountains lead to an enormous golden dome surrounded by eight minarets soaring eighty metres. The Saparmurat Turkmenbashi Mosque is seven thousand square metres. It has an underground parking lot, a kitchen to feed five thousand and a prayer hall for ten thousand worshippers. As Tatyana explained, its construction and symbolism are intricately tied to Niyazov's life. The president was born on February 19, 1940, in Kipchak. His father was killed in the Second World War and his mother and two brothers died in a devastating earthquake in 1948 that killed more than 110,000 people. He was raised in a Soviet orphanage, climbing his way to become the top apparatchik of the Turkmen SSR and later president of the independent republic. His miraculous survival and success led Niyazov to believe that he was a prophet.

"Muslims have a holy book, the *Koran*," Tatyana explained earnestly, "and we have a holy book, *Rukhnama*. *Rukh* means 'soul' and *nama* means 'book.' It tells the history of the Turkmen from the very beginning. Unlike a traditional mosque that has passages from the *Koran* inscribed around the dome, the Turkmenbashi mosque has passages from *Rukhnama*."

This "sweet spiritual fruit," as Niyazov described his quixotic musings, was to Turkmens what Joseph Smith's book is to Mormons. Niyazov infused his personality cult with a godly aura. He certainly appeared all-powerful (he systematically crushed his enemies) and all-knowing too: phones were tapped, informants lurked everywhere, email was monitored, offices and hotels were bugged. Yet on this day, Niyazov appeared to be a shepherd without a flock. The coliseum-sized prayer hall was empty. Three small birds circled above in the vast, gilded dome. Niyazov could now lay claim to another superlative: world's largest birdhouse.

Ashgabat was only ten kilometres away. It has been called the Las Vegas of Central Asia. The nickname did not disappoint. The capital of 700,000 is completely styled after Caesar's Palace. The themed city is replete with fountains, statues, domes, white palaces, sweeping concourses, mirrored emerald glass, Corinthian columns, Romanesque archways and Italian marble. A thirty-three-hectare amusement park of Turkmen folk art and fairytales—with a Ferris wheel, magic carpet ride, puppet theatre and roller coaster swooping over a miniature of the Caspian Sea—was nearing completion. What wasn't Romanesque was otherworldly. One ten-storey tower called the House of Free Creativity resembles an opened book. Another government high-rise looks suspiciously like a phallus penetrating a vagina.

Niyazov even looked like one of the Rat Pack—"a fat and grinning Dean Martin," as someone once described.[4] And like Julius Caesar, who named July after himself, Niyazov bestowed his own moniker upon the month of January. He was, after all, the only act in town. His image was plastered on everything: buildings, books, postcards, stamps, TV screens, billboards, the currency, even bottles of vodka.

One day I hired a twenty-two-year-old taxi driver to take me around the city. "Turkmenbashi is watching you," joked Arslan as we passed a massive roadside billboard.

"What do you think of the president?"

"He's a nice man, a good man," Arslan said. "For all the world he wants peace. Do you understand me? Peace. For everyone. He's a very intelligent man."

"Don't you think there are too many statues, monuments, billboards and posters of the President?"

"We are a young country," he explained matter-of-factly, "and he is our first president. We need to celebrate our independence."

"Okay, but don't you think Niyazov has gone overboard?"

"No, it's normal."

I DISCOVERED JUST how "normal" Turkmenistan was on my first night in Ashgabat. Tatyana had booked me in the Hotel Rahat on the city's famed resort strip—another borrowing from Vegas. I appeared to be the only guest. In Ashgabat, foreigners are allowed to roam freely without a minder. So I was happy to ditch Tatyana, who was terse and cold.

I took a taxi downtown for a late dinner. The six-lane highway, lined with gleaming white marble-clad condos, was eerily empty. Just before 11 o'clock, I finished some lamb chops and wandered the downtown looking for a taxi back to the hotel. At the Arch of Neutrality, a towering monument shaped like a toilet plunger crowned with a gold statue of Niyazov that rotates with the sun, I was confronted by a soldier.

"Passport?" he asked.

I showed him my travel permit and photocopy of my passport. The young man frowned at me.

"*Polis,*" he said.

I smiled innocently.

He clasped his wrists, as though putting on handcuffs, and pointed at me. I was apparently under arrest.

The previous month Niyazov had accused French diplomats of spying and fomenting popular unrest. The secret police arrested several human-rights activists and a journalist, who was drugged, interrogated around the clock and beaten. (A few weeks after I left Turkmenistan, her battered corpse was handed over to family.) A Russian journalist had also recently spent two weeks in a Turkmen jail. I tried not to look nervous and strained my facial muscles into an expression of benign innocence.

A blue, unmarked BMW with tinted windows pulled up. I was ordered to get in. I felt like Alice going down the rabbit hole. I was driven first to a dark, wooded complex next to the Presidential Palace, where my pockets and bag were searched. One bemused policeman held my digital camera to his ear.

"Mobile?" he asked.

"No. Camera. *Photo aparat,*" I replied.

Two plain-clothed agents arrived to transfer me to a police station, a dingy Soviet building back near the restaurant. A large wooden desk sat in the dilapidated entrance hall. The staff sergeant glared at me, barked a few orders and laughed at his attempts to frighten me. I smiled weakly. My pockets and bag were searched again.

"What are you doing, Eric?" Tatyana screamed, storming into the station. "What foolishness?"

It was a good question; I had yet to figure out why I had been arrested. Tatyana began translating and answering questions in Russian. I slumped on a wooden bench with a wailing drunk and two beautiful women in traditional velveteen gowns and matching bejewelled shoes who appeared to be prostitutes. After an hour of questioning, a frustrated Tatyana went out to her SUV for a cigarette.

"This is serious," she said, coming back inside. "I'm going to have a stack of paperwork on my desk in the morning."

It was now past 3 AM. I drifted uneasily into semi-consciousness. Loud noises echoed in the halls and in my head: footsteps, shouts, whispering, shuffling paper, rattling keys, slamming doors, a scream. Then, suddenly, everything quieted. I opened my eyes. Officers put on their caps and stood stiffly to attention. In strutted a senior commander, a silver-haired apparatchik, his epaulettes dripping with gold braiding. He took off his oversized Soviet-style hat and carefully opened his spectacle case. His glasses hung on the end of a bulbous nose as he read paperwork on me. Tatyana translated my story once again. He scowled, snapped his spectacle case shut, saluted and left.

"Now what's happening?" I asked.

"We have to wait for some more officials."

"Who are they?"

"They are like the KGB."

My stomach knotted and bowels loosened.

"I need to go to the toilet."

A friendly officer with protruding ears led me to an outhouse behind the station. The light was broken and the officer pinched his nose, suggesting that I do the same. Faint moonlight streamed through a small window. At first, everything was stark black. What should I do? The police had, in fact, overlooked two notebooks full of journalistic jottings in the side pockets of my cargo pants. Should I throw them down the shit hole? What would the secret police do if they discovered them? Would they beat, torture or imprison me, as had happened to others? In the end, as I rezipped my pants, I stuffed the small notebooks in my crotch, hidden within my baggy pants.

Three agents from the National Security Committee, known as the KNB, arrived. They were in their forties, had short cropped hair and wore white short-sleeved dress shirts and black pants. One had a pistol holstered to his belt. The senior agent, a thickset man with a pitted face and hollow eyes, looked through my belongings and photographs. He made me read aloud my travel diary while Tatyana translated. At the end of the first page, Tatyana rolled her eyes and said in Russian something that sounded like: "Is this really necessary?"

He then began interrogating her: "Are you his lover? Are you a prostitute?"

"Come on, guys!" she snapped. "I work for the state tourism agency. This is business. Nothing else!"

"Now what?" I asked after the KNB agents had left.

"They say they are going to hold you overnight at the Immigration Bureau."

The bureau was about five minutes away. "You're going to have to stay the night here," Tatyana explained before leaving. "They said that you won't be mistreated."

That she had to reassure me was unsettling. It was now 4 o'clock. I was delirious from a lack of sleep. I began sensing bugs crawling all over my body. A soldier assigned to guard me came over and, in fact, began picking ants off my neck. They were biting me all over. Horrified, I ran outside tearing off my shirt and brushing off the chomping ants, much to the amusement of the soldier and a lingering KNB agent.

Ant-bitten, paranoid and exhausted, I propped myself in the corner of an office sofa and tried to sleep. Three hours later I woke to bright sunshine flooding the room and stinging my eyes. More officials came with more of the same questions. *Where are you from? What were you doing? Why were you out so late?*

"I made an honest mistake," I told one immigration officer.

"So, do you confess?" he asked.

"Yes, I confess. It was my fault, my mistake."

By this time, I had learned what I had done wrong. I was handed a piece of paper and told to write a confession. After reading it, an immigration officer dictated one more paragraph that I added at the bottom:

> I was not aware that foreigners are not allowed to be outside in the city after 11 PM without a tour guide. I confess my mistake and promise to obey all rules and regulations in Turkmenistan. I have no claims against the immigration officers.

Tatyana arrived with bags under her eyes, wearing the same clothes as the night before but with fresh crimson lipstick. She drove me back to the hotel. As soon as I closed the door to my room, I blurted out: "That was a fucking nightmare..."

Tatyana's disapproving gaze stopped me cold. She slowly rolled her eyes up to the ceiling and then back down into my weary eyes. She leaned toward me and whispered: "Someone could be listening."

MANNERHEIM HAD LITTLE to say about Ashgabat. It was, he wrote, "a little town in a green oasis. The horses are strikingly beautiful and elegant. Regrettably I had no opportunity to take pictures of them. The Turkomans are tall and thin and wear high sheepskin caps and long *khalats* (gowns) of subdued colours. After Ashkhabad, the sand plains begin again."

British secret intelligence reports at the time draw a more troubling picture. I sifted through the massive, leather-bound volumes of the Political and Secret Department archived at the British Library in London. In 1906, the British army was occupying Afghanistan to the south (they were back occupying Afghanistan during my journey as part of the NATO force that ousted the Taliban) and, fearing an invasion, closely monitored Russian military activity.

Ashgabat, like so much of the Russian empire at the time, was in chaos. A large bomb-making factory, run by Armenian revolutionaries, had been discovered in the oasis. Two weeks before Mannerheim arrived, the rifle battalions mutinied. Disgruntled troops overran the officers' club, took over the railway station and threatened to kill the local governor. "The situation in Russian Central Asia seems grave again," a British report begins. "There is no safety in the towns, murder and rapine being rampant, and the troops everywhere are reported to be disaffected. Numerous attempts have been made to wreck and rob trains..."[5] The unrest went on for months, including an assassination attempt, "in open court," on the governor. "Reports from Askabad show that a serious state of disorder and insubordination continues to prevail," states a dispatch from November 1906.[6]

Given the mayhem, Mannerheim's train journey from Ashgabat to Bukhara in what is now Uzbekistan was surprisingly uneventful. I had wanted to follow in his footsteps by car, but my travel agent had botched my booking by adding an obscure place called Darvaza to my itinerary. I couldn't find it anywhere between Ashgabat and Bukhara on a map. When I finally realized its whereabouts, I begged Tatyana to change my official travel itinerary.

"That's not possible," she said churlishly. "You've upset the authorities."

"ARE YOU A hardy man?" asked Zamina, my new minder. Tatyana had apparently tired of me.

"Why?"

"It will be an incredibly hot and uncomfortable trip. We have no air conditioning."

It would have made little difference anyway. The decrepit vehicle didn't even have side windows. It was a dirty yellow UAZ-469 all-terrain jeep originally built for the Red Army in the 1970s. Only a black canvas ragtop protected us from the blazing sun of Central Asia's hottest desert during the hottest month of the year. "We don't enjoy our summers," the hotel desk clerk told me. "We fear them."

A wizened, wiry Russian named Sergei was our driver. Zamina, a short, plump Azeri, wore fake Chanel sunglasses, a pink top and black exercise pants. As we set out, the afternoon temperature was hovering just above fifty degrees Celsius. Our destination lay 260 kilometres north of Ashgabat in the heart of the Karakum Desert. Darvaza was known as the "Gates to Hell."

The road out of Ashgabat led through cotton fields, mills, vineyards and cornfields that quickly gave way to sand and gravel. There were few cars on the highway. The air was so sand-ridden that I couldn't distinguish between heaven and earth on the horizon. An arid, dusty breeze blew in my face the entire five hours. Near the halfway point, we reached a military checkpoint and the tiny oasis of Bahardok. Black sheep and camels lingered around earthen huts and yurts in the desolate landscape. The desert, a gravel plain, soon turned into an ocean of dunes. Waves of sand lapped over the cracked, disintegrating asphalt. At one point, we passed bulldozers, dump trucks and graders trying to rebuild a section of the eroded highway. "The southern part is in the best condition," Zamina said, foreshadowing hardship ahead.

I sat in the back seat with jugs of petrol jammed under my seat and water bottles stuffed into the hollow door panels. The jeep rattled like a jackhammer. I tried to read *Rukhnama,* but the book is a sophomoric pastiche of pseudo-religion, revisionist history, memoir, dietary tips (you should "not eat greedily"), bland exhortations— in short, the meanderings of a madman. I stalled at page 51.

Shortly after 8 o'clock, we reached Darvaza. There were no streets, no houses, no sidewalks, no waterworks. Only a lonely yurt and an earthen hut sat by the roadside. At the beginning of June 2004, while flying over the desert, Niyazov commented on the village's unattractive appearance. He ordered it razed. About three weeks later, two hundred soldiers and policemen arrived and began forcefully removing the 350 residents. "We were given one hour to pack our belongings," said one victim. "Soldiers stopped the trucks heading for Ashgabat and loaded them with household goods and other belongings. Nobody even tried to protest, knowing that it was useless."[7]

We left the highway, following a rutted track in the sand up and over a hill. The jeep slid and fishtailed in the cascading sand. Sergei frantically steered to keep the jeep upright. At a rusting gas valve sticking out of the desert, we swerved to the left, off the track, and up another ridge. Below, I spotted a Nissan Patrol SUV beside a campsite at the foot of a rocky hill. It belonged to another guide, who was escorting a retired British journalist with a patchy white beard and a sunburned face.

"A strange country," Mike said, shaking my hand.

"Strange indeed," I said. "And this is the strangest place of all."

Sergei and I collected firewood on a ridge. Small dead shrubs were scattered everywhere. Their dried, brittle branches snapped like toothpicks. Sergei built a fire to cook *shashlik* (mutton kebabs) while Zamina rolled out a Turkmen carpet and laid out dinner.

In the twilight, I saw an eerie orange glow in a depression behind the hill. Mike and I went down to investigate. The burning gas crater must have been at least a hundred metres in diameter and twenty metres deep. Near the crater, a strong wind blew scorching heat and the smell of natural gas in our faces. The earth was dry as powder, crumbling under every step. I cautiously made my way to the edge to take a photo. The heat was overpowering. The skin on my face tightened. I peered down into the crater. Huge flames leaped up from burning rocks and licked the night air. I had indeed arrived at the Gates to Hell.

Back at the camp, Zamina and Sergei had already drunk half a litre of vodka. They were grinning mischievously. As we ate dinner on the carpet, Zamina told us that an explosion in the 1970s at a Soviet gas mine had created the crater. Many people were killed. "Unofficially," she added. She also told us about Darvaza's resettlement.

"Don't you think your president is crazy?" I asked after a mug of vodka. Mike perched in his cot to hear the answer.

"I would never move to Russia or Azerbaijan," Zamina began, echoing what Tatyana had said to me. "I can buy one of those new high-rise apartments in Ashgabat for $35,000 U.S. Gas is cheap. Electricity and phones are free. It's like Communism."

Despite her forced bromides, I knew Turkmenistan was far from utopia. I was figuratively and literally at the Gates to Hell, a godforsaken land haunted by an evil. At midnight, tucked into my sleeping bag, I stared up at the blinking stars and fell asleep awash in the demonic glow of the burning gas crater.

We departed early the next morning. The asphalt was so crumbled and potholed that we drove off road most of the way. Five hours later, we reached the desert's northern edge, ringed by cotton fields and the ancient ruins of Konye Urgench, a centre of Muslim civilization destroyed by Genghis Khan. We visited some twelfth-century ruins, but the maddening midday heat drained my enthusiasm. I politely suggested that we press on to a remote border post where I said a perfunctory goodbye to Zamina and Sergei.

A young soldier in a cut-off T-shirt and army cap greeted me. He looked like a teenaged conscript, boyish with oversized ears, fair skin and dirty blond hair.

"Are you an ethnic Russian?" I asked.

"I am Turkmen," insisted Sapa, whose name, he explained, means "hero" in Turkmen. He spoke broken English and kindly helped me exchange my Turkmen *manat* for Uzbek *som* at a café where I bought two bottles of frozen water. Surprisingly, the border guards didn't search my bags, and even politely offered me a seat in the shade. They entertained themselves scrolling through the photos on my camera.

My most indelible memories of Turkmenistan aren't the outlandish architecture or even the "Gates to Hell." Rather, they are the warm smiles and friendly glances I unexpectedly experienced wandering bazaars and snapping photographs. Even junior policemen, during my overnight detention, greeted me with *"Salam aleikum.* Peace be with you," placing their right hand over their heart. This gesture was followed invariably by a soft handshake and generous smile.

"Do you have any English language newspapers?" Sapa asked as we strolled to the last border checkpoint.

"Sorry," I said.

Once safely out of earshot of his superiors, Sapa quietly asked for my email address. In the dark delirium of Turkmenistan, in an oppressive state where the Internet is virtually banned and where contact with foreigners gives rise to suspicion, Sapa seemed to be living up to his name with this seemingly innocuous but utterly herioic act.

UZBEKISTAN

The Great Game Redux

The Game is so large that one sees
but a little at a time.—RUDYARD KIPLING, *Kim*[1]

THE TAXI DRIVERS had seen me coming, stumbling out of the Uzbek border post over the cracked asphalt. I was sweaty, dishevelled, tired and wobbling under the crushing weight of my backpack. I slumped at the roadside under a broiling desert sun. Where was I? Three Uzbek drivers hovered over me, snatching and pointing at my map. I shooed them away. The word "Koneürgenç" was handwritten in my Turkmen exit visa. On the map, I found Konye Urgench about six hundred kilometres northwest of Bukhara, my desired destination. The nearest town was Nukus, the capital of a destitute region called Karakalpakstan, in an utterly bleak part of Central Asia.

I waited for twenty minutes but no car and driver appeared, despite assurances from Zamina, so I hired one of the beat-up Daewoo sedans and raced into Nukus. Once home to a biological weapons institute run by the Red Army, the drab Soviet-era town now stands watch over the dying Aral Sea to the north. Its waters are being drained at an astonishing rate to irrigate Central Asia's massive cotton industry. Dust storms, soil erosion and contamination from pollution and sea salt are turning the region into a briny wasteland. With only thirteen dollars in my pocket, I found a branch of the National Bank of Uzbekistan, got an advance on my credit card and hired a taxi.

After an hour of haggling, theatrics and yelling, a chubby, unkempt taxi driver agreed to drive me, for $113, to Bukhara. We left at 8 PM, picking up one of his friends as a relief driver on the way. The two men couldn't have been more different. The driver looked like a Mongol with a round, flat face and slits for eyes. His friend had a face wrinkled like a dried apple, a straight nose and high cheekbones, suggesting Persian ancestry. They may not have been ethnic Uzbeks at all, but rather Karakalpaks, who speak a Turkic dialect closer to Kazak than Uzbek.

Khanates of blended races and tongues traditionally ruled Inner Asia. People identified themselves according to their local oases, their ruling dynasties and their allegiance to Islam. That didn't quite fit the Soviet concept of nationality. So in 1924, Stalin split Turkestan, as it was then known, into five new "national" republics—the "-stans" as they've come to be known—that defied history, geography and culture. His mapmaking resembled an elaborate jigsaw puzzle with arbitrary borders and oddball ethnic enclaves. He effectively divided and conquered the multi-ethnic Muslim populations and attempted to mould them into a new breed, *Homo sovieticus*.[2]

Uzbekistan, the largest republic, was an especially alien nation. Prior to Russian conquest, it was divided among three khanates centred in Kokand, Bukhara and Khiva, the last just south of Nukus. The Soviets imposed nationhood on a population with no concept of it and standardized regional Turkic dialects into the modern Uzbek language. Mannerheim, in fact, never used the word "Uzbek" in his diary. Instead, he referred to the local settled population as "Sarts," meaning "town dwellers" or "merchants," which at the time referred to ethnic Uzbeks, Persian-speaking Tajiks and even Uyghurs, the Muslims of Western China.[3]

The six-hundred-kilometre journey to Bukhara followed the Amu Darya. The river, also known by its classical Greek name Oxus, drains the meltwater of the Pamir glaciers and is the lifeblood of oases strung along its banks between the Karakum and Kyzyl-kum deserts, as well as Central Asia's cotton industry. We passed through a dozen police checkpoints and made a pit stop at a smoky roadside café before arriving in Bukhara at 3 AM.

Uzbek authorities are a heinous lot. Grisly human-rights reports on the country describe people being boiled to death, raped, tortured and murdered. A gruesome massacre of unarmed protestors in the town of Andijan the previous year had left observers aghast at the barbarity of the regime. "Things have deteriorated to the point where foreigners really have to watch their back, especially when they decide to travel on a tourist visa and wind up meeting with human-rights activists and journalists and interviewing people," an official at the International League for Human Rights in New York cautioned me. He suggested I discreetly meet a lawyer at the Bukhara Legal Humanitarian Centre.

"Do not speak in Uzbekistan to whom or about our meeting!" the Uzbek lawyer emailed back in broken English. "I hope you understand a situation in the country."

He agreed to meet and recommended a comfortable inn in Bukhara's ancient quarter. However, another activist exiled to Washington, D.C., warned me that this lawyer was probably on the payroll of the secret police. "A mole," Nozima Kamalova told me over the telephone. "Be very careful. He will immediately give any information about you to the security forces." Alarmed by this intelligence, I broke off communication with this suspected operative and picked a different hotel from a list in my guidebook during the drive from Nukus.

In the morning, from the Caravan Hotel's rooftop, the holy city of Bukhara stretched before me: domed markets, madrasas, ancient mosques and tiled minarets that looked like ornamental candlesticks. The town, a second Mecca, was remarkably quiet: the midday heat had driven residents indoors. The only foreigner I met that day was, like me, an undercover journalist. We went for a beer at a café next to Lyabi Hauz, a large stone pool in the heart of the ancient quarter. "People are very fearful," the American told me in a hushed tone. "The situation is getting worse. Watch for agents who may follow you around." In the afternoon, I wandered through the quarter of clay homes, doglegged passages and shaded markets that sold tourist trinkets, jewellery, handicrafts and traditional clothing.

That evening, I met Sanjar, a young tour guide with a bouncy gait and friendly demeanour, in the hotel lobby. I invited him for food at the poolside café. Over a plate of *shashlik* and red beet salad, he complained about all the oppression in his life, from a domineering mother to the tyrannical President Islam Karimov and his brutish clique who have a stranglehold on the state-controlled economy.

Sanjar found freedom, paradoxically, in forced labour: university students in Uzbekistan are obliged to pick twenty kilograms of cotton per day for several months each year. He relished his new-found independence. "It's the only time you have freedom from school and parents," he said. "There was a greater chance to meet girls and we even set up a disco one night for entertainment."

Throughout the day, I kept looking over my shoulder but never found that I was being followed.

"Of course," Sanjar told me. "They even follow me because I work with foreigners and my sister lives overseas and I've been to Europe. There are a lot of spies at this café because so many foreigners drink and dine here." That last comment cast a chill over me and quickly brought the evening to an end.

BUKHARA WAS "a fertile district," the Baron wrote as he rode the train from Ashgabat, "with villages and towns surrounded by shady gardens and groves." Larger flocks of sheep signalled an "evident prosperity." The local men were "tall and stout" and wore "long, well-trimmed beards" and turbans cocked over the left ear. Their *khalats,* or gowns, were made of "bright and beautiful colours." Mannerheim was now entering ancient centres of Persian civilization, magnificent oases of merchants and mullahs. The train stopped only briefly in Bukhara, then reached Samarkand at dusk. Among those who squeezed into the coach in Samarkand were the deposed Turkmen khan and Paul Pelliot, the leader of a French expedition.

The young French scholar—ten years Mannerheim's junior—was a philological genius. He had an astounding memory, indefatigable drive and acute intellect. Pelliot is widely considered the greatest Sinologist of the twentieth century.[4] He was also a megalomaniac. "Modesty was not Pelliot's strongest point," recalled one assistant. "In fact he had none."[5] At age twenty-three, after displaying legendary bravado during the siege of the Peking Legations in 1900, he was appointed full professor at L'École Française d'Extrême-Orient in Hanoi. In 1905, Pelliot attended the Fourteenth International Congress of Orientalists, where he was charged to undertake an expedition to Chinese Turkestan. He was accompanied by Dr. Louis Vaillant, a thin and pale thirty-year-old medical officer with a bushy beard and intelligent appearance. Valliant was tasked with mapping and natural history research. Charles Nouette was the expedition's photographer. In manners and dress, according to Mannerheim, he resembled "a retired sergeant."

Mannerheim introduced himself to Pelliot, who had a thin face, wispy moustache and long, Roman nose. They had just met in St. Petersburg, but Pelliot had difficulty recognizing the Baron, who now wore civilian clothes and had shaved off his fashionable officer's moustache.

Back in March 1906, Palitsyn had contacted the French Foreign Minister to request that Mannerheim join Pelliot and even travel on a French passport. The latter was denied, but Pelliot fully endorsed Mannerheim's participation and even offered himself as an informant to the Russian General Staff. In return, the Frenchman demanded free passage on the Trans-Caspian Railway, a personal and confidential payment of ten thousand francs and a Cossack escort. These were granted, and the payment even doubled. In June, the Tsar personally approved Mannerheim's covert mission.[6]

A French scientific expedition was, in many respects, not the ideal cover for Mannerheim. The British always suspected French complicity in Russian intrigues in Central Asia. In fact, Napoleon Bonaparte made the first move against Britain in the Great Game. In 1807, Napoleon proposed to Tsar Alexander I that they invade India. Some fifty thousand French troops would join Russian Cossacks to march across Afghanistan and Persia into British India—a brazen plot that alarmed London. Instead, Napoleon turned on the Tsar, attacking Moscow in 1812.[7] The British later seized French explorer Gabriel Bonvalot in 1888, mistaking him for a Russian spy. And in Rudyard Kipling's classic Great Game novel *Kim,* a young British spy outwits a Russian and French agent on a "hunting expedition" in the Pamirs, stealing their maps and papers. Mannerheim and Pelliot, travelling together in sensitive borderlands, would certainly arouse British suspicions.

The Great Game was ultimately about one-upmanship, about moves and countermoves to secure commercial advantage and feed imperial hubris. Each side, British and Russian, wanted to monopolize Central Asia's untapped markets and raw cotton and to create a buffer against their adversary's advancing armies. In 1831, the British dispatched their first secret agent, Lieutenant Arthur Conolly, disguised as a doctor. (Conolly coined the phrase "Great Game" in a letter to a friend.) He returned the next year to try to convince the three powerful khans of Khiva, Kokand and Bukhara to unite against Russian invasion but he was imprisoned and executed in Bukhara. All the khanates eventually fell, becoming Russian vassals. With Central Asia in the Tsar's grip, the Great Game now shifted eastward to China, Mongolia and Tibet. In 1904, the British invaded Lhasa, a preemptive strike against Russian intrigues.

In this context, Mannerheim's mission was to collect military intelligence on China's vulnerable borderlands and, if possible, make contact with the Dalai Lama, who was secretly corresponding with Tsar Nicholas II.

In an odd twist, Mannerheim later became a good friend of one of his British adversaries. F.M. Bailey was a Tibetan-speaking subaltern and member of Britain's military expedition to Lhasa. In 1918, he was sent to Turkestan to undermine Bolshevik revolutionaries and aid the *basmachi,* or Islamic fighters. Upon his return to England, Bailey became a national hero, recording his brazen and bizarre exploits in *Mission to Tashkent*.[8] Mannerheim met Bailey during a hunting expedition in South Asia in 1928.[9] They remained friends long afterward.[10] Bailey ultimately failed to undermine Bolshevism, and Turkestan became locked behind the Iron Curtain. For the next seventy years, the Silk Road was a geopolitical backwater. But the fall of the Soviet Union opened a new and gruesome chapter in the Great Game.

I ARRIVED IN Samarkand at midnight after a four-hour taxi drive through the dusty steppe from Bukhara. Exhausted, I lay in bed reading Mannerheim's diary the next morning. "The town is ancient," he wrote. Alexander the Great installed his colourful court here during his conquest of Central Asia in the third century BC. Genghis Khan razed it to the ground in the twelfth century, but it was "rebuilt with renewed splendor" by Tamerlane, the great Turco-Mongol conqueror. "The most beautiful and wonderful ruined mosques," the Baron wrote, "are of the 14th and early 15th century." The city's centrepiece is the awe-inspiring Registan, an ensemble of madrasas and mosques offering an overload of majolica tiling and well-proportioned spaces around a central square. Mannerheim thought that its "wonderfully beautiful" mosaics gave "a touch of inconceivable splendour to the enormous mosques that venture to raise their minarets and mighty cupolas so unexpectedly above the indescribable monotony of this town of grey unbaked bricks or lumps of earth."

From my inn, I walked the block to the Registan. "People stopped praying here in 1918 because Lenin wanted to separate school and religion," said my young guide Raihon, who had shimmering black hair and a flowing traditional silk dress. We were entering the Ulugh Beg Madrasa. The oldest of the Registan's three madrasas, it was built by its namesake in 1420. "He was a famous astronomer," Raihon explained, "and had the madrasa built with starburst mosaics on its facade." The school's imposing entrance consisted of a huge lancet arch, carved mulberry doors and twin minarets. Inside, we wandered through the dim, cavernous corridors. The cool air was a relief. A passageway took us into an inner courtyard ringed by a decrepit two-storey gallery, which had once housed student dormitories and classrooms. It was still a working Muslim school in 1906. Mannerheim noted how the mullahs "are very pleased to see visitors and never refuse baksheesh [gratuity]."

The small, vaulted dorm rooms were now stuffed, floor to ceiling, with tourist souvenirs: silk scarves, wooden tobacco pipes, pencil boxes, carpets, silver jewellery inlaid with coral from China, skull caps, postcards, camel-wool slippers. The rear of the madrasa formerly housed the mosque but was now an art gallery selling Impressionistic oil paintings, animal figurines and hand-painted chess sets with khans and mullahs replacing kings and bishops. The mosque had been turned into a temple to commerce.

"Isn't it offensive to have depictions of people and animals in a mosque?" I asked.

"It's not a mosque anymore," Raihon said dismissively. "The madrasa was turned into storage rooms by the Soviets, and during the Second World War, Russian painters came to Samarkand and were housed in the Registan. The square became a horse yard."

Like me, Mannerheim was shocked "at the lack of outward reverence" that locals showed toward these sacred monuments. A century ago, the Registan was in a "semi-ruined" state with large cracks in building facades and collapsing minarets. At this rapid rate of destruction, the Baron lamented, Samarkand's "magic glamour" would soon vanish. Mullahs were more than willing to profit from the destruction. "For a consideration," he added, "many a mullah would, no doubt, be prepared, under cover of darkness, to pull down a slab of mosaic of lovely colour with his own hands and hand it over to an irreverent tourist."

After the tour, I stood out front of the Ulugh Beg Madrasa in the exact spot where Mannerheim framed a photograph. It was taken on Friday, July 27, 1906. Inspecting the photograph, I could tell the time, about 12:30, by the sharp shadow on a minaret. The scene was, the Baron described, "marvellously impressive" as thousands of Muslims came to worship on the holiest day of the week. "They hurry to the mosque from all sides, some stopping to rinse their feet in an ariq [canal], spread their cloths and carpets in long rows on the pavement outside the already filled mosque and proceed to make their obeisances and prayers. The monotonous voice of the mullah breaks the silence now and then and a sea of white turbans rises and falls with surprising uniformity."

The scene in my camera's viewfinder—a century later on the same fourth Friday in July—couldn't have been more different: many of the mosaic tiles had been restored, but missing were the worshippers. My photograph captures an empty square. The arched entranceway, covered in a black shadow, looks like a gaping maw. A man in a white shirt squats in the archway while a policeman, hat cocked back, leans lethargically on the stone terrace. The chiming minarets and melodic calls to prayer had been silenced.

THE OVERNIGHT TRAIN from Samarkand arrived in Tashkent, the capital of Russian Turkestan, in the early morning. Mannerheim and Pelliot took a comfortable carriage, drawn by a pair of horses, to the Grand Hôtel. "Straight and wide unpaved streets shaded by poplars and acacias divide the town into large, regular blocks," wrote the Baron. "In the evening, when the Russian part of the town is lit up by electricity, it gives the impression of a large, shady park." He settled into a room and then called on General Sergei Markov, Acting Chief of Staff of the Turkestan Military District, whom he had known from the war against Japan. Mannerheim also met his interpreter for the expedition, a Manchurian named Liu.[11] The next morning, he returned to the military headquarters "to study the secret files." At noon, he was received by Governor-General Subbotich.

The Baron described Subbotich as "a young and alert general, with a pleasant and intelligent face, but he seemed to be stressed and preoccupied." Indeed, within a few months, Subbotich, the third governor-general in fourteen months, would resign in disgrace as Turkestan descended into violent unrest and chaos.[12] "He is a man of education and intelligence, his ideas are liberal, and he has probably not been sufficiently energetic in repressing revolutionary thought and action," states a British intelligence report at the time.[13] The *New York Times* later reported that he was discharged from the army for his "all-round laxness."[14]

In the afternoon, Mannerheim toured Tashkent's picturesque Old Town, a warren of narrow, winding lanes connecting lively bazaars, shops and courtyard homes. Their walls were made of clay mixed with straw and crude sun-baked bricks, which were "flimsy and thin." However, he admired Tashkent's "unrivalled" water-works, a network of canals. He found the local Sarts to be "strikingly neat." Wearing "dazzling white" turbans, they lay about on beautifully carpeted platforms in front of the teahouses, mosques and shops. They gossiped and smoked. Quarrels were seldom heard in the bazaar, which thronged with thousands on Wednesday each week. The merchants were, the Baron wrote, "unenterprising and lazy, but good natured and obliging."

The women, on the other hand, were mysterious. They were "closely veiled, with a black net-like veil shrouding their faces and breasts" and long garments from head to toe. "You see them flitting along a dusty road or street like ghosts, never stopping or being spoken to in the lively throng of loud voiced men," Mannerheim wrote. "In the heat that often exceeds 50°C, when no breath of wind refreshes the parched vegetation, this heavy, closed garb must be a torture."

TORTURE IS SOMETHING Craig Murray knows a lot about. From 2002 to 2004, he was the British Ambassador to Uzbekistan, an infamously undiplomatic diplomat. He had a taste for strip clubs, young belly dancers and late night parties. A sensational swirl of innuendo and scandal engulfs his career. The *Sunday Times* called him a "rebel envoy," "rogue diplomat" and "kilted philanderer of heroic recklessness."[15] He sounded like someone I should meet.

On my way to St. Petersburg, I stopped for several days in London to do research in the British Library. I also called Murray, who invited me to his West Kensington flat. He had fair skin and strawberry blond hair greying at the temples. He wore a striped blue polo shirt, khaki shorts and no socks. A "Happy Birthday" sign and deflated balloons adorned his living room. The party was certainly over for him: fired from his post, he'd been forced to downsize from an ambassadorial mansion in Tashkent to a cluttered flat. Allegations—sexual misconduct, boozing and selling visas for sex, all unproven—plagued the former ambassador, who had recently sold his sordid tale to a movie studio and was about to publish a memoir, *Murder in Samarkand*. He was affable, intelligent and blunt, the last getting him into all sorts of trouble. Indeed, the Foreign Office was threatening to sue him for releasing state secrets in his memoir.

Murray's downfall, curiously, started the day he received photographs of a mutilated corpse. It belonged to Muzafar Avazov, a member of Hizb ut-Tahrir, a banned Islamic party. Avazov had been imprisoned in Uzbekistan's notorious Jaslik prison. Murray sent the photos to the pathology department of the University of Glasgow. The pathologist report described something out of a medieval torture chamber: Avazov had been immersed in boiling liquid up to his torso, creating a tidemark of cooked, jellied flesh, and had all his teeth smashed and fingernails ripped out.[16] Murray was soon inundated with torture cases: beatings, drownings, smashed limbs, electric shocks applied to genitals, asphyxiation, chlorine gas poisoning, rape. One man, he discovered, died after being sodomized with a broken bottle.[17]

What troubled Murray most was that American and British security forces seemed complicit in this gruesome activity. After the attacks of September 11, 2001, Uzbekistan granted the U.S. military use of a former Soviet airbase to launch sorties against the Taliban in Afghanistan. In return, Uzbekistan received military aid and a veneer of legitimacy in the West. Murray quickly discovered that the CIA and Britain's MI6 were using Uzbek intelligence obtained through torture. Horrified, he sent an ambassadorial telegram to London: "Tortured dupes are forced to sign confessions showing what the Uzbek government wants the U.S. and U.K. to believe— that they and we are fighting the same war against terror... This is morally, legally and practically wrong." He pleaded that the West shouldn't use Uzbeks as "just pawns in the new Great Game."[18] Like many human rights activists, Murray blamed President Karimov's brutal persecution of independent businessmen, political opponents and religious worshippers for radicalizing Islam. Uzbeks are Sufis, followers of a mystical and moderate Islam. "It is not a country in danger of falling to Islamic radicalism," he explained.

Yet it was overly simplistic, he said, to assume that American co-operation in Central Asia was only about fighting militant Islam. "The fundamental motives are more basic than that," Murray told me. "It's about oil and gas contracts." That, according to Murray, is the prize in the New Great Game. A century ago, the game was quite simple: two players, Russia and Britain, competed to control hapless khanates that were economically and militarily backward. Today, the United States, Russia and increasingly China are attempting to exert influence and control over the region's rich resources. Corrupt autocrats have used these petroleum deposits to become obnoxiously wealthy and powerful, crushing domestic movements that challenge their authority and playing foreign powers against each other. As Murray explained, Enron, the American energy giant, had initially paid $100 million in bribes to President Karimov's family for lucrative petroleum contracts. However, when Enron declared bankruptcy as a result of massive fraud, the contracts were resold to Russia's Gazprom.

"How do you know this?"

"That's your job as an ambassador," he said. "People in the regime tell you stuff. I'm very sure of this."

At the end of our interview, Murray gave me the name of an outspoken human-rights activist I should meet in Tashkent. "If you are travelling independently, you'll likely be followed at some point," he warned. The city was crawling with tens of thousands of undercover agents and informants. "You can't trust anyone. Be very wary."

THE *REGISTAN EXPRESS*, the comfortable evening train from Samarkand, brought me to Tashkent shortly after 9 PM. Tashkent is the most cosmopolitan and Russian-speaking city in Central Asia. Broad avenues clogged with Ladas, Daewoos and the occasional donkey cart radiate out from Tashkent's large central park, which is crowned with a statue of Tamerlane. In 1966, an earthquake flattened the city, which was rebuilt as a model Soviet city with a modern subway, prefab concrete apartments and grand boulevards. I stayed at a comfortable tourist hotel that looked like a baronial manor.

The next day I was instructed to take a taxi to Il Perfetto, a busy Italian eatery in Tashkent's downtown. The restaurant was abuzz with Japanese tourists. I sat on a bar stool at an elevated table and waited. Ten minutes later, Andrea Berg and her husband, Detley, slipped in. Berg, a German with sandy blond hair and an earnest demeanour, ran the local office of Human Rights Watch, one of the last foreign non-governmental organizations operating in Uzbekistan. She had just come from observing two criminal trials in which alleged Hizb ut-Tahrir members were being tried for "anti-constitutional" activities. This was the same party that Muzafar Avazov allegedly belonged to. I told her I wanted to meet local activists. "That will be difficult," she replied. "Many people fear for their safety."

But a half-hour later, a tall man with a goatee and skullcap joined us. Akhmadjon Madumarov had just returned from Dublin, where he had received a human-rights award. He was with his youngest son. His other three sons and two nephews were all in prison on trumped-up charges of Islamic militancy.[19] Then Berg's translator, Umida Niazova, arrived. (Within six months she too would be tried, convicted and imprisoned on bogus charges.) They chatted in Russian and quickly ate before Berg rushed off to more trials. She advised me to wait ten minutes, staggering our departures to avoid suspicion in case the secret police were monitoring the restaurant from the street. I spent the afternoon sightseeing, careful to watch for anyone following me.

The next day, I met up with Pierre, a contact I had made through a Western embassy. He had been a left-wing radical at Cambridge and in 1979 moved to Tashkent to study Soviet politics. He left briefly after the Soviet Union's demise, but returned in 1993. Pierre was astonishingly thin, with sunken cheeks, pale skin and greying hair. He wore a wispy moustache and oversized glasses and espoused conspiracy theories about a Zionist plot to rule the universe. We chatted about the country's gory politics over lunch in one of Tashkent's leafy parks. He also agreed to help me contact Surat Ikramov, the activist Murray had recommended.

Ikramov was currently in court defending Uzbek bard, folk-singer and dissident Dadakhon Khasanov, age sixty-six, who had grown infamous in the 1960s when his lyrics landed him in a Soviet prison. After the massacre in Andijan on May 13, 2005, Khasanov had written a ballad about the government's brutal suppression of protesters there. One stanza is particularly grim:

Children died on the streets
Bright red like tulips
Shattered mothers were weeping,
There was a massacre in Andijan.

Khasanov was under house arrest and was being tried for "unconstitutional" activities. Two men had already been thrown in jail for possessing tapes of the song.

That evening Pierre telephoned Ikramov on my behalf and successfully arranged a meeting for me the next morning. However, ten minutes after talking to Ikramov, Pierre got a call himself— no voice, just heavy breathing. He figured it was the secret police. About a month later, his suspicions were confirmed: Pierre went to renew his residency visa but was denied. After thirteen years in Uzbekistan, he was being expelled. "I should have searched out a payphone," he later lamented to me in an email, "but it was already late [in the evening]." The secret police, he figured, traced the call to his apartment.

I WAS JOLTED awake by the unnerving sounds of machine-gun fire and explosions. I had fallen asleep watching BBC World News. Israel had just recently launched a war against Hezbollah in Lebanon. The TV filled my hotel room with the terrifying noises of modern war.

I already felt on edge. I worried that the secret police—certainly spying on Ikramov—might detain me on my way to meet him. I could be interrogated, deported—perhaps worse. As a precaution, I couriered photocopies of my notebooks home to Canada. I then flagged down a taxi, handed an address to the mustachioed Uzbek driver and slumped low in the passenger seat. But he quickly got lost, had to ask a passerby for directions, picked up another stranger to show us the way, then stopped at a teahouse to consult yet another group of idle men. Any one of these might have been a secret informant. At this point, I insisted that the driver call Ikramov for directions. Eventually, we arrived at a courtyard surrounded by three Soviet-built prefab towers. I quickly went up to his third-floor apartment.

"The reason I became a human-rights defender was because my rights came under attack," explained Ikramov in his airy home office. He wore white cotton pants and a beige linen shirt. He looked relaxed with a tanned face, salt-and-pepper hair and a trimmed beard. He had a deep, raspy voice. We sat at a desk spread with dossiers. Speaking through an interpreter, he said that corrupt officials had defrauded him in a business transaction years ago. He found no justice in Uzbekistan's notorious courts. Instead, he began monitoring judges who were sentencing political activists and Islamic worshippers on the thinnest of evidence or completely fabricated charges. Soon friends and family of the persecuted came to him with horrifying stories—and photographs.

He pulled out a dossier on a trader who ran afoul of security forces. "First they shot him and then they beat him," Ikramov said. A bullet fragment became lodged in the man's head. He was then tried for smuggling and sent to prison. "He was innocent, but the authorities imprisoned him anyway to silence him." The dossier contained identity papers, court documents, interviews and photographs of the bloodied victim.

"How many files like this do you have?"

Ikramov threw up his hands. "A thousand," he said grimly. "With most of the political opposition driven out of the country, Islamic worshippers and businessmen are the main targets now. Imprisoned activists number about twelve thousand."

He then opened his own file. It included a dozen photographs of Ikramov with a swollen, bandaged head. In 2003, four men abducted him from his car. "They laid me down, tied my hands behind my back, and put a hood over my head. They brought me to the countryside and beat me," he said calmly. "They broke my ribs and smashed my skull. They beat me unconscious. After I was beaten, I came home and the next day the Second Secretary in the American embassy came to my home and offered to allow me to go to the United States as a political refugee."

"Why didn't you go?"

"If I went to the United States, who'd work in Uzbekistan? We have to fight against this regime. If other governments help us, we can defeat the government. The regime must be stopped."

He randomly selected another file. A dozen photographs depicted a dead young man. His skull was cracked open, his face bloodied, bruised and contorted. Ikramov spread the photos in front of me. I had to look away.

"Karimov used the money from the United States to persecute the people," he said of $60 million in U.S. military aid. "He didn't use this money against terrorists, but against the people. I have never seen any facts relating to terrorism in any of the criminal cases that have gone to the courts. There are no terrorists in Uzbekistan."

He paused, realizing this last statement was an exaggeration; the Islamic Movement of Uzbekistan, for example, is a well-known terrorist group. "Actually," Ikramov conceded, "there's one terrorist in Uzbekistan and he is the President."

IN JULY 1906, Tashkent was on the brink of insurrection, although you wouldn't know it from reading Mannerheim's diary. He and Pelliot stayed in the city for six days, touring neighbourhoods and procuring supplies. They visited an artillery general to obtain rifles, gunpowder and cartridges. Their good Russian impressed the general.

"Pelliot speaks excellent Russian and you almost as well— marvellous where Frenchmen are concerned," the general said.

"No wonder, after an alliance of so many years," Mannerheim replied.

Pelliot and Mannerheim, in fact, held up the Russo-French alliance's tradition of pettiness and backstabbing. The bickering began in earnest in St. Petersburg: Mannerheim proposed that his brother-in-law, Louis Sparre, join the expedition as its artist but they could not agree on the financial arrangements. In Tashkent, Pelliot became irritated "by the formality and slowness of the Russian authorities." He complained constantly that officials were not providing him with enough support. A power struggle emerged about who exactly was in charge.

The day before he left Tashkent, Mannerheim wrote a peculiar note in his diary: "The news of the unexpected dissolution of the Duma forced me to hasten my departure and complete my purchase with feverish speed." In Pelliot's diary, the Frenchmen also wrote upon hearing this news that "we must leave quickly."[20] Something seemed amiss.

I found the reason for the Baron's hasty departure in dispatches from the Political and Secret Department of the India Office archived in the British Library in London. Dated July 27, 1906 — the day after Mannerheim left Tashkent—one report describes "a serious mutiny at Tashkent in which practically the whole garrison, except the Cossacks, joined, and as a result of which authorities had to grant all the men's demands. It is said that in the course of the fighting one hundred soldiers were killed, and that the mutineers attacked and defeated the loyal portion of the garrison and captured the fort."[21]

Mannerheim, whose fellow Finnish countrymen were also fighting Russian oppression, was careful not to write anything in his diary that could be misconstrued as disloyalty to the Tsar. In fact, he wrote rather glowingly about Russian rule. The Tsar had given Central Asia "two railway lines, better roads, a flourishing cotton industry and probably much besides," including "security and peace." He even belittled Muslim complaints. "Illogicality, child-ishness and inability to take a broad view of a thing are typical of the Muslims of Turkestan," he wrote. "It is certain that large classes among the people of Turkestan entertain political dreams and hopes that no longer seem to them utopian after the unfortunate outcome of the last Russo-Japanese war."

Mannerheim recognized growing "demands for reforms, extended rights and other aims and ambitions" among Central Asians. The question now, he figured, was whether Russia, "by enlightened leadership, can succeed in guiding this process in a direction consonant with imperial policy, or whether the leadership of these people who scarcely read anything but the Koran at present" would launch an "Anti-Russian Mohammedan movement."

Leaving troubled Tashkent, Mannerheim returned to Samar-kand, where he called on the Second Ural Cossack Regiment. The colonel was flattered that two of his Cossacks were to be placed at Mannerheim's disposal by order of the Tsar. Almost nothing is known about Ignati Yunusov and Shakir Rakhimjanov. (Yunusov is mentioned only twice by name in the Baron's diary and a note-book.[22]) "The men looked smart, the horses were small, strong, plump and too well fed," Mannerheim wrote. "After explaining the privations and hardships that awaited us, I asked if the men had carefully considered that the journey would take fully two years."

"If it took three or four instead of two, we should be willing to go," the Cossacks replied. They left Samarkand in the evening for Andijan, where the party's French companions were waiting.[23]

Andijan was the terminus of the Trans-Caspian Railway, nestled at the eastern end of the fertile Ferghana Valley. This rich agricul-tural plain, coveted for its cotton fields, was the most unruly region in Russian Turkestan. Disastrous Imperial policy had brought about growing landlessness and indebtedness among disgruntled farmers. Led by a mystical Sufi religious leader, a mob of two thou-sand Muslims attacked the local Russian barracks in 1898, killing twenty-two soldiers. The Andijan uprising shocked the Russians, who blamed it on Islamic fanaticism. While Ferghana's religious conservatism played its part, the rebellion had more to do with power struggles and the economic plight of peasants.[24] The unrest persisted long afterward. Within a few months of Mannerheim's visit, the Russians imposed martial law in the district.[25]

Mannerheim saw little of the small town. He was too busy collecting his luggage and hiring *arbahs* (two-wheeled, horse-drawn carts) to carry his belongings and supplies for their continued journey on horseback. At their hotel, he and Pelliot met a wealthy merchant. Said Khani invited them to dinner that evening. Mannerheim thought his host was "talkative, good-natured and outwardly sincere." Khani telegraphed an employee and instructed him to meet the expedition on the road and escort them to the bazaar town of Osh the next day. Khani was, Mannerheim wrote, "exceedingly obliging and he really did me many a good turn."

I HAD BEEN repeatedly warned not to visit Andijan. It was unsafe, everyone said, especially for journalists. An Agence France-Presse reporter, visiting on the one-year anniversary of the massacre on May 13, had been held captive in his hotel room and beaten by vigilantes.

I nevertheless hailed a random Daewoo in front of the hotel and negotiated a fifty-dollar ride to Andijan, five hours away. The landscape outside Tashkent turned into a checkerboard of gold and green, fields of cotton and sunflowers, framed by the crimson Chatkal mountains. A gauntlet of military checkpoints and tunnels guarded by soldiers with machine guns protected the strategic pass over the mountains to the Ferghana Valley. An army convoy loaded with troops, howitzers and mobile radar equipment inched its way down a gnarly switchback. Cresting the rocky pass, we soon entered Ferghana's high alpine valley. I was trading the dry steppes and deserts of Central Asia for a lush, densely populated plateau fed by two rivers. A slight moistness and the pungent smell of fertilizer hung in the brisk evening air.

It was dark by the time we reached the Andijan Hotel, fronting the town's central square. A theatre, which had burned down during the uprising, was under reconstruction across the street. The hotel had a Russian colonial facade and opulent marble foyer with murals and plaster reliefs, a misleading first impression. Upstairs, it looked more like a skid-row boarding house: swarthy young men, stripped to their underwear, lay in dorm beds watching TV and smoking cigarettes. An old woman wrapped in a headscarf shuffled between rooms delivering tea. At the end of the hall, I found my room: two lumpy cots, no shower, no toilet.

I ate at the Golden Chicken Restaurant next door. Its back courtyard was nearly empty, but a small, boisterous group—laughing, joking and guzzling vodka—enlivened the air. I ordered some barbecue chicken.

"May I join you?"

I looked up from my greasy plate and was greeted by Rashid, a thirty-year-old English teacher. "We have very good theoretical classes about the English language and literature, but we don't get much practice," he lamented. "Few foreigners come to Andijan anymore."

"Many people warned me not to come," I said. "They said it wasn't safe."

"No, no, that's not true. There's no problem here," Rashid said. "It was foreigners who caused the problems in Andijan." As it turned out, Rashid also worked as a government translator and was just mouthing the official line about "foreign" troublemakers, meaning militant Islamists living across the border in Kyrgyzstan. But the Andijan uprising, like the one in 1898, was largely precipitated by the ruling regime's ruinous economic policies and power struggles. Authorities had imprisoned twenty-three businessmen who were part of a co-operative movement of Muslim merchants. When an armed group stormed the Andijan prison, freeing the entrepreneurs and many others, the regime reacted swiftly and violently.[26] Security forces killed hundreds of unarmed protesters, including children, assembled in the central square.

One Thursday every month, Rashid and his three childhood friends—a banker, a taxi driver and a businessman—go out for dinner and drinks. He invited me back to their table for more chicken, tomato salad and vodka, and offered to escort me to the Kyrgyz border crossing the next day. Their hospitality was uncannily familiar: Mannerheim had received similar generosity from an Andijan merchant.

Gulp by gulp, the vodka bottle emptied. Waitresses began stacking chairs on top of the tables and sweeping the floor. "Let's go for a tour of Andijan," Rashid declared. It was 11 PM.

We piled into a white hatchback parked out front. The banker, who appeared the most intoxicated, drove. He pulled out an illuminated taxi sign and attached it to the roof. "The police don't pull over taxi drivers and they would never suspect that a taxi driver is drunk," he grinned. I fastened my seat belt. We breezed through a police checkpoint at the edge of town and then turned right into a park and hilltop museum. All the while, Uzbek music blared and the banker gyrated in his seat as though the car were a disco.

The museum is dedicated to Babur, the great Mughal conqueror whose lineage stretches back to both Tamerlane and Genghis Khan. He became ruler of Ferghana at fourteen. "He was a great conqueror, but not a great ruler," Rashid said, sipping a beer. "Uzbeks celebrate him today, but in fact the Uzbeks were the ones who drove Babur from Andijan." Conniving uncles and rebellious *begs* (Muslim magnates) robbed him of his throne. Babur eventually conquered Kabul in Afghanistan and expanded his empire into Northern India, establishing the Great Mughal Dynasty. We walked up a stone stairway to his mausoleum. Some dirt from Babur's grave in Kabul had been brought here and entombed in a stone vault under a gazebo.

From here, I could see Andijan's lights twinkling like fireflies below the black silhouette of the Tian Shan range in the distance. These are the famed "Heavenly Mountains" that wall off China from the West. As I pondered my difficult journey ahead, I felt cold raindrops hitting my face and looked up to see thunderclouds. After four weeks of desert travel, the rain felt like manna. We ate *shashlik* and drank more vodka at a café next to the turnoff for the museum. With my tongue loosened by alcohol, I quietly asked Rashid about the massacre. He said his brother, who is an army officer stationed in Tashkent, called one morning to tell him not to go outside for three days. "I had no idea what was going on," he muttered. "The 'events' were really restricted to the city square." He knew nothing more, or so he professed.

We took side streets back into town. On Babur Square, where the massacre occurred, we stopped at a monumental gate crowned by a turquoise cupola, the entrance to an amusement park. It was 1 AM. As the banker shut off the motor, a white Volga full of policemen pulled up beside us. The banker and taxi driver got out. I was squeezed in the backseat between Rashid and the businessman, who also got out. "Stay in the car," Rashid whispered. In the dark, I heard voices and out of the corner of my eye I saw scuffling as the police wrestled someone to the ground. There was yelling and the scraping of shoes on concrete. I looked over my shoulder to see another police car arrive.

"Get out of the car and start walking to your hotel," Rashid whispered.

During the commotion, I slipped out of the car and nervously started off in the direction of the hotel a block away. My heart was pounding. "Not so quickly," Rashid cautioned.

As I neared some shrubbery, a teenage boy jumped out of nowhere and began yelling. I turned around to see a half-dozen police glaring at me. They motioned for me to return and put me in the back of the Volga. We drove to a one-room police post. Rashid and the rest of my newfound friends arrived separately. An officer looked at my passport and flicked his finger hitting a vein in his neck, a gesture for drunkenness. I shrugged and smiled, resigning myself to a long night of questioning that, thankfully, never happened. Rashid was well connected to the mayor and had apparently negotiated my release. As I left, I shook Rashid's hand. "Terribly sorry," he said, turning his eyes away in embarrassment.

My tour of this police state came to a fitting end. A senior policeman drove me back to the Andijan Hotel in his unmarked Volga. During the short drive, he kept repeating three words in English to me: "I am sheriff."

KYRGYZSTAN

Travels on the Synthetic Road

While the splendid pictures of the past, one by one, sank beneath
the western horizon, new and glorious prospects rose up daily in the east
under the morning sun.—SVEN HEDIN, *The Silk Road* (1936)[1]

"SILK ROAD" IS a misnomer. There was never one road, but rather a network of routes connecting China to the world across the scorching deserts and dusty steppes of Central Asia. And by the time German geographer Ferdinand von Richthofen coined the phrase in 1877, five hundred years had passed since the luxurious fabric had been the mainstay of the overland trade routes. The name was always meant to evoke a storied past, visions of endless caravans laden with the riches of Cathay.

In the second century AD, an imperial envoy, Zhang Qian, was sent west to establish an alliance with a Central Asian tribe against China's fiercest enemy: the Xiongnu, or Huns. Although Zhang's mission failed, the intelligence brought back, especially about a breed of warhorse in Ferghana, sparked the commercial beginnings of the Silk Road. The Han Dynasty pushed westward, establishing military garrisons to protect their newfangled trade routes. By

AD 380, so much Chinese silk was flowing to Rome that the Senate tried, in vain, to ban the material that had come to symbolize the empire's decadence and decay. The lopsided trade also drained the Roman treasury of gold. The trade routes flourished for more than a millennium but began to decline in the thirteenth century as a result of the Black Death in Europe, the collapse of the Mongol empire and the rise in maritime trade. By the time Marco Polo arrived, the Silk Road was losing its lustre.

At one time, China had the most skilled craftsmen and advanced technology in the world. Silk, satin, musk, jade, pearls, paper, the compass, gunpowder, printing, the astrolabe—all were prized in the West. But China's fortunes dimmed as the Enlightenment set off an explosion of rapid scientific advancement in Europe. Industry and empire sent Europeans on a global quest (and conquest) for raw materials and markets. At the same time, China's stubborn insularity had turned it into a medieval backwater. Overland trade was especially sluggish. China had little to offer but raw materials, particularly silk and cotton, which were exported to India over the Karakoram Pass and then imported back as manufactured goods.[2] Camel caravans also brought raw cotton, wool and leather over the rugged alpine pass from Kashgar in China's far west to Osh in Russian Turkestan.[3]

Mannerheim found Osh's "motley bazaars full of life and movement," but bemoaned the lack of quality goods. "There is little to buy and prices are high," he wrote. "Anyone travelling in Central Asia would be well advised to obtain little of his equipment as possible in Turkestan." At the time of Mannerheim's journey, the most valuable and sophisticated manufactures in local bazaars were Russian, including stained-glass oil lamps, sugar wrapped in blue paper packaging, scents and soaps. To bolster trade, the Russians agreed to lend the Chinese a large sum of money, interest free, to build a road for wheeled traffic over a mountain pass to Kashgar.[4] At the same time, Russia's domestic turmoil was causing a slump in trade. Still, darker days lay ahead for the Silk Road.

Trade limped along during China's decades of revolution and warlordism. Ironically, as the Silk Road's fame grew, its fortunes declined. Mannerheim never used the phrase "Silk Road" in his diary; the moniker came into popular use later, after his friend Sven Hedin titled one of his wild adventures *The Silk Road*. "We now saw the Silk Road at its lowest ebb," wrote Hedin in 1936, "with dormant life and dying trade, the connecting towns and villages in ruins, and populations languishing in a state of permanent insecurity and miserable poverty."[5] During the Sino-Soviet split in the 1960s, borders were sealed and the Silk Road, after more than two thousand years of commerce, ceased to exist altogether.

EVERY MORNING, AROUND 8:30, I watched half the city descend on the Jayma Bazaar in Osh. I came to Kyrgyzstan's second-largest city via taxi from Andijan, only thirty kilometres away. I rented an airy two-bedroom flat in a mid-rise built of prefab concrete. Some residents kept chickens in pens and tended small vegetable patches on the ground floor. The residential block was hemmed in on three sides by Osh's chaotic central bazaar. My fourth-floor balcony overlooked a street clogged with melon and kebab stands, shops, money exchanges and lively cafés that served flatbread and chopped noodles with spicy mutton.

The scene was the same every day: young boys pulled carts and makeshift trolleys heaped with mountains of melons, onions and rice sacks. Uzbek women in colourful headscarves—40 percent of Osh is ethnic Uzbek—set up stalls to sell soaps, toiletries, bras and clothing. Old Kyrgyz men, in traditional felt *ak kalpaks* (white hats) and goatees, browsed bootlegged DVDs, electronics and shoes—all made in China. There were Russian, Kazak and Tajik traders too. And blacksmiths, cobblers, seamstresses and bakers. Their rickety stalls of clapboard, rough-hewn timbers and scrap metal numbered about fifteen thousand.

Jayma is the oldest bazaar in Central Asia, dating back three thousand years. For decades, collectivization had hobbled its freewheeling spirit. But when the Soviet Union collapsed, former accountants, teachers, factory workers and technocrats suffering unemployment and unpaid wages made their way here. They hawked their personal possessions, homegrown veggies, goods shuttled over the mountain passes from China and whatever else they could scrape up. Feverish commerce quickly returned to Osh's famed bazaar, which now stretches a kilometre along the Ak-Buura (White Camel) River. Each day, some fifty thousand shoppers shuffle through the intimate alleyways, shaded by cotton sheets strung overhead.

I toured another newer bazaar with Amanda, an American professor on secondment to an international aid agency in Osh. The American journalist whom I first met in Bukhara was now in Osh and introduced me to Amanda. She was a young, astute woman with a lean physique and intense demeanour. Southern Kyrgyzstan, Amanda explained, was hit especially hard by the closure of Soviet factories. The economy virtually collapsed. However, in 2002, the Irkeshtam Pass between China and southern Kyrgyzstan reopened. Cross-border trade exploded and the number of bazaars across Kyrgyzstan quadrupled.[6] By 2006, China's trade with Central Asia had grown twenty-fold to almost $10 billion. "The south is now mostly a trading economy," Amanda said. "Products are being brought in from China and sold in wholesale markets such as Karasuu and then distributed throughout Central Asia."

Karasuu is, in fact, the largest wholesale bazaar in Central Asia. It's about twenty-five kilometres from Osh on the Uzbek–Kyrgyz border. It started as a simple farmers' market in Soviet times. "The wholesale market developed over the past ten years and it has boomed in the last five years," Amanda said as we approached by taxi. Some three thousand steel shipping containers and corrugated warehouses form a labyrinth of wholesale stalls. Stacked two high and forming cavernous aisles, the containers are crammed with Chinese-made goods. The bazaar was dim and muggy. Its vast scale makes even the largest Wal-Mart superstore look like a mere kiosk.

About 70 to 80 percent of the traders are ethnic Uzbeks, Amanda explained. We stopped at one container spilling brilliantly colourful silk.

"Do you have any Uzbek fabric?" Amanda asked the middle-aged Uzbek merchant in Russia.

The man chortled. All the fabrics looked Uzbek. They had that whimsical arrow-shaped pattern of tie-dyed colours, called *ikat*, that I had seen in Samarkand. "No," he said, "about 80 percent of the fabric is from China and 20 percent from Korea." I rubbed the radiant fabric between my thumb and fingers. It felt waxy and slightly stiff. It wasn't silk at all, but rather synthetic material probably made in Chinese petrochemical plants. Almost everything was fake, bootlegged or poor quality. At another container, I browsed cheap grey polyester suits; the material was as shiny as a silver dollar. In the shoe section, off-gassing glues, dyes and polymers—combined with the sweltering midday heat—were asphyxiating. We quickly escaped the feverish market to explore nearby border posts.

In 2002, Uzbek authorities demolished a bridge at the Karasuu border. That didn't stop the flow of goods, however. A kilometre down the road, desperate Uzbek traders drove out local authorities during the Andijan massacre and constructed their own rickety footbridge across the Shakhrikhansay River, which divides the two countries.[7] From here, merchandise passes from trader to trader, from wholesaler to retailer, spreading west through Eurasian bazaars. The handmade burqa market in Afghanistan had even reportedly collapsed because of cheap, mass-produced Chinese imports, which probably flowed through Karasuu.[8] At the footbridge crossing, the scene was chaotic and tense. Donkey carts, trucks and Volgas were loaded high with bundles of goods. These were being broken down and hoisted onto the backs of men, teenagers and even old Uzbek women—human packhorses. Kyrgyz border guards stood by as the traders shuffled across the bridge. On the other side of the narrow river, Uzbek soldiers toting Kalashnikovs sat in the shade of a tree. Attempting to take a photo, I was immediately accosted by two soldiers. "Documents," one scowled. A senior officer was more apologetic: "We have to be like this because the situation is difficult. The Uzbeks are very touchy."

Security forces had recently been in running gun battles with Islamic militants along the border. Karasuu has become a centre of drug trafficking, smuggling, militancy and corruption. Hizb ut-Tahrir, the banned Islamic party, has a large presence in the market. And in 2005, a violent struggle for control of the bazaar led to the assassination of a parliamentarian. Now the Chinese were weighing in by financing a competing wholesale market at Dostuk, twelve kilometres away.

The Chinese are reasserting themselves in Central Asia in a way not seen since the days of Marco Polo. Amanda had recently seen Chinese workers with "rice-picker" rattan hats rebuilding the highway to Bishkek, the capital. Some twenty thousand Chinese also work in bazaars across Kyrgyzstan.[9] "There's a lot of fear that Chinese businessmen are taking over the role of local traders," Amanda said. I even heard an absurd local story that the Chinese were going to buy Solomon's Throne, a sacred Muslim mountain in the centre of Osh, to build a resort casino atop its peak. This paranoia has a long history. "The Kirghiz," Mannerheim wrote, "apparently believe that a day will dawn when a great hero will arise in powerful China and reconquer them."

We dined at Hundali that evening. The Chinese restaurant is housed in an old Russian theatre. Its interior was adorned with red paper lanterns. A rowdy party of a dozen Chinese businessmen sat on the outdoor patio. From a teenaged Kyrgyz waitress who wore a synthetic cheongsam, we ordered eggplant with garlic sauce, starch noodles and beef with banana. We also bought a bottle of "Chinese vodka," as the waitress described, for a nightcap. It turned out to be *baijiu,* a horrific-tasting overproof liquor. Distilled from sorghum, the exotic drink is popular among Chinese businessmen. Its bitter taste is something that Central Asians are apparently going to have to get used to, along with the roasted squirrel on the menu.

MANNERHEIM AND PELLIOT stayed their first night in Osh in the home of Said Khani, the wealthy Uzbek merchant whom they had met in Andijan. They feasted on traditional *dastarkhan,* literally a "tablecloth" that is spread on the floor with hard caramels, dried fruits, almonds, pistachios, melons and other candy. Then came heaping "dishes of greasy mutton." Mannerheim was not impressed. "Pelliot claimed that it would have been a grave insult to leave anything on the dishes," he wrote. "After a great deal of sighing and eating the dishes were emptied and we hastened to bid our host goodnight in fear and trembling lest there should be any more mutton fat."

In the morning, they called on Colonel Alexeyeff, the district commander—"a typical, petty official, afraid above all things of accepting responsibility for anything"—and moved to a more spacious caravanserai where they began to carefully sort and pack their supplies and equipment into cases, which would be loaded on packhorses.

Mannerheim and Pelliot then started for Uzgen, thirty kilometres away, where they bought more horses for their caravan. Uzgen, according to Mannerheim, was "a small town celebrated for the biggest horse markets in the district." The Baron was one of Russia's leading horse traders. In 1901, he had been appointed to head the Imperial stables.[10] He travelled all over Europe purchasing horses and even lunched with Kaiser Wilhelm II on one trip to Germany. His entire family, Mannerheim once wrote, has "the love of horseflesh in our blood." In Uzgen, he bought four packhorses and two riding horses, one for himself and the other for Liu, his Chinese interpreter. He named his own horse Philip.

The expedition stayed another ten days in Osh. On August 9, Mannerheim penned a revealing letter to his father. "It might be too early to evaluate them yet, but my impression after having spent more than 2 weeks together is not favourable to P[elliot]," he wrote. "Very niggardly and avaricious, extremely particular about his prestige as the chief of the expedition, a poseur, interfering in everything, an egotist of the first rate, in other words a character whom it will not be easy to get along with." They were squabbling about expenses, the route and his role in the expedition. Despite his payment from the Tsar, Pelliot refused to recognize him as an official member but rather just as a Finn travelling in his company and sharing a cook. The other Frenchmen made a more favourable impression: Vaillant "is calm and equable as P[elliot] is violent and capricious." And the photographer, Nouette, he told his father, had "a jolly Bohemian nature [and] is full of whims and very resourceful."[11]

The journey began inauspiciously that same day. Their caravan of some seventy-five horses started six hours late. As they set out on the highway to Kashgar, the Baron rode into a swift flowing canal to cool off his horse. Philip shied from the steep bank and then jumped awkwardly down. Both rider and horse plunged into the cold water. It must have been hugely embarrassing for Russia's leading cavalry officer, as Pelliot smugly watched the mishap unfold. Mannerheim's camera survived the tumble, but his papers did not. He lost one of his stirrups and straps too. The Cossack Rakhimjanov undressed and dragged the canal until he found them.

For two days, they trekked along the Gulcha River toward snow-capped mountains in the east. "The hills rise up, covered with verdure in beautiful, dark shades while small flowers similar to our heath blossom appear in the valley," Mannerheim wrote. Villages became less frequent as the hills grew into mountains. At one point, they came across a Kyrgyz family laden with their yurt, cattle and belongings. The women were dressed in brilliant cloth, high boots, galoshes and white scarves wound around their head and neck. They covered their faces as the party approached.

The road became very steep and zigzagged to the top of Chi-girchiq Pass, whose velvety dark green meadows were bounded by "stately snow-capped peaks." "Even the Cossacks could not restrain cries of delight," Mannerheim wrote, "and we tore ourselves away with difficulty from the wonderful picture and began the descent." At the bottom of the pass, they encountered the son of Hassan Beg, a Kyrgyz nobleman whom Mannerheim had met in Osh. His father, the son explained, had mistakenly ridden to Gulcha to meet them. So the French expedition accepted the son's hospitality and settled in for the night. "The spacious yurt, decked inside with beautiful carpets and colourful hangings, looked inviting," wrote Manner-heim. They ate a quick meal with tea and then slipped into "warm silken quilts."

They woke in the morning to a pleasant surprise: Hassan's leg-endary mother, Kurmanjan Datka, was in the yurt next door. The Queen of Alai, as she is known, was a Muslim noblewoman who reigned over the mountainous Alai region wedged between China and the Central Asian steppe. Led by two elderly servants, she came over to the yurt wearing a rich *khalat* of silk brocade trimmed with fur. A white headscarf framed her dark face. "Puffing slightly," Mannerheim recalled, "she sank to her knees and sat down on her calves, according to Kirghiz custom, on a fur spread out for her." Her grandson translated her customary pleasantries. Manner-heim took a few photographs and then everyone went outside. "I requested the wrinkled old lady of 96 to allow me to perpetuate her sitting on horseback," he wrote. "A brown horse, handsomely saddled, was led up and with little help from her grandson and a ser-vant she mounted with the confidence only possessed by one who has spent her life in the saddle."

Kurmanjan Datka then instructed her grandson to fetch a *khalat* of green velvet from her tent. Pelliot rushed forward to accept the gift, Mannerheim recalled, "obviously fearing to be preceded by me." The uppity Frenchman thanked her in the name of them both and promised to send a gift from their caravan. "The end of it," Mannerheim complained to his father in another letter, "was that he did not send anything at all."[12]

THE DAY AFTER touring Karasuu, Amanda and I went for lunch at a restaurant on Kurmanjan Datka Avenue in Osh. "There's a rumour that an imam has been shot in Karasuu," she told me. An hour after we had left Karasuu, as it turned out, security forces shot Muhammadrafik Kamalov, an ethnic Uzbek imam and one of Kyrgyzstan's top religious leaders. He had been transporting two suspected terrorists in his car, or at least that's what government officials claimed. It was impossible to make sense of the murky details and motives behind the shooting. I didn't stay to find out. That afternoon Amanda arranged a car and driver to take me to Gulcha.

Sardarbek Ismailov, aged sixty-nine, greeted me with a warm, grandfatherly smile that revealed a row of golden teeth. He had a strong, wiry build, sun-blackened complexion and a tender handshake. I climbed into the front seat of his beat-up, beige-coloured Volga. Aidai, my eighteen-year-old translator, jumped in the back.

"Kurmanjan Datka was my great-great-grandmother," Sardarbek began as we raced out of Osh. He held up four thick fingers. "Fourth generation," he said laying on the horn as we passed a car. We hurtled over a bumpy country road through parched golden hillocks rising gently above the Gulcha River. Here and there, small farming hamlets of mud-brick bungalows were tucked along the embankment. We swerved around potholes, cows and sheep. As he ground the gears, he began telling me about his fabled grandmother, considered "the mother of the Kyrgyz people." After Kyrgyzstan achieved independence, a statue of her was erected in Osh, and her image adorns stamps and the fifty-*som* banknote.

The story of her life, as I pieced together from Sardarbek and a few other sources, goes something like this: at age eighteen, Kurmanjan, the daughter of a stockbreeder, rejected an arranged marriage to an older man whom she did not love. Fearing reprisals, the fiercely independent youth fled to China. She later returned and married Alimbek Datka, the ruling nobleman of the Alai Valley. In 1862, he was murdered in an internecine palace coup in Kokand, and Kurmanjan took his title Datka, meaning "just ruler."[13] Her reign was short-lived. In 1876, the ruthless Russian General Skobelev, who later slaughtered the Turkmens, conquered the Ferghana Valley and pursued Kyrgyz holdouts into the mountains. Kurmanjan Datka's eldest son, Abdullabek, led the Kyrgyz rebels. The Russians captured his mother, who, realizing that their defeat was inevitable, brokered peace. The Alai region was incorporated into the Russian Empire.

Sardarbek said his great-grandfather was Kamchibek, the youngest son of Kurmanjan Datka. Even after conquest, the Russians found it difficult to rule the remote Alai region and its restive Kyrgyz nomads, who continued illegal trade with China. "Kamchibek ignored the Russians. So the Russians stopped Kamchibek's caravan on the way to China one day and they saw a chest of gold," Sardarbek recounted. The details of what happened next are sketchy, but the Russians accused Kamchibek of murdering a border guard. In 1895, despite the pleas of his mother, the Russians executed Kamchibek in Osh.

"I heard about Mannerheim's visit when I was a child," Sardarbek said. "My mother and father told me about their meeting."

The car shook violently as we bounced over potholes. I could barely take notes. "The road is very bad," Sardarbek complained. "The Chinese government is going to rebuild it. We are travelling the same route as Mannerheim, but in a car, and going much faster than Mannerheim on horseback." He pressed on the accelerator. Through the cracked windshield, I saw a car stopped at a police checkpoint ahead. Sardarbek began honking the horn. We swung into the oncoming lane and shot past two policemen while narrowly missing a truck and flock of sheep.

"I'm the King of Alai!" Sardarbek yelled slapping my knee and laughing. "The police don't bother me!" As it turned out, his two sons were police officers.

The valley began to narrow into a gorge. Sardarbek murmured folk songs as he navigated the wicked stretch of wildly zigzagging road. "This car is my bread," he said, smacking the dashboard, which was caked with dust. The vista atop Chigirchiq Pass was as Mannerheim described: an undulating green expanse studded with white yurts. We stopped to visit a relative, a hefty man with a moustache and hunched back. He invited us under a roadside canopy, where he sold *kumis,* fermented mare's milk. I drank two bowls. It had, as Mannerheim wrote, a "sharp, sour taste" but was nonetheless refreshing.

Back in the Volga, we drove off road onto a rutted path of red earth carved into the rolling green hills. We climbed above the pass to some yurts and a tent. A grandmother, mother and daughter— all relatives of Sardarbek—invited us into a yurt adorned with brilliant carpets and a tapestry depicting wildflowers and elk. I was instructed to sit opposite the doorway, the most honoured spot in a Kyrgyz yurt. The women brought out nan bread with *kaimak,* a buttery cream, and more *kumis.* I was obliged to drink two more bowls. I pulled out my camera and framed a photograph of myself, Sardarbek and his relatives sitting cross-legged in the yurt. Mannerheim had taken a similar photo with Kurmanjan Datka, her grandson and Pelliot exactly a century ago. That photo turned out to be the last one of the Queen of Alai. She died six months later.

We descended the pass and followed the road "along chasms and narrow valleys," as Mannerheim described, to Gulcha. A row of flat-roofed houses lined a dirt street. We pulled up to one nondescript house. Here, I met Askat, a tall, thin and swarthy twenty-one-year-old university student, and Jenish, a thirty-seven-year-old trekking guide from Uzgen. Jenish had a row of gold teeth and a lean, athletic build. I had hired them to take me on a

two-hundred-kilometre horse trek to the Chinese border. I wanted
to experience what travel must have been like for Mannerheim.

In the living room, everyone squatted on a plush carpet to eat
dastarkhan and a mutton stew. Askat and Jenish then studied my
map, making jottings and sketches in their own notebooks. We
would follow the old caravan route, as Mannerheim did, to China.

"What do you think about all this trade with China?" I asked
Sardarbek.

He mulled over the question. "I'm disappointed in the quality
of Chinese goods," he said. "They are very aggressive businessmen
nonetheless."

Sardarbek left at dusk, returning to Osh. I extended my hand
to bid him farewell. Instead, the affable old man wrapped his arms
around me in a heartfelt hug. "Good luck," he said.

Another college student—Talont, who spoke English—soon
arrived. He would accompany us for the first two days, since Jenish
had no English and Askat very little. Talont told me that Gulcha
has a population of seventy thousand. Some residents work for the
government, but most are herders or eke out a measly income farming thin strips of land along the river. But the ambitious student had
a plan to diversify the local economy through tourism, including
mountain trekking and horse riding. "You are the first tourist in the
Alai region," he said beaming.

MY HORSE TREK started the next day in a place called Juluu-suu,
or "warm waters." Dragonflies as large as hummingbirds bounced
off the windshield of the Lada on our way to the small hamlet a few
kilometres from Gulcha. We arrived at a bus shelter and kiosk and
unloaded our gear. Behind the bus stop, a group of villagers was
building a small, rustic inn and bathhouse next to a hot springs. The
dozen men gathered to pepper me with questions.

Talont told them about my plan. They were surprisingly familiar
with Mannerheim, although their facts were shaky. A jug of *kumis*

soon appeared and I was obliged, of course, to drink two bowls. Then a bottle of vodka and two glasses arrived. "We shall be as brave as Kurmanjan Datka," said Nurkamil, the village leader who wore a traditional felt hat, torn plaid shirt and jogging pants. We each downed a glass of vodka in honour of the Muslim Queen of Alai. My vodka glass was quickly refilled and another man stepped forward to toast my safe journey.

I was then offered *nasvai,* a mild narcotic. I slipped the doughy paste under my upper lip like chewing tobacco. The bitter juice seeped into my gums and bloodstream, creating a numbing sensation in my body. "It's made of tobacco and 'other' substances," Talont vaguely explained. I later learned that it contained slacked lime and, possibly, glue, oil, chicken droppings and camel dung. "The problem is that after four or five years, it will destroy your memory," Talont warned.

The Kyrgyz, with their love of fermented drinks, have the most liberal attitudes in Central Asia. These nomadic herders, grazing livestock in high alpine pastures much of the year, traditionally lived beyond the earshot of the minaret. Islam never took root as deeply among the Kyrgyz as it did among the town-dwelling Uzbeks. In Osh, I saw Kyrgyz women swilling vodka shooters in a café, scantily clad girls at a public pool and few veils or headscarves. By Central Asian standards, Kyrgyzstan was economically and politically liberal too: a popular uprising known as the "Tulip Revolution" had ousted a corrupt, authoritarian president the previous year.

As we talked, a cargo truck sluggishly climbed the hill, belching black exhaust and kicking up dust. The prosperity of the New Silk Road was literally passing by villages like Juluu-suu. "I don't agree that China should rebuild the road," said Nurkamil. "The Chinese workers get less money. They are everywhere in Kyrgyzstan. It would be easy for China to conquer Kyrgyzstan." Like Sardarbek, he complained about the poor quality of Chinese goods. "Their shoes only last three months."

I sobered up over lunch and read aloud from Mannerheim's diary, with Talont translating for the assembled crowd. In the late afternoon, friends of Talont finally arrived with our horses. Mine was light brown with a blond mane. He was called Chabdar, a Kyrgyz word meaning "chestnut." He was only three years old, a bit skinnier than the rest and not as sure-footed. Coincidentally, Mannerheim's horse Philip was also a "chestnut gelding." We loaded our three riding horses and one packhorse, crossed the highway and ascended a path leading up a long, winding valley. That valley, dotted with yurts and grazing sheep, was pinched by two craggy peaks at one end. We reached the top after three hours. The final stretch was very steep with switchbacks. Chabdar grunted and wheezed; his back became soaked in sweat.

At the top, a *jailoo*, or "summer pasture," extended for five kilometres between the two jagged peaks. In the distance, the snow-capped Pamirs shot up like whitecaps on a tempestuous sea. A dozen yurts, tents and earthen structures were scattered along the bottom of the U-shaped valley, where sheep and horses graze from May until September each year. The grassy valley is called Tepshi, meaning "trough" in Kyrgyz, its alpine meadow rich with wildflowers and bumblebees.

Life here was rustic and had changed little since Mannerheim's time. We stayed in the yurt of a young man named Timur, whose wife served us a dish of mutton and noodles. She ladled *kumis* out of a leather bag hung on the wall. Entertainment consisted of watching two stallions fight under the silvery light of a full moon. For breakfast, I ate leftovers and drank *kumis* with black bits of charcoal added for flavouring. It tasted especially tangy. Visiting some elderly neighbours, I was obliged to drink two more bowls. "You must drink one kumis and then drink one more *kumis*. That's the tradition," insisted my elderly host, who watched me struggle to down the tepid brew. "If you throw up, then the host wins and you must give me one sheep."

My small caravan departed in the late morning. With Talont and several friends, we made a precarious descent on a winding gravel path cut into the side of the mountain. Chabdar slipped and stumbled on the loose gravel and we were forced to dismount. I tripped too, sliding on my ass several metres down the dusty path. After two hours, we reached a tributary that we followed to the Gulcha River. We had lunch in the shade of a poplar grove and swam in the cold glacier-fed tributary. We then bid farewell to our escort. Askat, Jenish and I began our trek eastward along the Gulcha River to China.

"The road follows the fairly swift river Gülchö faithfully in its innumerable windings down a valley of rare beauty," Mannerheim wrote of this spot. "The surrounding steep mountain slopes are tinged with very beautiful colours and assume very varied shapes."

After an hour, the valley narrowed between two bluffs at a place called Yangirik Pass. Here, Kurmanjan Datka's son fought twelve thousand Russian infantrymen. "The brave Kirghiz, armed with old-fashioned rifles, could not hold out against the guns and modern rifles of the Russians and retreated to the Alai valley," Mannerheim wrote in his diary. Abdullabek eventually escaped to Kabul where, according to one story, he was murdered by Russian spies.

On the other side of this narrow pass, we forded the river and camped at a grassy spot called Mazar Bulak, or "Tomb Spring." Askat found the clean spring bubbling up next to the silt-ridden Gulcha River. We pitched two tents, an old canvas one for Jenish and Askat and a domed one for me. Jenish then spread a red blanket on the ground surrounded by padded cushions and saddle mats. We ate coleslaw, cucumber, corn, a spicy mutton stew with carrots, onion and potato, tea, honey, nan, peanuts and vodka. The last item did wonders for my aching muscles and legs.

The days were long and lonely. We trekked in single file, and since Jenish couldn't speak English and Askat knew only a few phrases, the days were unusually quiet. We communicated with grins, laughter and gestures, pointing here and nodding there. In the evening, Askat and I usually gave each other language lessons. Our small vocabulary says a lot about the simple pleasures of a horse trek:

English	Kyrgyz
eat	*tamak jemin*
drink	*suu ichem*
sleep	*uktaim*
rest	*es alysh*
tired	*charchadim*
toilet	*tualet*
mountain	*too*
spring	*bulak*
river	*dariya*
horse	*ott*
stars	*jyldas*
friend	*dos*

I slipped into my tent at 10 PM. With a dim headlamp, I read Mannerheim's journal. "You see more and more camels," he wrote. "We met several caravans of about 100. You see them from afar with their up and down motion, mysterious and dignified." As I read, modern beasts of burden were roaring down the road a few hundred metres across the rushing river. They were Russian-built Kamaz trucks, heaped with bundles of Chinese goods wrapped in tarpaulins heading to the Karasuu bazaar. The whining sound of overworked engines woke me at 4 AM; I counted twenty-two trucks before falling back to sleep. The next day I counted 110 and the next 125. All day, thick billows of dust swirled behind the lorries, caking us in grime. In places, tire ruts had sunk the asphalt fifteen centimetres and in other places the road disintegrated into gravel. These trucks were the few signs of life along this rugged stretch of the Silk Road.

Two days' riding finally brought us to the most spectacular part of the journey: the Taldyk Pass at 3,630 metres. "This place is wonderfully beautiful in its wild grandeur," Mannerheim wrote. "The road continues along valleys, following the river Gülchö that has become a modest mountain stream making many curious bends . . . It was only when we reached its foot and saw the road worming its way in endless zigzags up the slope that we began to realise the considerable climb that was before us."

We began our ascent up a narrow ravine beside the switchbacks. The shortcut saved time, but it was dangerously steep and tiring on the horses. One misstep would have been fatal. Halfway up the mountain, we rejoined the zigzagging dirt road to the summit, where a herd of wild yaks grazed on a verdant *jailoo*. We were whipped by gusting winds and saw, as the Baron did, "a lofty chain of mountains, their peaks shimmering under their covering of perpetual snow." The high alpine pass sloped gently and swung to the southeast, delivering us down onto the lush grasslands of the Alai Valley. A hawk soared overhead. On the grassland, I immediately noticed the tranquility of not hearing clip-clopping hooves on asphalt or gravel. We wandered through the sleepy hamlet of Sary-Tash and camped on the wind-swept plain.

It had been an exhausting but exhilarating day. We had covered forty kilometres over wildly varied landscape. A muddy red river divides the emerald Alai Valley, which stretches from east to west for one hundred kilometres. Jagged massifs rise on all sides. Sprawled on a carpet in the evening, I sipped vodka and gazed at the majestic scene. An endless caravan of Kamaz trucks rumbled down the dirt highway from China. In their wake, clouds of dust danced across the grassland like apparitions in the twilight.

TENTS AND YURTS had been pitched at the entrance to the Alai Valley in anticipation of Pelliot and Mannerheim's arrival. Hassan Beg greeted them. The Baron seemed relieved to be among the Kyrgyz. Day by day, his relationship with Pelliot had deteriorated. "From as early as Tashkent, I have had the impression of finding myself in the company of a person who is definitely hostile towards me..." he wrote. "I clearly see that [Pelliot] takes pleasure in any difficulty that I encounter or in misfortunes I meet."[14]

Yet on the trek from Gulcha, Mannerheim seemed to take equal pleasure in noting Pelliot's foibles and misfortunes. The Frenchman was a terrible shot, failing to bag even a rodent during two hunting expeditions. Mannerheim also noted the wretched condition of his caravan. "Pelliot has the greatest difficulties with his horses and Vaillant's veterinary inspections become longer and longer." For his part, Pelliot noted in his diary Mannerheim's surliness toward locals and that his poor Russian prevented him from collecting as much information as the Frenchman.[15]

Their visit happened to coincide with a Kyrgyz wedding, which involved various games and competitions. One morning, a dozen Kyrgyz horsemen assembled to play *buzkashi*, literally "grabbing the dead goat," a game widely played throughout Central Asia. The goat had been gutted, beheaded and soaked in cold water overnight to harden the carcass. It was supposed to represent a bride. The horsemen competed ferociously to capture it. As Mannerheim described:

> Should the heavy and slippery carcase of the goat slide out of the arms of one of the Kirghiz, a hand-to-hand struggle ensues as to who will succeed in swinging the goat on to his saddle with a strong pull, and getting away with it. The crowd of struggling Kirghiz grows larger and larger, the blows of nagaikas (whips) resound, savage passion is reflected in faces until this strange struggle of some dozens of expert horsemen is interrupted once more by one of them, with the goat on his saddle, breaking through the crowd and converting the fight for a time into a race... The man who succeeds in carrying off the goat and casting it at the feet of the spectators is rewarded by their cries of joy and a sum of silver.

Mannerheim joined the frenetic game, but only briefly captured the goat. "It was not so heavy as I had thought," he wrote, "and on a really good horse I might have got away with it."

At one point, Pelliot asked to have the goat on his saddle. The Kyrgyz immediately obliged and, according to the Baron, "out of politeness refrained from chasing him." Pelliot struggled with the slippery goat and so the Kyrgyz took his reins and "galloping ahead, towed him to the spectators, where Hassan Bek's polite relative handed 1 rouble to him."

"It goes without saying," Mannerheim noted with evident sarcasm, "that during this 'wild game' he was immortalized on film by Nouette."

MY CRACKED LIPS bled as I ate porridge the next morning. The wind and scorching sun had burned them to a crisp. Cumulus clouds clung to peaks like cotton candy to fingertips as we set off eastward down the Alai Valley. We passed several herders grazing sheep on the sweeping grasslands.

Askat guided us to a spot where the chocolate-coloured river swung north against a mountain slope. A landslide, caused by road building, blocked our way. Our packhorse stumbled badly and fell between two boulders. Jenish grew angry, yelling at Askat. Fatigue had apparently frayed his nerves. We dismounted and hauled up the horse. We forded the muddy river. Beyond, the road stretched ahead for thirty-five kilometres, mountains on each side closing in. Cargo trucks crawled past at no more than thirty kilometres per hour over a rutted dirt road. "A great number of caravans with merchandise met us on the way," the Baron wrote of this stretch of the Silk Road. "One caravan of 500 or 600 camels moved across the plateau in a number of columns."

Chabdar bayed and grunted as I whipped him on. By evening, we reached rolling meadows and a series of ravines fed by snowy peaks ten kilometres away. We camped in a ravine with a babbling creek. It was littered with cow dung. Askat hid our horses beyond a bend in the creek for the night, since a black stallion from a nearby Kyrgyz family kept molesting our mares. Dinner consisted of the remains of five-day-old mutton wrapped in a dirty towel. It had turned greyish brown and tasted tangy in Jenish's pilaf, or *polo* in Kyrgyz, a popular Central Asian rice dish flavoured with vegetables, spices and mutton. Our bread was as hard as wood. Askat tried, in vain, to soften it by steaming it over the pot of pilaf.

That night I could barely write in my diary. My muscles ached and I shivered uncontrollably. Even worse, we had run out of vodka. Immobile in my sleeping bag, I heard yelling and hooves menacingly close to my tent, as Askat chased away the stallion. But I was too exhausted and cold to care. "Toward evening," the Baron wrote of this same spot, "the cold became fairly severe." It hailed and snowed that night, and some of Pelliot's horses broke loose and disappeared into the grassland.

In the morning, I found that a light frost had formed on my tent. I was stiff and numb with cold. We ate leftover pilaf, which stung my cracked lips.

As Askat assembled the horses, Jenish and I visited the Kyrgyz family down the ravine. We interrupted them dismembering a sheep. The mother, in a bright red gown, was squeezing excrement out of the sheep's intestine, and their four children were roasting its charred head and hooves over an iron stove. Thankfully, the father offered us only *kumis* for breakfast. "How was the Kyrgyz vodka?" Askat asked with a grin. I felt mildly buzzed and replied with a smile.

The day's ride climbed up and down verdant gullies and wild red river gorges. Formidable black mountains to the east marked the Chinese border. At one shallow spot, we forded the snowmelt-swollen Kyzyl-suu, or Red River. Chabdar struggled against the current. At a second gorge, we were forced to dismount and lead our horses down a perilously steep path to another river, following its bank to a bridge.

We climbed onto a new highway whose slick surface glistened under the blazing sun. We had finally reached the New Silk Road, an eighteen-kilometre stretch of tarmac financed and built by the Chinese government and Asian Development Bank. In the years to come, it will stretch all the way to Osh and perhaps beyond. Chabdar's horseshoes, polished smooth after five days of trekking, kept slipping on the oily asphalt. After four kilometres, we reached Irkeshtam Pass, the border crossing to China.

At 2,960 metres, the remote pass wasn't what I'd expected. Mannerheim had found a platoon of thirty Cossacks at the border post. "What a strange life in this little fort," he wrote, "shut in between high mountains." It seemed to me to have only grown stranger with time. Nowadays, Irkeshtam Pass is a bleak, sprawling truck stop, a dystopia of ramshackle buildings, canteens and rusted tractor-trailers converted into homes and travellers' inns. As we trotted into the settlement, drunkards staggered about and a crazed horse bucked wildly through the dirt streets. It felt like *Mad Max* meets *Bonanza*.

Jenish and Askat found me an abandoned transport trailer to sleep in and abruptly bid me farewell. There was no running water, no heating, no toilet. The beds consisted of carpets on the floor. I couldn't blame the two for wanting to leave. They had a long return journey and Irkeshtam was a disreputable place, a nexus for prostitutes and lecherous truck drivers. I was surprised at how choked up I became at their departure. Despite the lack of a shared language, we had bonded during the arduous trek.

"*Rahmat. Rahmat.* Thank you. Thank you," I croaked in Kyrgyz, handing them fifty dollars, the last of my American money, as a tip. I followed them to the road, caressed Chabdar's mane one last time and watched them disappear over a desolate hill.

I sat on an old tire in front of my trailer and stared at the abominable camp conditions. It was a grim end to an otherwise spectacular trek. I felt the first pangs of loneliness after seven weeks on the road. I wandered over to an overturned trailer and watched young men reload bundles onto another truck. Taking pity on me, four drivers from Jalalabad invited me to dinner at a dim canteen. The men were in their late thirties and forties. Two were ethnic Kyrgyz and the others Uzbek. We drank vodka and ate *laghman,* a spicy mutton noodle dish, and then drank more vodka. From their crude gestures, I surmised they were talking about the price of prostitutes. After dinner, they bought another bottle of vodka and I photographed each of them proudly posing in front of their Kamaz trucks. We then sat cross-legged on hay strewn on the dirt parking lot and swilled mouthfuls of warm vodka in the chill of the night.

The next morning, I woke up in my underwear, not remembering exactly how I got to bed. My head was throbbing. A young boy was sleeping on my left and a strange middle-aged man to my right. For breakfast, I drank tea with my host's family and nibbled on musty bread in a fog of buzzing flies.

At the customs house, the Kyrgyz officials were friendly and laid-back. A soldier flagged down a truck and arranged a ride for me across the no-man's-land to the Chinese side. We stopped at a small shack by a creek midway. I squatted next to the clear, rushing water and washed my face and hands. Not having showered after a week of horse trekking, I tried to make myself look presentable.

A gleaming white watchtower marked the Chinese border post a kilometre away. I was about to face the most difficult leg of my journey. At the Chinese consulate in Vancouver, I had been twice declined a visitor's visa. I was perplexed: why would they deny me a visa? "This initial refusal might just be a gentle slap, a reminder that THEY are in charge and that if and when you go to China, THEY will be watching you," a human-rights activist for China's Muslim Uyghur group wrote me in an email. "While perhaps you should be a little cautious about who you speak to before you go, I think it's more likely to be China's arbitrary bullying going on here rather than the influence of a 'mole.'"

On my stopover in London, I again applied for a visa at the Chinese embassy. I went back the next day to pick it up and was confronted by a thin, cagey Chinese diplomat with greying hair.

"You want to go to China?"

"Indeed."

"What is your occupation?"

I told him that I worked for a nonprofit environmental group. (I had taken a leave of absence.) He seemed skeptical, pressing me with many questions about the organization's name, its purpose and my career. "Have you ever done any work in the media?" he asked.

It was an odd question, since there was nothing to indicate on my visa application that I was a writer. I'd never been to or written about China either. I grew paranoid that the Chinese government had somehow collected other information on me. In preparing for the journey, I had interviewed Falun Gong, Tibetan and Uyghur human-rights activists, and sought advice from various academics, some of them born in mainland China. I now realized one of them may have been a snoop for the Chinese government.

"Is there any incorrect information on my application?" I asked. "What information do you need for me to obtain a visa?"

The official said that he didn't have the authority to issue me a visa. He slipped me my passport under the security glass. On the back page, I found two Chinese rejection stamps. The red inky marks were dated and their Chinese characters stated Wengehua (Vancouver) and Lundun (London). "Sorry," the Chinese diplomat added seeing my utter disappointment. "It's a pity."

WESTERN CHINA

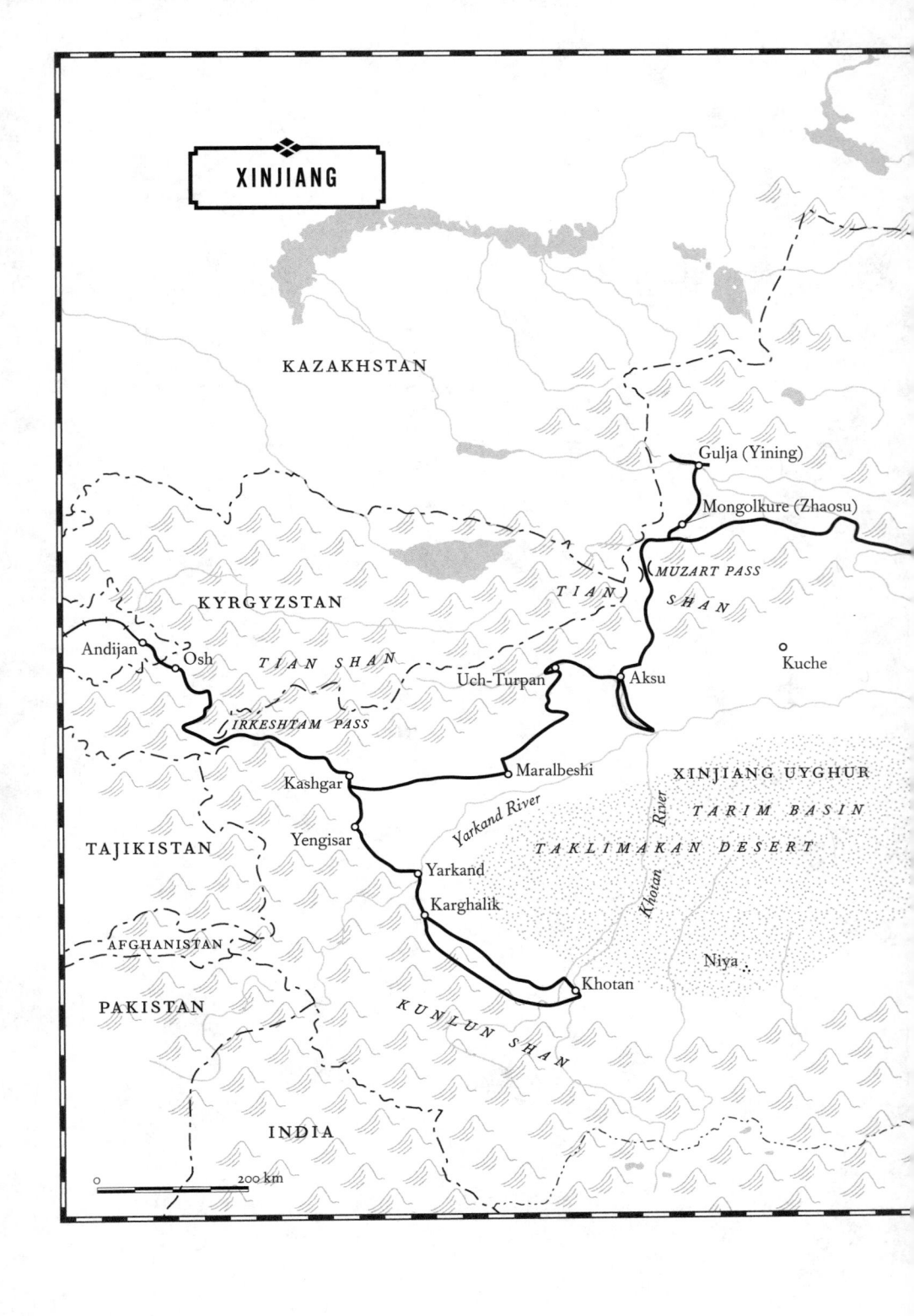

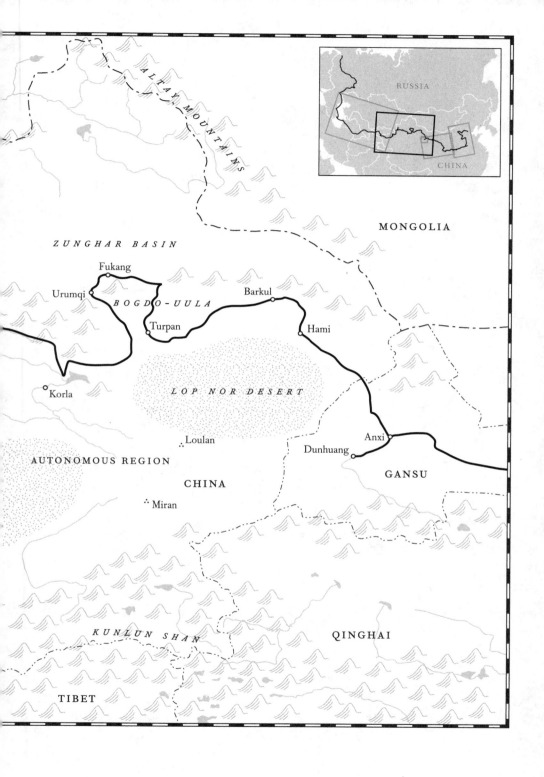

SIX

KASHGAR

Mission Impossible

It is a commonly accepted dictum that work amongst
Moslems is impossible.—REV. W. GOLDSACK, First Missionary
Conference on Behalf of the Mohammedan World (1906)[1]

IN ORDER TO remain "strictly incognito," Mannerheim did not
reveal his Russian military identity even to his Cossacks. He
wrote his diary, surveys, notes and letters home in Swedish.[2] In a
letter from Osh, he asked his father to secretly forward intelligence
from his personal correspondence to General Palitsyn in St. Petersburg: "Extract anything concerning my trekking route, geographic
circumstances, climate, politico-military observations, remarks
concerning the population, authorities, foreign agents, my circumstances towards Pelliot and the mission (in censored form), plans for
the future, disease and whatever else you think can be of interest to
him." He even assigned Palitsyn a codename. "If I need to mention
him in my letter, I will call him Feda."[3] To further conceal his identity, the Baron travelled on a Finnish passport.

I found myself following in Mannerheim's footsteps in a way that
I had never imagined. I hid my Canadian passport. A filthy cargo

109

truck, driven by a Kyrgyz man, took me across the no man's land separating the Kyrgyz and Chinese border posts at Irkeshtam Pass. At the first Chinese checkpoint, a machine gun–toting soldier of the People's Liberation Army stood in a watchtower above a gleaming white-tiled compound. I climbed down from the cabin and walked over to a trailer. Inside, two Chinese guards in impeccable green uniforms sat behind a wooden desk: "Passport?" I handed him an Estonian passport.

My father had fled the tiny Baltic state as the Red Army swept out the Nazis at the end of the Second World War. Upon independence in 1991, Estonia declared Soviet rule an "illegal occupation." My father's citizenship was restored, and I too was granted Estonian citizenship. On my way to St. Petersburg, I made a last attempt to apply for a visa at a Chinese embassy in Scandinavia under my Estonian identity. Thankfully, a consular official, unaware of my earlier attempts and Canadian identity, granted me a three-month visitor's visa to China. Like Mannerheim, I disguised myself as an innocuous Nordic traveller.

I may not sound like an Estonian—I have only a rudimentary knowledge of the Finno-Ugrian language, having struggled through lessons at Estonia's Tartu University one summer—but I certainly smelled like one that morning.

"Have you been drinking?" asked a puzzled official.

It was 10 AM. I hadn't showered since leaving Osh. The vodka from the night of drinking with Kyrgyz truck drivers soured my breath and oozed from my pores. A dull pain pulsed in my forehead.

The official wrote down my passport details and I continued several more kilometres to the main border post, a modern facility with metal detectors, video cameras, x-ray machines and more soldiers. A border guard, who had never heard of Estonia, stamped my passport and pointed to a door. My stomach knotted. Inside, two steely officers in immaculate black uniforms sat behind computers. They looked like Gestapo. One flipped through the pages in the passport.

He stared with bemusement at its cover, which read "Eesti Pass," or "Estonian Passport" in English.

"What nationality are you?" he asked.

My heart pounded. Did the border guard notice that my place of birth in the passport was "Kanada"? Did my name pop up on a blacklist on his computer monitor?

"Estonian," I replied.

I named all three Baltic states and then tried to illustrate Nordic geography on my hand: the space between my thumb and index finger was supposed to be the Gulf of Finland, and my thumbnail tiny Estonia. The official frowned at my odd geography lesson and waved me away. I had snuck through the back door of China.

A minibus and Chinese driver, which I had arranged, were waiting to take me to Kashgar. We ate a quick noodle lunch in a roadside café and then barrelled down the mountain pass on a new highway into a desert basin. A few Kyrgyz yurts and camels were the only signs of life. "A wild desolate landscape, wherever you look; the people, too, have disappeared," Mannerheim wrote. It was a hauntingly beautiful landscape, almost devoid of vegetation, a kaleidoscope of geology: gorges and mountains scarred in spectacular colours, shapes and patterns.

AT THE IRKESHTAM Pass border post, the Baron filled the bellies of his horses and replenished his stock of corn feed. "If you do not want to starve your horses, like Pelliot who seems to have a considerable inclination towards it," he wrote, "you must have plenty of corn on their backs." As this sniping at the Frenchman suggests, geography wasn't the only factor that made the journey to Kashgar particularly trying.

Pelliot insisted on long, strenuous marches each day that left the caravan in "a miserable condition." It rained the second day, making the trek more treacherous. The horses slipped in the mud and stumbled over wet stones. The route was littered with the skeletons and rotting carcasses of dead packhorses and asses. After another "exceedingly strenuous march," Mannerheim lost his temper. "Only a philologist, orientalist, archaeologist and, on top of that, a sinologist like Pelliot is able to divide his route in that way," he complained. Fed up, Mannerheim stopped for a day's rest, while Pelliot stubbornly plodded on with his caravan of injured and galled horses.

"Now when time permits," Mannerheim wrote on his day of rest, "I must in a few words touch on my relationship with Pelliot." He had sensed that "a certain coldness" had developed between them from the very beginning. Mannerheim attributed it to professional jealously and egoism, although Pelliot in his diary points out similar flaws in the Finn. "As to me," the Baron wrote of Pelliot, "I have been irritated by his unpleasantly self-important domineering, or character as a poseur, his pedantry which went so far that already in Osh he wanted to determine how many lumps of sugar each of us was allowed to put into his tea or coffee, his need to observe and control every step one took, whether it concerns him or not, his tactless habit . . ." And so on.

Even worse, Pelliot said he would not lie about Mannerheim's true identity if pressed by Chinese officials. Feeling betrayed, the Baron threatened to write General Palitsyn. "Mannerheim was very upset," Pelliot wrote in his diary. "I explained further that, given his complete independence, I could not take responsibility to officially count in my mission someone over whom I had no control."[4] If Mannerheim wanted to join the French expedition, Pelliot seemed to be saying, he would have to submit to the Frenchman's authority.

"This answer, in the context of his patently unfriendly attitude towards me," Mannerheim wrote, "made me realise that I could count on no help or support from him."[5] Indeed, he felt Pelliot was "definitely hostile towards me and my objective." The Baron was on his own.

IF THE XINJIANG Uyghur Autonomous Region is China's Wild West, then Kashgar is its Dodge City. The unruly oasis is locked between the vast sands of the Taklimakan Desert—"a Land of Death," according to one British explorer[6]—and a line of incisor-like peaks that form the Kunlun, Pamir and Tian Shan ranges. The surrounding geography is brutal, making Kashgar a welcome respite on the Silk Road.

Xinjiang's inhabitants, known today as Uyghurs, are historically a blend of Persian and Turkic tribes who converted to Islam in the fifteenth century. Culturally, their closest cousins are Uzbeks. This vast Muslim borderland—larger than Germany, France and Spain combined—was never historically under Chinese rule, despite dubious claims to the contrary.[7]

It was only in 1759 that the Qing Dynasty sent its armies west and conquered the scattered oases around the southern fringe of the Taklimakan Desert. The Qing established military and civilian administrations, promoted immigration and constructed irrigation systems for agricultural settlements, while staving off periodic uprisings. In 1862, Muslims revolted en masse in Gansu province to the east. The rebellion soon spread. Entire Chinese garrisons were massacred and Qing rule ended. In Kashgar, Yakub Beg, a charismatic warlord from Kokand, established a unified khanate over Xinjiang. To the north, Russian Cossacks conquered the Ili Valley in 1871 ostensibly to stop the Muslim uprising from spilling over into Russian Turkestan.

Alarmed by the Russian conquest, the British sent an envoy to Kashgar for an audience with Yakub Beg. The British sought trade opportunities and an alliance against the Russians. However, the British also hedged their bets by financing a Chinese military expedition to oust the Muslim ruler. General Zuo Zongtang swept westward, slaughtering Muslim rebels and crushing resistance. The Emperor dubbed his newly conquered territories the "New Dominion," or Xinjiang, and in 1884 formally integrated it into the imperial administrative system.

The Russians agreed to give the Ili Valley back to China in exchange for an official consulate in Kashgar and trade privileges.

In 1882, Nikolai Petrovsky arrived in Kashgar with his wife, son and forty-five Cossack guards. Petrovsky, a militant Anglophobe, was domineering, preposterously rude, ambitious, petty and supremely egotistical. He became the "virtual ruler of Kashgar," and fought a covert war against his British counterpart, who arrived in 1890.[8]

George Macartney had a Scottish father and Chinese mother. Born in Nanjing, he spent his first ten years in China before moving to Britain and then France for his education. The Chinese offered him a single-storey house and garden known as Chini Bagh, or the "Chinese Garden." He was a reserved, scholarly and unassuming man. His mission was to create friendly relations with the Chinese, promote trade with British India and act as an intelligence agent. He fought a bitter battle against the conniving, tyrannical Petrovsky and single-handedly thwarted Russian territorial ambitions.

"The Chinese are conscious that strategically the Kashgarian province is at the mercy of Russia," states a confidential military report from the British Intelligence Branch in 1907, which Macartney helped to write. "An invasion is thoroughly realized by them as within the sphere of possibility, but since the [Russo-Japanese] war the prevailing idea seems to be that Russia no longer has designs on the country."[9] Mannerheim's secret mission to Kashgar, however, was evidence to the contrary. "Russia is clearly preparing to take Chinese Turkestan," an American traveller, who visited Kashgar in 1904, warned.[10] A year later, the *New York Times*—incorrectly as it turned out—even reported that the Russians had invaded and seized Kashgar.

On the evening of his arrival, Mannerheim cleaned himself up and a bearded horseman announced his entry into the Russian consulate. "I was welcomed by a man of middle age with an expressive, though delicate and nervous countenance," he wrote. Sergei Kolokolov had recently replaced Petrovsky as consul. He was a progressive man who believed in constitutional government and even condemned (in private, of course) his own government's war in Manchuria. Mannerheim found him cheerful and fond of joking. The Baron frequently dined with Kolokolov, who spoke both Chinese and Uyghur and who maintained a network of spies. Pelliot and Mannerheim also met the *daotai,* or governor of Kashgar, the next day.

He was "a thin old man of distinguished appearance and manners." Pelliot, who spoke Chinese, led the conversation and, Mannerheim complained, "naturally considered it beneath his dignity to ever let us get a hint of the matters discussed." For a month, Mannerheim gathered news and gossip, reviewed "very defective" maps and secret reports at the consulate, studied Chinese and met with local mandarins. He even called on Macartney. Not to meet the British agent—a tradition among foreign travellers—would have certainly aroused suspicion.

The British consulate overlooked the Russian compound. "Here," the Baron wrote,

> Mr. Macartney, the British Political Agent, has lived for 16 years. His Chinese blood, inherited from his mother, and his long service have bound him closely to this country. When you watch his self-controlled, correct, dark-complexioned figure and hear him talk with sympathy and devotion of this community with its mud huts and peculiar conditions, you realise that he belongs to this country more than any European could and that, if fate should ever remove him to some other place, he would pine for his quiet, his books and his flowers in the Chini Bagh gardens. He knows the country and its people and history as no other European does.

Chini Bagh was essentially a British listening post. Macartney ran a network of paid informants scattered across Xinjiang and Russian Turkestan. Caravans travelling from Osh would bring intelligence on the latest political intrigues, ethnic unrest, troop movements, geographical surveys and railway and road construction in the Russian borderland. Nothing went unnoticed. He gathered the intelligence into monthly reports that were sent first to India and then London.

I found Macartney's dispatches bound with other intelligence reports in the British Library in London. Cracking open the cloth-covered volumes, I almost sneezed from the musty smell and fine dust particles rising from the frayed, yellowed pages. These massive volumes are a detailed play-by-play of the Great Game: each move and countermove, rumour and intelligence tidbit is recorded in painstaking detail. In one of the monthly memoranda, Macartney reported on Pelliot's mission: "The party travelled to Kashgar with a Finn, named Baron Mannerheim, who is making an archeological collection for the Helsingfors Museum."[11] There was no mention of Mannerheim's military identity. So far, the Baron had slipped through Macartney's dragnet.

REMORSELESS COMMERCIALISM welcomed me to Kashgar. The minibus crossed a bridge over the Tuman River. My first sight was a big-box furniture store festooned in Chinese banners. We entered the oasis on a broad new boulevard lined with faceless buildings clad in tile and mirrored glass. Gaudy signage and billboards hung on every storefront and rooftop.

I stayed in the Seman Hotel just west of the walled ancient quarter. It was adorned in Uyghur architectural flourishes: a baby blue domed entranceway, Ottoman arches and a lobby full of fanciful plaster reliefs. Sore and soiled from the horse trek, I headed straight for a steaming shower. I fell into a deep sleep the minute my head hit the pillow. The next morning I scrubbed more dirt and oily horse stains off my bags and clothes and made my way to the Caravan Café. "If you want to know what's going on in town," my guidebook stated, "make this your first port of call." It also served the best coffee in Kashgar, a morning pleasure I desperately craved.

Greg Kopan, the café's American owner, had arranged my pick-up at Irkeshtam Pass the previous day. In his late thirties or early forties, he wore a moustache, glasses and neatly quaffed hair—a conspicuously tidy and polite man. He reminded me of Ned Flanders, the evangelical neighbour on *The Simpsons*—and in more ways than one. I asked what brought him to Kashgar.

Kopan said that he was originally from Idaho and majored in music in college, where he became interested in traditional lute-plucking Uyghur music. He first visited Kashgar in 1989 and in the 1990s moved to Urumqi, the regional capital, where he studied the *dutar*, a long-necked, two-stringed instrument native to Central Asia. He continued his studies in Kashgar, where he attended the Kashgar Teachers College. He must have been deeply devoted to the *dutar*, I figured, since he dragged his wife and their three daughters to this unruly backwater bordering Pakistan and Afghanistan. Kashgar is, to borrow a biblical expression, "the ends of the earth." It is a curious home for a wholesome Midwestern family. He then set up the Caravan Café, serving caffeine-deprived Westerners lattes, mochas, granola and pizza. He had been in business now for six years and also organized guides and camel-riding excursions into the desert.

I showed Kopan a 1908 map of Kashgar that I copied from a military report at the British Library. He was currently rereading, and enjoying, Peter Hopkirk's *The Great Game: The Struggle for Empire in Central Asia,* which chronicles the intrigues of Macartney and Petrovsky in Kashgar. (Mannerheim doesn't warrant a mention.)

"The Caravan Café seems like the new Chini Bagh," I said. "You have become the go-to place for foreign travellers, tourists and expats."

"We aren't in the same business," Kopan said defensively. He insisted that he stays clear of snooping foreigners who pose indelicate questions about Chinese repression and Muslim unrest. Since 9/11, the Chinese government has been fighting its own "war on terrorism" in Xinjiang. As part of a so-called "Strike Hard" campaign, Chinese security forces have cracked down on Muslim worshippers and Uyghur nationalists and executed alleged terrorists.

"You may be in a different business," I agreed, "but you are still the centre of foreign life in Kashgar just as Macartney was a century ago."

Macartney's former residence stands next door to the Caravan Café. It is hidden behind the Chini Bagh Hotel, a five-storey monstrosity with a distinctly dreary facade. In the hotel's backyard, the charming old consulate squats atop a loess ridge. Part of its garden is still alive with bushy acacia and poplar trees, overgrown hedges and a trellis of ivy. A two-storey tower trimmed by a red parapet makes it look like a small castle. By the time I visited it, the building had seen better days—its paint was chipping and stucco cracking—but amazingly had escaped destruction.

The former British outpost is now a Uyghur restaurant with fanciful reliefs depicting grapes, vines and curlicues adorning its walls and cornices. I ate alone in the eerily quiet dining room, imaging all the great explorers—Sven Hedin, Sir Aurel Stein, Paul Pelliot, Albert von Le Coq—who had graced its halls. Chini Bagh had certainly lost its legendary status as a haven of hospitality. The Caravan Café had also replaced it, I would come to learn, as a nest of foreign intrigue in Kashgar.

KAHAR, A twenty-one-year-old waiter, greeted me in the Seman Hotel's foyer one morning. I had met him in a teahouse the previous day. He spoke English well and earned extra money showing foreigners around Kashgar. "I want to find the old Kashgar hidden behind all the billboards and commercial facades," I said, showing him the 1908 military map. This piqued his curiosity. He agreed to show me around the ancient city—or what was left of it.

From the hotel, Seman Road skirts the old city wall. It is made of rammed earth and stands some six metres high. The wall was once part of a Manchu fortress, which protected the *yamen* (residence) of the local military commander, barracks and a parade ground. Now two Chinese soldiers guarded a gate with a sign identifying the area as Kashgar's "military administration zone." Behind the wall stands a gloomy grey high-rise topped with a steel telecommunications tower. It's the headquarters of the Public Security Bureau. The building's disproportionate height, compared to Kashgar's low-slung neighbourhoods, had the desired effect: I felt like I was being watched.

"I don't like the new Kashgar," Kahar grumbled about all the bleak, Soviet-style buildings obscuring the wall. "It doesn't even feel like Kashgar. When I was a little boy, I could see a lot more of the wall. Even ten years ago, you could see more of the old, typical Kashgar. It was not like this with these kinds of buildings."

Yet there were drawbacks to Ye Olde Kashgar that even Kahar couldn't deny. "The architecture here is, if possible, inferior to that in Russian Turkestan," Mannerheim wrote. Traditional houses are made of unbaked mud bricks, dirt floors and flat roofs caked in clay mixed with straw. According to the Baron, "a slight earthquake is sufficient to demolish this unstable dwelling entirely." Indeed, an earthquake that hit Kahar's hometown to the north a few years ago reduced traditional Uyghur houses to heaps of dust, killing thousands. "My parents almost died," he said.

Nowadays, central planners, not periodic cataclysms, are wreaking havoc on Kashgar. A dreary modernism is devouring the city's ancient charm. Engineers have ploughed a six-lane thoroughfare, Jiefang Road, through the wall's northern gate, splitting the old town in two. At one spot, the flesh-coloured clay wall juts out between two Chinese shops like a severed limb.

We walked north on Jiefang Road toward the Tuman River in search of the old Russian consulate. The entire neighbourhood had been replaced by a windowless big-box store and an industrial zone of building supply stores, warehouses and factories. I figured a plumbing shop was where Mannerheim stayed.

"This is like a different world," Kahar said as we toured a vast furniture warehouse. "Absolutely different. Uyghurs don't have much furniture in their homes. We mostly sit on carpets around low tables."

In 1907, Kashgar's population was about 320,000, only slightly lower than current estimates. However, more than 90 percent were Uyghurs. Only about 750 Han Chinese, not including soldiers and mandarins, lived in the city. Kahar figured the Han population had swelled to 45 percent, up from 15 percent about a decade earlier. That was probably an exaggeration. But in 1999, a new railway to Kashgar opened, which has since caused Han Chinese migration to explode, sparking a residential construction boom.

We walked south toward the Old Town's central plaza. Donkey carts driven by bearded Uyghurs clip-clopped along the smoggy thoroughfare choked with buses, motorcycles, trucks and taxis. In the heart of Kashgar sits Idkah Mosque, the largest in China. It can accommodate up to twenty thousand worshippers. Originally built in 1442, the mosque has been renovated many times. An official sign near the entrance boasts, unconvincingly, that the renovations are evidence that "freedom of belief is protected" and that "all ethnic groups live friendly together." The mosque has an open-air layout: covered verandas carpeted with richly patterned prayer rugs surround a central garden courtyard shaded by poplars. Dozens of Han Chinese tourists—many of them women in tank tops, skirts and shorts—blissfully roamed the mosque.

"They are silly," Kahar said of the Chinese. By the end of our tour, his annoyance grew to anger. "It's absolutely rude!" he snapped, pointing to several scantily clad, giggling Chinese girls. "Look at their clothes. And I really don't like it when the Han Chinese make noise in the mosque. That's the difference between the Chinese and foreigners. The Chinese make so much noise."

We found respite in a traditional teahouse on a narrow street behind the mosque. These establishments, Mannerheim wrote, were "where the events of the day are discussed over several cups of weak tea without sugar." We sat on a second-storey wooden veranda, joining two old men on a wooden bench. They were dressed in crisp white shirts, grey jackets and traditional embroidered *doppa* caps. The pair had thin goatees and dipped bread into milky tea. "Even six years ago, there were a lot more buildings like this in Kashgar-style," Kahar said of the teahouse whose pillars and sunscreens were carved in arabesques and interlaced tendrils. At another table, Kahar said, the four gentlemen were "complaining about the destruction of the old-style Kashgar house, which is happening at an alarming rate." Nobody, he added, liked living in the "matchbox" apartments that the Chinese are building.

We silently watched the bustling bazaar scene below. Food vendors crowded the sidewalks with their small trolleys, umbrellas and stools. Smoke from a kebab stand stung my eyes and the musty smell of mutton hung in the air. "A large number of evil-smelling kitchens," the Baron noted, "prevent the rural population from dying of starvation." Melon sellers, butchers, craftsmen and bakers created a curbside cacophony. Uyghur women in colourful headscarves and the occasional brown burqa slipped gracefully through the melee. "I like this street," said Kahar. "It reminds me of Old Kashgar."

We continued south on Kumdarvaza Road, which appeared to lead to "Sand Gate" on my 1908 map. The old fortress wall had disappeared and been replaced by a new wall, of sorts: block after block of commercial towers housing Chinese banks, telecoms and state-owned enterprises on Renmin Lu, or "People's Road."

"Maybe the road should be renamed Wall Street," I joked.

People's Road leads, of course, to People's Square, where a gigantic statue of Mao Zedong—the largest in China—looms over a sterile concrete concourse. Mao is the size of Godzilla, with one arm raised like a club.

"What do you think of Mao?" Kahar asked.

I quietly mumbled a few disparaging remarks about the erratic, murderous despot.

"My grandparents said that Mao let many of the minority peoples starve and would not provide them with any food," Kahar said with remarkable candour. Such utterances can land Uyghurs in prison or before a firing squad. "Nobody likes Mao."

A passage next to the statue led into Old Kashgar. Only a few of these dense, honeycombed quarters remain in the city. All around the neighbourhood's periphery, clay houses were being knocked down to widen roads or build modern buildings. We wandered the narrow, serpentine alleyways. Wooden doorways in the walls led to courtyard homes—tranquil and intimate abodes compared to the Chinese apartments fronting noisy, car-clogged streets. Mannerheim noted the "extremely simple" living conditions: floor rugs for beds, a hole in the wall for a fireplace, a "metal pot of glowing coals" for a heater.

We ate lunch at a Uyghur restaurant near Idkah Mosque. Over fried noodles with mutton and sweetened yoghurt, I broached another politically sensitive subject, especially for Kahar, a devout Muslim. He had spent two years studying Arabic in a state-run madrasa. "Have you ever met Christian missionaries in Kashgar?" I asked.

MISSIONARIES ARE NOTHING new to Xinjiang. Religious conversion is central to the Silk Road's storied past. As early as the second century AD, Buddhist monks from India made their way over the Pamirs to the scattered desert oases, eventually introducing Buddhism to China. Zoroastrians, Nestorian Christians, Manicheans and Muslims followed. The latter effectively wiped out the thriving Buddhist civilization, whose remnants were unearthed from the desert sands by explorers such as Sven Hedin, Aurel Stein and Paul Pelliot.

In 1603, a Portuguese Jesuit priest visited Yarkand, two hundred kilometres south of Kashgar, but it took almost three hundred years for the next Christian missionary to arrive in Xinjiang. In 1887, a Dutch Catholic, Father Hendriks, installed himself in a mud hut in Kashgar. The bedraggled cleric died a month before Mannerheim's arrival, having reportedly converted only one Muslim.

Besides officials and guards at the Russian and British consulates, the only other resident Europeans in Kashgar a century ago were five Swedish missionaries. In 1892, Nils Fredrik Höijer, a preacher with the Mission Covenant Church of Sweden, and Johannes Awetaranian, a converted Ottoman Turk, arrived in Kashgar. Both Petrovsky and Macartney warned Höijer that "it would be utterly impossible to begin a mission in Kashgar as the Mohammedans were more fanatic than anywhere else."[12] Discouraged, Höijer returned to Sweden. But Awetaranian, who learned the local Turkic dialect, took a room near the bazaar, where he began proselytizing.[13] He cleverly read parts of the Gospel that were the least offensive to Muslims. (Islam accepts Jesus as a prophet and miracle worker, but not as the Son of God.) He also translated the Gospels into the Kashgarian dialect, reading drafts to mullahs and *begs* who helped correct his grammar. "In this way," he slyly noted, "I read the whole New Testament to them."

His first convert—indeed the first known Uyghur convert to Christianity—was Awetaranian's Muslim servant, Omar Akhund, who wanted to be baptized. "It will mean a lot of difficulties for you," Awetaranian warned. "If you are baptized, the Muslims will persecute you and perhaps kill you."[14] At first he refused, but after a few years he relented. He dunked Omar's head in the murky Tuman River. His wife soon betrayed him to the mullahs, who threatened the convert with death. At one point, they tried to hang Omar, but Chinese authorities intervened. The mullahs became further enraged in 1894, when another four Swedish missionaries settled in Kashgar. Nobody would rent them accommodation and several riots, instigated by outraged mullahs, erupted. The Swedes were forced to live in a garden outside the city.

According to my 1908 map, the mission lay just outside the south gate, but Greg Kopan told me nothing remained. There had once been two stucco houses surrounded by beautiful gardens with tall trees. The missionaries kept busy running an orphanage, school and hospital. During one visit, Mannerheim counted thirty-seven patients. One emaciated Uyghur had a deep knife wound in his chest. With each breath, he expelled "a bowlful of matter out of his lung." The Swedes also tilled a small plot to grow food. "The soil is so fertile that, if you were to stick your cane into the ground," the Baron wrote, "a year later you would find a flourishing bamboo plant growing there."

Notwithstanding the rich soil, Kashgar wasn't fertile ground for church planting. Still, it was a heady time for global evangelism among Muslims. In April 1906, sixty-two Protestant missionaries held the First Missionary Conference on Behalf of the Mohammedan World in Cairo. "[The church] should see that in Islam she has her only rival for the conquest of the world," an American missionary told the conference.[15] The published proceedings—marked "For Private Circulation Only" on its cover—were a practical and theological guidebook to converting Muslims. Missionaries were encouraged to gain a fluent knowledge of the local vernacular, be thoroughly versed in both Christian and Islamic theology, avoid "unprofitable controversy and useless wrangling," and use Koranic references to describe Jesus. Schools, orphanages and medical missions were to be established as evidence of Christian charity and to win over converts. Awetaranian attended and spoke about his experience in Kashgar.

Delegates left the conference with "new hope and courage." They had reason to be confident. Within a few years, the Ottoman Empire collapsed, Persia was partitioned and much of the Middle East was under colonial rule. "No sane statesman need longer fear a general uprising of Moslems under a political leader..." stated an editorial in *Moslem World*, a missionary journal, in 1913. "Islam has lost its sword."[16]

For decades, the Swedes doggedly brought the "Good News" to reluctant Kashgarians. A church wasn't built in Kashgar until 1926. Fifty-six churchgoers were registered in 1932. Just as missionaries began to see a "breakthrough," especially among those Muslims who grew up in their orphanage or attended missionary schools, political instability swept away their meagre gains in a bloody wave of violence. The rise of a Muslim warlord resulted in the expulsion of all foreign missionaries in 1938. Many of their converts were executed. The few survivors disappeared into underground churches.[17] By the end of the Cultural Revolution—another period of brutal religious oppression—only a handful of known Christians remained among the Uyghurs.

"NOBODY LIKES THE missionaries here," Kahar said over lunch. "I heard that some volunteer English teachers here were secretly pushing Christianity."

"Is it true that the Han Chinese accept Christian teachings more readily than the Uyghurs?" I asked.

"The Chinese are a people without a religion," Kahar hissed. "The Chinese don't care about people. They care about money."

In truth, I had already confirmed that evangelicals were back in Kashgar. An official with the Mission Covenant Church of Sweden, who speaks Mandarin and regularly visits Xinjiang, told me that nearly every foreigner in Kashgar is a missionary. Some study or teach at the local college while others use businesses to front their religious work. Though foreign evangelism is officially illegal, they are tolerated, if at all, because they bring much-needed expertise— and foreign currency—to a hinterland where few foreigners dare to tread. "They are doing things in private, secretly," the official said of foreign evangelicals. "Five or six people praying is fine, but more than that and there will be troubles."

A young Uyghur whom I met late one night for beers explained the situation this way: "The Chinese know about missionary activities, but it's tightly controlled through the use of spies and informants. With labour so cheap, it's easy for the authorities to hire people to participate and keep watch on the underground churches. If the meetings get too large—over ten people—the Chinese authorities quickly shut them down. Freedom is just an illusion. There's a limit to Chinese tolerance of underground religious activities. This is, after all, a police state."

I was intrigued by this gossip and so I began digging after my return to Canada. Shortly after I left Kashgar, security forces launched a campaign against foreign missionaries, code-named "Typhoon No. 5." According to the China Aid Association, a Texas-based Christian rights group, authorities rounded up and expelled sixty alleged foreign missionaries from Xinjiang. Besides the deportations, police arrested and beat house-church leaders and closed several businesses purportedly used as fronts for illegal religious activities. It was part of "anti-infiltration" efforts to dissuade foreign missionaries from using the Beijing Olympics as a pretext to proselytize. I first read about the expulsions on the blog of an American businessman. Michael ran a sun-dried tomato business in Xinjiang. I met him later during my stay in Urumqi. His blog was scathing about the Christian missionaries, but also about China's repressive religious laws. Commenting on the blog, one expat was angered by "the shadow of suspicion that missionaries cast on all foreigners once they've been found operating in a certain area."

Missionaries are now everywhere in China, venturing to the most destitute regions to offer charitable works. "I'm sure many of you in other parts of China run into missionary types in your day-to-day lives," Michael wrote. "That young fresh-faced couple pushing their toddler through the streets of Lanzhou? *Missionaries.* That American girl you saw with her Chinese friends drinking Coca-Cola while the other foreigners were falling down drunk? *Missionary.* The owner of the Caravan Café in Kashgar who would never talk about his past and has recently been forced to close shop? *Ditto!*"

I had had my suspicions about Greg Kopan from the start, especially because of his unusual interest in Uyghur music. Missionaries have historically used the Uyghurs' love of music to push Christianity. "The Gospel was literally sung into their souls," one missionary wrote of the Uyghurs in 1920, "and caused many hearts to surrender, resulting in new birth or revival."[18] I eventually tracked down Kopan through the Cherry Creek Presbyterian Church in Englewood, Colorado.

The church, according to its website, brought "the Good News to ethnic groups that are especially unreached" and had adopted the "YOU" people of Central Asia for "special emphasis." An online newsletter mentioned that a missionary named Kopan with his wife and three teenaged daughters needed a place to stay during an upcoming visit. I rang up the church.

"Who are the YOU?" I asked Al Johnson, the church's mission elder.

"It's a code word," he said.

"Code for what?"

"For Uyghurs."

"What happened to the Kopans?"

"It's rather confusing," he said. "There doesn't seem to be any real sense to it. They were running a legitimate business and employing people in [Kashgar]. They were accused of being evangelists and were expelled from China. I guess they were kicked out of China because they were sharing the Gospel of Jesus Christ with the people of China."

Johnson explained that his church helped finance the Kopans, but wouldn't say much else. He gave me Greg Kopan's email and referred me to a Chinese evangelical church in Vancouver that had hosted a secret conference on converting Uyghurs in 2006.

"The missionary work over there is very sensitive," said the Vancouver church's mission pastor, who asked me not to identify him or his congregation. "We all use code words . . . We need to be very careful."

The pastor, originally from China, said that police in Xinjiang were clamping down on any activity that threatened the region's stability, especially leading up to the Beijing Olympics. The number of Uyghur converts, he explained, had soared from fifty to more than five hundred in the last few years. Estimates of Uyghur worshippers, however, remain sketchy. Still, Chinese authorities have reason to worry that foreign missionary activity—and the growing number of Uyghur Christians—could spark Muslim unrest.

Uyghurs who convert to Christianity risk double jeopardy. Not only are they ostracized by Muslim friends and family, but they may also face persecution from Chinese authorities. One Uyghur convert, Osman Imin, was sentenced to two years' "re-education" in a labour camp for assisting "foreigners in illegal activities." According to one missionary group, he had worked for "an outspoken Christian American businessman who was expelled from China and had his business shut down." Another Uyghur convert ran an agricultural business in Kashgar. He was arrested on charges of subversion and endangering national security, a crime punishable by death.[19] "Where are those people that first handed you the Bible now that you really need salvation?" Michael asked on his blog.

It is a good question and one that I wanted to ask Greg Kopan, who likely knows both men. I sent him a list of questions via email. He was living in Phoenix, and based on his email address appeared to be working with Frontiers, a missionary group focused on converting Muslims. Kopan refused to answer any of my questions, fearing further persecution of converts left behind in Kashgar. However, I found a newsletter from the Blackhawk Church in Verona, Wisconsin, that shed light on his double life in Kashgar. He had sent the church, which supported his missionary work, an update. In the newsletter, Kopan was quoted as saying that "the charges against us were trumped up and falsely based," but that he had:

1. Gathered and taught believers over a period of 13 years
2. Baptized people and celebrated communion with them
3. Distributed copies of local language Bibles and related materials . . .

"We are actually happy about these charges," Kopan boasted, "and would not want to be charged with any other crimes than those, since they are the things our Lord commanded us to do!! We have heard that 'investigations' are continuing even since we've left, so please pray for those who are currently being harassed."

Their expulsion will have little impact on evangelism in Xinjiang. In fact, the growth of Christianity in this Muslim borderland is piggybacking on Beijing's repressive policy to colonize cities such as Kashgar with Han Chinese. Currently, 5 to 7 percent of the Han population is Christian and that number is growing fast.[20] That means, proportionately, at least 400,000 ethnic Han Chinese Christians already live in Xinjiang. Churches have opened in Urumqi, Korla and Hami on the northern fringe of the Taklimakan Desert. Some thirty house-church leaders are active in Aksu, a town just north of Kashgar. Han Chinese Christians, I learned, had already applied to build a church in Kashgar, but were turned down. "The Chinese government are very sensitive about Christian missions seeing it as a destabilizing factor in Xinjiang province," the Swedish missionary official told me. Yet once Kashgar is "stabilized" with enough Han Chinese, this restriction on church construction may be lifted, as has happened in other cities in Xinjiang. Muslims who protest will likely face persecution as "Islamic militants" or "splittists" or both.

As early as the 1940s, followers of the Mainland Chinese church began setting out west to convert Tibetan Buddhists and Muslims. The Communist Revolution ended this native evangelism, but the so-called "Back to Jerusalem" movement has been reinvigorated in the past decade. The pastor in the Vancouver church told me that many Han Chinese are now taking up the mission to the Uyghur people. Foreign churches and missionary groups clandestinely fund their activities, he said. I contacted a half-dozen missionary societies active in Central Asia, but none would answer my questions.

However, a blog posting on the website of Reaching Unreached Nations Ministries captures the movement's zeal. Its founder, Eric

Watt, believed that the 9/11 terrorist attacks "have unlocked a 'great and effective door'" (1 Corinthians 16:8) for a "spiritual army" to descend upon the gates of the Muslim world. He wasn't talking about American soldiers invading Iraq and Afghanistan. A rather different vision came to him one night while in southwestern China: "I saw hordes of people, thousands of Chinese Christians walking back across the Silk Road proclaiming the Good News all the way back to Jerusalem."

LATE ONE MORNING, I headed to the Kashgar Teachers College in the northeast quarter of Kashgar, just beyond the old city wall. The Swedish church official had told me that more than half the foreign teachers and students at the college were missionaries.

I later tracked down one of the first foreign teachers at the college. Henryk Szadziewski, a Brit of Polish descent, now works for the Uyghur Human Rights Project in Washington, D.C. He came to Kashgar as an English teacher in 1994. On his first day at the college, another Westerner approached him.

"Do you believe in God?" he asked Szadziewski, whose answer proved unsatisfying.

"Well," the foreigner said, "I think you are going to go to hell."

Szadziewski soon discovered that almost every one of the college's twenty or so foreign students—Americans, Koreans, Australians, a Norwegian and a Swiss—were missionaries. The Kopan family turned out to be his neighbours. "Greg had the apartment above me," Szadziewski recalled, "and on a Sunday morning he'd lead the singing of Christian songs."

The overt missionary presence is difficult to explain in light of the harsh religious restrictions in Xinjiang. However, the college was expanding at the time and needed the hard currency paid by foreigners for tuition and rent. The latter was exorbitantly priced, and Szadziewski figured some of the cash likely paid off local officials who turned a blind eye to the missionaries' preaching. He also said there were rumours about "rice Christians" among the student population. The missionaries would pay each pupil fifteen yuan (two dollars) a month if they converted. "They were told that if they looked at the poverty around them this was because you are Muslims and if you look at the Christian countries they are in general economically better off because of their religion," Szadziewski explained. Two of his students—one Uyghur and the other Han Chinese—converted. Their attitudes toward him turned abruptly aloof. "The world that the missionaries live in," Szadziewski recalled, "was a very black and white one."

I took a taxi to the front gate of the college campus, but a guard prevented my entry. Rapket, a Uyghur student who spoke English, eagerly offered to sign me in and escort me around the campus. He was tall and dark skinned with thick black hair and a thin moustache. He evidently wanted to practise his English.

The tree-lined streets were deserted. The fourteen thousand students and faculty were on summer recess. We sat under the shade of a poplar near outdoor gymnastics equipment. I asked Rapket about campus social life. Every morning started with gymnastics at 6 AM, he said, followed by classes at 7:30. There were afternoon and some evening classes too. At night, students had to return to their dormitories within an hour of class.

"What about student pubs and drinking?" I asked.

"Being drunk brings you great shame," Rapket said. "It's a sin. We fear God, Allah, the Creator."

Allah should be the least of his fears. Szadziewski described how, during his stay at the college, three Uyghur students got drunk and started talking politics. An informant tipped off authorities about their apparently seditious views. The students were publicly sentenced to hard labour. The "ringleader" received fifteen to twenty years' imprisonment. The unwitting Uyghurs had been caught in an elaborate surveillance system, called *xinxi wang*, or "information network," set up by the Public Security Bureau to watch over both students and faculty. Xinjiang has the harshest restrictions on religion in China. Religious teachings and attire such as beards and headscarves are banned from schools. Students are forbidden to attend mosque. Authorities conduct periodic witch hunts for worshippers and separatist sympathizers.

Surprisingly, the repressive education system had not weakened Rapket's faith or resolve. The physics student had even reconciled Islam with the cold, hard facts of modern science. "Life is a mystery," he explained to me. "Physics is the root science. I believe that physics can help explain the relationship between the spiritual and material world. Have you read *God and the New Physics* by Paul Davies?"

"I haven't."

"You should read it," he went on. "Physics won't be able to explain everything. If it does, then the mystery of life will be gone. There won't be any more meaning to life." He was beginning to sound like Joseph Campbell. "The mystery is Allah; the meaning in life is faith. If someone does discover the mystery of the universe, I hope I won't be around."

In the meantime, he was studying English at a private night school so he could read online scientific journals and keep abreast of cutting-edge scientific discoveries. He was especially interested in Stephen Hawking's recent musings on string theory. Rapket was also about to begin two weeks of mandatory military training before the start of the fall semester. That surprised me given the restive nature of young Uyghurs.

"The Chinese actually train you to shoot?" I asked incredulously.

"No guns," Rapket said smirking. "The government is scared of us."

MISSIONARIES HAVE HAD a huge impact on the Uyghurs, but not in any religious way. "Education and spiritual life are at an extremely low level," Mannerheim wrote of Kashgar. The local

Muslim schools, in 1906, taught only reading, writing, religious poetry and bits of the Koran. "The height of education," Mannerheim noted, "is the knowledge of the whole Koran by heart." Only a few Uyghurs could read Persian or Turkish newspapers. In contrast, the Swedish missionaries ran the first modern schools for boys and girls, compiled textbooks and grammars in the Uyghur language and translated texts. They built the first modern hospitals and operated the first printing press. They introduced skills to construct better buildings, forge better tools and increase the productivity of farmland.

At a new mission school in Yarkand, south of Kashgar, Mannerheim even noted that the pupils learned their Islamic prayers under the guidance of a mullah. It was "excellent testimony to the toleration exercised by the Swedish mission," the Baron wrote. "The object of their work is evidently not to be able to boast of so and so many converts from Islam, but to develop the people, so that they can make their own choice between different religions."

The same is true of contemporary missionaries working in Kashgar. Even critics of Western evangelism—myself included—find it difficult not to admire the hard work and philanthropy of many missionaries. Greg Kopan, for example, hired local Uyghurs and ran a fund to provide relief for local Kashgarians who can't afford medical treatment and other basic necessities. Most missionaries work as lowly paid or volunteer teachers. Rapket told me that a group of American "volunteers" recently taught English at a local private school, but the lessons were halted once someone complained to police about their extracurricular Bible studies.

On my last day in Kashgar, Kahar invited me to the private English school for Uyghurs where he taught night classes around his restaurant work. The school was located above street-level shops in a nondescript commercial block. The few dimly lit classrooms consisted of wooden desks, blackboards and small platforms for teachers. Perfunctory posters of Mao and Politburo members adorned the walls. His five female and four male students were in their early twenties. He insisted that I teach the class.

We recited vocabulary from their textbook. For days, my visit had been eagerly anticipated. Most students had never met a foreigner. The class shouted each word—"Ice cream! Shop! University! Hardware store! Motel!"—with embarrassing enthusiasm. "I'll never forget you," one of the Uyghur girls told me during a break.

Another teacher insisted that I provide some instruction to his class too. There were a dozen students, including two middle-aged Uyghur businessmen and a six-year-old with large ears and a mousy voice. The students were in the middle of reading a short essay. About twenty words were written on the blackboard: unique, pigeon, built-in radar, trust, homing, ordinary, mission. We recited each one and then I provided a short definition.

"Homing," I said, "is an adjective and describes the ability to instinctively find your way home."

Some students had only a shaky grasp of English. So I tried to define each word using examples from their everyday lives.

"What's a pigeon?" I asked.

"A bird," someone blurted out.

"Correct," I said, "and you can get pigeon kebabs in the bazaar."

Everyone nodded.

"What is a mission?"

Blank stares.

"A mission," I explained, "is an important journey with a specific goal or purpose. When you go to Mecca for the Hajj, you are on a religious mission." A few heads nodded. "Christian missionaries also go on missions to spread Christianity around the world." More nods. "And soldiers can be sent on a mission to kill terrorists in the mountains." That, I figured, rounded off the relevant examples of the word "mission" for Uyghurs.

The short essay in the government-issued textbook was curious. The previous year, Nurmuhemmet Yasin, a Uyghur poet and writer, had been sentenced to ten years in prison for a story titled "Wild Pigeon." Authorities had interpreted it as tacit criticism of China's harsh rule over Xinjiang. A brave young pigeon narrates the story. It ventures far from home and is eventually captured and caged. The pigeon decides to commit suicide rather than lose its freedom. "Now, finally, I can die freely," the feisty fowl says.[21] The essay in the textbook was, by contrast, titled "Homing Pigeon." It describes a dutiful, loyal little bird with "built-in radar." It is released from its cage to perform various "missions" for its captors, but always faithfully returns.

"The homing pigeon," the essay concludes, "can be trusted with its freedom."

TO KHOTAN

Oases and Outposts

*Converting low ranking servicemen of disbanded military units
into colonists has been a favourite method of colonization for ages.*
—MANNERHEIM's military intelligence report (1909)[1]

K HOTAN IS ONE of the last Uyghur strongholds. It lies locked
between geographic extremes—one of the world's largest deserts to the north and highest mountain ranges to the south. Few
newcomers dare to settle here. Kara-burans, "black hurricanes,"
rolling in off the Taklimakan Desert's ocean of sand routinely lash
the remote oasis. One year, sandstorms were recorded on 202 days.[2]
Horrendously hot and arid, the oasis survives on the waters of two
rivers that tumble down from the Kunlun range ringing the Tibetan
Plateau.

Khotan (Hetian in Chinese) is both inhospitable and insignificant. It lost its importance long ago with the decline of the Silk Road,
which forks at Kashgar. One route, now connected by road and rail,
leads north along the foot of the Tian Shan range; the other—a tor-
rid stretch of tarmac known as Route 315—skirts the Taklimakan's
southern edge through poor, dusty oases. Even in Mannerheim's

day, Khotan was a commercial and geopolitical backwater where, in the words of one British traveller in 1906, even the mosques were nothing more than "miserable mud hovels."[3]

Mannerheim had mixed feelings about a five-hundred-kilometre reconnaissance trip from Kashgar to Khotan. It would be a difficult detour, taking months. And upon arriving in Khotan he would have to turn around and head back to Kashgar to continue north—strategically the most important leg of his journey.

He was also doubtful of the military importance of this southern desert region. But Russian consul Kolokolov showed Mannerheim "curious reports" about British and Japanese movements between Kashgar and Khotan. There were rumours that twenty-six Japanese agents had recently appeared in Khotan and established an arms cache.[4] "However," Mannerheim wrote skeptically, "all of this seems to me more a product of pathological suspiciousness than reality." Nonetheless, he decided to verify these "incredible rumours" himself. Since the area bordered British India and Afghanistan, he also wanted to collect intelligence on "mysterious English travellers in the southern part of Kashgaria—almost all of them military persons."

Military value aside, Khotan was one of the most mysterious and elusive places in the world. As late as 1863, one British spy, murdered on the Karakoram Pass on his way back to India, wrote in his notebook that Khotan "was long ago swallowed up by the sand."[5] Local merchants and traders stirred up endless tales of ancient buried cities—and treasure. In 1889, a scroll scratched on birch bark made its way from Xinjiang to a linguist in India. A scholar deciphered it as a Sanskrit text using the Brahmi alphabet. It dated from the fifth century. The so-called Bower manuscript, named after the Indian intelligence officer who discovered it, turned out to be one of the oldest written works in the world and evidence of a lost Buddhist civilization in the Muslim stronghold of Chinese Turkestan. Its discovery shocked archaeological circles worldwide.[6]

Sven Hedin, the daring Swedish explorer, was the pathfinder. From 1895 to 1899, he went on three expeditions searching for ancient relics in the Taklimakan Desert. Its name, from *taqlar makan* in Turki, means "the place of ruins."[7] Ruin is what many explorers faced in the Taklimakan, including Hedin, who lost men and camels and almost died of thirst on his first foray. In the Ethnographic Museum in Stockholm, I saw the tall leather boots that he filled, after five days without water, in the Khotan River to carry back to his dying Uyghur guide. Hedin's discoveries, including the lost city of Loulan, created a sensation in Europe. Expeditions from Germany, Britain, France, Japan, the United States and Russia followed.

In 1906, Mannerheim found himself in the midst of an archaeological free-for-all. The Baron had met two Russian architects, the Beresovsky brothers, on the Irkeshtam Pass returning from investigations of ruined cities near Kucha, where the Bower manuscript was unearthed. Albert Grünwedel of the Ethnological Museum in Berlin was nearing the end of his third expedition to Xinjiang at the time too.[8] And only two months before Mannerheim and Pelliot arrived in Xinjiang, Aurel Stein, the great Hungarian-born British explorer, had left Kashgar for Khotan.

Stein has been described as "the greatest explorer of Asia since Marco Polo." His expeditions, "the most daring and adventurous raid upon the ancient world that any archaeologist has attempted," began in 1900 when he crossed the Karakoram Pass from India to Kashgar.[9] He travelled south to Khotan and then ventured to a desert ruin called Dandan-oilik. After eleven days' march into the desert, he reached its "ghostly wrecks of houses."[10] Here he hit pay dirt. His excavations unearthed ancient Sanskrit manuscripts of the Buddhist canon, Chinese documents, coins, frescoes and painted panels from buried Buddhist shrines. He also found Buddhist artwork blending Indian and Chinese influences, a style he coined "Serindian."

The Japanese were particularly interested in discovering their spiritual ancestry in these lost and buried Buddhist cities. Learning of Stein's discoveries, Count Kozui Otani, the leader of the Jodo Shinshu, or "Pure Land," Buddhist sect in Japan, dispatched two scholar-monks from his monastery in Kyoto in 1902. A second expedition sent in 1908 aroused considerable suspicion from the British, who suspected the monks of being secret intelligence agents. The British had used similar covert tactics themselves. Bower, an army officer, cloaked his clandestine survey as a hunting expedition. In two years, Mannerheim noted, thirty Englishmen "have crisscrossed certain parts of Kashgaria, especially its southern parts" toward Khotan. Petrovsky, the feared Russian consul, even tried to thwart Stein's expedition by telling Chinese officials that he was a British spy. Everyone was suspect, even Sven Hedin.

In the summer of 1906, Hedin was waiting in Simla, India, for permission to lead an expedition to map the vast "unexplored" Tibetan Plateau. The British refused, barring the Swede from entering Tibet from India. Even if Hedin wasn't a spy, the British had good reason to worry that whatever he learned would end up in the ear of the Russian Tsar. The explorer had a chummy relationship with Nicholas II, writing him letters in French and calling on the autocrat whenever he was in St. Petersburg. An egomaniac and celebrity-seeker, Hedin relished his forays into the glamorous world of geopolitics. He left Leh, India, on August 15, 1906, and, ignoring the British, disappeared into Tibet.[11] Twenty-two months later, not even George Macartney's far-reaching network of informants could locate the elusive Swede.[12]

Macartney tracked everyone, and not just for political reasons. Through the native mail service, he informed Aurel Stein about the movements of his archaeological rivals, especially Pelliot. Indeed, the British consul tipped off Stein about Pelliot's arrival in Kashgar. Alarmed, Stein quickly departed Khotan moving east to keep ahead of Pelliot. "The true race," Stein wrote in a letter to a friend, "will be with the Frenchmen."[13]

Stein described Macartney as a man "who can read human character in general with rare penetration."[14] Macartney, however, had a lapse in judgment when it came to Mannerheim. The Baron escaped serious scrutiny. Macartney noted Mannerheim's arrival in Kashgar and his return from Khotan several months later, describing him innocuously as a "Finnish traveller" in intelligence reports.[15] Ostensibly, the purpose of Mannerheim's Khotan trip was to gather ethnographic items and visit mountains "famed for their shooting." In reality, "more serious reasons" motivated this Russian spy. On October 7, Mannerheim sent his first secret dispatch to "Feda" through a letter to his father. He informed General Palitsyn of his covert plans and departed for Khotan that same day.[16]

THE DESOLATE SOUTHERN reaches of Xinjiang are wild in a number of ways. Prevailing winds are driving the dunes, like a conquering army, southward by as much as three metres a year.[17] Desperate officials have been constructing a "green wall" of drought-resistant tamarisk, olive trees and other shrubs to stop the dunes' incessant advance.

The isolated Uyghur population is equally untamed, at least in Beijing's eyes. A few months after my visit, Chinese security forces raided a camp on the Pamir Plateau, a sprawling high-altitude zone near the Afghan and Pakistani borders. Eighteen alleged Uyghur terrorists were killed and another seventeen arrested after a fierce gun battle.[18] Chinese authorities are particularly paranoid about this last bastion of Uyghur purity. It is one of China's few remaining regions where, as in Tibet, an ethnic minority population is larger than the Han Chinese.

I was especially mindful while trekking through this unruly borderland. Two Japanese scholars had recently been caught illegally surveying Khotan with satellite global positioning systems. According to the state-run Xinhua news agency, their equipment could map locations to within twenty centimetres, "exact enough for military use."[19] (Of what military use it would be to the

Japanese went unmentioned.) They were fined ten thousand dollars and deported, a warning to all foreigners not to probe too deeply in China's back of beyond.

I hired a car and Uyghur driver to take me on a four-day return journey to Khotan. (Mannerheim's trip lasted four months). My first stop would be Yengishar, literally "New City," just south of Kashgar. In 1906, Mannerheim reported that the frontier fortress was home to fifty thousand Chinese soldiers and their descendents who had quashed the Muslim revolt thirty years earlier. "Foreigners are forbidden in Yengishar because there's an army base and many Han Chinese," the tour company manager explained to me. The manager, a Uyghur, also warned me to stay clear of a small village outside Khotan. "The local Uyghurs here don't like the Han Chinese," he said. "There's been trouble."

Kasim, my Uyghur driver, was in his mid-twenties and spoke English sparingly. He had thick, wavy hair, a sparse moustache and pointy cheekbones suggesting Indian or Persian influences in his ancestry. He was polite, good-natured, but reticent.

Kasim cautiously drove through the streets of Yengishar, or Shule in Chinese, keeping well below the posted speed limit. It was a typical Chinese town with concrete plazas, wide boulevards and block after block of garishly commercial facades. Its outskirts consisted of windswept strips of farmland planted with corn, wheat, cotton and sunflowers. The soil was yellow and sandy. Fields quickly gave way to meagre tuffs of reeds and desert shrubs grazed by camels, cows and sheep. Then, beyond a poor village of poplars and clay huts, I found myself on a barren plain that, as Mannerheim wrote, seemed "to burn under the hoofs of the horses"—and now under the tires of the car.

A half-hour later, we arrived in Yengisar (also Yengi-hissar and not to be confused with Yengis*har*), one of the green oases that sit like lily pads on the wastes between Kashgar and Khotan. A century ago, a crenellated wall with turrets on four corners surrounded the garrison town. Fortresses like this one were built all over Xinjiang after the Muslim revolts of the 1870s. Two streets were laid out on the east–west and north–south axes "with the precision characteristic of the Chinese in matters concerning the points of the compass," Mannerheim wrote. It was a sleepy outpost whose bazaar was "usually empty and lifeless" except for once a week. There were houses for a few Chinese inhabitants, a couple temples, infantry barracks, a covered bazaar street and several caravanserais. Traders came from India and Afghanistan. "One caravan succeeds another," the Baron wrote. "The shouts of the drivers and the dull tinkling of the camel's bells herald the approach of a fresh caravan from a distance."

Disappointingly, the Yengisar of yore was nowhere to be found. A new six-lane boulevard, lined by drab government buildings and apartment blocks, now cuts through the downtown. A few scooters and motorized three-wheeled carts zipped along the desolate thoroughfare. At the town's main intersection, we turned south toward a large sandy grey wall. Engineers had ploughed the boulevard right through it. We parked and climbed a sloping, dirt path to the top. From here, I realized the wall was actually a long loess ridge. I looked north over the town trying to spy anything resembling the old fortress, but saw only faceless modern buildings and poplars poking up from mud-brick neighbourhoods. In an odd way, the outpost's wide boulevards reminded me of Paris.

Almost every town in Xinjiang is being modernized along the exact same lines: medieval walls, narrow bazaar streets and labyrinths of low-slung courtyard homes are being razed to make way for a network of grand boulevards, modern apartments, shops and monumental public spaces. It is a scheme pioneered and made famous in Paris by Georges-Eugène Haussmann. In 1852, the civic planner modernized the French capital by demolishing entire blocks and laying out a spectacular axial grid over Paris.

Yengisar's modernization is supposed to improve residents' standard of living, yet authoritarianism, as in Haussmann's Paris, underlies China's new urbanism. Haussmann designed boulevards so infantry could easily circulate and control the city, and fire artillery at unruly citizenry if need be. The French brought this scheme to their own colonial outposts, ploughing grandiose boulevards through the ancient Muslim quarters of Algiers and Tunis. Chinese city planners are now effectively doing the same. Yengisar is even crowned with a monument to modernity: a steel telecommunications tower in the centre of town pierces the skyline like a miniature Eiffel Tower.

The road out of Yengisar skirted a dry reservoir and abandoned fields cut with irrigation ditches. We drove across a desert landscape scattered with grimy villages where donkey carts trotted along dirt streets lined with poplars, chalky fields and earthen abodes. The only signs of modernity were telecom towers that dotted the terrain every sixty kilometres or so. They reminded me of *paotai*, the massive clay watchtowers that Mannerheim saw spread out every four kilometres along the route.[20] In ancient times, flagpoles atop the towers were used to relay warnings about enemy activity or approaching caravans. Nowadays, these telecom towers serve the same purpose for Chinese security forces.

Since Kasim was so quiet and withdrawn and since there was little to look at—"Nothing but sand and some gravel as far as the eye can see," Mannerheim wrote—I passed the time reading the Baron's diary.

MANNERHEIM'S PROSE IS as dry of titillating details as the Taklimakan is of water. He comes across as aloof, impersonal and even churlish at times. One would expect bonds to form between men during such a long, arduous voyage, but the Baron displays little warmth to or interest in his travelling companions. For his desert trek to Khotan, he hired two Uyghur *yigits*, or horsemen, but never mentions them by name. He complains about Liu's poor grasp of Russian and notes that he hired an "elderly Chinaman" to teach him Chinese during the monotonous ride. He briefly mentions Rakhimjanov, but the other Cossack, Yunusov, is never heard of again.

Mannerheim, a cavalryman, is far more effusive about horses. In Yengisar, he writes of Afghan traders as being "distrustful and shy," but goes on at length about their "very beautiful" horses whose heads are "lean and noble." Finnish novelist Markus Nummi even drew on this idiosyncrasy in *The Chinese Garden,* a novel about a Uyghur orphan raised by Swedish missionaries in Kashgar. Mannerheim makes a telling cameo, in which Nummi depicts him as a lonely figure who shuns people. Instead, he confides in his horse Philip about his feelings of love and longing—personal musings that are nowhere to be found in his actual diary.

About 175 kilometres southeast of Kashgar, calamity struck Mannerheim. He was forced to dismount. Nothing is mentioned in his original travelogue published in 1940, but his handwritten journal, now in the archives of Helsinki University, is revealing. "I fell so severely ill that I was compelled to stay in the village of Qaraqum," he wrote. Rheumatism brought about during the Russo-Japanese war crippled him. A Chinese cart was brought from a nearby village and he unceremoniously "trundled along" for the ten kilometres to Yarkand. Here, Mannerheim called upon the Swedish missionary Gustaf Raquette, who was also a practising doctor.

After a month in Yarkand, he was still unwell and decided to purchase a cart to continue his trip. The idea was "deeply repugnant," but there was no other way. Overall, the expedition was turning into a catastrophe: he'd had a falling-out with Pelliot, lost a team member, accidentally broken his camera and now fallen ill with rheumatism and fever. His translator Liu was threatening to quit. He had no intelligence on Japanese or British spies and had done no ethnographic collecting. "My two months long stay in Chinese Turkestan," he wrote from Yarkand to Otto Donner, his patron in Helsinki, "has no interesting results to show."[21]

WE ARRIVED IN Yarkand just in time for Friday's noontime prayer. Kasim parked on a narrow street crowded with motorcycles, vendors and worshippers flooding into the open-air Altunluq Mosque. He told me to watch from across the street. Kasim and hundreds of men in beards and white embroidered *doppas* crouched behind the mosque's iron gate. A woman and teenage boy sold disposable plastic prayer mats at the entrance. An imam droned over a crackling loudspeaker as a sea of white caps bobbed rhythmically under the blistering noontime sun. Afterwards, the hungry worshippers swarmed street vendors selling mutton, *polo* (pilaf), melons and flatbread. An eager crowd thronged one unusual merchant. "He's selling medicine for rheumatism," Kasim said, "but it's not real. Throughout China, even in big department stores, you can buy things that aren't real. He's just trying to take their money."

We strolled through the adjacent bazaar street, but the afternoon heat was unbearable. We retreated to an air-conditioned hotel and agreed to meet for dinner in the early evening. "I've been in China for more than two weeks and I haven't had any Chinese food. Let's go to a Chinese restaurant tonight," I suggested.

"You can go," Kasim replied flatly. "I don't eat Chinese."

I apologized for my unthinking suggestion; as a devoted Muslim, Kasim ate only in halal restaurants. Instead, we had chopped noodles with spicy mutton at a Uyghur café around the corner from the hotel. The next morning Kasim refused even to set foot in the hotel's Chinese restaurant for tea or a steamed bun. He sat in the lobby as I ate breakfast. On the way out of Yarkand, we stopped at a roadside Uyghur vender. Kasim bought two hard-boiled eggs and flatbread to eat on the road to Khotan.

The Yarkand oasis stretches southward for nearly fifty kilometres. We crossed a bridge over the Yarkand River, whose churning waters were the colour of putty. Farming hamlets become scarcer. The gravelly desert plain eventually turned into shifting dunes. Gusts of wind swept rivulets of sand across the highway. So far, I hadn't yet seen the sun's glimmer or a patch of blue sky. Everything was eerily awash in a sepia monotone, like one of Mannerheim's old photographs. Just outside Khotan the Baron also noticed "a kind of haze in the air that curtailed the view extremely."

We stopped at Kasim's home in a Khotan suburb for lunch. An alleyway shaded by grape trellises led to the modest abode. His mother, donning one of the colourful silk headscarves for which Khotan is famous, served us nan, spicy bread-dough pies filled with mutton and onion, plump red and green grapes and bowls of *polo* which we ate, in traditional style, with our fingers. Kasim performed his midday prayer, and then we drove down a series of dirt roads that wound through agricultural hamlets. We woke an old man who was sleeping under a tree at the roadside. His beard, skin, hair and clothes were caked in powdery yellow soil. He looked like a castaway. He pointed us down a rutted road. We drove on a bit farther and then Kasim parked under a tree. "I'll stay with the car," he said. I climbed a nearby mound overlooking a swath of reeds ringed by poplar and mulberry trees. It looked like dried swampland. This is all that is left of Yotkan, the site of an ancient Buddhist city, now buried under metres of accumulated alluvium.

The process by which ancient settlements such as Yotkan disappeared took centuries. Climatic shifts shrank glaciers in the Kunlun Mountains which, in turn, shortened rivers, leaving remote oases on the margins of the Taklimakan stranded. As the desert expanded, many outposts had to be abandoned. Over time, the encroaching sands buried stupas, houses and monasteries. In Yotkan's case, canals and streams silted up over centuries, choking off the oasis's water supply until it died.

Yotkan was effectively lost below the silt until the 1870s, when a deep irrigation canal was dug through the area. Soon, valuable gold bits, terracotta figurines, glass, coins and other antiquities started surfacing in the canal. Local treasure seekers descended on the rich soil. Sven Hedin was the first European to visit the site in 1895, followed by Aurel Stein in 1900. Mannerheim conducted no excavations of his own. Instead, he bought a modest collection of items from local diggers, including several reliefs depicting monks or perhaps the Buddha, and numerous animal figurines.[22] "Any discoveries of value had, no doubt, already been secured," Mannerheim wrote.

Europeans have plucked much of the Taklimakan's archaeological sites clean. As a result, the collection at the downtown Khotan Museum was relatively modest. I browsed its two rooms, which house Islamic arts and handicrafts, ancient scripts in strange languages (Sanskrit and Khotanese Saka in Brahmi script), Buddhist ceramic figurines and pottery fragments. The museum's centrepiece is two mummies, Buddhist nuns who lived about fifteen hundred years ago in Yotkan. This centre of Buddhist civilization—in AD 399 the pilgrim Faxian recorded fourteen large monasteries and thousands of monks—slowly withered until the sword of Islam delivered a deathblow in the eleventh century. A new Muslim oasis began to flourish in the present location of Khotan about ten kilometres to the west. Over the centuries, shifting sands and waves of migrants—travelling merchants, Muslim crusaders and pilgrims—transformed this desert region. Yet its tumultuous ancient history was nothing compared to the rapid change that Khotan had experienced in the last ten years.

THE SAND STILL threatens Khotan. Early one morning, Kasim drove me to Jiya, a village on the edge of the Khotan oasis that sticks out like a headland into the Taklimakan's tempestuous sea of sand. The poplars disappeared and soon we were on a hard-packed sand road. We stopped at the first dune, unable to go on. I walked out into the desert and climbed a high crest. I spotted two slender minarets and a green dome poking above a golden dune about a kilometre into the desert. This is the mosque and tomb of Imam Asim, one of the first martyrs to bring Islam to Khotan. Over the course of several centuries, it has become engulfed by the Taklimakan.

Khotan seems hardly worth saving from the encroaching desert, at least by the brutal calculus of modern economics. Its only real industry is handicrafts whose techniques haven't changed in centuries. On our way back into town, we stopped at the Atlas Silk Factory in Jiya. In the first century, a Chinese princess, betrothed to a Khotanese king, smuggled mulberry seeds and silkworms in her headdress to this remote oasis. The kingdom grew wealthy on the silk trade. Nowadays, the primitive factory looks tragically anachronistic. A Uyghur woman boiled white, furry cocoons in a smoking cauldron and another spun the strong filament on a pedal wheel. The local carpet factory—the largest in Khotan, I was told— employed only seventy women (and a dozen of their children) on twenty-two looms. The scene inside the factory looked almost identical to a photograph that Mannerheim snapped of a local carpet factory a century previous.

More than anything else, however, Khotan is famous for jade. The town is wedged between the Yurungkash (White Jade) River to the east and Karakash (Black Jade) River to the west. During the summer months, precious nephrite stones are washed down from the Kunlun Mountains by snowmelt. Jade shops line the main boulevard and hotels are packed with Han jade traders from Eastern China. I visited a jade factory next to the bazaar. It consisted of a half-dozen Han craftsmen carving ornaments, jewellery and lucky charms. "Uyghurs don't carve images of Buddha," Kasim explained. "Islam forbids it."

But Uyghurs are jade diggers. I saw them wandering the rocky riverbanks searching for the motherlode—the only hope for economic advancement for many Uyghurs. Kasim took me twenty-six kilometres upriver to a massive excavation site along the Yurungkash. We arrived at a ragtag jade-prospecting settlement. The scene on the floodplain was no different than a century ago: "As far as you can see," Mannerheim wrote, "there are large heaps of sand, gravel and stones, as if the plain were inhabited by

gigantic rodents." Nowadays, the rodents are backhoes and excavators operated by Han Chinese and rented for up to five thousand
dollars a month by groups of Uyghur men who sift through buck-
ets of mud and rock. Mannerheim counted several hundred diggers;
most were addicted to opium and gambling. "The finds are irregu-
lar," he wrote. "Few men have been able to earn a fortune, but many
have lost all they possessed" and were forced to collect asses' dung
to earn a living.

We drove back to town and visited the home of Kasim's fiancée
in a Khotan suburb. Gulnar, who was studying traditional Uyghur
medicine at a local college, was a homely girl with plump, rosy
cheeks framed by a headscarf. Her home was a typical courtyard
house with colourful wooden doors, sculpted plaster ceilings and
no furniture. We sat on vibrant red carpets and plush cushions. She
offered green tea, mutton pies and melon.

"The house used to be a lot bigger. Last year the government
widened the road and destroyed part of the house," Kasim said with
surprising candour. "The officials didn't even pay them compensation for this. It's terrible."

"Four rooms were completely bulldozed," Gulnar added shyly.

Yet Gulnar's family was lucky that even one room remained
standing, given the massive destruction I saw in the city centre. We
drove back into town on the rebuilt road. Kasim dropped me off on
Khotan's main street, Beijing Road, by a section of the old city wall.
It was about two hundred metres long and stood along a new river-
side park still under construction. There was also a stretch of wall
running a block south of the road toward my hotel on Unity Square.
Otherwise, the old fortress was obliterated, replaced by wide thoroughfares, gated Chinese apartment compounds, jade shops, malls,
hotels, administrative buildings and military barracks. Khotan's latest transformation was unfolding at an unprecedented speed.

"There's an army base over there," Kasim said pointing north to
a gated compound guarded by soldiers. "Be careful."

"I'll take photographs to the south," I said.

"There's army over there too. Be careful," he implored.

I discreetly snapped a few photographs of the crumbling wall and then walked back along Beijing Road to my hotel. On Unity Square's north side stands a statue of a domineering Mao Zedong shaking the hand of Kurban Tulum, a frail-looking Uyghur and Communist stooge known throughout China fittingly as Uncle Kurban (think Uncle Tom). A billboard advertising new condominiums covered one side of the statue's plinth. On the other was a kitschy montage depicting soldiers of the People's Liberation Army, smiling ethnic minorities and the Great Wall. A slogan read: "The army and the people, bound together like fish and water, can build the Great Wall." But in this wretched desert region, the Han Chinese are more like fish out of water.

IT TOOK WELL over a century for the Chinese to begin seriously colonizing southern Xinjiang. Mannerheim, wherever he travelled on his way to Khotan, noted the saliferous soils, the lack of water and a population suffering from venereal diseases, gambling and opium addiction. The region was so backward by Chinese standards that it had even kept its former Muslim administrative organization. While Chinese governors reigned in Yarkand and Khotan, Muslim *begs* ruled districts, and mullahs settled disputes and petty crimes. Mannerheim also noted the ridiculous condition of Chinese garrisons. There were only three Chinese officers and 104 soldiers in Khotan. The soldiers conducted a drill with bamboo lances in Mannerheim's honour. Their fighting technique, the Baron wrote, was "most comical."

Mannerheim left Khotan the next day. He travelled back to Kashgar along the foot of the mountains. He hunted, practised surveying, conducted ethnographic research on two obscure tribes (the Pakhpo and Shiksho) and spent Christmas with the missionary Raquette in Yarkand.

It was impossible for me to retrace his route along the rugged foothills. Kasim and I had to stick to Highway 315. From Khotan, the road was freshly paved for eighty kilometres. At the end of this slick surface, out in the desert, lies Kaifa Qu, a new settlement under construction. The name means literally "development zone" and was probably taken from the slogan *Xibu Da Kaifa,* or "Great Western Development." The strategy was launched in 2000 to lure Han Chinese to Xinjiang's hinterlands. Critics refer to it as the "Great Leap West."

Kaifa Qu was so new that it wasn't on my map—nor can you yet spy it on Google Earth. We pulled into the nascent settlement. There's a telecom tower, a collection of gaudy coloured apartment buildings and an idle factory. Two paved streets intersect at its centre. We turned onto a gravel path toward the settlement's reservoir, an elevated square structure built of concrete and sand. It is about three hundred metres long on each side and is called Sha Qing Shui, or "Sand Pouring Water." A sturdy Chinese attendant with a buzz cut came out of a nearby hut. He wore a camouflage jacket and red armband. He looked like a militiaman. The reservoir was built three years ago, he said, and is fed by a long canal from the Karakash River. It provides drinking water and irrigates an orchard of date trees that sits hidden in a haze about a half-kilometre into the desert.

"My uncle says that bad Chinese live here," Kasim said as we were leaving.

"What do you mean by 'bad' Chinese?"

"I don't know," he said. "That's what I heard."

Several weeks later I would discover just who these "bad" Chinese were: members of the Fourteenth Division of the Xinjiang Production and Construction Corps (xpcc) operating the Hetian Kunlun Mountain Chinese Date Company. I happened upon their booth at a tradeshow in Urumqi. In 1954, xpcc was founded with demobilized pla and Guomindang soldiers. The paramilitary agro-industrial corporation runs its owns towns, cities, judiciary, prison labour camps, public security apparatus, newspapers, hospitals and universities. The corps's divisions and regiments have been set up on the margins of troubled borderlands and along strategic transportation arteries in Xinjiang. It consists of 2.5 million members, 88 percent of whom are Han Chinese. It has jurisdiction over 740,000 hectares, or 48 percent of Xinjiang's landmass. It's an economic powerhouse, fuelling Xinjiang's export growth and doubling cultivated land.[23] Answerable only to Beijing, it's a state within a state.

XPCC's roots go back thousands of years to the ancient *tuntian* system of settling farmer-soldiers on China's restless borderlands. Around Yarkand, Mannerheim noted that former soldiers expanded irrigation canals, opening new land for Chinese settlement. "The desired impact however was not achieved," he concluded. "Old soldiers turned out to be unsuitable for colonization and they had to give a greater part of those plots of land to the [Uyghurs]."[24] He saw the same pattern in the hamlet of Zawa on the edge of the Khotan oasis and not far from present-day Kaifa Qu. Poor soil, scarce water and a lack of irrigation technology prevented serious colonization. "If they want to increase the Chinese population," Mannerheim wrote, officials "will have to take away land from the [Uyghurs] and give it to the Chinese."[25]

Between 1950 and 1978, the Communist government cajoled, induced or ordered 3 million Han Chinese to settle in Xinjiang.[26] It was difficult to keep these new settlers in such a desolate, hostile region. It was only after the 1990s—with the weakening of the *hukou* (residency permit) system, construction of a railway to Kashgar, cheap land leases and tax abatements—that Han Chinese started pouring into the desert oases. A thousand years ago, Muslim crusaders and shifting river patterns obliterated Buddhist towns. Now Muslims face the same peril: Chinese workers at Kaifa Qu were digging irrigation canals and building a new settlement that is draining water—and ultimately prosperity—away from the Uyghurs.

As we left Kaifa Qu, I asked Kasim what Uyghurs think of all this Han Chinese settlement. He cracked a thin, ambiguous smile. "How can I answer this?" he asked rhetorically.

Just down the highway, Kasim pulled to the side of the road and washed his face and hands in a swift-flowing canal. We drove on in silence. At one point, we passed two eight-wheeled PLA tanks with gun turrets—a new class of combat vehicles designed to respond at lightning speed to civil unrest. Just past noon, Kasim stopped again at a godforsaken spot between two oases. He walked out into the vast desert, unrolled a small rug, slipped off his shoes and knelt defiantly in quiet prayer.

EIGHT

TIAN SHAN RANGE

The Horse That Leaps through Clouds

*The beginning of wisdom is to call
things by their right names.*—CHINESE PROVERB

FOR A WESTERNER, selecting a good Chinese name is tricky. Ideally, you want it to be meaningful, euphonic and phonetically similar to your Western name. Transliteration is the most obvious means, so that Mary becomes Mali and Colin becomes Kelin. However, the results are occasionally less than satisfactory: the two characters for Kelin (克林) translate as "subdue" and "forest," respectively. Unless you are a lumberjack, the name probably doesn't resonate. There are also undesirable homophones. Simon can become Siming, meaning "talented" *(si)* and "brilliant" *(ming),* but if *si* is pronounced with the incorrect tone it can also mean "death," which is why the number four, also *si,* is so unlucky to the Chinese. The safest strategy, then, is to have a Chinese friend bestow on you a Chinese name.

A month before departing on my trip, I had dinner with Charlotte, the mother of my partner. Over fried rice, chow mein and shrimp stir-fry, she told me about her family's flight from Shanghai in 1957.

By this time, Mao had turned himself into a wily tyrant with a crazed personality cult. He bloodily purged the party of rivals and launched various terror campaigns against "counter-revolutionaries." Charlotte's father, a businessman and a Christian, no less, fled to Hong Kong, leaving behind his wife and children. PLA soldiers periodically raided their home. One day, her mother put on her most expensive jewellery, gathered her young children and left for a "day trip" to Hong Kong. They never returned. Although her mother tongue is Shanghai-ese, Charlotte quickly learned Cantonese during her childhood years in Hong Kong before immigrating to Canada.

Picking the character for my surname was easy. Although there is only one listing for Tamm in the Vancouver telephone directory, there are 278 listings for Tam, a popular Cantonese surname. Considering my visa problems, long journey ahead and stubborn disposition, Charlotte chose Yilik for my Cantonese given name. It can loosely be defined as "perseverance" or "willpower." The first character, *yi* (意), means "idea, intention or thought" and the second, *lik* (力), means "power, force or strength." It sounds similar to "Eric," especially to Cantonese who have difficulty pronouncing "r." So, I became Tam Yilik, or Tan Yili in Mandarin. "It suits you," Charlotte said.

MANNERHEIM OBTAINED HIS Chinese name in a different way. Returning from Khotan, he realized that his passport, issued by the Chinese Minister in St. Petersburg and on its way via Peking, had still not arrived in Kashgar. Foreigners were not permitted to travel beyond a sixty-five-kilometre radius of any treaty port without a passport *(huzhao)* from a district mandarin.[1] The Russian Consul suggested that Mannerheim request a new one from the local governor.

Mannerheim visited Yuan Hungyu, "a thin old man of distinguished appearance and manners," in Kashgar's Chinese quarter. "*Ma* is horse in Chinese," the Baron later recalled, "and as these first letters of my name made a good beginning of a sonorous Chinese name, my host suggested it should be entered into my pass. The Chinese are in the habit of adding two more syllables, which, in combination with the first one, express some pleasing poetical idea." Yang seized a fine brush and delicately added two "beautiful" characters after *ma*. These were *da* (達) and *han* (漢). Mannerheim was now called Ma Dahan, which he translated to mean "the horse that leaps through the clouds."[2]

Mannerheim employed literary licence in his interpretation. Depending on the context, *da* can mean "to attain, pass through, achieve or reach," but the character for *han* refers to the Han people or what we commonly refer to as ethnic Chinese. To suggest that it means "cloud" is, well, a leap. A more appropriate translation would be "the horse that travels to [the land of] the Han," an equally meaningful name.[3]

There was, however, something "curious" about Yang's inscription in the new *huzhao*. The "artistically decorated card" was addressed to "the Russian subject, the Finn Baron Mannerheim, whose Chinese name is Ma Dahan."[4] Only a few days before, Yang had never even heard of a Finn and now, somehow, he identified Mannerheim as both a Finn and "Russian subject." "In my opinion," the Baron wrote in his diary, "Macartney has definitely a hand in it."

The British Consul certainly had close ties to Yang, but Macartney never suspected Mannerheim of espionage or referred to him as a Russian, at least not in his intelligence reports back to London. Nevertheless, Yang may have asked Macartney about the Finn's imperial allegiance. Pelliot may have also spoken indiscreetly about the Baron's identity to his compatriots. Their Chinese translator may have, in turn, overheard a chance remark and passed on the information to Chinese officials.[5] Thirty years later, Mannerheim expunged every reference to the untrustworthy Pelliot from his published journals, an indication of his deep disdain for the Frenchman.

The Baron relished his Chinese name. "Whenever my pass was inspected by the authorities," he recalled, "my new name was much admired."⁶ Fittingly, since Mannerheim was a baron and a cavalryman, "ma" also refers to the knight on a chessboard. With his new *huzhao* in hand, Mannerheim was now ready to make his next move in the Great Game.

The formidable Heavenly Mountains lay ahead. The Tian Shan range stretches 2,800 kilometres from the Kyrgyz/Kazakh border region to Urumqi, splitting Xinjiang into two distinct basins: the Tarim with its sweltering sweep of sand to the south and Zungharia (also Jungaria) with its wind-torn steppe to the north. Mannerheim would have to literally leap through the clouds to cross the Heavenly Mountains. Its treacherous passes spiral up peaks soaring higher than seven thousand metres. Even in late spring and summer, conditions could be bleak. As Tang Dynasty poet Li Bo once wrote:

> Tian Shan in May
> No blossoms gay,
> Snow on the hill
> And winter chill.⁷

Mannerheim planned to zigzag across the ragged range three times, an exhausting six-month journey. His first crossing to the Ili Valley would be in the dead of winter, in freezing temperatures and over a perilous glacier—a foolhardy endeavour, it would seem.

The Russians had controlled the Ili Valley in the 1870s during the period of Muslim unrest. The town of Gulja (Yining in Chinese) near the border would likely be the first target of an invading Russian army. From here, Cossacks would quickly ride eastward and overwhelm Urumqi, the regional capital. A greater challenge would be subduing Kashgar and oases to the south. General Palitsyn ordered Mannerheim to scout the Muzart Pass across the Tian

Shan range. This strategic corridor, very close to the border, could be used to quickly send Russian cavalry into the Tarim Basin to cut off the communications and supply route between Urumqi and Kashgar. Mannerheim was to assess road conditions and gauge the allegiance of various ethnic tribes living in the mountainous region.

Mannerheim was happy to leave Kashgar, even though he enjoyed "lively social intercourse" with its European residents. One newcomer, a bright young Swedish woman, had caught the Baron's eye. He hoped that her "joie de vivre" and "silvery laugh" would win the day over Kashgar's gloom. On January 27, 1907, Mannerheim set off with his interpreter Liu, a new cook named Ismail and the Cossack Rakhimjanov. They rode north of Kashgar over an "ugly and monotonous landscape." Misery and poverty were everywhere. In one village, Mannerheim came across Dolans, a poor tribe of nomadic pastoralists closely related to Uyghurs. In another, he discovered a lost tribe of Persians, the mysterious Abdals who were Shiite outcasts. "They live by themselves, despised by the people in the neighbouring villages," he wrote. He took anthropological measurements and photographs, then quickly departed.

He pressed northward, out of the desert and into the foothills of the Tian Shan. One night he came across Kyrgyz yurts on an alpine grassland. One was jammed with a dozen adults, four children and forty sheep. The other was even less inviting. "My entrance was not welcomed with cries of delight, as I had expected, but an old woman yelled something unintelligible that sounded like abuse," he wrote. They made themselves at home anyway among bleating sheep and a screaming child. The Baron treated his hosts to some bread since there wasn't enough meat to go around. The hungry Kyrgyz, however, "got busy with the bones that had fallen on the ground."

The next day's ride took him to yet another Kyrgyz camp where Mannerheim became "more than usually anxious" about Ismail, his randy Uyghur cook. "I was afraid," he wrote, "that the sheepskin coats of the rosy-cheeked Kirghiz women would not be strong enough armour to protect their hearts against the gaiety and attractive looks of my cook."

His small caravan then descended to Uch-Turpan, a town locked in a river valley between the Tian Shan and Karateke ranges. He followed a tributary to the Aksu River, which spills into the Taklimakan Desert. General Palitsyn had instructed Mannerheim "to make a military and statistical description of the Aksu oasis."[8] It was, the Baron wrote, "the most important district in Chinese Turkestan from a military point of view." Aksu protected the entrance to Muzart Pass and the strategic crossroads connecting Urumqi to Kashgar and Yarkand.

Mannerheim quickly set about gathering intelligence. The Baron surveyed the Aksu River while he waited for the local military commander to return. General Tang Yongshan was a "lively man of 60 of herculean build" who was a firm believer in modernization and reform. "Japan's amazingly rapid development was proof of the possibility of China's awakening in the near future from her centuries of sleep," he told Mannerheim. He had introduced new exercises, uniforms, military schools and armaments (including Winchester rifles) to the Aksu garrison. However, the critical factor for Xinjiang's security, according to the astute general, would be the construction of a railway. It would permit speedy deployment of fresh Chinese troops in the event of ethnic unrest or foreign invasion. "Once that is completed," General Tang explained, "we need not fear anyone."

MUZART PASS APPEARED impassable. On my map, it looked like a thin crack in a five-thousand-metre-high wall topped with peaks as jagged as barbed wire. A red dotted line—described as a "path" on the legend—vaguely suggested that it was traversable. A mountaineering guide in Urumqi informed me, via email, that caravans used the pass in ancient times. "However," he warned, "the road has been given up lately since it is too close to the border and Muzart

Pass is very dangerous. To my information, there is snow and ice on the pass all year round and caravans used to lose some pack animals while crossing the pass. So, I am sorry to say that we can't make it."

About two hundred kilometres to the east of Muzart, the Chinese had built Route 217 over the range. "The road is in disrepair," Greg Kopan had told me in Kashgar, "and hasn't been open for two years." Farther east, another route required an expensive four-wheel drive. Dangers and costs aside, these routes also necessitated special travel permits from the Public Security Bureau. I dreaded facing Chinese officialdom and their probing questions about my obscure nationality and curious itinerary. If I wanted to skirt China's security apparatus, I'd have to skirt the Tian Shan too.

Kasim, my Uyghur driver, met me outside the dreary Chini Bagh Hotel, where I stayed the last few nights in Kashgar. I hired him for an eight-day road trip to Gulja on the north side of the Tian Shans. He said he could take me to the mouth of the Muzart Pass but not beyond. Mannerheim had marched a hundred kilometres across the pass, but we would have to go around the rocky range— a 2,300-kilometre detour. Jappar, a friend of Kasim, came along as well. He had fallen ill with migraines and lost his appetite. He was pale and rail-thin, with sunken eyes. The gaunt young man silently slumped in the backseat for most of the journey to Gulja, his hometown. In exchange for the free ride, Jappar agreed to host me at a friend's farmhouse in the Ili Valley.

The morning was warm, the air sticky with dew. Under an overcast sky, we left Kashgar on a concrete highway, Route 314, labelled "Silk Road" on my map. About a hundred kilometres outside Kashgar, we turned north onto a secondary road that allowed me roughly to retrace Mannerheim's trek through the foothills of the Tian Shans to Aksu. The road weaved through sandstone hillocks that looked like the folds of a golden blanket. The hills were pockmarked with brackish pools and saltlicks. On a grassy plateau, camels roamed across the road. Just before noon, we stopped at the village of Karajol for refreshments. Swarthy Kyrgyz in stubby white felt hats loitered around a roadside kiosk. A refrigerator contained only cold beer. "Kyrgyz!" Kasim scoffed disapprovingly of his free-spirited, alcohol-drinking co-religionists.

An ominous black range, the Karateke Mountains, lay ahead. The highway snaked up a mountain pass. In places, erosion had taken large bites out of the new asphalt. Dark, heavy clouds loomed overhead. A thunderstorm suddenly broke. Huge rain-drops bounced off the hood of the car like marbles. Lightning flashed. Kasim hunched forward, his grip tightening on the steering wheel. We slowed to a crawl for our descent. The Volkswagen skidded down a wicked road overflowing with ochre-coloured mud. In the torrential din, I could faintly hear Kasim repeating a soothing Uyghur folk song. We were soon delivered into the Tushkan River Valley, squeezed between the majestic snow-capped peaks of the Tian Shan and Karateke ranges. "The whole valley is lovely, set in its frame of endless mountains," the Baron wrote. The river's churning, yellowy waters meandered through lush green pastures dotted with white Kyrgyz yurts that looked like mushroom caps. At one point, the rains abated. Kasim quickly pulled over to pray. The wind howled and he placed stones on the corners of his prayer rug lest it become a flying carpet.

The wild grasslands soon gave way to cultivated cornfields, orchards and Uyghur farmsteads. The valley progressively widened and sloped down toward Uch-Turpan. It was immediately clear to me why Mannerheim wanted to survey and sketch this outpost: a citadel sits atop a rocky prominence in the middle of town. It's a tourist attraction now, but an army barracks lies on its northern foot.

"Be careful," Kasim said as I was about to get out of the car to take a photograph of the old military fortress. "There's an army base right there."

"I don't want them to think I'm a spy," I said. "I'll take the photo from inside the car."

"Are you a spy?" Kasim asked.

"What do you think?"

Kasim chuckled, but we both knew that it was no laughing matter. Chinese authorities regularly harass Uyghurs who befriend or interact with foreigners. Poking around military bases in China's Muslim borderland was fraught with peril, especially for a pious Muslim in the company of a foreigner carrying old military maps and intelligence reports.

It was now 5:30 PM. Kasim and Jappar slipped into Uch-Turpan's central mosque for the day's final prayer. We then left the fertile valley for the desert wasteland to the south, following Mannerheim's path. It was dark by the time we reached Aksu, an unremarkable town that stands at the base of yellow loess cliffs. The majority of its population is Han Chinese. Its streets are devoid of charm. "There is little of interest for the modern tourist," states my guidebook. Aksu is still of strategic import, but not as a defence against foreign invasion. It is home to an entire division of the paramilitary Xinjiang Production and Construction Corps. The heavy concentration of these farmer-soldiers, who are overwhelmingly Han Chinese, is intended to fortify the region against Uyghur unrest and separatism.[9] That night we stayed at the Great Wall Business Hotel. A sign at the reception desk curtly stated, in English, "Soldiers first."

We left Aksu at 7 AM. The morning was clear and chilly. I could see the awesome silhouette of the Tian Shan range to the north. The road out of town was lined by dirt-poor villages. Jam, where Mannerheim camped, wasn't much more than a few shops, a truck stop and shabby clay homes. At a melon stand, a Uyghur truck driver gave Kasim directions to a road, about fifteen kilometres to the east, that would take us north to Muzart Pass.

"Road" is an overstatement. The route consisted of broken pavement, gravel patches and potholes the size of bomb craters. In a few places, it wasn't much more than a rutted trail. After an hour of jangling, I was relieved to arrive at the village of Awat, in part because I recognized the name from Mannerheim's diary. The road forked here and an old Kyrgyz man with yellow teeth pointed us east into a spectacular river gorge framed by flaming red mountains. We eventually ended up at a coal mine called Pochengzi, dug into the base of the Tian Shan range. A black, soot-covered path led past open coal pits and concrete hovels for miners and then along the mountain slope to another river gorge. From Mannerheim's photographs, I immediately recognized the massive chasm that seemed to split the Tian Shan in two: we had arrived at the mouth of the Muzart River Valley.

The car rattled and skidded as Kasim navigated an abrupt gravel path cut into the cliff. It brought us to several farmhouses below. Golden wheat and barley were planted above the river. Just beyond the hamlet stood an outpost and gate. An ancient wall of clay and stone, which Mannerheim described, still runs from the outpost up the mountain slope, blocking passage to the valley. About three kilometres farther on, the road steepened and deteriorated. The Volkswagen bottomed out in a dry creek that cut across the gravel road. Kasim threw me a worried look. "We shouldn't go on."

While Kasim inspected the car's undercarriage, Jappar and I walked toward the rumbling torrent. "The river sounds strong," Jappar said. We climbed down to the boulder-strewn riverbank. Mannerheim described the Muzart as just a "mountain stream," but now, in summertime, it was swollen with silt and snowmelt. The ribbon of silver wound its way toward shrouded peaks and windswept glaciers. I stared down the long, steep valley, imagining a small horse caravan zigzagging up its dramatic slopes toward the heavens.

MANNERHEIM'S RIDE across the Tian Shan took five days. It was the most dangerous leg of his journey. Before even reaching the river valley, he got lost for several hours in a snowstorm of "unabated severity." The bad weather lifted, but he now faced gruelling geography: the trail into the mountains became "quite breakneck, winding along narrow ledges." In places, stones were piled up to form staircases on the path. "Philip, my horse, was equally fascinated by the view," he wrote, "and kept going along the extreme edge, so that I began to suspect him of contemplating suicide."

They stayed at a rundown caravanserai at the foot of a glacier. A heavy mist obscured the surrounding peaks and a cold wind blew through the open windows. "Three men with bandaged and frost-bitten faces, and a few carcases of horses reminded us of the seriousness of our undertaking," he wrote. His men woke at 5 AM and set off on a long, punishing ride to the headwaters of the Muzart River. "There was a regular gale throughout the journey," he wrote. "Whenever we rode close to a mountain wall, the horses were almost blown over." At another rundown hovel that night, Rakhimjanov complained of a headache and the bitter cold.

They got off late the next morning. Despite the extreme conditions, Mannerheim was tempted to hunt ibexes. Liu had spotted the "beautiful creatures with their bright, sabre-like horns" grazing on a slope. The Baron failed to bag any, but later shot an eagle for sport. At the foot of the glacier, they reached Muzart's infamous ice steps, cut daily by eight labourers. These men unpacked Mannerheim's horses and carried the sacks and chests up the twenty steps. The unburdened horses still slipped and fell on the treacherous staircase. At the top, two gigantic mountains pinch the glacier, whose icy expanse glinted under bright sunshine. "The weather was lovely," the Baron wrote as if he were holidaying.

Rakhimjanov, however, wasn't so chipper. He had developed a high fever and could scarcely stay in his saddle. But the Baron ordered everyone to press on through the "muddle of icy pinnacles, short ridges and open crevices." The horses couldn't find footing on the icy path. "The ascent went on incessantly," he wrote. At one point, Rakhimjanov's horse fell into a cleft, but was pulled out, luckily unhurt. "Large numbers of carcases and skeletons of horses are convincing proof of the difficulty of the road," Mannerheim wrote. "I counted 30 during the day and Philip, who had been scared by these grinning horse's skulls at first, got so accustomed to them that he no longer wasted a glance on them." With darkness approaching, he had "an unpleasant feeling of being responsible for the men who might easily freeze to death on the glacier without fuel." Their descent soon brought them into scenery that was "unusually magnificent and beautiful." The mountainsides were covered in grass and stubby fir trees. The path was stony, narrow and steep, with patches of ice. "A false step would be fatal," the Baron wrote. Off the glacier, they ploughed through deep snow until they saw "a fire twinkling at the foot of the mountain."

They found "tired wanderers" camping inside two hovels built of logs. Fierce winds had caused the cabins to "lean over more than the tower of Pisa." The cabins, warmed by open fires, were full of smoke. "The soot hung in large flakes from the roof and wall," he wrote. Rakhimjanov could "scarcely stand." While pilaf was being prepared, the Baron took a walk to keep warm. In the moonlight, he reflected on how the bitter landscape had hardened the people. In the cabin, he met an old Uyghur with frostbitten hands who had left his wife and one of his daughters, both frozen to death, atop the glacier. The Uyghurs lived such an "exceedingly hard life," Mannerheim reflected, that they were "almost justified in not being tender-hearted towards other people and animals."

His ill Cossack and exhausted horses rested the next day. Mannerheim, ever the outdoor enthusiast, did some hunting but failed to shoot any ibexes before a snowstorm set in. They then carried on down the north side of the Tian Shan range. A two-day ride brought them to grassy slopes dotted with felt yurts that belonged to Kalmyks, a tribe of Western Mongols. At the village of Shato, "a celebrated old Kalmuk hunter" named Numgan guided Mannerheim on another shooting excursion. They trudged through deep snowdrifts up a "breakneck" mountain, where Mannerheim, exhausted but exhilarated, spotted a roebuck with seven-branched antlers. "My Mauser made short work of it," he wrote with glee.

I WAS DISAPPOINTED to stray from Mannerheim's route, but Muzart Pass had long since lost its military significance. Railways, as General Tang had predicted, and airfields were now the military's preferred transportation mode. In fact, my circuitous journey to Gulja would take me along vital railway and pipeline arteries. We followed a dirt road out of the crimson-coloured gorge that descends from the Tian Shan and eventually rejoined the newly rebuilt Route 314. The Silk Road highway skirts the Taklimakan, connecting cities, power plants, coal depots and oil and gas refineries. Some 11 billion tons of oil reserves lie under the desert's sands. Beijing's primary military objective is to keep Xinjiang's rich mineral and petroleum wealth, and pipelines to Central Asia, under tight control.

Between the towns of Kucha and Korla, we stopped at a roadside stand late one morning. A young Uyghur woman was lying on a platform bed in the shade of a mulberry tree. She sold sweetened green tea, peaches and three types of melons to passersby. Kasim selected an extraordinary specimen. "I've never seen anything like this before," he said. The fruit was actually two melons fused in the middle. "I'm going to buy it for my girlfriend," Kasim smirked holding it up to his chest. But the buxom melon reminded me of a different kind of bombshell.

A few hundred kilometres from Korla, in the Taklimakan Desert, is the world's largest nuclear testing base. Here, between 1964 and 1996, the Chinese detonated forty-five nuclear bombs, both underground and atmospheric. During my stopover in London, I met a Uyghur political refugee and surgeon named Enver Tohti, a talkative, pudgy forty-three-year-old. As a doctor in Urumqi, Tohti saw a shocking number of Uyghur children born with cleft palates, under-developed brains, deformities and cancers such as leukemia and malignant lymphoma. While studying medicine in Istanbul in 1998, he met a British documentary crew from Channel 4. He travelled back to Xinjiang with the undercover journalists, who secretly visited Uyghur villages near the nuclear testing zone. The exposé, titled *Death on the Silk Road,* showed a young man with a chronic muscle-wasting disease, and a teenage girl twisted like a pretzel and in constant agony from a crippling bone disease. Outraged at the inaction of Chinese authorities, Tohti smuggled statistical reports from a hospital showing that Uyghur communities near nuclear test sites had cancer rates 30 percent higher than the national average. I now wondered whether these same nuclear tests had any effect on Kasim's mutant melon.

We continued on through inhospitable terrain. We crossed two small mountain chains to the Turpan Depression. It is the second-lowest point on Earth and felt like a boiling cauldron. I was relieved once we began climbing back out of the basin through a wide pass splitting the Tian Shan and Bogdo-uula ranges to Urumqi.

"The weather in Urumqi isn't very good," Kasim complained.

"Is it too hot?" I inquired wearily.

"No, it's dirty. The air is the second worst . . ."

"In China?" I asked.

"No, I think it's the second worst in the world."

A filthy haze did indeed hang over the dense modern city of high-rises and expressways. We rested the night, leaving early the next morning. We were now on the northern flank of the Tian Shans. A busy highway swung northwest through Sanji, an industrial town of petrochemical plants and oil refineries. From here, a highway, railway and oil pipeline run along the foot of the Zunghar Basin, an arid steppe bounded by mountains to the south and the borders of Kazakhstan, Russia and Mongolia to the north. This strategic corridor is China's main artery to the oil and gas reserves of Central Asia. After six hundred kilometres, we reached Sayram Lake. The briny lake is brilliant turquoise. It looks like a gemstone set more than two thousand metres high in a knot of mountains. Pastures slope to its shores and are dotted with yurts and grazing animals. From the lake, a steep pass snakes through evergreen forests to the Ili Valley. For miles along the side of the road into Gulja, the valley's bustling centre, golden sunflower seeds and corn had been laid to dry. We continued to a Uyghur farmstead about fifteen kilometres from the city.

We stayed in a typical Uyghur abode with clay and brick walls and a flat roof. A veranda connected individual rooms piled with silk cushions and plush carpets. The house belonged to friends of Jappar, who seemed overjoyed to be back in his home village. The wife and grandmother served us a dinner of bread, dumplings, watermelon, sunflower seeds, tea and chocolate. Jappar then took me to a nearby hamlet. It had one paved street and a new police station with gleaming white tiles and blue trim. Overnight visits by foreigners must be registered with authorities. Kasim stayed in the car. "I don't like police," he said.

The Ili Valley has always been a trouble spot for the Chinese. North of Urumqi, Mannerheim came across a caravan of five hundred camels heading to Gulja with rifles and ammunition. A few months later, thousands of Uyghurs threatened to sack the Chinese garrison and administrative *yamen* there.[10] In the 1940s, the Ili Valley also faced a Muslim rebellion. Uyghurs founded a short-lived breakaway republic. The last major upheaval in Gulja was in 1997: thousands of Uyghur youths protested for better jobs and the release of jailed religious leaders. Police and soldiers arrested thousands and executed nine ringleaders. (This incident has since been overshadowed by a violent clash in Urumqi in 2009: Uyghur rioters killed almost two hundred people—most of them ethnic Han Chinese, according to officials—and injured about eleven hundred others.[11]) On the way to Gulja, we passed thirty army transport trucks and buses full of troops. They were part of a massive anti-terrorism exercise in the Ili Valley. Seven hundred policemen and soldiers had been dispatched to fight mock battles against the "three evil forces" of terrorism, religious extremism and Uyghur separatism.[12]

Inside the police station, two Uyghur policemen perfunctorily questioned and fingerprinted me. A plainclothes Chinese officer, probably a Public Security Bureau agent, took Jappar into another room. He came back and held up his fingers, smudged with ink. "They got me too," he said.

THE NEXT DAY, I caught up with Mannerheim at the Mongolküre lamasery, the spiritual heart of a lost Mongol tribe. The steppe and valleys north of the Tian Shan range had once been ruled by the Oirats, a Western Mongol tribe. In 1640, they allied with Tibetan Buddhist clerics in a loose confederacy. The so-called Zunghar Empire fought off Russian advances, plundered fellow Mongol tribes in the east and threatened the Chinese Empire, which launched several failed military expeditions to suppress the wily Mongols. After a century of rule, the Zunghar state, divided by squabbling princes, fell into disarray. In the 1750s, Emperor Qianlong ordered the massacre of the Oirats. A million Mongols were slaughtered, died of smallpox or fled to territories controlled by Russia. The Qing conquerors set about colonizing the verdant valleys north of the Tian Shan with Uyghur farmers, Chinese Muslims, loyal Mongols, Han Chinese and even a regiment of Manchu-speaking Xibo warriors. In 1771, about 70,000 exiled Mongols returned to their homeland, which was now firmly under Chinese rule. Nowadays, the surviving Oirats are called Kalmyks and those who remained in Russia live in the Republic of Kalmykia.

In Xinjiang, the Kalmyks' main settlement of Mongolküre (Zhaosu in Chinese) lies in the Tekes Valley. We drove 120 kilometres over a mountain pass into the neighbouring valley, whose rolling hills were blanketed in an autumn harvest. Tractors hauled huge bushels on trailers as poplars showered golden leaves over the road. A sign outside Mongolküre welcomed us to "the hometown of heavenly steeds." We found the lamasery on the edge of town.

It was small and lifeless. The temple buildings are hidden behind high walls. I peeked through a wooden door. Although Kalmyks are Tibetan Buddhists, the temple's architecture looked Chinese. "All the buildings have the Chinese tiled roofs with their gracefully curved corners and richly decorated roof-timber," Mannerheim wrote. Obscured by large trees, the main temple—faded and caked in soot and dust—looked ghostly.

Jappar went inside. He came out saying a Kalmyk caretaker had waved him away. Kasim also came back disappointed. "The lamasery is closed and under repair," the caretaker had told him. "No visitors." But then the caretaker himself came out: a short Kalmyk with a round dark face and grey felt cap. I showed him Mannerheim's photographs of the lamasery's interior festooned in Buddhist images, banners and *thangka* artwork. He snatched the book from my hands, flipping curiously through its pages. I asked to see the senior lama. With the caretaker, we drove to a nearby walled complex of modern buildings. He led me into a small courtyard compound with several residences where, instead of meeting the lama, I was introduced to a teacher and local historian.

Baying Kixik was in his fifties with thinning hair. His jacket, slacks and shirt were various shades of grey. We sat on a platform bed in a small room with a TV. I pulled out Mannerheim's journal.

"I know all about this man," began Kixik, speaking a mix of Kazak and Uyghur dialects that Kasim struggled to translate. "He came here in 1907. He stayed for two days and then went to Gulja. He returned after ten days and then went hunting in the mountains for billy goats." The "man"—Kixik didn't know his name—later became the President of Finland, he explained. "He gave the senior lama a clock and a telescope as a gift, and the senior lama gave him a Buddha charm."

Kixik's account was astonishingly accurate with one small exception: the telescope was in fact a magnifying glass.

"Where did you hear all this?" I asked.

"My wife's brother told me the story," Kixik said.

Kixik brought out a book, which he had authored, about Kalmy-kian history. The current monastery, he explained, is the thirteenth and largest ever built here. Construction started in 1886, after Russians destroyed the previous one. It was last renovated in 1927. Five hundred lamas had lived and worked at Mongolküre, but in 1947 an epidemic swept the lamasery and the town, killing eight out of ten residents. Luckily, 317 monks survived. Mao's Cultural Revolution whittled that number down to thirty. Now, only eight were left.

"The name of the last great lama, a living Buddha, was Dandar Butrun," Kixik said. "He died in 1985. Last year, the other senior lama died and now there's a twenty-seven-year-old lama who runs the lamasery. His name is Amur."

"Can I meet Amur?"

"I saw him this morning, but he left town," he said.

Kixik also knew about Mannerheim's hunting expeditions with Numgan. The baron made a short visit to Gulja, where he reorganized his expedition, firing Liu, "whose caprices were beginning to disturb me," and hiring a sixteen-year-old Chinese boy named Zhao as translator. A Cossack named Lukanin also replaced Rakh-imjanov, who almost died on the Muzart Pass.[13] When he returned to the Tekes Valley, he reunited with the old hunter. Together, they trekked for a month and a half along the grassy slopes and high alpine valleys of the Tian Shan. Mannerheim gauged the loyalty of Kyrgyz, Kazakh and Kalmyk tribes, conducted anthropological research, surveyed mountain passes and hunted. A country boy at heart, Mannerheim watched escaping gazelles and ibexes with delight. "The graceful animals were a lovely sight," he wrote, "as they leapt from spur to spur in short bounds." They ended their shooting expedition at Bayanbulak in the Yulduz Valley, an alpine pass that leads down into the Tarim Basin. It had been a successful hunt: four ibexes, one wild sheep, one gazelle and one deer. Numgan carted the heads back to Gulja, where they were shipped back to Helsinki. These hunting trophies and a faded prayer rug still reside in Mannerheim's Helsinki home.

As we drove by the lamasery on our way back, the Kalmyk care-taker waved us over. Two new silver Mitsubishi suvs sat out front. Communist Party officials were inspecting the renovations. The stocky Kalmyk grabbed Mannerheim's journal and showed it to a hefty Chinese official.

"Ma Dahan," the official said.

"Yes, yes, Ma Dahan," I said, repeating Mannerheim's Chinese name with excitement.

"I've read the Chinese translation of Ma Dahan's diary," the official said.

"Do you think I could look inside the temple?" I asked, hoping that 2,300 kilometres and six days on the road would not be in vain.

"Sorry," he said. "It's closed for renovations."

I WOKE EARLY the next morning. My body felt terribly stiff and sore from days of driving. My shoulders and neck were knotted. Fatigue and my disappointing attempt to visit the lamasery put me in a gloomy mood. Kasim, Jappar and I ate breakfast with the house's grandfather. We sat on carpets and cushions around a low-slung table. The grandmother served us tea, rock-hard bread and pilaf. A huge plate of pilaf topped by a bony chunk of lamb was set before me. I dug a hole into the rice and a pool of grease quickly filled it.

The grandfather wore a wispy white beard that trimmed his jaw and chin. He had rosy cheeks, oversized ears and a generous smile. In a warm, caramel voice, he recited a poem to me that he had once heard about honeybees. Gulja is renowned for its honey, he explained. On the mountain pass into the Ili Valley, I saw dozens of honey stands lining the road. The golden jars glinted in the sunshine. They were hard not to miss.

The grandfather wrote the poem in a beautiful Uyghur script, which looks like decorative curlicues, strokes and dots. I asked Kasim to translate the verse. "It's impossible to translate," Kasim said. I was growing tired of his aloof behaviour and insisted that he translate each line word for word:

In a tiny hive, many busy honeybees live
There is no goodness in humans as in the honeybees
The honeybees have stingers, but do not fight each other
Humans live together, but constantly fight.

The grandfather, a septuagenarian, had lived through Xinjiang's bloody history: the breakaway Islamic republics, warlords,
civil war, revolution, repression and unrest. Upon my departure, he
clasped my hands in his own. They were surprisingly soft for a man
who'd spent a lifetime tilling fields. "You and I are the same," he
said to me. "We cannot let nationality divide us."

Nationality never did divide the Uyghurs, who historically
had no understanding of this concept. Mannerheim spent fourteen
months in Xinjiang, but only once used the word "Uyghur" in reference to an ancient coin that he dug up at an excavation site eighteen kilometres northeast of Gulja. According to a 1907 British
intelligence report on Kashgaria, the local Muslim population had
"no knowledge of national unity, but regard themselves as members of various tribes which correspond with the oases inhabited
by them, e.g., Kashgaris, Yarkandis, Khotanis, etc."[14] The term
"Uyghur" did not reappear until 1921, when Soviet advisers in
Tashkent proposed that the term be used to describe oasis dwellers
in Chinese Turkestan. In 1934, the Xinjiang provincial government
adopted the term, which was later taken up by the central government in Beijing.[15]

Ironically, it was Beijing's minority nationalities policies and
colonization of Muslim borderlands that both awoke and inflamed
the Uyghur nationalism that authorities are now ruthlessly trying
to suppress.

MOST UYGHURS WILLINGLY complained to me about the Chinese,
but not Kasim. Including my trip to Khotan, I had spent, in total,
nearly two weeks with Kasim, but barely got to know him. He was

so reserved that he even slept in his clothes—and socks!—when we bunked in the same room. "I don't like questions," he kept replying to my queries. He was reticent, suspiciously so. He was, by far, the most pious Muslim I met in Central Asia. Our road trip was punctuated by roadside prayers several times a day.

Kasim had gained a level of freedom that few Uyghurs enjoy. He spoke a bit of English, which allowed him to communicate with the outside world via tourists and the Internet. He worked for a private company, and thus wasn't restricted in his religious practices as state employees are. He also had access to a vehicle, giving him remarkable mobility. He told me that he now hoped to earn enough money to purchase his own car and become his own boss. He thus kept to himself lest a careless remark—that the Chinese would surely see as seditious—jeopardize these meagre freedoms. This restraint made for a long, unusually quiet journey.

Our return trip to Urumqi took two days. At the Chinese town of Jing, on the fringe of the Zunghar Basin, we stopped to rest. The next morning, we found a Uyghur café and ate *laghman*. The burly, mustachioed owner was from Kashgar. He sat with a group of Uyghur men. Surprised to see a foreigner, he asked where I was from and my name. "His name's Iraq," joked Kasim, mispronouncing my first name. The men chuckled.

"You should have a Uyghur name that sounds like your English name," one of the men suggested. "We'll call you Ärkin."

The men burst out laughing again. They shook their heads as though something mischievously funny had been uttered.

"What does it mean?" I asked.

"It means freedom," Kasim smirked.

NINE

URUMQI

The Banquet

The Province's traditions of hospitality
are all its own, and the death-rate at banquets is appalling.
—PETER FLEMING, *News from Tartary*[1]

"ARE YOU CANADIAN? I heard through the Foreign Ministry in Beijing that a Canadian was coming from Kyrgyzstan retracing Mannerheim's route."

I was startled by this comment from Wang Jiaji, the former Chinese ambassador to Finland. I bumped into the wily diplomat as we left a banquet in an Urumqi hotel. The feast ended the first day of the International Symposium for the Study of Mannerheim's Journey to Xinjiang. Waiters stacked plates upon plates of pickled radishes, barbecue pork, spicy sausage, lamb soup, chicken with bean jam, Peking duck, steamed broccoli and more on our table. I had stuffed myself, thinking a lull in service marked the end of the banquet. Then, unexpectedly, a second and third sortie of servers descended on our table, dropping more succulent dishes. Our Chinese hosts made a half-dozen toasts with *baijiu,* the 120-proof liqueur made of grain alcohol. I stumbled from the banquet feeling bloated and drowsy—and now paranoid.

How did Wang know that I was a Canadian? I had, in fact, crossed the border using my Estonian passport. Did authorities know I was travelling with two passports? How exactly did Wang find out? I was afraid to ask.

I'd had doubts about even attending the symposium, knowing that it would put me in contact with Chinese officialdom. Wang had written a biography of Mannerheim in Chinese and translated his Asian journal. He now worked for the Research Centre for China's Borderland History and Geography in Beijing, a co-host of the symposium. I had been warned about both Wang and this research centre.

"Always try to avoid embassies, diplomats, politicians, because you can never count on them," Harry Halén cautioned me during my stopover in Helsinki. Halén had just retired after more than thirty years as the secretary of the Asian and African Studies Department at Helsinki University. A wiry, intense man with a dry wit, Halén is a philologist and the foremost expert on Mannerheim's journey to Asia. He has written numerous articles, prepared an "analytical index" of place names and foreign words in Mannerheim's journal (an invaluable resource in trying to determine where Mannerheim actually travelled) and edited a third edition of *Across Asia*, published in 2008.

Halén is deeply wary of Chinese officialdom. In 2001, a group of Chinese scholars visited Finland to research Mannerheim's Asia collection. The Finnish Ministry of Defence called Halén to lend the Chinese delegation a hand. "Of course, that's something that I would never do," he told me. It was only a matter of time, he reasoned, until this rising global power would start to throw its weight around, demanding the repatriation of Chinese artefacts from foreign archives. Halén was also highly critical of Beijing's policies toward ethnic minorities. "In China, they are 'modernizing' areas against the will of local populations," Halén said. "Look at what they've done to Lhasa. It is an ordinary Chinese town with some tourist spots—the Potala Palace. The Tibetans want to preserve their own culture and identity, not become Chinese."

Halén wanted nothing to do with the Borderland Research Centre, which is part of the Chinese Academy of Social Sciences. It is, he said, "a kind of intelligence service." Gardner Bovingdon, another academic who specializes in Uyghur studies at Indiana University, also told me the research centre was subject to "thorough politicization" and that its "work did not deserve the name of scholarship." Halén recalled one research paper, written by the Research Centre's hawkish former director Ma Dazheng, that describes how the task of Chinese scholars is "to expose and criticize" those explorers whose objectives had "Imperialistic ends concerning the invasion of China." The paper, he added, accused Mannerheim and other Europeans "of obscure things which are history."

MANNERHEIM ARRIVED in Urumqi from the south on a broad avenue flanked by garrisons and European-style buildings. The regional capital is wedged in a valley between the Bogdo-uula and Tian Shan ranges, a strategic corridor connecting the Tarim and Zunghar basins. Snow-capped peaks and hills surround the town. The Russian consulate with its spacious courtyards, gardens and beautiful Orthodox church stood in the southern district. The Baron stayed in its chancellery. After the trying six-month ride crisscrossing the Tian Shans, he "revelled in the possession of a bed with sheets."

I stayed in the same district. Today, the southern area of Urumqi is still the Uyghur quarter. But little Russian architecture remains. The former Russian consulate is now a complex of decaying buildings and overgrown grounds. Still, many billboards are written in Cyrillic, targeting businessmen from Kazakhstan and Russia. Trade with these neighbouring countries has exploded in the past few years. During my visit, the regional capital was especially abuzz because of the annual foreign trade fair. The northern part of Urumqi, where the Manchu fortress once protected Xinjiang's administrative centre and army garrison, is home to the Chinese and an evident prosperity: glitzy shopping centres, condo towers, high-rise offices and posh hotels that were far too pricey for my slim budget. Hiring Kasim and his Volkswagen for eleven days had drained me financially. Urumqi's poorer ethnic 'hood fit my budget.

Mannerheim too had arrived in Urumqi almost flat broke. After hunting in the Tian Shans, his caravan was in a wretched state. "My poor skeletons of horses wandered about like shadows," he wrote, "unable to find a blade of grass to appease their hunger." After one arduous day, one of his horses "collapsed at the gate [of an inn], and had almost to be carried into a stall." Fodder was exceedingly expensive. And so he had to leave his Cossack and nine horses in Turpan while he continued on to Urumqi. "It was rather comical to be so hard up in China as to have to leave my horses in pawn for the fodder they consumed," he wrote. By the time he reached Urumqi, he had only half a *liang* (one ounce of silver) in his pocket and joked that he "might have been forced to pawn myself." He immediately wrote his brother Carl asking him to advance "a couple thousand marks." The Baron would pay him back the following summer with dividends from his Nokia shares. (Nokia, the largest mobile phone company in the world, began in 1865 as a pulp mill along the Tammerkoski River in Finland.)

Mannerheim would have recognized the cheap hotel where I stayed in the Uyghur quarter. The Yihe Hotel was a modern-day caravanserai with eighteen-wheelers replacing camels and pot-bellied Pakistanis who wore pajama-like trousers, baggy tunics and thick black beards taking the role of nomadic traders. Rooms doubled as trading offices and the Pakistanis prayed on small mats at the end of hallways. A young man in a sparsely furnished office told me they mostly ship textiles, clothing and shoes to Pakistan over the Karakoram Highway and bring fruit back to China. By noon each day, the courtyard was a flurry of activity, labourers loading and unloading large bundles and boxes.

I timed my visit to Urumqi to coincide with the Mannerheim symposium, which was held at the Shihezi Mansion, a three-star hotel in a well-to-do Chinese district in the northwest. For two days, some eight Finnish and fifty Chinese researchers crowded into a small conference room on the hotel's ground floor. "Mannerheim is a household name in Finland," Li Sheng, the new director of the Borderland Research Centre said in his introductory remarks, "but is getting better known by Chinese scholars, and the public in Xinjiang." In 2000, he explained, the research centre launched an intensive study of Mannerheim. Chinese scholars translated and published his memoirs, Asia journal, two photographic books, a biography and more than a dozen research papers. "Mannerheim's research is full of prospect," he said.

Three Finnish scholars delivered the symposium's first papers that morning, focusing on his horse trek from Osh, a visit to a Tibetan lamasery and Mannerheim's "many hats" as secret agent, amateur archaeologist, anthropologist, horseman, hunter and cartographer. After a steaming Chinese buffet in the hotel's restaurant, we boarded a bus for the Xinjiang Regional Museum. It is located in a new building just up the street, a postmodern pastiche worthy of Las Vegas: mirrored glass, Ottoman arches and an emerald dome. The museum's former director, besides committing various architectural crimes, was recently sentenced to ten years of penal servitude for corruption.[2]

The museum's exhibits were even more outlandish than its architecture. An introductory sign unabashedly tells visitors that the museum is "for safeguarding the reunification of the motherland" and for mass education "in patriotism." Exhibits on each dynasty leave the impression that Xinjiang has always been "an inalienable part of the territory of China." What's missing is Xinjiang's long history of bloodletting, ethnic slaughter, Mongol rule and Yakub Beg, the independent ruler of Kashgaria. Chinese propaganda infects almost every exhibit in a bald-faced attempt to rewrite the past that is worthy of Orwell: "Who controls the past controls the future: who controls the present controls the past." A Han Dynasty exhibit, for example, showcases an official seal (dated 220 BC to AD 24), a chop, various coins and Chinese scrolls. These artefacts are evidence that Xinjiang "became an inalienable component of the great motherland" long ago. In reality, the Chinese empire had only marginal control over their western borderlands until the Qing conquest in the eighteenth century. Even then, breakaway Islamic republics, however short lived, beset the region. "Current Chinese claims that Xinjiang has been part of China 'for 5,000 years' have only rhetoric on their side," write two American scholars.[3]

Back on the bus, we headed to a cultural hall and theatre run by the People's Liberation Army. A large red banner hung outside: "Finnish Scholar Mannerheim: Hundredth Anniversary of His China Journey." Inside the hall's atrium, some sixty black-and-white photographs adorned the walls. I'd seen most of them in one of two publications: Mannerheim's published journal, and a book by Peter Sandberg, a Finnish photographer who happened to be at this conference. Mannerheim took more than thirteen hundred photographs, one of the richest collections for the time.

I introduced myself to Sandberg, who wore glasses, a blond goatee and black attire head to foot. Sandberg explained to me that photography was in vogue among St. Petersburg's high society at the turn of the century. Mannerheim's Ernemann Klapp was a German-made, state-of-the-art camera. It was collapsible, with a wooden, self-casing enclosure. Its glass-plate film was so insensitive, Sandberg said, that in the smoky, dim interior of the lamasery at Mongolküre, Mannerheim counted to sixty while the monks held steady, pretending to beat drums and blow on their copper trumpets.[4]

"As a photographer," Sandberg told the symposium the next day, "Mannerheim is at his best in his portraits. These pictures still exude a refreshing spontaneity, the persons seem so alive and the situation so vivid every time you look at the photos. The portraits also bear witness to his skilful direction: the sessions appear to have been quite relaxed in spite of the fact that many of his subjects certainly had never seen a camera before, and perhaps not even a Westerner."

MANNERHEIM STOOD HOLDING his camera in the courtyard of a modest house inside Urumqi's fortress. At the other end, double doors swung open to reveal Duke Lan, a cousin of the Emperor. The Manchu nobleman was balding and wore a long, thin moustache. Mannerheim was not the first Westerner the Duke had seen—in fact, during the anti-foreign uprising in 1900 known as the Boxer Rebellion, the Duke had ordered the mass slaughter of Westerners. The Baron fumbled with his camera, whose shutter jammed. Lan smiled pleasantly about forty paces away. Mannerheim continued to struggle, but the device "seemed bewitched and would not budge." A few servants hurried toward the Baron, whispering "*Qing* [please], the Duke is waiting."

Mannerheim explained his predicament to Duke Lan, who "laughed and said that he, too, was an amateur photographer and quite understood my difficulty." Food and refreshments—"rather more sumptuous and European than usual"—were set on a round table in a room hung with traditional Chinese paintings. A dozen breach-loading rifles fixed with bayonets were also mounted on a wall. Lan had been the deputy chief of the Peking gendarmerie. With his even more notorious brother Prince Tuan (whose son was heir to the throne), Lan had been sent into exile for inciting the Boxer movement. This obscure, ill-organized sect of dispossessed and disgruntled peasants lashed out at Westerners in a terrifying wave of nationalistic violence. The Boxers—who got their name from the martial arts and calisthenics they practised—massacred Christian converts, beheaded foreign missionaries—as we'll later see—and besieged the Peking legations, which were eventually rescued by an Allied expeditionary force. The Western powers called for Lan's execution, but Empress Dowager Cixi exiled him to Xinjiang instead.

"Sitting at table with him," the Baron wrote, "you would scarcely believe that this modest and outwardly very charming man of fifty was one of the leaders of the Boxer rising, the object of which was nothing less than the massacre of all Europeans residing in China. He has easy and elegant manners and much natural dignity."

Mannerheim was surprised that the Duke "spoke with less restraint than is usual in China." It also appeared that Lan's once rabid xenophobia had turned to admiration for foreign ways. "The Japanese were a wise and bold nation," he told Mannerheim. "They fought [in Manchuria] from conviction and were united as one man, whereas the Russians suffered from internal dissension and insufficient conviction." He also admired the Germans who were "well armed and possessed excellent organization."

Duke Lan was smitten enough with Mannerheim that a week later he invited him to his country residence. Five kilometres northeast of the fortress, the villa was, Mannerheim wrote, "delightful, with a rapid little river flowing between the shady trees and bushes that climb the slopes." The Duke's residence was a cool respite from the summer heat. A modest temple stood a dozen paces up the slope and a graceful pavilion sat at a bend in the river. Together, they walked along the river taking photographs and visited a nearby mint and cartridge factory run by an Austrian army officer named Bauer.

Dinner was served on the veranda of the Duke's villa. It was a typical banquet, according to Mannerheim, "exactly the same as in the houses of the mandarins." Duke Lan invited his neighbour, a miller, to join them. Together they drank "a great many glasses of very strong Chinese brandy of a poisonous green colour." During dinner, the children and wives of local mandarins arrived to spend the boiling afternoon in the Duke's shady garden. Mannerheim wanted to photograph "this group of gaily coloured and mincing little women," but the towering Finn restrained himself. "The sight of me almost scared them away."

IN TRUTH, THE Finns ignore, or at least underplay, an uncomfortable historical truth of their own. Most Finnish scholarship on Mannerheim's trek across Asia is either ethnographic or biographical, putting the journey in the context of his life. There has been relatively little Finnish scholarship on the military and geopolitical significance of Mannerheim's journey. "This Finnish attitude," said Alpo Juntunen, a senior researcher for the Finnish National Defence College, on the symposium's second day, "is largely because of a reluctance to admit that their national hero worked for Russian Imperialism."

Which, in fact, is exactly why the Chinese are so fascinated by Mannerheim. His intelligence-gathering offers a rare glimpse into detailed foreign plans for invasion and attempts to conspire with minority nationalities to "split" China. Mannerheim saw Xinjiang, with its scarce population and non-existent industry, as a geopolitical bargaining chip. In his report to the General Staff, he argued that it would be Russia's "great blunder" not to invade Xinjiang.[5] The region was China's vulnerable underbelly, with lame military capabilities, poor communications, no railway links and restless ethnic populations. "The picture which I saw during my travels round Chinese Turkestan was, for a soldier, an extremely sad one," Mannerheim wrote in his diary. He figured local Muslims and Mongols may even turn against their Chinese rulers and support Russian conquest.[6] The Baron sketched a plan for Russian Cossacks to easily conquer Urumqi and then ride as far east as Lanzhou, sacking the capital of Gansu province. During peace negotiations, Russia would then trade off these vast western wastelands for more valuable concessions in Manchuria.

The scholar who launched China's intensive research on Mannerheim—and set its tone—is Ma Dazheng. The former director of the Borderland Research Centre travels the country advising military and civilian officials on threats to China's borders. Ma had published an influential book, *The Interest of the State Is Greater Than*

Anything, justifying the suppression of Uyghurs as part of China's "war on terror."[7] In a 2003 internal report intended for government leaders, Ma called for the expansion of the Xinjiang Production and Construction Corps. More paramilitary settlements, he argued, would "prove an excellent conduit for changing the *minzu* [minority] population ratio in [Khotan], which has gotten out of balance."[8] He opposed true autonomy for Uyghurs, advising that the party's cadres should be filled with ethnic Chinese. "Hans are the most reliable force for stability in Xinjiang," he wrote.[9]

Ma chaired the second day of the symposium. He gave a fascinating talk on Tsutomu Hino, a Japanese army officer and spy. Hino, only a year younger than Mannerheim, fought in the Russo-Japanese war and was awarded a merit of honour. That wasn't the only uncanny parallel in their lives. "There was a dramatic coincidence: Hino stepped into Xinjiang at almost the same time as Mannerheim," Ma said. "One moved westward; the other moved eastward." And both, Ma pointed out, were serving foreign Imperialism. "Hino's inspections were precise," Ma said. "He left no stone unturned."

Hino is not mentioned in Mannerheim's published journal and the two spies never did meet, but the "hostile Japanese major" does show up in other notebooks and in his intelligence report. While crossing the Tian Shan at Bayanbulak, in fact, Mannerheim discovered that Hino had passed through only twelve days earlier.[10]

Ma ended his presentation by talking about future research. The Borderland Research Centre, he said, was planning to publish three or four more books on Mannerheim and, perhaps, conduct a modern investigation of Xinjiang just as Mannerheim did. "I think if Mannerheim were alive today," Ma said, "he would beam with a smile."

IT IS DIFFICULT to overstate Mannerheim's hatred of Communism, the "cruellest despotism the world has ever known." The Baron was the only White general to successfully defeat the Bolsheviks, liberating Finland from their terrifying grip. In 1919, Winston

Churchill, then Secretary of State for War, hatched a plan with Mannerheim to invade St. Petersburg. The objective was to smash the heart of Bolshevism. Mannerheim was Commander-in-Chief of Finnish forces at the time and, according to Churchill, was "a real *man*, strong like a rock."[11] And with that "rock," Churchill planned to crush Communism for good. Mannerheim drafted up detailed plans and undertook secret negotiations with Russia's counter-revolutionaries. In London, the Finnish General met Churchill who agreed that "a lasting Bolshevik regime—assuming it were not stamped out now—would constitute a danger for practically the whole of the world."[12] Alas, Mannerheim and Churchill were unable to convince their compatriots of their audacious plan. "Europe and the whole world have had to pay a heavy price for allowing Bolshevism free play in 1919," Mannerheim wrote in his memoirs.[13]

Even in his retirement in Switzerland after the Second World War, the Baron clipped stories from Geneva newspapers about Mao Zedong and Soviet scheming in Xinjiang. In the Finnish National Archives in Helsinki, I found one undated article, circa 1949, among the Baron's personal letters, notes and clippings. He had underlined in red pencil the headline, "Soviet Advance in the Far East," and a sentence, "Xinjiang is bigger than France, Spain, Germany and Italy combined." He seemed to be underscoring just how much this "world menace" had spread in his lifetime.

A half-century later, Chinese Communist Party members were celebrating a man who spent his entire life trying to expunge their creed from this earth. In my six-month journey through China, nothing—not even the KFC, McDonald's, Pizza Hut and Starbucks outlets—heralded the death of Communism more than this symposium and banquet honouring Baron Gustaf Mannerheim—aristocrat, Imperialist spy and the twentieth century's most sabre-rattling crusader against Communism.

Other paradoxes marked this symposium and centennial celebration. In 1809, Finland became an autonomous Grand Duchy of the

Russian Empire. The country had its own army, parliament, administrative branches, national language and so on. By 1899, however, Tsar Nicholas II began rescinding Finland's autonomous status and "russifying" the country. The repressive policies led to acts of Finnish terrorism and open rebellion. Two decades later, Mannerheim led Finland's "War of Liberation" and fought to keep his countrymen free from Russians, an "alien race . . . with a life philosophy and moral values different from ours."[14] For Uyghurs, who supposedly live in one of China's "autonomous regions," there is much to be admired—and perhaps even emulated—in Finland's bloody struggle for independence against a repressive neighbouring empire.

An even more glaring paradox of this centennial celebration, which included two sumptuous banquets, was that Mannerheim actually disliked Chinese food. Not that he was a gastrophobe. Mannerheim was a well-known gourmet. He had an eclectic palate and was immensely knowledgeable about international cuisine. He developed his culinary interests at a young age thanks to his bon vivant father, who enjoyed fine French food. His knowledge was enriched during his years among St. Petersburg's aristocracy. He collected restaurant menus as mementoes and even created menus and seating plans for his own lavish dinners in his Helsinki residence. "Nobody ever forgets a Mannerheim dinner party," his daughter Anastasie remembered. "His guests used to be Royalty from neighbouring states, great men of science, medicine, literature and art from all over the world."[15]

Mannerheim's visits to Helsinki restaurants became legendary. He was rumoured to be a demanding customer: butter had to be served hard in a ceramic dish, and he frowned upon waiters' suggestions. To this day, Helsinki hotels still serve dishes inspired by Mannerheim. A recent cookbook, *Dining with Marshal Mannerheim*, also contains dozens of recipes and a full culinary history of his life from his childhood to his final days at the Valmont Clinic on Lake Geneva—where, in a fitting twist of fate, he died from an intestinal ailment. Recipes cover a variety of national cuisines: Finnish, Swedish, Russian, French, English, German, Polish, Ukrainian, even Nepalese. Noteworthy is the absence of any Chinese recipes.

Whenever Mannerheim visited a mandarin, a banquet was usually held in his honour. (This tradition is still upheld in China today for visiting scholars, businessmen and foreign officials.) Yet Mannerheim disliked the long, tiring dinners. In Yarkand, he and Gustaf Raquette, the Swedish missionary, attended an extravagant feast hosted by the local governor. They sat at a large, round table laid with a white cloth, ornamental tin plates, miniature china bowls and ivory chopsticks. The latter he found difficult to use, "seeing that most of the dishes are very flabby." "The dishes succeed each other in surprising numbers," he wrote. He counted twenty-four unique dishes all "floating in gravy" or "roasted in dripping." At first, he went on, "many of the dishes seem repulsive. The sameness in the taste, in particular, is wearisome. Everything has the same flavour of steam and fat."

The Baron was also put off by Chinese etiquette—"energetic slobbering," as he described it—and entertainment that usually consisted of "a noisy play" or "whining music." The banquets often lasted for hours. After a six-hour banquet in Aksu, he complained of being "more exhausted than if I had spent 12 hours in the saddle."

The day after arriving in Urumqi, the Baron called on a man who would become one of the most notorious banquet hosts in modern Chinese history. Yang Zengxin was Urumqi's mayor and Xinjiang's supreme judge. He was a "tall, exceedingly thin figure, with an emaciated face and clever eyes, and thin moustaches hanging from the corners of his mouth."

Mannerheim quickly discovered "dissension and intrigues" among Urumqi's mandarins as they backstabbed each other, jockeyed for promotion and wrestled over the pace of reform. "Blackmailers and informers seem to flourish among the mandarins more than anywhere else," the Baron wrote. "Everything is done in an exquisite way, under a shower of smiles, gifts and compliments." At the time, rumours were swirling about who would be Xinjiang's next governor-general. A knife-wielding assassin had recently attacked the region's highest official in his *yamen*. Within a few years, as reform gave way to revolution, Yang would ultimately win Urumqi's power struggles. But he would come to rule Xinjiang not with "smiles, gifts and compliments," but with the sword.

When Mao said, "Revolution is not a dinner party," he obviously was not well acquainted with Yang Zengxin. In 1912, Yang, a cunning and ruthless tactician, seized control of Xinjiang as the Qing Dynasty collapsed. The new governor stacked government positions with loyalists and executed opponents.[16] In February 1916, Yang caught wind of a coup. He invited the plotters to a Chinese New Year banquet. After the first toast, Yang left the banquet hall and returned with a soldier brandishing a sword, who beheaded two unsuspecting rivals. Yang called for more wine, coolly explained his actions and then dug into a bowl of rice.[17]

In 1928, Sven Hedin, who had a soft spot for ruthless despots, dined with Yang at several sumptuous banquets overflowing with champagne. "With an iron hand," Hedin wrote, Yang "has for 17 years suppressed all attempts to rebel against his power."[18] But a few months later, the strongman would be served his just deserts. An ambitious, Japanese-educated modernizer named Fan Yaonan crafted a bloody showdown, according to one historian, "like the plot of grand opera, with tragic symmetry."[19] Governor Yang was, fittingly, invited to a banquet. His bodyguards were seated in a separate room and quietly disarmed. Yang, in high spirits, was preoccupied entertaining those seated next to him. Fan made a toast. As they drank, seven gunshots rang out. "Who dares do this?" a defiant, wounded Yang screamed. Revolver in hand, Fan stood over the dying Governor and fired two more shots, completing the crime.[20]

A proverb soon arose in Urumqi about Yang's death: "He who slays at a feast shall at a feast be slain."[21]

THE CENTENNIAL BANQUET celebrating Mannerheim's ride through Xinjiang began at 7 PM. It was held at the Yindu Hotel, a luxurious facility whose huge marble atrium has a gurgling fountain stocked with colourful koi. The banquet hall was hung with red banners and glittering chandeliers. A massive round table, with a huge glass turntable, could seat all nineteen guests. I sat by Teemu Naarajärvi, an up-and-coming young scholar from the Finnish Institute of International Affairs.

Cold dishes were already on the table: figs, a spicy cabbage salad, sliced barbecue beef, fresh vegetables. We sat down and Wu Fuhuan, Director of the Xinjiang Academy of Social Sciences, made a quick opening toast. A petite waitress came around and filled small shooter glasses with fiery *baijiu*. I gulped it quickly, but the alcohol's noxious fumes burned my nostrils. The waitress hovered behind us immediately replenishing the glasses from a tin kettle with a fish head for a spout.

"You had better bottoms-up like Mannerheim did," Wu laughed, as everyone sucked back a second glass.

"According to Chinese tradition, I must make three toasts to show my respect," he said. Naarajärvi turned to me. "If this is how it is going to start," he said, "then I think we're in for a night of heavy drinking."

A course of hot dishes soon arrived: a warm flatbread, spicy lamb with hot red chili, and diced horsemeat. (The latter dish wasn't exactly what Mannerheim meant by having a "love of horse-flesh.") The banquet was a seemingly endless series of dishes and toasts, dishes and toasts. At one point, an exotic fish platter was set on the table. Roars of laughter came from the Chinese. The fish's head was pointing at Kauko Laitinen, director of the Confucius Institute at Helsinki University, which apparently meant that he had to drink a glass of *baijiu*. The tall, calm Finn gulped a shooter and then rose to toast the strengthening of ties and friendship between Finland and China.

A cup of pilaf was then set down in front of everyone. This spicy rice dish was Mannerheim's favourite. He called his Uyghur cook Ismail "a master of his art" and his *polo* "indispensable." He and Ismail parted ways in Urumqi, but after two days with a Chinese cook who proved "quite incapable" Mannerheim sent for Ismail again.

Dr. Alpo Juntunen, the military historian, then got up to make a toast. "A century ago," he began in Finnish, "Mannerheim understood the geopolitical importance of Xinjiang, and look today at just how right he was ... I propose a toast to the memory of Marshal Mannerheim."

Before we could stand up, Altan Ochir leapt to his feet. The ethnic Mongol with the Borderland Research Centre wanted to add to the toast. He recited a famous quote from Zuo Zongtang, the great Chinese general who reconquered Xinjiang during the Muslim uprisings of the 1870s: "To defend the Imperial Court in Peking, you need to defend Inner Mongolia. To defend Inner Mongolia, you need to defend Xinjiang. If you can't defend Xinjiang, you can't defend Peking." He then held up his glass. Everyone rose to their feet. "To Mannerheim," he said.

Servers then dished out a noodle soup, followed by even more toasts and more speeches. Finally dessert arrived, plates of Xinjiang melons, grapes and cherry tomatoes.

Director Wu made the eleventh and final toast. "I hope you will enjoy yourself," he said, referring to a week-long tour to Kashgar that was to begin the next day. "I hope after your inspection tour, you can write notes and publish a diary like Mannerheim did, and introduce Xinjiang to the rest of the world. For many, Xinjiang is still a mysterious land yet to be known. I hope that along the way you can use your notebook and camera to document what is happening in Xinjiang." He held his glass aloft. "For Xinjiang," he said.

I had been drunkenly scratching notes all night. Altan Ochir leaned over as I wrote down Wu's last words. "Whatever you write," he said politely, but firmly, "don't write East Turkestan. Write Xinjiang."

"East Turkestan," of course, is what Uyghur nationalists call their homeland. Uttering the term could likely land a Uyghur in front of a firing squad. Despite Wu encouraging us to make detailed notes of modern Xinjiang, I figured that the symposium's Chinese organizers would plan the field trip to Kashgar in such a way as to minimize the Finns' contact with Uyghurs, who might air unseemly opinions about the Han Chinese. I decided to opt out of this charade.

"I hope you're having a fantastic trip to Southern Xinjiang," I emailed one of the Finnish participants.

"'Fantastic' is not, regrettably, the word I would use to describe our trip to Xinjiang," he replied while still on the road. "Due to 'fantastic' Chinese organizing ability we sat 10–14 hours in the bus every day except for one in Kashgar. We started at dawn from one city and reached the next after sunset, perhaps stopping once or twice at some historical monument. A couple of times we even had supper after midnight."

My suspicions proved correct. Chinese authorities loathe foreign scrutiny over their borderlands, particularly Xinjiang and Tibet. One night I met an American academic at Fubar, an expat watering hole next to People's Park in Urumqi. He agreed to talk with me as long as I did not reveal his name or affiliations. Conducting research in Xinjiang, especially about ethnic minority issues, he explained, was perilous. He knows one Western scholar who was constantly harassed. The police kept making her come to the station at all hours of the night, saying she wasn't properly registered. "They made her pay a 'fine,'" he said. "She finally decided to leave." In another case, a foreign researcher left Xinjiang and then heard that police had rounded up his Uyghur friends. A few were jailed for six months.

Gardner Bovingdon, the Indiana University professor, later told me that almost all American scholars researching Xinjiang, including himself, have been, at some point, banned from China. The Chinese apparently took issue with their contributions to *Xinjiang: China's Muslim Borderland,* the most authoritative work on the region. In the book, published in 2004, Bovingdon wrote an essay on Xinjiang's "contested histories." He pointed out how ancient conflicts between Han Chinese and Uyghurs live on in contemporary scholarship. Authorities have censored Uyghur writers and "lavished funds" on official histories that depict Chinese territorial expansion into ethnic borderlands as "unifications (*tongyi*), never as conquests (*zhengfu*) or annexations (*tunbing*)."[22] Yet the Uyghurs have stubbornly resisted the Chinese Communist Party's ideological claims, Bovingdon writes, in "an enduring struggle over history that is also a battle" over the future of their land and their own fate.[23]

TO DUNHUANG

Treasure Hunt

From several different countries, England, Germany,
France, Russia, America, expeditions have been sent out, but one
can hardly talk of any competition.—SVEN HEDIN,
Speech to the Royal Geographic Society, London (1909)[1]

THE "FIELD INVESTIGATION" retracing Mannerheim's trek began on a crisp late summer morning. Eight Finnish and six Chinese researchers boarded a bus in Urumqi for the week-long excursion to Kashgar. I decided to hitch a ride as far as Turpan, the first stop on the itinerary. Staccato Finnish chatter filled the bus.

"We are wondering where this large mountain is that Mannerheim kept mentioning in his diary when he left Urumqi," Teemu Naarajärvi, the young analyst with the Finnish Institute of International Affairs, explained to me.

To the northeast, I could see a snow-capped peak poking above Urumqi's gleaming skyline of towers. That must be it. "On the right," the Baron wrote, "at a great distance, the magnificent, white-topped head of Bogdo-uula rose like a giant among a group of mountain ridges that descended slowly in ledges towards Urumchi." These mountains form the easternmost spur of the Tian Shan range.[2] Mannerheim had already scouted the pass between the two ranges on his way north to Urumqi. So he ventured west to the fortress town of Fukang. From here, he surveyed a river valley into the imposing Bogdo-uula range whose "striking views" were, he wrote, beyond "my wildest imagination." "The mountain peaks and slopes simply sparkle in the sun as though strewn with thousands of diamonds," he described. His caravan clip-clopped along stony, serpentine paths through a knot of rocky gorges and peaks. The trek to Turpan took one month. Our air-conditioned bus ride lasted two hours.

Halfway to Turpan, we stopped at a "scenic spot" called Dabancheng, which sits pinched between the Tian Shan and Bogdo-uula ranges. On his trek north, a furious windstorm forced Mannerheim to halt here. It seemed, he wrote, "as if all the winds of Asia had conspired to prevent our crossing the pass." Dabancheng is now the site of China's largest wind farm. Stepping off the bus, I heard the din of swooshing blades cut through the air. Some 120 turbines generate one hundred megawatts of electricity. Gales tear through this spot as air rushes from the sizzling heat of the Turpan Depression north into the cool Mongolian steppe.

Turpan (also Turfan) is a surprisingly pleasant town given its climate. Its economy revolves around tourism and grape growing. It is so hot and so dry—it receives a mere twenty-two millimetres of rain per year—that its ancient inhabitants built a unique subterranean irrigation system, or *karez*, that taps snowmelt from mountains to the north. Some sixteen hundred kilometres of underground channels ingeniously use gravity to carry water down into the depression. While the surrounding landscape is a sterile dust bowl, Turpan itself is lush. Mannerheim too was surprised by its "numerous murmuring ariqs, luscious verdure and shady trees." Trellises of grapevines still shade its main promenades and sidewalks are cooled by the shade of low bushy trees and swift-flowing *ariqs*.

The Turpan Depression's arid microclimate is perfect for archaeological preservation. Which is why Europeans have been coming here for more than a century to harvest treasures from ancient ruins and from Buddhist caves carved into dramatic gorges.

Our first stop was the Turpan Regional Museum, with its rich display of items from local sites. A red and yellow wool blanket dating back two thousand years had such vivid colours that it looked like it had just been purchased in the nearby bazaar. Nine well-preserved mummies, dating to the birth of Christ, looked eerily alive. One of them, our museum guide explained, died giving birth. "The baby is still inside her corpse," she said. The mummy's face had a horrifyingly pained expression, as though she'd been in labour for the past two millennia.

Next, we ventured ten kilometres west to the ruined city of Jiaohe (Yarkhoto in Uyghur). It was established as a western outpost of the Han Dynasty. The fortress was built atop a thirty-metre-high terrace, shaped like a willow leaf, at the confluence of two rivers. The fortified outpost was well protected against marauding Xiongnu horsemen. It came to be ruled, at various times, by Tibetans and Uyghurs and was eventually abandoned after the Mongol conquest in the thirteenth century.

Our odd group of towering Finns and short Chinese scholars climbed off the bus and ran a gauntlet of vendors selling cowboy hats, faux artefacts, postcards, stuffed animals and other trinkets. We entered the ruins through the eastern gate, climbing a sloping path onto the loess plateau. Jiaohe now looks like a gigantic ruined sand castle, its sun-bleached clay creating a blinding glare. "I must say that I expected something grander in the way of architecture and decoration," Mannerheim wrote of Jiaohe. "These clay buildings, worn smooth and stumpy by rain and wind, certainly look more imposing in a photograph than in reality." Worse, Buddhist murals in the underground abodes were badly damaged. He found three wall paintings, but "resolved to leave them to more qualified collectors." A century later, not a painting can be found.

The midday heat was brutal, so we retreated to a downtown hotel for a hearty lunch and air-conditioned siesta. At 5 PM, when the heat began to abate, we resumed the tour. The bus headed east across a sandy, desolate plain. A road wound up a gorge into the crimson-coloured Flaming Mountains. In a dramatic canyon cut by the Murtuk River, we found the Bezeklik Thousand Buddha Caves. Dating back to the fourth century, the caves are tucked beneath sandstone cliffs accessed by a twisting path. Of the sixty-seven caves, only a half-dozen are open to the public.

In Cave 20, we found six framed, life-sized photographs of Buddhist frescoes hanging on bare sandstone walls, the original artwork spirited away. In fact, no cave is unscathed: Buddha portraits have had their faces rubbed out, statues were gone or severely damaged, and most wall murals had been either sawn or hacked away. Signs in two damaged caves stated that the murals were "stolen by Stein." It's understandable why the Chinese loathe Aurel Stein, whose raids robbed China of so much of its physical heritage.

Stein visited the Turpan Depression and Bezeklik in November 1907, but did not excavate here. In fact, he was shocked at what he saw: "Big temples, monasteries, etc, were dug into with the method of a scholarly treasure-seeker, barely explored with any approach to archaeological thoroughness."³ He did "save" some frescoes in 1914, but by then most of the damage had already been done.⁴

The real "foreign devils" at Bezeklik and most other sites in Turpan were Germans. It was Albert Grünwedel and Albert von Le Coq of Berlin's Ethnological Museum who were responsible for much of the plundering. They conducted four expeditions to Turpan between 1902 and 1914. Alas, many of their finds were later destroyed when a bomb hit the Berlin museum during the Second World War. Mannerheim briefly visited Bezeklik, which, he wrote, "is still worth a visit in spite of all the destruction it has suffered."

After dinner at the hotel, I slipped out with a few Finns to wander Turpan's trellised streets without a Chinese chaperone. Next to the main square, rows of billiard tables, illuminated by strings of incandescent light bulbs, bustled with young Uyghur men. Kebab barbecues billowed smoke and outdoor cafés were packed with chattering locals drawn out by the inviting evening air. Back in the hotel lobby, we sat around drinking cold Tsingtao beers.

"Did anyone see any beggars today?" asked Peter Sandberg, the Finnish photographer. "Mannerheim said he saw a lot of beggars in Turfan." The Baron, in fact, counted ninety-two.

"I think I saw an old man begging," replied Teemu Naarajärvi, "but I passed him twice and he did not ask me for money."

"I think I saw an old woman begging," Sandberg added, "but was unsure."

Ari Mäkelä, a researcher with the Finnish Environmental Institute, came over to our table. He pulled out a small coin with a hole in the middle that he bought for fifteen yuan (about two dollars) at a tourist shop. Juha Janhunen, a linguist at Helsinki University, inspected it carefully.

"It's worth maybe one or two yuan," he said.

"You can tell people back in Finland that Mannerheim overlooked this 'precious' coin during his collecting in Turpan," I joked.

"Mannerheim went hunting instead," Mäkelä replied.

The Finns all roared at this inside joke. Hunting, as it turned out, did sidetrack the Baron. The diversion, in fact, cost him one of the greatest archaeological discoveries of the twentieth century.

SILK ROAD EXPLORERS were a cordial lot—at least publicly. They heaped praise on one another in the drawing rooms and lecture halls of Europe. But privately, in diaries, letters and secret dispatches, they talked of "campaigns," "rivals," "ransacking" and "raids." It sounded like war, and at one point almost turned violent.

In early 1906, the Russian Beresovsky brothers claimed that a German expedition was violating their archaeological sphere of influence at a site near Kucha, six hundred kilometres east of Turpan. The competitors nearly came to blows, until the Germans graciously backed off.[5]

European rivals spied on each other through informants, agents, Chinese officials and local gossip. Macartney, for instance, received dispatches from his *aksakals* (literally "white-beards," or local Muslim elders) on the whereabouts of foreign expeditions. The British consul then secretly forwarded this information to Stein. It was a note from Macartney about Pelliot's arrival in Kashgar, for example, that hastened Stein's departure from Khotan. The British explorer raced eastward "to raid desert sites" before his rivals could catch up.[6]

Mannerheim maintained the Russo-French alliance against the British despite his dislike of Pelliot. After leaving Kashgar, the Baron sent word to Pelliot that Macartney had news from Stein in Lop Nor, a desert in eastern Xinjiang that Pelliot had publicly announced his intention to dig up. Mannerheim reported that Stein had excavated sand-buried ruins of an ancient Chinese garrison at Loulan and then raided Miran, another lost Chinese garrison on the southern leg of the Silk Road.[7] At the latter site, Stein unearthed a hoard of Tibetan documents, dating back to the eighth century, from a rubbish heap. "The number was said to be something considerable," Mannerheim told Pelliot. Rumour had also gotten back to Kashgar, the Baron wrote, that Pelliot had collected "a fortune of gold objects."[8]

"I'm not surprised that someone had spilled the rumour of a find of gold..." Pelliot wrote back. "The natives don't understand that one can search for other things than precious objects. In reality, we have only cleaned out one considerable ancient Buddhist temple which had not been recognized up to now. We have here reaped a lot of sculptures, but very few documents." He also thanked the Baron for "intelligence" on Stein.[9]

Pelliot stayed in the Kucha area for more than six months—a strategic blunder, as it turned out. Meanwhile, Stein frantically excavated desert sites to the south. After clearing this area, he raced farther east, paranoid that Pelliot might already be at his next destination. Mannerheim doesn't warrant a mention in Stein's correspondence, but it was the Finn, not the Frenchman, who was speeding east toward Stein's most coveted archaeological site.

In Turpan, Mannerheim collected information on the strength of the local garrison and picked over the archaeological dregs in the wake of German operations. He bought 1,971 document fragments from local treasure hunters. "Many fragments are so minute that I never would have purchased them had I not in Kashgar had the opportunity to see Mr. G. Macartney buying considerably smaller pieces of paper for the learned societies in England," Mannerheim wrote to Otto Donner. "Now I have a small box full of such fragments."[10] Only 204 were more than sixteen centimetres long. Most of Mannerheim's purchases are ancient Buddhist texts in Chinese dating back as early as the fourth century.

While in Turpan, Mannerheim received disturbing news: Pelliot's baggage had arrived from Urumqi, suggesting the Frenchman was on his way. The Baron immediately dispatched a letter to Pelliot. "If I knew that your stay in Urumqi would only be a short duration," he wrote, "I would have waited for you."[11] That hardly seems likely, given his distaste for the Frenchman. Indeed, a few days later, Mannerheim hightailed it out of town.

He headed east across the barren plain to Astana, the site of an ancient graveyard, and the ruined fortress of Gaochang (Karakhoto in Uyghur). At the latter, he rode around the stumpy clay ruins for several hours. "Everything was in an exceedingly bad state, which is not surprising when one knows that during the two years' sojourn and excavations of the Grünwedel expedition it recently suffered fresh destruction," he wrote. "Of the paintings on stucco there is practically nothing left." A greater treasure awaited him to the east.

I BID FAREWELL to the Sino-Finnish group the next day. They continued on their way to Kashgar; I returned to Urumqi for a few days' rest. I had been on the road for over two months and felt exhausted. I was struck down with the flu and lay in bed for two days eating melons and drinking green tea. Blustery winds rattled my hotel room window and the temperature dipped noticeably. On the morning I left Urumqi, golden poplar leaves were showering the street like confetti. Autumn had arrived.

Aboard the bus back to Turpan, I met a Uyghur tour guide who arranged a car to take me to the ancient ruins of Gaochang, which Mannerheim had found so rapaciously raided. It had originally been established as a Chinese garrison in the second century BC, but like Jiaohe later fell into the hands of the Huns. Nowadays, local Uyghurs run donkey carts full of mostly Han Chinese tourists to a large temple complex a kilometre inside the disintegrating ruins. The Chinese donned so much protection—sun visors, hats, parasols, sunglasses, facemasks and headscarves—that they looked like they were entering a quarantine zone. They were certainly well protected from my lingering flu. In the desert heat, dripping in sweat, I climbed aboard a donkey cart for the short jaunt. The temple, now nothing more than a few eroded brick walls, was covered in scaffolding and off-limits. I scaled a crumbling rampart nearby that surrounds the ancient fortress. It was a hauntingly panoramic view: hundreds of remnant walls, whittled down over time, looked like the tombstones of a vanquished kingdom.

After visiting Gaochang, I told my Uyghur driver to head a half-hour east to a spot where I was sure to witness more contemporary ruins. Given the widespread destruction of Uyghur Old Towns in Xinjiang, I cringed at the thought of what I'd find left of Toyuk. The small village is carved into a sandstone gorge that leads into the Flaming Mountains. Its farmers are famous for their oval-shaped seedless grapes, the raisins of which were once sent to the Emperor's table in Peking.[12] Mannerheim counted 350 houses and fifty shops in the village. "The terraced village with its crooked walls, old-fashioned lanes, verandas and terraces looked charming in the sunshine," he wrote. "Decidedly the most attractive Sart village I had seen."

A lick of new asphalt swung up into the Flaming Mountains from the gravel plain. The highway cut right through a graveyard of large domed *maẓars* (mausoleums) and clay tombs along some foothills. Below the cemetery, in a lush gully, lay Toyuk. We pulled into a parking lot surrounded by tourist shops. At a kiosk, I paid fifty yuan (seven dollars) for a ticket to enter the village, which now appeared to be a tourist attraction. I was pleasantly surprised at how little had changed. The village and vineyards are cut like steps into the ravine. A wooden footbridge connects both sides. Everything is constructed in rough-hewn timbers and pinkish clay. I followed a tour guide with three Han Chinese men in tow. One wore a cowboy hat like Indiana Jones. We crossed the bridge and came to the entrance of a traditional Uyghur home. An elderly couple was lying on an iron bed outside their front door. The Chinese tourists barged into their home. Was it now an exhibit? The old man, thin and frail with weary eyes, looked like he was on his deathbed. He craned his head to look at me. His elderly wife smiled and nodded for me to go inside.

The home was of traditional construction: unbaked brick, clay, straw and log beams. With a vaulted ceiling and dirt floor, the dim main living room looked like a cave. A large clay oven for winter heating and cooking stood in a corner. The second floor with wooden lattice windows was used for drying raisins, a feature common to many homes in Toyuk. Exiting, I bought a bottle of water and bag of sweet red raisins from a merchant, and followed a marked path to a beautiful waterfall at the back of the village. From here, a boardwalk led me through a ravine to crumbling Buddhist caves (pillaged by von Le Coq in 1906 and Stein in 1914). They were dug precariously high into the sandstone cliff.

Toyuk was still the most attractive town in Xinjiang, but I left with mixed feelings. Some residents were courteous and curious—a boy even ran out with a gift of grapes for me—but others gave me sidelong glances or ignored me altogether. One Uyghur woman in a silk dress threw me a surly look and waved her hands disapprovingly when she saw me point my camera. One can hardly blame them for their menacing looks. The Uyghurs must worry that one day a busload of Han Chinese will arrive in Toyuk and not leave— a fate that has befallen most other Uyghur towns in Xinjiang.

MANNERHEIM'S NEXT DESTINATION was Hami, a large town in the northeast corner of Xinjiang. He took a convoluted route via Barkul, a rundown Chinese garrison town famed for "resisting the repeated onslaughts of the insurgents" during the Muslim uprisings in the 1870s. He ventured out of the desert basin into a knot of mountain ranges that protected Barkul on all sides. Velvety slopes were covered in wild grasses where sheep, boars, gazelles and goats grazed. "Shooting must be splendid in these parts," Mannerheim wrote. A fit of rheumatism kept him in Barkul for five days. He then left the high alpine valley, via a southern pass, into a wasteland between the Taklimakan and Gobi deserts. His crossing was slowed by a wintry blizzard. "The snow was an unpleasant surprise," he wrote with characteristic understatement. The next day, with the help of Chinese labourers, they cleared a path through the two-metre-deep snow to allow his cart through. A day later, after much exertion, he reached Hami.

There, the Baron later wrote to Otto Donner, "my path crossed with Dr. Stein on his return from the southern desert region. He had some twenty camel-loads of 'treasures' in the keeping of the local military Mandarin, while he set out on a long tour of the mountains."[13] Their paths, in fact, didn't quite cross. Mannerheim arrived one day *after* Stein had left for his alpine excursion and the Baron departed Hami two days *before* Stein's return. In his published journal, *Ruins of Desert Cathay*, Stein reported only to have heard "rumours of the arrival of a Cossack officer," which was most likely Mannerheim.[14] As for Stein's "treasures," Mannerheim told Donner that he heard that Stein's expedition "achieved excellent results," including the discovery of "hundreds of documents" at Dunhuang, an oasis just beyond the Xinjiang border in Gansu province.[15]

Stein's cases contained, according to one contemporary British scholar, "perhaps the greatest of the archaeological finds of the Silk Road."[16] Stein received a knighthood for his daring exploits. He also won the Gold Medal from the Royal Geographical Society and honorary degrees from Cambridge and Oxford. The archaeological find was so massive—and its removal so tricky—that Stein left half the treasures behind.

Since the Germans had already returned to Berlin, the race to Dunhuang was now between two archrivals: Pelliot and Mannerheim. Pelliot heard about the Dunhuang find from Duke Lan in Urumqi shortly after Mannerheim's departure. The two had a bittersweet reunion. Pelliot had been in the French Legation in Peking while Duke Lan and his soldiers were besieging the foreigners during the Boxer Rebellion. "We had fought one another in 1900, but the passage of time heals all things," Pelliot wrote afterwards, adding: "We sealed our friendship with many a glass of champagne."[17] Duke Lan also presented Pelliot with a sample Dunhuang manuscript. "Pelliot had hardly unrolled this," Vaillant, his travelling companion, later recounted, "when he realized that it dated from before the eighth century."[18] Pelliot quickly set off for Dunhuang, but with his considerable lead—Mannerheim was only a two-week ride away from Dunhuang—the Baron appeared to be heading into the history books.

THE BUS WAS crowded with Uyghur labourers, a half-dozen women and two young Han Chinese soldiers. I could barely squeeze my backpack into the luggage compartment among all the bundles of merchandise, a steel grinder and an oily piece of machinery. As we departed Turpan, I pulled the dark blue curtains shut to keep out the scorching sun. There was little to see anyway, just a broiling gravel wasteland. Over seven hours, the bus became humid with the stench of warm bodies, cigarettes and garlic breath. I was sweaty and sore by the time we reached Hami, a dreary, uninteresting town. I left early the next morning on another bus.

The makeup of the passengers changed markedly from Uyghur to mostly Han Chinese and Hui (ethnic Chinese Muslims). We barrelled south toward Dunhuang. Black hillocks rose out of the red gravel plain, marking the border between Xinjiang and Gansu province. Beyond the low-slung range, we drove across a salt flat and crossed, according to my map, "an ancient boundary wall." It had once been the most western extension of the Great Wall. I was now in the outer reaches of Han civilization. A half-hour later we were in the ancient outpost of Dunhuang.

I got a cheap room next to the bus station. The room was small but had air conditioning, a TV and hot water. My head felt tight and my shoulders ached. I took two Tylenol and laid down to rest, but the din of the station—shouting, banging doors and rumbling diesel engines—kept me awake. I went for a stroll instead.

Chinese soldiers settled and fortified Dunhuang—which means "blazing beacon"—in 121 BC. It was the last caravan halt before leaving China proper. All merchants and pilgrims had to pass through the oasis, where the Silk Road forks into southern and northern routes. In the second century AD it was a prosperous oasis of seventy-six thousand. But by the time Mannerheim visited, Dunhuang had lost its verve. "With its memorial gates, temples with bells tinkling in the wind, cramped official buildings and centuries-old gnarled trees, the little town possesses a charming air of antiquity," he wrote. "The streets are lifeless, nothing is visible but a couple of debilitated old opium smokers and a crowd of loitering street-boys." I found Dunhuang almost as quaint and sleepy. The narrow streets were lined with poplar and mulberry trees, hotels and restaurants. Tourist shops sold jade, paper scrolls, wall hangings, books and postcards. A lively night market served up lamb skewers and spicy hotpots. The sidewalks were broad and clean. The architecture was more endearing than in most towns in Xinjiang. Winged and tiled Chinese-style roofs top many modern buildings, attempting—however awkwardly—to evoke the romance of the Silk Road. The old fortress, which Mannerheim sketched and described in detail, had been bulldozed. However, by the old western gate, I found three shiny new towers with fanciful roofs and tapering walls constructed of beige stone and mirrored glass. They were supposed to evoke the ancient watchtowers of yore. Although not usually an admirer of this sort of kitschy postmodernism, I found them oddly inspiring given the bleak aesthetics of most Chinese towns.

I hardly slept that night. The mattress, as thin as a sanitary napkin, felt like concrete and the pillow was like a lumpy beanbag. At 5 AM, with a bag full of dried fruit, nuts, crackers and water, I went across the street to John's Café, where I had booked a camel ride across the desert to the famed Mogao Grottoes, or Caves of the Thousand Buddhas. An idling taxi was waiting to take me to the edge of the oasis.

In the dark, I almost stepped on the massive camel sitting on the walkway to my Chinese guide's house. I climbed atop the animal, feeling my way between its furry humps. The beast stumbled to its feet and my faceless guide led me on. The only sound was the crunch of hooves and the shuffling feet of my guide. A few clouds were streaked white with moonlight in the starry sky. At one point, my guide handed me the reins, but the disobedient beast wandered all over the place. I heaved aggressively, not realizing that the reins were joined to a wooden bit drilled through the camel's nostrils. The animal squawked like a duck with laryngitis. It immediately began to kneel in protest, suggesting I should figuratively and literally get off its back. The guide grabbed the reins and glared at me. For the rest of the journey, I sat bobbing atop the shaggy beast like a child on an amusement ride. I felt ridiculous.

At dawn, a blistering orange sun came up, casting a peachy glow over a black ridge. A wicked wind rose too. I crouched in the saddle, tucking my hands into the camel's warmth. We climbed into rolling, barren hills and eventually came to a green valley. I dismounted after four hours, bid farewell to my guide and descended on foot into a dry riverbed. Looking up, I spotted sandstone cliffs pocked with darkened cavities that looked like eye sockets. It felt as if the Caves of the Thousand Buddhas were watching me.

Bus after bus roared past as I walked into Dunhuang's famed tourist attraction. I counted eighty buses and hundreds of taxis, vans and private cars in the parking lot. Several thousand Chinese tourists squeezed through the gates on guided tours. I waited an hour for a group of foreigners—two Australians, two young Israeli backpackers and a dozen middle-aged Americans—to assemble for an English-language tour. The long lines to view the caves made me feel like I was queuing at Disneyland.

Mr. Mao, our tour guide, wore a dark blue suit and pink shirt. He was in his mid-thirties and gregarious. We began the tour in front of a seven-storey pagoda-like structure clinging to the cliff. Built in the 1920s, the red wooden tower with Chinese-styled eaves houses the largest Buddha statue in the world.

"Why wasn't it destroyed during the Cultural Revolution?" someone asked.

"Dunhuang is far from China's political centre," Mr. Mao began. "The people here are far more conservative." That meant the caves largely escaped the widespread destruction that has robbed China of so much of its physical heritage. "Buddhist monks wanted the caves to be preserved as a sacred religious site," Mr. Mao said, "but they are actually a state treasure which everyone can enjoy." So in the 1960s, he explained, the caves' crumbling facade was reinforced with sand-coloured concrete. Balconies, stairways and wooden doors were added, making the caves look like a Flintstones attraction.

Inside, the Buddha stood almost forty metres. Light poked through small windows into the dim chamber. Monks first dug the three windows into the side of the cliff, one on top of the other, and then began hollowing out the cave and shaping the Buddha inside, Mr. Mao explained. The industrious monks caked the rough form in straw and clay to create the statue's detailing: fingers, eyes, earlobes and so on. With bright red lips, small but noticeable breasts and black slits for eyes that could have been mistaken for streaks of mascara, the Buddha looked like a transvestite. It took sixteen years to build during the Tang Dynasty (AD 618–906).

"The Chinese are very proud of this dynasty, the Golden Age," Mr. Mao said.

"The Chinese are like the Americans," the young Israeli girl said as we stepped outside into the blinding desert sun. "They have to do everything the biggest."

In another cave with the world's second-tallest Buddha, I noticed a chunk of missing fresco by the entrance. "What happened here?" I inquired.

"One hundred years ago some foreigners came here and took away some murals, but not many, not many," Mr. Mao said, pointing his flashlight beam at the small bare patch.

Stein, to his credit, realized that chopping down frescoes would stir popular unrest. "In view of local religious feelings—Tun-huang people are all pious Buddhists—excavations . . . were out of the question," Stein wrote in a dispatch to Macartney. The culprit in this case was Langdon Warner, a Harvard professor and one of the models for Indiana Jones. He used strips of tape to peel off the frescoes.

"Thankfully," Mr. Mao added, "he didn't have much tape. But when he came back the next year the locals found out what he was up to and almost killed him."

In another cave, I saw evidence that I'd reached the historical outer reaches of Chinese civilization. In Cave Number 148, a massive Shakyamuni Buddha is reclined in nirvana pose and surrounded by seventy-two clay statues of disciples, devas, princes and Bodhisattvas. "There were seventy-two disciples who toured the countryside with Confucius and who are mentioned in the *Analects*,"

Mr. Mao explained. "It's not a coincidence. When Buddhism came to China from India, the Chinese tried to make it more and more Chinese." Stein too had noticed this Chinese influence in the art-work, especially "their love for ornate landscape backgrounds, graceful curves, and bold movement."[19]

We ended the tour at a temple that has been renovated into a small museum. Wang Yuanlu, a Daoist monk and the self-appointed abbot of the Mogao Grottoes, constructed the Trinity Temple (San-qingong in Chinese) a century ago. How he funded its construction is a matter of great controversy.

ON MARCH 16, 1907, Aurel Stein made his first visit to the Caves of the Thousand Buddhas. (Mannerheim was in Aksu, preparing to leave for the Muzart Pass). He had heard "vague rumours about a great hidden deposit of ancient manuscripts which was said to have been discovered accidentally some years earlier in one of the grottoes."[20] He found the cave, but its caretaker, Wang, was away begging for alms in Dunhuang. Stein returned two months later, pitching his tent in front of the grottoes. He introduced himself to Wang, who "looked a very queer person, extremely shy and ner-vous, with an occasional expression of cunning which was far from encouraging."[21]

Wang had discovered the hidden library in 1900, while he was cleaning sand out of what is now Cave Number 16. The monk was attempting to restore the caves to their former glory. Stein soon dis-covered that the suspicious Wang had not only locked the hidden library behind a wooden door, but also blocked it with brickwork. Stein mentally prepared himself "for a long and arduous siege."[22]

First, Stein suggested a "liberal donation" in exchange for an opportunity to view the library. Wang showed him a few speci-mens, but became perturbed when Stein's Chinese assistant hinted at purchasing some manuscripts. "To rely on the temptation of money alone as a means of overcoming his scruples was manifestly useless," wrote Stein, who then launched a charm offensive.[23] He told the monk that he had followed in the footsteps of Xuan Zhang, a Buddhist pilgrim whose travels to India in the seventh century are well known in China. Stein spoke of his devotion and admiration for Xuan. Wang's eyes "gleamed with lively interest." Stein had found a way into Wang's heart—and soon into the library.

Late one night, Stein's Chinese assistant came, "in silent elation," with a bundle of scrolls that Wang had secretly brought him. The specimens turned out to be ancient Buddhist sutras translated by Xuan Zhang himself—"a most auspicious omen," Stein declared.[24] The explorer plied the monk with more pious words about how, as a loyal disciple of Xuan Zhang, he had been brought to Dunhuang by fate to shed light on the ancient manuscripts for Western scholarship. The sentimental, unsuspecting monk led Stein to the hidden library.

"The sight of the small room disclosed was one to make my eyes open wide," the cunning explorer wrote. "Heaped up in layers, but without any order, there appeared in the dim light of the priest's little lamp a solid mass of manuscripts bundles rising to a height of nearly ten feet, and filling, as subsequent measurement showed, close on 500 cubic feet."

Stein's assistant brokered a late-night deal to exchange manuscripts for a donation. For seven nights, bundles were clandestinely brought to Stein's tent. The antiquarian treasures included Buddhist sutras in Chinese and Tibetan, Sanskrit manuscripts on palm leaves, rolls in Indian Brahmi, ancient Uyghur scripts and texts in Sogdian, Runic Turkic, Mongolian, Tangut and other mysterious languages. One of the greatest archaeological finds of the twentieth century netted Stein some twenty thousand ancient manuscripts and fragments. The haul included the *Diamond Sutra*, the world's oldest block-printed book, made in AD 868. The cost was "relatively trifling" (Stein's words), a mere £130. Wang used the money to build his small temple, which fell into disrepair until 2000 when it was renovated into the Hidden Library Museum.

STEIN'S FANTASTIC HAUL is now housed in another secret location, this one deep in the bowels of the British Library. While passing through London, I visited Susan Whitfield, director of the International Dunhuang Project. Two storeys underground, locked behind an aluminum door in a fireproof vault within a vast concrete bunker, sits Stein's collection. "It's an immensely important find for world history," Whitfield told me. "I don't think historians, except the Chinese and Japanese, have awakened to its significance."

Inside the vault, nine rows of custom hardwood cabinets with glass doors hold some twenty thousand manuscripts. Whitfield pulled out a seventh-century scroll, which happened to be a copy of the *Diamond Sutra*. The sacred text chronicles a dialogue between the Buddha and his elderly disciple Subhuti. Only eight centimetres wide, it stretches eight metres in length, with seventeen painstakingly neat characters per column. The paper is heavy and yellowed, but surprisingly soft. Stein meticulously numbered each bundle, roll and scroll. Realizing that constant handling threatens the delicate manuscripts, Whitfield broached a bold idea at a landmark conference in 1993 that brought together Chinese and European scholars. "Digitization was the solution," she explained, "although nobody believed me at the time." There are now 159,821 images (and counting) in the digital Dunhuang database from collections in Britain, China, Russia, Japan and Germany. The physical location of the manuscripts now seems less important. "We've never had a formal request [for repatriation]," Whitfield told me.

While the Chinese may be understandably bitter, the Hidden Library Museum is surprisingly tactful in reference to the foreign explorers who ransacked Dunhuang. The exhibit matter-of-factly states how Stein "by playing on Wang Yuanlu's reverence for the eminent monk Xuan Zhang" acquired the ancient treasures. Pelliot, who absconded with ten thousand for a mere £90,[25] is described as a "brilliant Sinologist and linguist." There are no bad words for the Japanese Otani expedition (four hundred scrolls), Russian

Oldenburg expedition (two hundred scrolls) or Langdon Warner either. From the gargantuan heap, only 8,697 documents remained for the Chinese.[26]

Mannerheim doesn't warrant a mention anywhere in the museum. The reason is rather curious. He left Dunhuang to visit the Caves of the Thousand Buddhas but became sidetracked along the way. Forty years later, he attempted in his memoirs to explain away this odd oversight. "To examine this find," he wrote, "exceeded my competence and even otherwise I would by no means have undertaken it as I heard that a French scientific expedition was on its way there in order to tackle the task." This excuse is unconvincing. Otto Donner had specifically commissioned him to collect manuscripts, not judge their scientific worth. Despite his lack of "competence," he had already amassed thousands of text fragments from Khotan and Turpan. Furthermore, it's beyond incredulity that he graciously stepped aside for the hated Pelliot, who finally arrived four months later. Although Mannerheim had little money, even buying a few scrolls would have delighted Donner.

It appears that the Baron's finicky palate was the real reason he never visited the sacred grottoes. He hunted for his dinner on his way to and from Dunhuang. The wild game, he wrote, was "a welcome change from our monotonous diet." On his way to the Buddhist grottoes, he therefore could not "resist the temptation" of shooting a brace of pheasants and two gazelles. "After losing much time in shooting," he wrote, "we reached the mouth of the gorge, when the sun was already so low that there was nothing for it but to give up the 'thousand gods' and discover the sarai [inn] before dark."

"Thus," concludes Helsinki University's Harry Halén in a monograph on Mannerheim's "hunt" for Central Asian manuscripts, "a great scientific treasure was exchanged for roast pheasant and gazelle."[27]

The Hidden Library is now numbered Cave 17. It is an elevated antechamber on the right side of the entranceway to Cave 16.

Mr. Mao said it was originally built as a meditation room for the great monk Hong Bian. "Sometime in the eleventh century," he said, "the chamber was stuffed with manuscripts and sealed." It may have been done to protect the sacred texts from Muslim warriors or to archive old scripts. Nobody really knows, he said.

In the main chamber of Cave 16, Mr. Mao pointed his flashlight at a large, blank wall. American and Chinese researchers, collaborating in the 1980s, discovered that the wall in this spot is hollow too. It may be another hidden library, Mr. Mao explained, but authorities have refused to open it.

"I'm very curious about what's behind the wall," Mr. Mao said, "but the Dunhuang Academy is not. Maybe one night I'll come and open the cave myself."

"You'll be the new Wang," I said.

"And you," Mr. Mao smiled wryly, "look a bit like Pelliot."

ELEVEN

HEXI CORRIDOR

Barbarians Inside the Gate

They cannot much longer resist the onset of progress:
as victors or vanquished they must at least suffer change.
We shall have known the .last Barbarians.
—MAJOR HENRI D'OLLONE, *In Forbidden China*[1]

ABOARD THE TRAIN from Dunhuang, I spied in the distance the
Great Pass Under Heaven, an ancient fortress of ramparts and
parapets crowned by three towering pagodas. It stands in the
centre of a barren valley, wedged between snow-capped peaks.
From each side of the fortress, tamped earth walls dip and thrust like
a dragon's tail, extending into the distant mountains. The lonely military outpost, known in Chinese as Jiayuguan, historically protected
a strategic pass to the Middle Kingdom from the barbarian world
beyond. I had reached the beginning of the Great Wall of China.

Known as the "golden section" of the Silk Road, the Hexi Corridor runs a thousand kilometres from Jiayuguan through a thin,
marginally arable zone between geographic extremes: the Gobi
Desert to the north and the Tibetan Plateau to the south. Here, Han
Chinese, Mongolian, Tibetan and Turkic cultures have collided
(or "blended," in official Chinese parlance) in Gansu province for

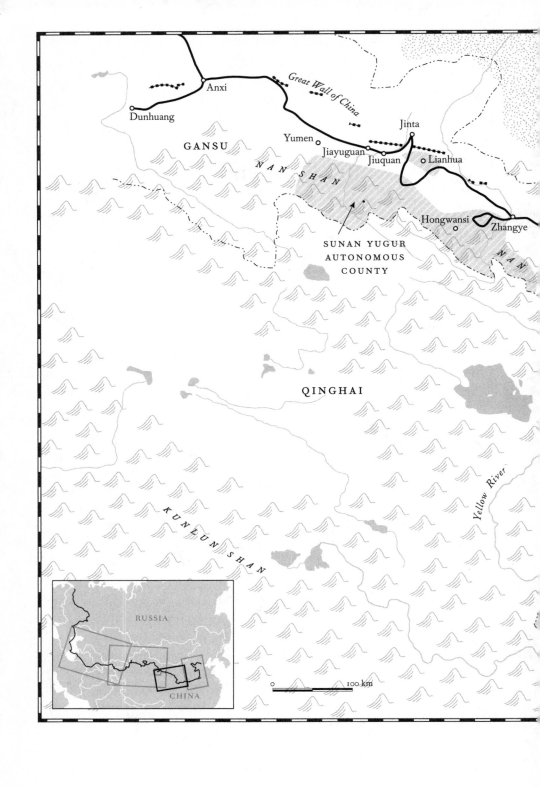

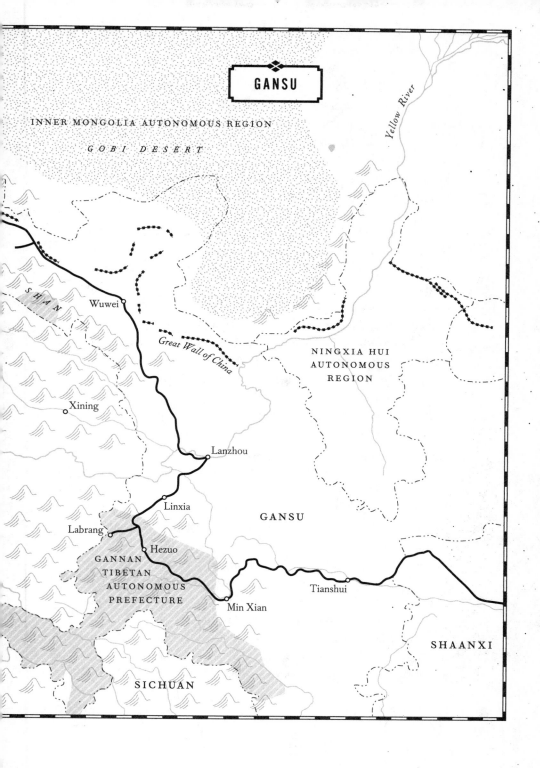

centuries. A half-century ago, Chinese engineers easily punched a hole in the wall's crumbling clay and laid the railway tracks upon which my train sped into town.

I stayed in a quaint inn designed as a replica Qing-era villa, with upturned eaves and ceramic roof tiles, set just below the fortress. Archways led into interlocking courtyards with tranquil gardens and pavilion-style guesthouses. The inn was overpriced, deserted and, apparently, contaminated. A chicken stir-fry from its restaurant sent me dashing for the toilet. I rested for several hours before wandering up the hill to the ancient fortress and a modern museum.

Despite its name, the Great Wall of China is not great. It is certainly long—some ten thousand kilometres—which is why the Chinese dub it Chang Cheng, the Long Wall. China's first emperor unified the country through its construction. The Qin Dynasty (221–206 BC) began building the wall after all else failed to deter "barbarian" invaders. However, a chink soon developed in the dynasty's armour. "The strength of walls depends on the courage of those who guard them," Genghis Khan once said. Indeed, the wall failed to keep out the marauding Mongols, who conquered China in 1279. After routing the Mongols, the Ming Dynasty revived wall building. Jiayuguan was completed in 1372, during a period when the Ming rapidly expanded the wall westward to protect against another invasion. But by the end of the dynasty, the wall had become a symbol of military weakness and ineptitude. "Up went the Long Wall and down came the empire," wrote one seventeenth-century official.[2]

Yet the wall wasn't just defensive. In the museum, I saw not just bows, battleaxes, spears and swords but a rich collection of farming implements too: iron ploughs, stone mills, hoes, ceramic jugs. "The Qin Dynasty saw the start of farming garrisons," states a display, "when a large number of peasants were immigrated to border areas for both cultivation and defence of the frontiers." The Ming Dynasty expanded this system on a "vast scale" in the Hexi

Corridor. Through irrigation and sheer tenacity, Han Chinese farmers turned steppe, alpine and desert—traditional territories of Mongol, Tibetan and Turkic peoples—into settled agricultural lands. The Great Wall fortified these farming garrisons. "These walls look less land-protecting than land-grabbing," writes one historian, "designed to enable the Chinese to police peoples whose way of life differed from their own, and to control lucrative trade routes."[3]

The Jiayuguan fortress is practically empty now. Outer ramparts protect an Old Town that consists of a few tourist shops, restaurants and a dim, smoky temple dedicated to the God of War, a red-faced deity whose crazed expression looks like something out of Japanese manga. Inside the fort, I wandered an expansive gravel yard where barracks and warehouses once stood. Only a replica *yamen* of the military commander remains. It was nearly closing time, and so the massive fort was unusually devoid of visitors.

I climbed a wide brick staircase to the three-storey pagoda over the main gate. Like a sentry, I stood looking out over the parapet into the desert valley. A soft, orange sun was slipping toward the hazy horizon. The earthen ramparts turned tangerine in the glow. A train shooting in from Xinjiang reminded me of the long, bobbing camel caravans of yore laden with melons, spices, jade and gold. I squinted into the sunset and imaged Mannerheim's small procession trotting toward me over the undulating plain.

I then turned around to look at modern Jiayuguan. The contrast was jarring. The scene was out of a Charles Dickens novel: clouds of steam, inky trails of smoke and a brown fog oozed up over concrete apartments, a forest of brick chimneys, power plants and industrial mills. Thanks to Mao Zedong, Jiayuguan leapt from medieval farming garrison to military-industrial complex virtually overnight. In 1958, waves of workers flooded in to build steel mills for armaments factories and to exploit rich coal and ore deposits in the surrounding mountains. After six hundred years, Jiayuguan still protects China against the world. "A pass built here," General Feng Sheng, Jiayuguan's founder, once said, "must be as strong as iron."[4] That's now literally true: the town of 150,000 is effectively run by the Jiuquan Iron and Steel Company.

Back in my room, I pulled out the Baron's journal for bedtime reading. Mannerheim stayed in a caravanserai below a corner tower inside the fortress. His Uyghur cook prepared pilaf and murmured his evening prayer over a gurgling pot. As the sun began to set, the Baron heard the "monotonous drawn-out notes" of the evening tattoo, an army drum call, echoing in the night. "These were followed by gunfire warning all honest folk to hasten home," he wrote, "and then I heard the Chinese Empire being locked up securely behind five massive iron gates, and there we all were safe and sound under lock and key."

BEFORE LEAVING Helsinki, Mannerheim consulted his cousin Erland Nordenskiöld, an anthropologist, and his mentor Otto Donner, a professor of comparative linguistics at the Imperial Alexander University (later Helsinki University), about ethnographic collecting. Donner advised Mannerheim to focus his research on the "innumerable people" of Inner Asia, "which have been studied very little or not at all."[5] If Mannerheim was to make a contribution to world ethnography, he'd need to seek out obscure tribes along the Silk Road.

One of the most obscure and mysterious ethnic groups Mannerheim came across eked out a grim existence on the margins of the Gobi Desert. Their villages lay just inside the Great Wall not far from Jiayuguan. His investigations among these people—now known as Yugurs—would arguably be the Baron's greatest contribution to the field of ethnography. Nowadays, finding these people, whose population had dwindled over a century of war, revolution, colonization and repression, would be a feat.

I stumbled upon help while asking some kids for directions in front of Jiayuguan's bus station. The youths stared at me as I mangled the few Mandarin phrases I knew trying to ask about the bus to Jiuquan, a town twenty kilometres to the east. Fortuitously, a taxi pulled up and out jumped a young man in an army jacket, jeans, thick-framed glasses and scraggily long hair. He looked Bohemian.

"How can I help you?" he asked in impeccable English.

"I'm trying to catch a bus to Jiuquan," I said.

John, as my luck would have it, owned the only expat bar in Jia-yuguan. He was picking up crates of tonic from the bus station's cargo depot. Desperate for a local guide, I told him about my plans to find Mannerheim's "little, lost, Turkish tribe." John had never heard of them, but suggested I call one of his friends for help.

At 10 PM I met Bing in the dim lounge of the Jiayuguan Hotel. She was a tiny woman, barely five feet tall. Her petite frame was hidden under an oversized T-shirt emblazoned with "FIFA World Cup Germany 2006." She had a slender face and a bridged, distinctly un-Chinese nose. "My father is Tibetan; my mother, Chinese," said Bing, who grew up in a Tibetan town in southern Gansu. At sixteen, she ran away from her abusive father. "I refused to cry in front of him," she said, "and so he'd beat me harder." She escaped first to Lanzhou and then moved to Beijing, Shanghai, Xi'an and even as far west as Urumqi. She had been in Jiayuguan for the past two and a half years, slinging beers in John's bar. Bing was feisty, talkative and worldly. I liked her immediately.

"Let's go for a drink at the Aidingbao Pub," she said. "It's just down the street."

"How did you learn to speak English so well?" I asked.

"The Germans taught me."

There was little Scottish about the Aidingbao (Edinburgh) Pub. Tucked in an alleyway, the bar was festooned with pendants in German yellow, red and black, and a massive German flag hung on the wall. Bing grabbed two bottles of Snow beer from behind the bar. Within a few minutes, twenty burly German engineers, plus a Dutchman, Englishman and Croat, stormed in. They were followed by two pretty Indonesian girls and a Chinese woman named

Miss Liu. The bar filled with the din of grating German chatter, clinking glasses and loud rock music.

"My friends in Shanghai warned me not to come here," said Miss Liu, who had just arrived after a thirty-four-hour train ride. "There are men with knives." A reference, no doubt, to Gansu's Muslims.

In her early forties, with a wild perm and caked in cosmetics, Miss Liu hung off the arm of Rolf, a barrel-chested engineer with Düsseldorf-based SMS *Demag*. The company, he explained, is modernizing the Jiuquan Iron and Steel Co. mill with new machinery to produce high quality steel coils and thin metal sheets. Production was set to soar, but officials had run into a snag. "There are occasional blackouts in nearby villages," Rolf explained. JISCO, which supplies power to Jiayuguan prefecture, was now doubling the number of coal-fired power plants. "China is growing too big, too fast," he said. "It can't be sustained."

The engineers were mostly pot-bellied, middle-aged men far from home on tours of duty in China's impoverished hinterlands. "Some of the Germans have whores and some marry them too," a twenty-three-year-old apprentice told me. He had a shaggy, Britpop haircut and had grown up in East Germany. Miss Liu saw us chatting at the bar. She slithered toward us.

"You look wealthy," she said, caressing the silk scarf that I had bought in Khotan.

"Looks are deceiving," I said.

"You're very handsome," she gushed, brushing an unruly curl from my bangs.

"Oh, that's okay," I said, politely pushing her hand away.

"No, no," she insisted. "I used to be a hairdresser. Let me do this."

I glanced nervously in Rolf's direction, hoping that the thickset engineer wasn't watching her brash advances. Miss Liu wasn't a treasure worth fighting over, so I slipped out of the pub before trouble could brew. Besides, it was already past 2 AM. Bing followed me outside and flagged down a taxi to take me to my hotel. "I'll see you tomorrow," she said. "I'll help you find those strange people who live in the desert."

A CENTURY AGO, the Germans had already made inroads into Gansu province. About twenty kilometres from Jiayuguan, in the town of Jiuquan (then called Suzhou), Mannerheim heard that German engineers were building an iron bridge in Gansu's provincial capital and running a modern textile mill there too. European goods were relatively plentiful in Jiuquan's shops, and two Belgians, a chemist and a foreman, were helping the Chinese set up enterprises there. The Baron also met a young Roman Catholic missionary, a Dutchman named Jozef Essens, who helped him enormously with advice and information. "It gave me great pleasure to meet a European again after three months of solitude," he wrote.

After a week in Jiuquan, Mannerheim ventured fifty kilometres north to Jinta. It was, he wrote, "one of the most northerly outposts of Chinese civilization, in the sand and gravel ocean of the Gobi Desert."[6] His Chinese cart driver showed up hours late on the morning of their departure. Furious, the Baron snapped and turned violent. "In the heat of the moment," he wrote, "I gave a thrashing to the wrong driver, an injustice that I tried to make good by giving the man 1 liang. The example frightened the culprit, however, and he did his utmost to make himself useful." One horrified spectator may have been the mandarin who drew up Mannerheim's travel permit to Jinta. The official added two strokes to the first character in his Chinese surname. The new character (傌) is also pronounced *ma* but with a falling tone. Its meaning changed from "horse" to, in Mannerheim's words, "a term for abuse." It may have been a subtle warning to other officials about this hot-headed foreigner.

A wintry day and a half of riding brought Mannerheim to Jinta. To his surprise, the son of a local mandarin spoke German. Zeng had lived in Germany and "had learnt a little German which he murdered unmercifully," Mannerheim wrote. The young man was "tall, thin, with deep-set eyes and hollow cheeks," and was "a strong supporter of European reforms in China and vehemently attacked the old system without the slightest respect for princes or other great people in the Empire." In a few years, the embittered young man added, the entire imperial system would collapse. Corrupt officials, especially those in Xinjiang, would be wiped away. "His cheeks glowed, his eyes shone and with an elegant gesture he indicated each one that would, in his opinion, be executed." Zeng dreamed of becoming viceroy of Xinjiang himself and believed Western technology would help to restore China's lost glory. "China should be run by the Chinese," he told Mannerheim, "but Chinese with a western education." Mannerheim was "pleasantly surprised" by his new German-speaking friend. "He was a wholly unexpected phenomenon to me," the Baron wrote, "a son of that new China whose doings were being followed with rapt attention by the powers of the Old World, particularly Russia." They parted "like old friends."

After a day's ride south, over a landscape of sand, gravel ridges and salt flats, Mannerheim arrived at homes scattered outside a village called Mazhuangzi, meaning "horse hamlet." He dismounted to get a closer view of three hardy women busily working in a yard. "They wore a strange costume such as I had never seen before," he wrote. The women turned out to be Huanghu, or "Yellow Barbarians," as he called them.

At the time, Western science knew almost nothing about these people, known nowadays as Yugurs. In 1893, Russian explorer Grigory Nikoleyaevich Potanin published a small glossary of Yugur words, along with notes on their administration and geographical situation. Mannerheim would be the first to conduct a detailed ethnographic investigation of the Yugur, drawing on nothing more than two methodological textbooks—*Notes and Queries on Anthropology* by Francis Galton and *Hints to Travellers* by E.A. Reeves—to guide him in his research. In 1911, he published his findings in an article for the Finno-Ugrian Society.[7] "[I]t is without the least claim to authority," he wrote, "that I present this very unpretentious material to the kind consideration of the reader."

Mannerheim offered the women gifts of mirrors and took their photographs. "[They] were fairly talkative at first," he wrote, "but as soon as I got out my pen and began to take notes, they changed as though by magic and became extremely reticent." He continued into Mazhuangzi, where he found forty homes, a small temple and an ancient Mongol ruin. The monks were absent, so his caravan settled into one of their cleanest houses. "When the lamas returned," he wrote, "they accorded me rather a cool reception at first, but they soon grew hospitable and talkative."

They called themselves "Sarö Yögurs" or Yellow Yugurs. "They did not know of a written Yögur language," he wrote, "nor could they tell me anything of their past history, princes, wars, etc." They appeared to be a blended race. They spoke a Turkic dialect closely related to Kyrgyz, Mannerheim noted, but were followers of Tibetan Buddhism, not Islam. Their meagre houses and clothing looked Chinese, but some Yugur men wore Mongolian fur caps. They also drank Mongolian-styled tea with roasted wheaten flour, salt, butter and cream.

"Altogether the people gave an impression of being dejected and readily complained of their money troubles," he wrote. The richest had no more than seven horses, ten cows and a hundred sheep. They ate mostly flour, various cereals and little meat. He noted some Yugurs with prominent cheekbones and others with "an oval shaped face." Most were short and broad, and some women had thick "potato" noses. Unfortunately, he made no anthropological measurements in Mazhuangzi. "I was on this occasion without my craniometer—which always had the effect of depriving even the boldest among them of all courage," he wrote.[8] He took notes on their customs and colourful costumes, including the women's "very peculiar" hats and plait pendants hung "with a couple of silver ornaments and thickly embroidered with small pieces of coral, glass beads or stones in various shades of violet."[9]

More peculiar to Mannerheim were the men, whom he found at home knitting stockings and weaving baskets. These were, he scoffed, "hardly to be called masculine occupations."[10] The women, by contrast, worked outdoors herding cattle and fetching water. "It seemed to me that there was a great lack of energy and one was surprised at the want of manliness, especially among the young men," he wrote in his article. "There is no kind of sport, no races, no wrestling, even none of the games on horseback which are so usual in Central Asia."[11]

After a few days, he left Mazhuangzi for another Yugur tribe living in a southern mountain range that forms the outer edges of the Tibetan Plateau. His Yugur host, a lama named Kua, acted as an escort and "rode a small pony which more resembled a rat than a horse." It trotted quickly, even outpacing Philip. Kua frequently asked for Mannerheim's matches, and then would dismount to light a small fire to warm his hands.

"I am sure any of the Yögur women would have shown more power of endurance than this young man of twenty-eight," the Baron wrote, "and at the moment of parting with him, it appeared clearer than ever to me that this little, lost, Turkish tribe, living at the foot of the Nanshan mountains, with its stocking-knitting men, void of all energy and manliness, was on its way to certain annihilation."[12]

BING AND I bought several provincial and prefecture maps and studied them intensely in my hotel room. Bing read aloud the Chinese characters of various villages and I compared them to the list of places Mannerheim visited. We could not find Mazhuangzi anywhere. Marti Roos, a Dutch linguist who studied the Yugur language, had set up a website that provided a list of Yugur villages. Unfortunately, only one of those names appeared on our many maps. Huangnibao lies twenty kilometres outside Jiuquan. Perhaps someone there could point me to Mazhuangzi.

Bing hired a car driven by a Chinese man and his nagging wife. We set off on Route 312, China's "mother road" that ends in Shanghai. A few kilometres outside Jiuquan, we turned north onto a gravel country road. For the next hour, we wandered aimlessly through the countryside. The stench of manure and onions hung in the hot air. Bing smoked cigarettes and listened to Santana on her MP3 player. I listened to the squabbling couple.

"Let's look at the map," the husband said in Chinese.

"Forget the map," snapped the wife. "You don't understand the map. It's better that we ask people for directions."

We eventually came to one of the hamlet's few paved streets. We stopped along a block of a dozen new Chinese-style homes clad in white tile. Each had a flowerbed overflowing in lavender, red and pink. About 150 families lived in the immediate vicinity, farming corn, squash, onion and sunflowers. An old woman came out to greet us.

Tian Guifeng identified herself as a Yugur and said her family had been living in Huangnibao for about three hundred years. I asked about the Yugurs' history and language.

"The young people haven't a clue about history and most of the elders are in their eighties with poor memories," she said. "I don't know anything about history and nobody in the village can speak Yugur either."

A half-dozen women and girls gathered. A seventy-two-year-old man also wandered over. He said there was a Buddhist temple in Lianhua, a village fifty kilometres away, where people speak Yugur.

"What about a place called Mazhuangzi?" I asked.

"Never heard of it."

That evening, back in Jiayuguan, Bing and I went to an Internet café to do more research. Marti Roos, the linguist, had replied to my email. He informed us that Mazhuangzi was "in Lianhua Township in Minghua District, [but] not on any map." Luckily, we found Minghua on one of our local maps. The road leading to the Yugur village, out in the desert, appeared to be a dead end.

BING, UNFORTUNATELY, could not accompany me to Lianhua. She had just started a new job at a tourism agency. Instead, she introduced me late one night to a thirty-one-year-old bar owner and musician named Mel. He spoke English and had travelled China for six years playing guitar. He loved jazz and opened the only bar with live music in his hometown of Jiayuguan. Our driver was the obnoxious wife from the previous day.

We followed the map, driving east on Route 312 for forty kilometres and then turning north on a country road shrouded by poplars. We passed clay ruins, farmhouses and Han Chinese in rattan hats driving donkeys with ploughs. The pavement soon disintegrated into gravel and the farmland too disappeared. We were venturing into a desert plain with tuffs of reeds and scraggily shrubs. Here and there, sheep dotted the bleak horizon.

A crew was rebuilding the road outside Lianhua. Dump trucks, a grader and a front-end loader kicked up a dust storm. The village too looked like a construction site. Workmen were erecting new power poles. One of two dirt streets was dug up to lay waterworks. And dozens of new homes, built with plaster and brick by Hui workers, were under construction. The village government was housed in three low buildings arranged in a horseshoe. Here, we found a one-room school, offices for family planning and the village leader.

"I feel like time has turned back twenty years," Mel said as we got out of the car caked in dust.

The village leader's office had a wooden desk, two chairs and four illustrated Communist Party posters on the wall. "I haven't seen that picture of Mao in years. Cool!" Mel said, pulling out his digital camera. The poster depicted Mao in a long greyish blue overcoat surrounded by pink flowers and futuristic skyscrapers in the background. Thirty years after Mao's death, Lianhua was finally taking its own Great Leap Forward.

The leader wasn't around, but his young female cook, Maerjian, agreed to introduce us to a village elder. We found Khan Zhouchit down the street in a back courtyard. In her seventies, Khan had thin, pursed lips and the prominent, rosy cheekbones of a Kyrgyz. Like rivulets cut into loess, deep wrinkles carved her face. She wore a brown Chinese jacket, a chunky stainless steel watch, silver bracelets and amber earrings. Her thick, muscular hands reminded me of Mannerheim's description of hardy Yugur women. We sat in her dim hovel to chat. The two-room house had cracked clay walls, a woven reed roof, a bed in the corner, a small yellow wooden table, two chairs, a few stools and a clay fireplace. "A very old house," Mel said.

Khan was born in the village and said she had never left. I showed her Mannerheim's photograph of an old Buddhist temple's interior festooned in banners and *thangka* artwork. Lianhua means "lotus flower" in Chinese, which was probably the name of the village temple. She held Mannerheim's article in her hands, squinting at the grainy photocopy.

"I remember this temple," she said. "It was torn down in 1958 by Maoists." A new temple was later erected in another Yugur village, twenty kilometres east. She goes to pray there three times a year. "A lot has changed," she said. "The youngsters no longer pray at the Buddhist temple."

In the past, she explained, the Chinese were farmers and Yugurs were herders. But in 1958, under forced collectivization during the Great Leap Forward, each Yugur family was granted twenty *mou* (1.3 hectares) of farmland. Some still grow corn, maize and cotton, but Yugurs are mostly shepherds. They also gather roots and wild grasses in the desert that are sold for Chinese medicine. "One root looks like a penis," Mel explained to me in an aside, "and is supposed to improve your sex drive."

"Life is changing," Khan went on. "Some young Yugur go to Jiuquan to sing and dance in Mongolian yurts making money entertaining Chinese. They are even eating chicken too [traditionally a taboo]. These Yugurs want to be like the Chinese."

The sturdy old woman rose out of her rickety chair, grabbed a butcher's cleaver and began chopping in vain at the lock on a yellow armoire. "I've lost the key," she explained. She then grabbed a pair of heavy steel scissors and pried the cabinet doors open, pulling out a package wrapped in turquoise cloth and several layers of tissue paper. Inside was a traditional Yugur costume.

"Yugur girls would usually marry at about fifteen years old," she explained, "and our parents would make us a wedding dress. We would wear it for our entire lives. I was married in 1949, but had to stop wearing my traditional clothes in 1958."

She pulled on the royal blue gown and tied it with a pink and red sash at the back. She hung two pendants around her neck and down the front of the gown. These were thickly embroidered with red, white, yellow and green beads, forged silver ornaments and tassels. She topped the outfit with a white, cone-shaped felt hat covered in red tassels. Maerjian also attached a long pendant made of bone buttons to the back of her hat. It hung down to her feet. The outfit looked exactly like those described by Mannerheim.

"I made the dress last year with the help of some old photographs," she said, smiling radiantly. "It's just like a dress from a hundred years ago."

"Why did you decide to make the dress after all these years?" I asked.

"I don't want Yugur traditions to die," she said.

That was only partly true. "The old lady told me that the reason she made the dress is so that when she dies she can be buried in it," Maerjian told me after we left. Indeed, Mannerheim noted how Yugur women wore their traditional plait pendants and embroidered clothing every day of their lives and beyond. "Even in the grave," he wrote, "it is not all removed."[13]

MANNERHEIM'S CARAVAN must have looked motley: a Finnish nobleman, Uyghur cook, teenaged Chinese interpreter and Russian Cossack. He was also now accompanied by the Yugur lama Kua. They were on their way to Ganzhou through the Hexi Corridor's arid, dusty plain. Mannerheim had heard of another Yugur tribe living in the Nan Shan, or "southern mountains," a rugged chain that forms the border between the provinces of Qinghai and Gansu. These Yugurs apparently spoke a Mongol dialect, not Turkic. They were called "Shera," or "Eastern" Yugurs. (The Sarö Yögurs are nowadays referred to as Western Yugurs.) Intrigued, Mannerheim stopped briefly in Ganzhou, where he provisioned his caravan, then saddled up for an alpine expedition.

About thirty kilometres from Ganzhou, they arrived at the mouth of the Da He (Big River) gorge. They zigzagged across a frozen riverbed all day (it was December 27), heading into the mountain range. They saw Han Chinese driving donkey caravans of logs from the forested valleys.[14] The gorge grew narrower and steeper. They finally reached a fork in the river and took the southern tributary. Mannerheim spotted the bulbous form of a Buddhist stupa up the valley. As he approached, a monastery came into view. It stood on the lower slopes of some small hills, "a mass of buildings out of which rose a large, massive temple in red and brown and grey and white, with the usual gilded Buddha roof-decorations."[15] He had arrived at Kanglesi.

In size and style, the temple reminded Mannerheim of the Kalmyk monastery in Mongolküre, "but the details showed signs of Tibetan influence." The central temple hall, two storeys high, was draped in banners of bright colours and Buddha designs. Cupboards for Buddhist texts written in Tibetan covered the sidewalls. A colonnade of wooden pillars led to an altar, behind which stood a one-metre bronze statue of the Buddha wrapped in red cloth. The temple was filled with statues, paintings, Buddhist icons, scarlet mantles and high-combed headdresses. On the hillside immediately above stood tombs and stone cairns in memory of highly respected lamas. The *gegen,* or "living Buddha," of the monastery was still a child and resided in a village three days' ride to the south. Fifteen lamas worshipped at the temple.

"Several of the lamas... disappeared as soon as they saw me produce my craniometer," Mannerheim wrote, "and no gifts of knives, mirrors and so forth to those who were brave enough to face the peril of being measured, would tempt them to cross the threshold of my room." Despite the "great difficulty," Mannerheim ultimately convinced a dozen Yugurs to be measured.

Their *toumu,* a hereditary governor, agreed to be his guide. Mannerheim visited his residence, a day's ride south across forest-covered heights and snow-capped peaks. Renchen Norbu's "princely dwelling," a large wooden house, lay at the bottom of a forked ravine. From here, the Yugurs' administrative leader dispensed justice, levied taxes and managed the tent settlements in the district. Norbu complained "of the arbitrariness and extortion of the Chinese officials," and in particular how one mandarin recently redirected the royalties from a local coal mine to his own pocket.[16]

Mannerheim prodded Norbu about his people's origins, to little effect. "It is a strange fact," Mannerheim wrote, "that this little mountain tribe who not only consider themselves, but, without doubt, are, Mongolian, say that in spite of the difference of language they belong to the same tribe as the Sarö Yögurs."[17] While they spoke a Mongolic dialect—Mannerheim recorded some 250 words in Eastern Yugur—and adopted some Mongolian songs, they lived in canvas tents, not Mongolian yurts. Mannerheim, in fact, recorded a tremendous volume of ethnographic information on their burial rites (similar to Tibetan Buddhists'), births, marriage customs, hygiene and culture. The material was later published in his seventy-seven-page article. He thought the Yugurs were "much sharper" in intelligence than Mongolians and Tibetans, and were "very fond of jokes." He took more than three dozen photographs—of people, animals, dwellings and temples—and collected as many objects:

caps, embroidered garments, a saddlebag, trousers and so on. He also noted their decorative hats, which women wore "coquettishly" to one side.[18]

It was, he wrote, "almost with feelings of regret" that he left Norbu's residence after four days. He knew that he'd never return. The future of this mysterious Mongol tribe looked bleak. "Their numbers have been reduced both by amalgamating with the Chinese element," he wrote, "and by dying off."

I LEFT JIUQUAN on the evening train, heading 230 kilometres to Ganzhou (now Zhangye) to organize a sojourn to the mountainous home of the Eastern Yugurs. At 9 PM I stepped off the train to the waiting smile of Steven, a university student clad in a sharp blue suit and tie. He had spiky hair, glasses and crooked, stained teeth. Through a contact in Jiayuguan, I had arranged for him to be my translator and guide.

"Water is a big problem here," Steven said as we drove in a hired taxi across the parched plain toward the mountains the next morning. Throughout the rail journey to Zhangye, I had seen a low-lying mountain range to the north that acted as a breakwater holding back an ocean of sand. In one spot, the Gobi had spilled over the rocky ridge into the gravel plain of the Hexi Corridor. Every year, little by little, the desert creeps in on the region's meagre farmland. "Farmers are constantly fighting against drought. The land here is largely desert."

Thirty kilometres from Zhangye, we came to the mouth of a dramatic gorge. Crimson-coloured outcrops licked at a clear blue sky. For a hundred kilometres, the taxi wound its way along the Liyuan River. At a bulge in the river gorge, deep in the mountains, sits Hongwansi. The capital of the Sunan Yugur Autonomous County is a case study in ethnic kitsch. On the way into town, we passed two roadside pagodas in the shape of Yugur women's hats. The compact town, population seven thousand, consists of dreary mid-rise buildings accented with Yugur architectural flourishes: bright pink, red, orange and turquoise colours, polka-dot trim that echoes the bone buttons on Yugur pendants and several roofs shaped like Yugur hats. Large billboards also depicted smiling Yugurs donning their garish ethnic garb.

At the foot of a cliff, hidden behind the Soviet-styled municipal building, we found the Yugur National Minority Cultural Institute. Inside, four researchers were busily preserving the remnants of Yugur culture for posterity. They sat at large wooden desks cataloguing personal narratives, oral histories, folklore and songs, and constructing an Eastern Yugur dictionary.

Timur, the director, wore glasses, a thin moustache and long scraggy hair. I began to explain to him what I was doing.

"Mannerheim!" he blurted out.

"Yes, Mannerheim!" I repeated with excitement. "I'm following in the footsteps of Mannerheim."

He gave me a recent copy of *Yugur Culture* magazine in which Mannerheim's article had been translated into Chinese. He then pulled out a thick encyclopedia of Yugur culture and history written in Chinese. Over the years, a small group of scholars has pieced together the puzzling history of the Yugur. The official Chinese version identifies the Yugurs as descendents of ancient Uyghurs who controlled a vast empire in what is now Mongolia. In AD 840, these Uyghur were driven from their homeland by a tribe known as the Yenisei Kirghiz. One diaspora settled in the Hexi Corridor and became known as Yellow Uyghurs. After the Mongol invasion in 1227, their population declined and scattered. At this time as well, some Yellow Uyghurs in the mountains south of Zhangye abandoned their native Turkic dialect for Mongolic, splitting the tribe into two distinct linguistic groups. Over the course of the next seven hundred years, the Yellow Uyghurs absorbed traits from neighbouring ethnic groups, evolving into modern Yugurs.

Yet even today, nobody is exactly sure of the Yugurs' ancestry. Linguists such as Juha Janhunen at Helsinki University and Marti Roos have linked the Yugurs' Turkic dialect to the conquering Yenisei Kirghiz, not to the ancient Uyghur who are allegedly their ancestors.

In 2003, Janhunen toured Sunan county collecting saliva samples from Yugurs to determine their genetic ancestry. Analysis has yet to be done, but it may someday conclusively clarify whether the Yugur are descended from the ancient Uyghur, Yenisei Kirghiz, Mongols or other ancient tribes.

Nowadays, the Chinese have stopped referring to Yugurs as Uyghurs (Weiwu'er in Mandarin). The government calls them Yugu: *yu* (裕) means "abundant" and *gu* (固) means "strong," but the Yugur appear to be neither. Officially, there are only 13,719 Yugurs in China—about 0.00001 percent of the population. They are one of the country's smallest ethnic minorities. Some 4,600 speak the Mongolic dialect and 2,800 Turkic. The others have lost their mother tongue and speak only Chinese.

"Most of the language has been preserved, but over the years it has been influenced by Tibetan and Chinese," Timur said. "The trend is that the culture will disappear."

"Disappear?" I said.

"It's difficult to say," he amended. "Maybe it will disappear, but it could be preserved in remote villages where it is not affected by economic development and influenced by other languages."

"During the period after 1958, the traditional culture of the Yugur almost disappeared," added An Yubing, the deputy director who goes by his Chinese name. "But since the introduction of the openness policy, the Yugur have gradually brought back many of their traditions. Of course, some cultural traditions have changed."

"What's changed?" I asked.

"I can't tell you exactly what has changed because there is no historical database or records of the culture," he explained. "There's only oral traditions. Many people were too afraid to talk about the loss of their culture because of the government. Compared with the past, Yugur culture has changed. It's a new culture: a bit of the old, a bit of the new."

The lack of a documented history has made Mannerheim's investigation particularly important in Yugurology. "Mannerheim's diary could help us bring back old customs which we can't see now in our daily lives," added Sarangua, a young researcher. "The ultimate purpose is to preserve our own Yugur culture. Mannerheim came to this place before the abolition of the culture. His diary reflects the original culture and other aspects of Yugur lifestyle. The overall value of the diary is quite considerable."

Following Timur's directions, we drove back down the river gorge and turned off onto a gravel road in search of a Yugur village that Mannerheim had visited. The road followed a narrow, barren ravine that gradually climbed to alpine pastures. A large Buddhist stupa with a golden crown appeared on a crest. Two Yugur men were whitewashing its bulbous top. From here, I peered at a stunning view of forested slopes and craggy peaks. A wicked road with hairpin turns and no guardrail led down into the Da He valley. We drove along a tributary into a side valley, following Mannerheim's route. We passed a few earthen houses and parked in front of a small Buddhist temple at the base of a hill. We had reached Kanglesi, the Peaceful Happy Temple.

A motorcycle roared up, and a withered old man, decked head to toe in army fatigues, climbed off. He was stooped and mangy with long dirty fingernails. His smile revealed only two teeth dangling from pink gums. His face was gaunt. He looked like Gollum from *The Lord of the Rings*. He held a jumble of keys knotted together with twine and strips of cloth. Limping, the ancient gatekeeper unlocked a series of iron gates and wooden doors that led to the temple. He opened three more locks and swung the temple's heavy doors inlaid with precious stones and painted gold and red. Sunshine streamed into the dark hall festooned in colourful silk banners and murals. The back wall contained a glass showcase with two golden Buddha statues and a black-and-white photograph of the former *gegen*.

"The head lama died in 1957," said Jalashjap, the gatekeeper. "The next year Kanglesi's three hundred Buddhist worshippers were arrested and the temple and its sacred texts written in Tibetan were destroyed. Gone with the wind."

"Who destroyed the temple?" I asked.

"Those who have no faith," he replied. "The worshippers of Mao Zedong's scientific theory destroyed the temple. It was an army officer sent by order of the central government."

In 1998, local Yugurs began Kanglesi's reconstruction. It took five years. "I was very glad to see the temple rebuilt and for the government to bring in its new policy of openness," he said. A twenty-two-year-old *akha*, a "knowledgeable worshipper," ran the temple for a few years then left. There were now no living Buddhas or even lamas left. "The temple is exactly the same, except that we did not rebuild the eight stupas around the temple. We didn't have enough money," he said.

"What do the people do here to earn money?" I asked.

"We can do nothing but raise sheep," he said.

"Is life getting better?"

"Compared to the past, our lives are greatly improved," he said. "But compared to life in the city, our lives can be improved a lot more." The gravel road has increased contact with the outside world. A new cellular telecom tower, recently installed next to the mountaintop stupa, was also revolutionizing life in the Big River Valley.

It was getting late, so Steven and I returned to Hongwansi. We stayed in a dank hotel with the ambience of an insane asylum. The echoing, concrete halls reeked of urine. We rose early. The town was bathed in a blue light, the air moist and cool. We found elderly Chinese, Tibetans and Yugurs practising tai chi in a picturesque square overlooking the river. Music blared from loudspeakers. After

Steven made inquiries, a Yugur man agreed to take us to the home of a friend who might answer a few questions.

Yuerjis, age twenty-nine, and her mother, Zaximso, sixty-six, greeted me with curious stares. They lived in a two-room house hidden behind a walled courtyard. A pink curtain was draped over its doorway. The main room had two beds, a dresser, washbasin, makeup stand and iron stove. A small window and bare light bulb faintly illuminated the dreary interior. The ceiling was plastered with old newspapers and flies buzzed about.

"Yugur culture is stronger today than in the past, but many young people are moving away from their villages. They are losing their culture," said Zaximso, who came to Hongwansi three years ago to help take care of her nine-year-old grandson.

"We are worried about this trend," her daughter added. "There are some young Yugurs working in Shanghai and Shenzhen and they are losing their Yugur national consciousness." One of her own sisters, in fact, worked in Beijing.

Yuerjis put a lump of coal in the stove, and made me some milky tea with butter and roasted wheat—Mongolian-style, as Mannerheim was served. I stirred the brown bits in the murky bowl and cracked dried bread into the tea. I fished for the soggy bits with chopsticks.

"Of course," the grandmother went on, "in the future there will be more and more people going to the outside world." Yugurs have lived, she admitted, an insular existence. "We are very afraid to eat shrimp," she said, citing just one example, "because we've never seen that type of creature before."

Traditionally, Yugurs were herders, but many now work for the government or at the smelter, owned by Han Chinese, at the entrance to town. The mountains are rich in coal, copper and iron. "We get along well with the Chinese in our daily lives," the grandmother said.

"We can even get married to each other," said the daughter. "Many Yugur marry Chinese."

"What about your language?" I asked. "Don't the kids in these families speak Chinese instead of Yugur?"

"It's a great pity that the children don't speak Yugur," the daughter said.

As it turned out, Yuerjis had recently separated from her Han Chinese husband. Her son only knew about 20 percent of the words in the Yugur language, but Grandmother Zaximso was teaching him more. It's difficult to teach Yugur, Yuerjis explained, especially since kids start learning English in grade 3 and Mandarin even younger.

"The Yugur have preserved their language so well because they have lived in isolated areas," He Weiyuan, a Yugur professor at the Northwest University for Nationalities in Lanzhou, later explained to me. "Nowadays, especially after the policy of reform and opening up, Yugur living standards have gone up, but the population speaking the Yugur language has declined. After Yugur nomads move to the towns, they seldom speak their native language." Most Yugur speakers are thirty or older. "My kid is too busy studying English to learn Yugur," He said.

In 2003, while touring Sunan for genetic samples, Juha Janhunen found an environment that "favours a rapid decline" of the Yugur language. Past repression, Han Chinese migration and the decline of nomadism have weakened the roots of the Yugur language. "Those Yughur who have been unwilling or unable to assimilate to the Chinese society have become victims of impoverishment and alcoholization," Janhunen wrote. His article was published in the *Journal of the Finno-Ugrian Society*, which had also published the Baron's article in 1911. And like Mannerheim, Janhunen isn't optimistic about the Yugurs' future. The language's only hope of survival is preschool and parental education. Yet Janhunen discovered a tragic irony among the Yugur: the first to abandon their ethnic language "are the relatively well-educated activists themselves."[19]

THE RAILWAY SOUTH of Zhangye skirted several sections of the Great Wall. It was a pathetic sight: eroded clay ramparts and stumpy watchtowers, nothing like the iconic brick fortification that tourists climb in the mountains north of Beijing. "There is nothing to indicate that, even in the imagination of the Chinese, it could serve as an actual defence of the realm," Mannerheim wrote.

Trekking through the Hexi Corridor, the Baron constantly came across Han Chinese settlements and young soldiers walking alone or in pairs along the wall. "Moving slowly to the west along the slope of the Nanshan Mountains the Chinese little by little have inhabited all cultural oases in that direction up to Dunhuang forcing out all other tribes," Mannerheim wrote in his military report. "Though they had to undertake a difficult struggle with harsh natural conditions and a lack of water, the borders of oases [and the Chinese Empire] have been expanded."[20]

Nowadays, the Great Wall symbolizes the glory, and for some even the superiority, of Chinese civilization—"One of the greatest cultural and architectural miracles in the history of world civilization," as described by an exhibit panel at the Jiayuguan museum. Yet the wall also casts a long, dark shadow, particularly over the Yugur and other ethnic minorities whose cultural fates look grim in the face of Chinese domination.

The train from Zhangye to Lanzhou followed the wall's ancient remnants for three hundred kilometres. As I watched the relic roll by and reflected on my visit among the Yugurs, I was reminded of a strange short story written by Franz Kafka titled "The Great Wall of China." An anonymous official who oversees the construction of a small section narrates the story. He describes building techniques and speculates about the mysterious motives for its monumental construction. He mentions an ancient scholar who believed the wall was built to unite humanity. The Great Wall certainly helped the Chinese conquer ethnic borderlands and ultimately unite many disparate races—Uyghur, Mongol, Yugur, Hui, Tibetan, Manchu—under a lingua franca: Mandarin. Indeed, the old scholar claimed, wrote Kafka, that the Great Wall "would create, for the first time in the history of mankind, a secure foundation for a new Tower of Babel."[21]

LANZHOU

The Chinese Renaissance

China is not poor in resources but poor in men of ability,
not weak in troops but weak in will.—VICEROY
ZHANG ZHIDONG, *Memorial on Education Reform* (1901)[1]

A THIN FOG HAD settled over the Yellow River. The train crept cautiously above the serpentine riverbank. Through the mist, I could make out picturesque fields and orchards tucked between terraced mountains and the churning river. The scene looked timeless, idyllic, like a classical Chinese watercolour. The train then plunged into a pitch-black tunnel and a few minutes later popped out into the horrific haze of another world.

We crawled through a canyon of dilapidated workers' apartment blocks, industrial mills, factories and belching smokestacks. Garbage thrown from balconies choked narrow ravines. Leaden clouds released an acidic brew that streamed down the train's window. It was a sad sight, but not unexpected. I had arrived in Lanzhou, the capital of Gansu province, and reportedly one of the world's most polluted cities.

A "thick mist" had greeted Mannerheim too. That fog rose not from oil refineries, auto exhaust, plastics factories and petrochemical plants, but from fields of melting snow that had fallen the night before. A century ago, Lanzhou was still an archaic outpost whose fortified clay walls ran for two kilometres along the Yellow River. It lay pinched at a narrow spot in the dramatic river gorge, surrounded by mountaintop temples, terraced farmland and fruit groves. Towering pagodas poking above crenellated walls marked its "mighty gates." Inside the fortress town, streets recently paved in cobblestone were the only sign of modernity.

Today, a dense mass of office towers and residential condos rests on the fortress's ruins. Lanzhou's population is 3 million. Sprawling suburbs, concrete roadways and a vast industrial zone—home to one of the largest oil refineries in China—spread along the river for forty kilometres, smothering all signs of nature and any vestiges of the past.

ZHAO, MANNERHEIM'S Chinese interpreter, arranged his accommodation in a dark "hovel" inside the fortress. As they unpacked, Father Leon van Dijk, a Belgian Catholic missionary, called on the Baron. The father was appalled at the filthy quarters and insisted that the Baron and his men move to a caravanserai in the European quarter just outside the wall.

His entire caravan soon fell ill. Mannerheim himself had a fever and pain in his right lung and legs, and suffered a "terrible headache." He stayed in bed listening to the "rumble of drums, the clash of cymbals and banging of percussion caps" during the Chinese New Year festival. Influenza plagued one of the missionaries too; after his fever broke, the priest declared that he had died and come back to life. Mannerheim would have none of it. "I cannot imagine how such a strange idea is to be got out of the head of a Catholic, who believes in miracles," he wrote.

A fortnight passed before the Baron was well enough to call on Sheng Yun, the viceroy of Gansu.[2] Sheng was scarcely fifty years old, and had served as a diplomat in St. Petersburg and as the governor of Xi'an, "where he enjoyed a good reputation." An ethnic Manchu, Sheng was "rather a stout man with the swaying waddle that the Chinese covet so much," the Baron wrote. Sheng resided in a spacious *yamen*, its walls decorated with Chinese scrolls and ink drawings. He and Mannerheim sat on stiff chairs around a low table for tea.

Although Sheng wasn't exactly "pro-European," he did employ several Europeans as technical advisers who helped to reform the three vast provinces of Gansu, Qinghai and Xinjiang under his jurisdiction. "To anyone coming, as I did, from the west," the Baron wrote, "Lanchow is of interest at present for the reason that the reforms planned in [Xinjiang] were introduced here 2 or 3 years ago and it is possible to observe not only the manner in which they are being carried out, but also their extent and success."

The "cut and dried" program of reform, Mannerheim explained, had been mandated by Peking, but its execution depended on the viceroy. "Should any of his undertakings miscarry, he may be sure that willing tongues will lose no time in reporting the matter to headquarters," the Baron wrote. The viceroy had "to wage an incessant war with slander and intrigues at court. His every step is watched by spies and in order to cope with them he is forced to keep an eye on proceedings in Peking by means of his own spies."

Besides corrupt, incompetent and backstabbing lower officials, the viceroy also contended with popular resistance to his reforms. He had proposed to build an aqueduct from the Yellow River into the fortress, but some three hundred Sichuan water carriers, worried about losing their jobs, threatened unrest. "A single riot," Mannerheim wrote, "is enough to ensure [the viceroy's] removal and ruin his future career."

The viceroy's plan was to develop mines and industry that would, in turn, help finance the construction of the railroad from Central China. Sheng figured it would take twenty years for the railway to reach Lanzhou. (The first train actually arrived in 1952.)

He also brought officers and NCOs from Zhili and Hubei provinces, whose armies had been reorganized on European lines. But in Lanzhou, target practice was neglected, training was poor and modern weapons were lacking. The all-powerful Yuan Shikai, a viceroy and trusted adviser of the Empress Dowager, accused Sheng of neglecting military reform. "On closer examination," the Baron noted, "you really come to the same conclusion as Yüan Shih-k'ai, that very little attention has been devoted to the military sphere."

Mannerheim saw the most tangible progress in education reform, which dated to the Self-Strengthening Movement of the 1860s. After the Second Opium War, the Great Powers forcibly opened China to further trade, concessions and foreign evangelism. In response, a cadre of progressive provincial officials—Li Hongzhang, Zeng Guoquan, Zou Zongtang and Zhang Zhidong—built modern shipyards, armaments factories and new military and technical schools to strengthen the Empire. Protestant missionaries also founded schools and colleges teaching Western science and foreign languages in the treaty ports. In 1872, Li and Zeng sent the first thirty Chinese abroad to study in the United States,[3] and in 1893 Zhang opened the first Self-Strengthening School in Hubei province.[4] Yet, overall, reform was piecemeal and never fully embraced by the Manchu Court in Peking. It would take China's humiliating defeat at the hands of the Japanese in 1895 to galvanize support for systematic reform.

In 1898, Kang Youwei, a scholar-adviser, called on the young Emperor Guangxu to introduce exhaustive reforms, modelled on those of Japan, throughout every sphere of Chinese society. Feeling their power threatened, hard-line conservatives in the Manchu court orchestrated a coup d'état to reinstate the Empress Dowager Cixi, who had effectively retired. The young Emperor was put under house arrest and his "Hundred Days of Reform" stalled. It would take yet another foreign invasion—this time to crush the Boxer Rebellion in 1900—to demonstrably show Peking's utter impotence and to dispel any remaining doubts about the need for reform. The Empress Dowager soon began to introduce the very reforms she had originally rejected.

A towering figure with a keen intellect, Zhang Zhidong advocated extensive but moderate reform that appealed to the Empress. He outlined his vision in a memorial—later translated as *China's Only Hope: An Appeal*—that focused largely on education. "The fate of China depends upon the literati alone," he wrote.[5] The entire Chinese school system was geared to training students to take the Imperial civil service examination. Graduates could write stilted verse and recite the sages, but not much else. Zhang urged the teaching of Western sciences, government, history and foreign languages, but on the bedrock of traditional Confucian ethics and Chinese culture. He summarized his approach in a famous dictum: "Chinese learning for fundamental principles [*ti*] and Western learning for practical application [*yong*]."[6] It has become known as the *ti-yong* dichotomy.

In 1905, an edict abolished the Imperial exam after six hundred years and called for "the establishment of schools of modern learning throughout the Empire."[7] A new Ministry of Education in Peking began to oversee the transformation, which would be modelled on Japan's successful adoption of Western learning and would bring learning to 40 million boys and girls throughout the Empire. Mannerheim detailed the new education system in his Russian military report. High school curriculum included chemistry, botany, zoology, physiology, hygiene and mining. The study of Japanese was obligatory, while English and French were optional.

Mannerheim stayed in Lanzhou for a month and a half, touring the local schools and colleges with Father van Dijk. A "very curious industrial school" was located in the complex where the ancient civil service exam used to be held. Van Dijk taught French and another Belgian taught chemistry. The industrial school had silk and cotton weaving mills, a furnace for glass blowing, craftsmen making copper teapots and leather goods and a small vegetable garden for agricultural studies. The goods produced were of such bad quality, however, that officials deviously dispatched Japanese and Indian goods to Peking as samples from their school.

The new military school was more impressive, a very beautiful complex with large courtyards and tidy one-storey pavilions. Long wooden tables lined the dining hall, which was decorated with paintings from the Russo-Japanese War. "It is scarcely necessary to add that the feats of the Japanese are depicted in not too modest a manner," noted Mannerheim, a decorated veteran from that war. "In fact, Japanese propaganda [is] everywhere." Chinese instructors, who had recently returned from Japan, taught at the local academic colleges, and most textbooks also came from Japan. By 1906, some fifteen thousand Chinese were studying in Japan, which had become a sort of mecca for China's new intelligentsia.[8]

The changes were monumental: officials opened "thirty to forty thousand schools across the entire Empire within some two years," Mannerheim noted.[9] More than a million students were enrolled in these new Western-style schools, which were funded through provincial revenues, scholarships and tuition. Whatever the schools' shortcomings—a lack of teachers, poorly educated students, corrupt administrators, shoddy instruction, backward facilities—the Baron felt one "should be fair and give the government its due for its persistence, decisiveness and foresight."[10]

In 1907, Zhang Zhidong, seventy-one, was appointed Grand Councillor and Minister of Education. Mannerheim described him as "a zealous follower of new educational methods."[11] Others hailed him a genius for combining classical Chinese learning with Western technological know-how. Zhang was "a giant in intellect and a hero in achievement," gushed one American educator.[12]

However, the fine balance between old and new, between *ti* and *yong*, had begun to tip. A growing number of schools was dropping classical studies altogether. Zhang himself feared that he had unleashed forces that would undermine the ancient Confucian order and perhaps even Imperial rule.[13]

DR. YANG SHU, vice-president of Lanzhou University, invited me to stay at the university's International Guesthouse. Yang is the director of the Institute of Central Asian Studies and worked as a diplomat in Moscow during the dissolution of the Soviet Union. A widely quoted expert on terrorism and China's energy and security interests, Yang also translated a book on Mannerheim's expedition to China. He had missed the Urumqi gathering, but I read a paper he published in the symposium's handbook. Mannerheim's photography, geography surveys and extensive data collection were, Yang wrote, "unmatched by the Chinese of the time," because the country "was unable to carry out scientific investigations in the modern sense."[14] In Urumqi, I had emailed Yang, who replied immediately, saying he had booked me a room, had found me an interpreter and was looking forward to my arrival.

The campus looked like your typical Western university, with sports fields, leafy promenades and modern, albeit rundown, lecture halls and dormitories. Students carried rucksacks, wore track suits and even held hands. Young men in baggy clothes shot hoops in basketball courts. At the end of a quiet lane, I found the guesthouse. It was a new facility with a sky-lit atrium, clean rooms and a superb cafeteria. I arrived on a dull, wet evening. The verdant, tranquil campus was a welcome relief from the heat and dust I had experienced trekking the fringes of the Gobi Desert.

"You're lucky. The air is much cleaner after it rains," said Linda, a graduate student in human and economic geography, who would be my guide and translator. Originally from Sichuan province, Linda had taught herself English, and spoke the language with ease. That summer she had spent nearly two months in the United States working as a translator for twenty Chinese mayors who were studying American government. She was energetic, opinionated and not much over five feet tall. She picked me up the next morning for a walking tour of the city

Lanzhou's downtown is dense with tedious towers, shopping plazas and monolithic malls. New concrete skyscrapers were sprouting like bamboo shoots. "Most Chinese cities look the same," Linda sighed. "The government thinks that the high-rises are a symbol of modernization. It's a pity." I lamented how Old China—the whimsical Buddhist temples, Manchu fortresses, winged pagodas and *yamens* of yore—have all been replaced by a stultifying new urbanism. This two-millennia-old city had less built heritage than my hometown of Vancouver, founded in 1886. How could so much be razed so quickly? I wondered.

"From our perspective today," Linda explained, "people seemed so irrational back then. From 1958 to 1976"—the year of Mao's death—"China was in chaos."

A monument by the Yellow River illustrated just how utterly chaotic and irrational that period was. A six-metre-tall rusted iron column stood above the riverbank. It was one of four posts used to secure the Zhen Yuang Floating Bridge, originally built in the Ming Dynasty. Each year, floods would tear apart the bridge, which consisted of boats tethered to ropes strung across the river and anchored to the iron posts. By March 1908, when Mannerheim arrived in Lanzhou, the pontoon bridge had already been dismantled and a new fixed bridge with five iron arches was under construction. It was completed in June 1909. Mannerheim dined with its American designer, Mr. Goldman, and "Herr Delo," a representative of the German engineering firm that was constructing it. Spanning 234 metres, it was the first fixed bridge over the Yellow River. The four blackened, iron columns were all that remained of the ancient floating bridge—until 1958.

That's when two of the columns were melted down. Mao demanded that the entire country make steel to overtake Britain's production in three years. Some 90 million Chinese built backyard furnaces during the Great Leap Forward. Everything was melted: cooking utensils, iron door handles, nails, women's hair clips and, apparently, two Ming-era monuments. People even tore down their wooden homes to stoke the fires. Production doubled in a year, but most of the steel was lumpy pig iron of little worth. Meanwhile, 20 to 30 million people died of starvation. Survivors in one Gansu county turned to cannibalism. "People were just driven crazy by hunger," remembered one villager.[15]

Mao followed up this mayhem with the Cultural Revolution in 1967. The Great Helmsman worked up millions of rebellious teenagers to destroy the "Four Olds": old customs, old culture, old habits and old ideas. Red Guards rampaged through schools and universities, beating, humiliating, torturing and killing teachers, writers, artists and other "bourgeois" elements. Universities simply closed down and young intellectuals were dispatched to work in the countryside. In Lanzhou, a "Fifth Old" was also attacked: old architecture. The Manchu fortress, Imperial *yamen*, pagoda towers, courtyard pavilions and temples were all bulldozed. The only built cultural heritage that I saw was a single pagoda, like a lone tsunami survivor, sitting atop a mountain across the river.

Linda and I decided to visit this relic. We crossed the historic Zhongshan Bridge. It was clogged with cyclists and pedestrians. (In 2004, the rickety old structure closed to car traffic). Many Muslim Hui in white caps were heading to a mosque across the river. On the other side, we climbed one of two stone paths that snake up the mountain. The path led through ornate gateways, beautiful pavilions and restored Buddhist temples set in a verdant mountainside park. At the top, we reached the crowning seven-storey White Pagoda, now stained brown by pollution. It was originally built in 1228 in remembrance of a Tibetan lama who died en route to the city to visit Genghis Khan. We sat at an outdoor café sipping Eight Treasures tea made of sugar crystals, rose petals, dates, jujubes and various herbs.

The Yellow River was as red as copper. (It acquires its eponymous colour as it swings north through the loess plateau of Ningxia and Inner Mongolia, becoming saturated with mustard-coloured mud and sand.) From the riverbank, fringed with trees, towers were tightly packed against a mountain range. A dozen construction cranes worked to fill the few gaps in the skyline. The downtown is so congested that government authorities are moving to a new suburban administrative centre on the north side of the river, Linda explained. "There's a problem trying to find space to green the city. It's very dense with all the buildings, and plants have a hard time surviving on rooftops and in vertical gardens. The winters are dry, cold and windy. Occasionally there are sandstorms too."

For lunch, we slurped down bowls of spicy beef noodle soup at a famous Hui restaurant downtown, then rushed back to campus. We arrived sweaty and panting for a meeting with Vice-President Yang. He looked youthful and relaxed, wearing blue jeans, a dress shirt, tie and navy jacket. We sat in a conference room at the guesthouse and chatted about education reform over cups of steaming green tea.

In 2000, Dr. Yang explained, Beijing launched a massive program to reform education across the country. In five years, the number of new teachers in higher education had doubled, and university enrolment had tripled to 4.1 million.[16] The number of students going overseas, mostly to Japan and the United States, had also tripled. The scale and scope of reform hadn't been seen in China since the days of Zhang Zhidong.

"The first thing we did in the reform was change the content of the courses," Dr. Yang said. "We've cancelled a lot of courses that were politically biased. By Western standards, you may think that there is a lot of political bias, but it's nothing compared to when I went to university."

The quandary for the Communist Party—identical to the one faced by the Qing Dynasty—is how to promote new Western-style education to strengthen the country without weakening the fundamental belief system that legitimizes Communist rule. It's the classic *ti-yong* dichotomy all over again. Students still take compulsory courses in the "fundamental principles," including Marxism, scientific socialism and "Deng Xiaoping Thought." However, new emphasis has been placed on the humanities, social sciences and foreign languages.

The results of this reform have been modest. "Chinese universities have failed to produced distinguished talent," Qian Xuesen, the revered father of China's missile and space program, complained to Premier Wen Jiabao. "None of China's universities have adopted a model propagating creative and innovative minds."[17] Their meeting and candid conversation were widely reported while I was in China. Qian, age ninety-four, had studied at MIT and Caltech in the 1930s and lamented that the intellectual legacy he brought from these cutting-edge institutes had not taken root in his own country.[18]

"The problem is that we don't have applied research," Dr. Yang told me. "It's hard to get money from industry." In fact, he could not name one invention, patent, commercial product or groundbreaking idea that had ever come out of Lanzhou University.

One of the problems is the national college entrance exam introduced in 1977. It now serves the same function as the ancient civil service exam. High school education is geared solely toward preparing students for this exam, which will determine their university placement and career prospects. An elite education can earn students Party membership and more rapid advancement. Every student I met dreamed of one day strolling the hallowed halls of Peking University or Tsinghua University in the capital.

"By the time you are twelve, you've given up your life," Michael Pettis, an American professor at Tsinghua later told me. Students often study from dawn to 11 PM with only short breaks. "They go through this brutal schedule of memorization, memorization, memorization . . . There's no critical thinking, no questions." It is purely rote learning. "The more you can quote the sages' texts, the better you do on the examination." This has produced a copycat culture. "Plagiarism is so pervasive you can't even call it plagiarism," Pettis complained.

And it's not just students. While I was in China, several high-profile scholars at leading universities were sacked for fudging scientific data or lying about their academic record. Such dodgy behaviour is endemic. In a survey of six thousand Chinese academics, one-third admitted to plagiarism, falsification or fabrication. Many face incredible pressure to "publish or perish" and blame a culture of *jigong jinli*—seeking quick success and short-term gain.[19]

Every year, Pettis told me, the Chinese agonize over why they never win Nobel Prizes. "We must work harder" is their answer. "The real challenge is that they need to think differently," Pettis explained. That's difficult to do in a society where censorship is widespread and groupthink is official state policy. Linda pointed out to me that Gao Xingjian, a dramatist, novelist and critic, won the Nobel Prize for Literature in 2000, but his works—he wrote a novel titled *Fugitives* in 1989 that referenced the Tiananmen Square massacre—are banned in China. Gao himself fled to France. Even *Brokeback Mountain,* a movie about two gay cowboys that won Taiwanese director Ang Lee an Academy Award, is banned in China. "It's embarrassing," Linda said.

The very things that are vital to a vibrant economy and resilient society, and that China therefore needs to cultivate in students—creativity, individuality, innovation, critical thinking—are what the Communist Party is trying to contain. "Our students are brilliant and hardworking, but they have a real difficulty thinking for themselves," Pettis said. "If you want a flawless execution of Mozart, come to China; if you are looking for the next Mozart, don't come to China." Indeed, the journal *Nature,* in an editorial about China, questioned "whether a truly vibrant scientific culture is possible without a more widespread societal commitment to free expression."[20]

In this way, Ralph W. Huenemann, a Canadian professor at Peking University, later told me, the Communist Party's education reform echoes the inherent contradictions of Zhang Zhidong's *ti-yong* approach. "Their slogan 'Chinese learning for the essence, Western learning for practical application' meant 'We will borrow your technology but keep our cultural essence.' It was impossible then and it's impossible now," he said. "But the Chinese still think like that."

DR. YANG COULD think of only one historic building in Lanzhou that had survived the devastating chaos that is China's twentieth century. It happened to be an old hall that was part of the complex where the Imperial civil service examinations once took place. Linda and I went searching for this lonely relic the next day.

We found the tumbledown structure tucked in the dreary block of institutional buildings that make up Lanzhou Hospital No. 2. It was easy to spot. Its swooping gabled roof of wooden beams and clay tiles looked whimsical in contrast to the hospital's austere modernism. A vine-covered trellis led us to a locked red door. A sign said it was built in 1875. The hall was now covered in dust and soot. A patch of roof tiles had broken off like rotten teeth. It was in ruins, an ignoble end for a symbol of Chinese education that, at one time, had produced the most advanced civilization on Earth.

In an adjacent tower, the hospital's director of public information showed me an old newspaper article chronicling its storied past. The building was a *zhigong tang,* or "staff hall," for teachers and administrators. Mannerheim had visited the complex shortly after it became an industrial school. Its lanes and long, narrow buildings contained "innumerable small cabins" where up to three thousand students would write the ancient exam. In 1913, according to the newspaper article, it became the Gansu Law and Political College and then a medical school, which moved to Lanzhou University's current campus in 1956. The hall had been renovated inside, but the official didn't have the key.

Eight blocks away, behind The East Is Red Square, we found another reminder of Lanzhou's educational history: a modern Catholic Cathedral. It was Jesuit missionaries, after all, who first brought Western science, mathematics and astronomy to China in the sixteenth century. They became trusted court advisers, but were banned in 1721 because of a papal condemnation of Chinese rites. It wasn't until the nineteenth century, when the Opium Wars forcibly opened China to the West, that missionaries scattered throughout the country, bringing modern medicine, Western education and Christianity to its far reaches.

In Lanzhou, the Roman Catholic missionaries whom Mannerheim met lived a spartan existence. They toiled with little free time or income, eating only cereals and meagre meat. "This institution," the Baron wrote with admiration, "is held together and guided by iron discipline." The Belgian missionaries ran orphanages and schools in Gansu province. Two English missionaries also ran Lanzhou's first modern hospital, and several of the missionaries taught foreign languages and engineering. Mannerheim spent several "pleasant hours" with Bishop Hubert Otto and other priests.[21]

Nowadays, the Catholic Cathedral's architecture extols the glory of gaud: hot pink stucco, emerald mirrored glass, arches galore and a golden cross framed between two wedding-cake clock towers. An old lady directed us to the sixth floor, where we could find the resident priest. Linda tapped on the door. Nobody stirred. I knocked hard twice, but still no answer. Linda cracked open the door and peered in.

"*Duibuqi*. Excuse me," she said.

In one corner of the room, we saw a lumpy mass tucked under heavy wool blankets on a bed. A rotund man threw off the blankets, rolled upright and waved us in. The priest was clothed in brown pants and a dark blue shirt with white clerical collar. He was in his thirties with black hair neatly parted on one side. He put on silver-framed glasses, a blue blazer and loafers. The sparsely furnished room contained a dresser, bookshelf, night table and desk with a small picture of the Virgin Mary. He beckoned us to a small couch, then sat on a wooden chair with his hands gently clasped between his legs. He offered us green tea and bananas. Linda began by telling him about my journey and Mannerheim's meeting with Bishop Otto.

"Before 1949, the cathedral used to be quite splendid," the priest said. It was the largest in Northwest China, with 350 *mou* of land (about twenty-three hectares), and operated a hospital and school for girls. "After the liberation of China," he said, "the church found it difficult to survive. Since the 1980s, the government designated only nineteen *mou* of land for the church to organize its activities." In 2000, worshippers raised enough money to build this new cathedral, he explained.

"Did the government provide any assistance?" I asked.

"Not only did the government not provide us with financial support," he said with irritation, "but the government sometimes interferes with our activities." In 1957, he explained, Beijing established the Chinese Patriotic Catholic Association to act as a "bridge" to the church. "It was actually set up as a means to control the church," he said. The Vatican has disavowed the association, considering it a schism within the church. The government also severely restricts proselytizing, the priest said. "We can only hold activities in this yard, not beyond the iron gate."

Despite these difficulties, the congregation is growing, largely by word of mouth and the garish architecture that draws in curious onlookers. By the priest's estimates, Chinese Catholics number 10 million, twice as high as the official count. There are thirty thousand in Lanzhou alone. "Our numbers are increasing," he said, "particularly among the young, urban and well-educated."

"Those are the very people who are abandoning the Catholic Church in the West," I pointed out.

"People really need something spiritual to sustain them," he said. "There's now a crisis of belief among the Chinese. In the past, people were forced to believe in Marxism and its propaganda. Some people have come to realize that Marxist ideology isn't so helpful in their daily lives."

The priest politely declined to give his name, so we thanked him for his time and then went across the street for lunch.

"If you read the original Marxist texts, you can learn a lot of things, but not the way the government approaches it," Linda said, popping a steaming beef dumpling in her mouth. "They teach us that Marxism is better than capitalism, but that has proved to not always be the case. Yet the old textbooks still repeat this message."

But now even Marxist education is undergoing reform. One of her professors sat on a committee that was updating textbooks to be more consistent with contemporary China, she explained. "A lot of scholars today are researching the original Marxist texts to get valuable insights." Students and scholars are freer than ever to interpret Marxism beyond official orthodoxy. "Of course, the criticism is moderate by Western standards," she conceded. "You don't want to get yourself into trouble."

MANNERHEIM ARRIVED in Lanzhou just as the government was beginning to survey Gansu's rich mineral wealth for exploitation and industrial processing. About a dozen Belgian technicians were in the service of the viceroy. Mannerheim met one named Alphonse Splingaerd, "a grand faiseur [great doer], a kind of factotum to the Viceroy." The Baron thought him a fraud. With little field investigation and even less technical knowledge, Splingaerd would miraculously proclaim the percentage of mineral wealth in various mountains. "It is hard to imagine," Mannerheim wrote, "that such 'bluffing' should succeed for any length of time, but after all this is China."

He also met Robert Geerts, a more credible Belgian who had been scientifically testing the mineral wealth in the Hexi Corridor and near Xining, the capital of neighbouring Qinghai province.

"These investigations are said to confirm the view that large mineral wealth lies stored in the mountains of Kansu," Mannerheim wrote. They had found coal, salt deposits, lead, iron, copper, silver, gold and "whole mountains of gypsum." A copper mine was just starting, and at Yumen, near Jiayuguan, authorities were about to launch oil exploration. They'd eventually hit black gold, turning Lanzhou into a booming petroleum processing centre.

The most valuable natural resource—one people were willing to kill for—was water. Regulating water was so unpopular that wealthy officials would bribe others to do the job for them. In Jiuquan, Mannerheim noted "that most of the quarrels and fights, sometimes ending in murder, arise out of disputes regarding the distribution of the water."

Fast-forward a century, and environmental conditions in Gansu have deteriorated exponentially. In the Black River Basin, the heart of the Hexi Corridor between Jiuquan and Zhangye, the population has exploded fivefold in the last twenty years alone. This Han Chinese settlement has resulted in shortening of rivers, shrinkage of lakes and precipitous drops in groundwater levels. There had already been sixteen dust storms in Gansu, three times as many as the previous year.[22] The region was also experiencing the worst drought in half a century. One county in Gansu hadn't seen rain in thirteen months.

One morning Linda took me to see Professor Wang Nai'ang, dean of the School of Resources and Environmental Studies at Lanzhou University. Cracking open a cloth-covered atlas, he pointed to large-scale deforestation in the Qilian Mountains, growing soil erosion and desertification in the Hexi Corridor and a lake north of Jinta that has been completely drained since the 1980s. On my tourist map, he also pointed out a new farming settlement. His finger landed directly on the words "Anxi Extreme Arid Wilderness" just west of Yumen, an area where Mannerheim noted "common and very severe" sandstorms. "The government wants this project to be long term," Wang said, "but actually some of the farmers have moved back [to southern Gansu] because of the heavy winds and the harsh environment."

As for Lanzhou, drought and desertification manifest themselves here as fierce sandstorms, which aggravate the city's horrendous air pollution. That afternoon, Linda and I visited Xigu, a huge petrochemical district in a western suburb. In 1970, Lanzhou became the first city in China to experience "photochemical smog." It forms when sunlight cooks nitrogen oxides from fossil fuel-burning engines together with volatile organic compounds from petrochemical plants. A chemical reaction ensues that creates a noxious vapour of ozone and particulate matter. The smog causes breathing difficulties, headaches, fatigue and eye irritation.

On entering Xigu, where this smog first appeared, our taxi ploughed into a thick, bluish fog bank. Visibility dropped to no more than two blocks. On my map, I counted sixty-three massive oil storage tanks. Huge smokestacks and gas flares rose above smoky residential neighbourhoods. The taxi dropped us at the headquarters of the Lanzhou Petroleum and Chemical Corporation, a subsidiary of state-owned PetroChina, the country's largest oil company. More than forty thousand employees work at the refinery, which processes oil from Yumen, Xinjiang and Central Asia. For thirty minutes, Linda and I waited for a company spokesperson, but we both became nauseous from the aerosol-like air. I felt a throbbing in my temples.

"I think it would be horrible to live by these petrochemical plants," Linda said. "Most people work and live here, and they have children!"

Aghast, we retreated back toward the city centre. Our taxi driver was a madman, passing cars, honking his horn and swerving into oncoming traffic. From the back seat, I could see Linda's grim, pale face in the side-view mirror as she slumped against the passenger window. "I feel dizzy," Linda said, as we climbed out.

We ate a quick lunch of Sichuan spicy pork and rice, went on a perfunctory tour of a local science and technology university and then escaped east, away from Xigu, to Yantan Park. Our respite proved elusive. The park's entrance was a massive demolition site with excavators, dump trucks and Hui workers pulling apart rebar from broken concrete. The noise was deafening and the machines stirred grit into the air and belched inky plumes.

We made our leisurely way back to Lanzhou University's campus, strolling through the park then along the Yellow River. We talked about Chinese history. Linda explained that the reason so many young men took the Imperial examination was that they wanted to be government officials. "The mandarin was the top societal position, with the farmers next and then the merchants," she said. "It's never been clear to me why the merchants were so low in status in Chinese society."

"Do you think Confucianism paved the way for Communism?" I asked. "It seems to me that both stress the importance of the state bureaucracy, shun the merchant class and support autocratic rule. All that's old is new again."

"We have a Chinese saying," Linda said. "'You are using a new bottle to hold old wine.'"

A stooped old man in a blue Mao suit shuffled by. I gazed into his weary eyes. "How bewildering it must be for the older generation to watch the country embrace the market economy," I said. "It's like he worked his entire life for a lie."

"After the Cultural Revolution," Linda said, "there was a collapse in the Chinese belief system. People are improving their material wealth. They are making a lot of money, but they are confused. They don't know what will make them happy."

A transport truck rumbled by, spewing black clouds of diesel fumes. Linda paused and cupped her hand over her mouth.

When her parents joined the Party thirty years ago, she went on, they really believed in Communism. "In the 1960s, although we lived a life unimaginable in the West, people actually believed in something... But when people find out that they've been working for a lie their entire lives, you get a collapse in the belief system. You have to re-establish some kind of belief." Nowadays, cynicism has replaced Communism as the belief system that drives Party membership. "Most young people who join the Party are careerists," Linda said, "not idealists."

IN THE STATE-RUN Xinhua Bookstore the next day, I browsed the English-language stacks. I bought *Selected Writings of Deng Xiaoping* (Volume III, 1982–1992) and *Mao Zedong Poems*. Linda encouraged me to also buy *The Chinese Renaissance* by Hu Shih, a man I knew nothing about. "He's a well-respected scholar," Linda enthused.

Hu is widely recognized as one of the founders of Chinese liberalism and language reform. Born in Shanghai in 1891, he grew up in a fatherless household. In 1910, he won a scholarship funded through the Boxer Indemnity to study philosophy and literature at Cornell University in the United States. After graduating, he went on to Columbia University, where he studied under John Dewey, a leading progressive and stalwart of the philosophical school of Pragmatism. In 1917, Hu became a lecturer at Peking University and founded the iconoclastic journal *New Youth*, edited by Chen Duxiu, who cofounded the Chinese Communist Party a few years later. Hu became a leading intellectual in the nationalistic May Fourth Movement. He promoted vernacular Chinese, which made literature more accessible to the masses. He became ambassador to the United States and the last chancellor of Peking University before fleeing to Taiwan during the 1949 revolution. *The Chinese Renaissance* is a collection of lectures that Hu delivered at the University of Chicago in 1933. I was surprised to find the writings of an unabashed Communist critic in a state-run bookstore.

I spent the next two days devouring its contents. His prose is electrifying. Hu's writing is infused with a sense of optimism about the tenacity, pragmatism and inventiveness of the Chinese. He answered many questions that were gnawing at me. Why, for instance, did Mannerheim describe a China that was so scientifically backward more than a century after Europe's Industrial Revolution? With so many world-changing inventions to its credit,[23] how did the greatest civilization on Earth fall so terribly behind?

Hu argued that for centuries Chinese scholars focused on ethical and political theories, while the Enlightenment turned the West's attention outward to the physical sciences. "Galileo, Kepler, Boyle, Harvey, and Newton worked with the objects of nature, with stars, balls, inclining planes, telescopes, microscopes, prisms, chemicals, and numbers and astronomical tables," Hu wrote. "And their Chinese contemporaries worked with books, words, and documentary evidence. The latter created three hundred years of scientific book learning; the former created a new science and a new world."[24] The rapid revival of China's spirit of scientific inquiry, Hu believed, depended on "an intimate contact with the civilization of the West."[25]

Hu also saw democratic foundations in the traditional culture of China. The equal division of hereditary property among sons created a level of equality in wealth and property unheard of in feudal Europe. The civil service examinations also produced "a thoroughly democratized social structure" in which "men of poverty and lowly origin often rose to highest positions of honor and power."[26] Walking the streets of Lanzhou, Mannerheim was struck by the uniformity of the Chinese. "It is just as though they had been cast in the same mould, from the mandarin to the street porter, the same dress, the same manners, the same customs . . ." he wrote. "Class distinctions are far less striking here than among us." The Office of the Imperial Censor, throughout history, had also encouraged a measure of free expression, Hu wrote, creating "safety-values through which the complaints, protests, and grievances of the people are expressed and heard." Confucianism also provided a "scriptural justification" for ousting tyrannical rulers. These factors, Hu argued, made "a workable democratic constitution" almost inevitable for China.

It was only a matter of time until China caught up to the West. "Slowly, quietly, but unmistakably," Hu wrote, "the Chinese Renaissance is becoming a reality. The product of this rebirth looks suspiciously occidental. But scratch its surface and you will find that the stuff of which it is made is essentially the Chinese bedrock which much weathering and corrosion have only made stand out more clearly—the humanistic and rationalistic China resurrected by the touch of the scientific and democratic civilization of the new world."[27]

REACTIONARY CONSERVATIVES in the Imperial Court hated Zhang Zhidong's education reforms. They saw foreign languages and Western science as affronts to their power and traditions. It would bring about not a renaissance, the critics charged, but rather revolution that would tear asunder the Confucian order and ultimately Imperial rule.

One critic of Zhang thought grafting Western know-how onto Chinese values was unnatural, tantamount to using the body of an ox to perform the function of a horse.[28] Zhang too later realized his error. In 1907, he began drafting new decrees for the Empress Dowager stressing the superiority of Chinese studies to those of the West. He ordered schools to inculcate loyalty to the throne and revere Confucius as a deity.[29] He even established a School for the Preservation of Antiquity. China's lead reformer had become a reactionary.[30]

While the West was generally giddy about Zhang's initial reforms—"China At Last Awake to Western Progress," declared a *New York Times* headline in 1906—one foreign educator in Shanghai noted an unexpected side effect of Western teachings. "Perhaps the least pleasing feature has been the unruliness of the student class," he wrote. "The new ideas of liberty and equality have turned the heads of the young men and they have often proved an intractable body to manage. Many a school with bright prospects has been wrecked by rebellion against the authorities on the part of the students."[31]

New ideas were beginning to penetrate, Mannerheim observed, "into the remotest districts of the great Empire."[32] Teachers returning from Japan were spreading "progressive ideas," and literacy was growing. "Newspapers are spreading among the people, and they inevitably result in a national awakening," the Baron observed.[33] He recognized that the thousands of students studying abroad would, in addition to their technical knowledge, bring back to China "deep-rooted Western principles of incorruptibility" and an awareness of responsible government.[34] The very education reforms that were meant to strengthen China came to unravel imperial rule. The *ti-yong* dichotomy was, writes one contemporary historian, the "fallacy of halfway Westernization, in tools but not in values."[35]

China's Communist leaders undoubtedly had history on their minds when they ordered tanks and soldiers into Tiananmen Square in 1989 to crush student democracy activists. Since then, an unspoken truce has been in place. On campuses across China students have eschewed political activism—and daring talk of democracy—for new economic freedoms and opportunities created by an exploding economy. All the Chinese students I met obsessed about prestigious universities, foreign travel and the hot job market in coastal metropolises. Linda planned to become an urban planner in Shenzhen, one of China's biggest and fastest growing cities. Still, it would be wrong to confuse shunning politics with submissiveness, as *Nature* has editorialized: "Exaggerated deference to authority is clearly on the wane in China's younger generation of scientists— and who knows how far that pragmatic liberalization will go?"[36]

Quite far it seems. During my six-month journey, there were major riots and unrest on campuses throughout China. Some twenty thousand college graduates refused to move out of their dormitories in Guangzhou because they were unable to find jobs. At a private vocational college in Jiangxi, students accused officials of profiteering, and rioted and looted the campus after learning their diplomas were worthless. And at a business college in Henan province, police with water cannons fought thousands of students who smashed windows and threw stones after officials downgraded their diplomas. Across the country, students complained of skyrocketing tuition, misuse of educational funds, shoddy teaching and rote learning. Poorly trained for an economy with a tightening job market, a quarter of the new graduates, some four million students, were expected be jobless in the coming year. Students were not protesting for democracy—although that day may come again—but were rebelling against the education system itself.

LABRANG

Stoned

The bareheaded lamas, dressed in red, appeared
on all sides like an army of ants. Hooting,
jeers, stones.—C.G. MANNERHEIM, *Across Asia*

THE BLANK SPACES of the world's map are becoming so narrow;
there is so little left for the exploring enthusiast to mark with his
pioneer footsteps."[1] And what little remained, explained the
British journal *Nature* in 1904, was quickly being pencilled in.
Only the most harrowing environments—the polar icecaps, the
searing Sahara, the Tibetan Plateau—had yet to be fully surveyed.

A map of Tibet published by the Royal Geographical Society
in 1906, in fact, bore the word "Unexplored" north of the Hima-
layas. "It was my ambition to obliterate that word from the map of
Tibet," wrote Sven Hedin.[2] In early 1907, the Swedish explorer,
having snuck into the country despite British opposition, sent a
letter to the *Times of London* bragging about his exploits. "I have
discovered many new lakes, rivers, mountain ranges, and goldfields,
and the geographical results are extraordinarily rich," he boasted.[3]
Disguised as a shepherd, he was still trekking through Tibet, while

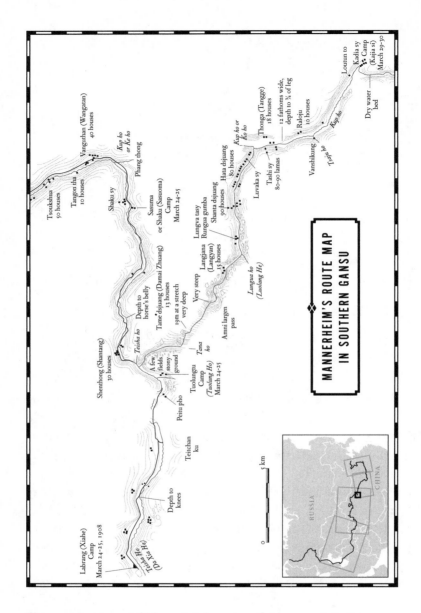

MANNERHEIM'S ROUTE MAP IN SOUTHERN GANSU

Tsoukshua 50 houses

Tangon tha 10 houses

Vanguthan (Wanguzan) 40 houses

Kup ho or Ke ho

Phang thong

Shaku sy

Sasuma

Sasuma or Shaku (Sasuoma) Camp March 24–25

Depth to horse's belly

Teisha ho

Tame dsjuang (Damai Zhuang) 13 houses

19m at a stretch very deep

Shenthong (Shantang) 30 houses

A few fields, stony ground

Tana ho

Tuolungtu Camp (Tuolang Ho) March 24–25

Peitu pho

Teitchan ku

Depth to knees

Labrang (Xiahe) Camp March 24–25, 1908

Teisha Ho (Da Xia He)

Very steep

Langjana (Langyan) 15 houses

Amni largen pass

Lungua ho (Luolang He)

Lungva tasy Rungua gumba

Shanta dsjuang 90 houses

Hara dsjuang 80 houses

Kup ho or Ko ho

Luvaka sy

Tashi sy 80–90 lamas

Thonga (Tangge) 18 houses

12 fathoms wide, depth to ¾ of leg

Vanshikung

Tseju ho

Kup ho

Raloju 10 houses

Loutun to

Kadia sy Camp (Kajia si) March 29–30

Dry water bed

5 km

RUSSIA

CHINA

This map depicts part of Mannerheim's southern Gansu route, including topography, villages, terrain and dates recorded. Place names in parentheses are modern pinyin spellings.

Mannerheim was in Lanzhou preparing for his own trek into areas traditionally inhabited by Tibetans.

In a modest way, Mannerheim was also filling in the blank spots of Inner Asia. He mapped 3,087 kilometres of his journey. While much of it was over well-trodden terrain—both Hedin and Aurel Stein had mapped the region between Kashgar and Khotan, for instance—other areas, such as the Tian Shan range, were not well surveyed. The scope of Mannerheim's maps, however, was rather narrow, literally so: he rarely surveyed and sketched topography more than a kilometre or two from his route. He marked villages, campsites and farmers' fields, drew contours of mountains, gorges, riverbeds and ravines, and wrote brief notes on travel times, road conditions and whatnot. His route maps look like long, wiggly ribbons surrounded by vast white space. Without surrounding context—mountains, rivers, lakes and so on—they are difficult to read.

He originally drew them on cardboard sheets and mapping notebooks at a scale of 1:84,000. To economize space, the maps were later reduced in size by more than 50 percent and then chopped up and confusingly rearranged like a jigsaw puzzle on fourteen map sheets for publication. Map XII covering the route south of Lanzhou, for instance, consists of eight disjointed sections. Even more confusing, Mannerheim's peculiar spellings and the fact that many place names have changed over the years often left me stumped about his exact route. Mercifully, Harry Halén, the retired philologist at Helsinki University, had published an "analytical index" of places, persons and general terms mentioned in the Baron's diary. He had also plotted Mannerheim's trek on a modern map of China, which he allowed me to copy. But even Halén, a meticulous scholar, was at a loss to figure out the Baron's route between Lanzhou and the Tibetan lamasery of Labrang, 160 kilometres to the southwest.

THE BUS WAS full of Chinese tourists decked out in knock-off North Face outdoor gear. They were heading to Labrang for some sightseeing during the national "Golden Week," seven days of holiday at the beginning of October. The bus rumbled through the same smoky ravine southwest of Lanzhou's downtown that Mannerheim took. The mountains were, he wrote, "all bare and grey with soft, curved outlines." His small caravan forded dry riverbeds, navigated deep gorges and scaled mountain passes. The terraced hillsides looked like "a great number of gigantic tongues" stacked atop each other. Small hamlets and farmsteads were nestled on ridges, where peasants burrowed cave dwellings into the steep slopes. It took four days for Mannerheim to reach Linxia, a village halfway to Labrang. Thanks to several new tunnels (one still under construction) my bus took only four hours.

Some things hadn't changed, though. Through a dirty window, I saw terraced farming plots cut into steep mountainsides, flocks of sheep grazing in the golden autumn foliage and villages of tamped earth houses. Farmers still used yaks, asses and horses to pull ploughs. During a later bus ride through southern Gansu—one of the poorest regions in China—I even saw two Chinese women harnessed to a plough with a man tugging at the reins.

Linxia is located in a fertile river valley. A massive emerald cupola crowned by a golden crescent and four candlestick minarets sits in the centre of "Little Mecca." From the bus, I saw local men with shaggy beards and snow-white skullcaps. Headscarves and veils adorned the women. Linxia has been a centre of Islam for centuries. It was a Muslim stronghold during the violent uprisings that swept Gansu in 1877. Throughout the Hexi Corridor, Mannerheim saw the ruins of homes, temples, fortifications and entire villages that had been levelled during the Muslim rebellion. Linxia wisely surrendered to the Chinese without a fight, and thus saved itself from ethnic cleansing. My guidebook said the locals were known for "their surliness, ill manners and hostile suspicion of strangers."

In Linxia, the Baron called on Ma Galian, a Hui general who had betrayed his fellow Muslims. During the rebellion, the Baron noted, "his energy and severity gained him considerable renown . . .

his name alone is said to be sufficient to instil terror and aversion." Mannerheim was surprised that such a ruthless warrior had agreed to be "a servile watchdog" for the Han Chinese. "It is strange that the Chinese so easily find men to undertake the contemptible part of a renegade," the Baron wrote. Ironically, one could say the same about Mannerheim, who joined an Imperial army that was repressing his fellow Finns.

Mannerheim doesn't explicitly mention why he ventured into this rugged region, but his assignment from Palitsyn instructed him to investigate the attitudes of ethnic minorities toward Peking. There's little doubt that the Hui—who are ethnically and linguistically related to Han Chinese—had some loyalty to the Emperor, but the Tibetans and their mischievous leader, the Dalai Lama, were a different matter.

From Linxia, Mannerheim's route followed the Daxia River, a tributary of the Yellow River. This mountainous region in southern Gansu touches the northeast periphery of the Tibetan Plateau and has historically been a part of the Tibetan province of Amdo. At first, the river valley was full of Hui and Han Chinese farmers, but after Mannerheim had been riding for a day, "Tanguts," or Amdo Tibetans, began appearing. Mannerheim saw Tibetan women in sheepskin coats working fields while their husbands herded. In villages, Tibetans gathered to witness the arrival of the "foreign devil." One night, Mannerheim gave a group of Tibetans "some brandy to make them sing" and was rewarded with "a monotonous, ugly snatch of song." It took four tiring days to reach Labrang. After a day of "incessantly" crisscrossing the river and climbing up and down rocky spurs, he arrived as "the numerous gilded roofs and spires of the monastery shone and reflected the last rays of the sun." Hundreds of curious Hui and Tibetans gathered to greet his caravan.

Mannerheim sent his calling card to the senior lama to ask if he could stay at the lamasery, but it was intercepted by an "intriguing" Muslim merchant named Ma-laoye. The merchant insisted that

Mannerheim stay in an uncomfortable inn. Ma inserted himself as a middleman for any request. The Baron bluntly—and mistakenly, as it would prove—rejected this arrangement.

Ma seemed to hold surprising sway over both Tibetans and Hui. His name provides a hint of his stature. Ma is a common Hui surname, and *laoye* means "grandfather" in English. However, the powerful merchant turned out to be more like a godfather. Mannerheim apparently crossed the Muslim mafia boss of Labrang.

XIAHE, THE TOWN tucked beside the Labrang lamasery, was prepared for my arrival. Xiahe itself is unremarkable. It looks like any small dusty Chinese town with wearisome, white-tiled architecture and tacky signage. The town, a county seat within the Gannan Tibetan Autonomous Prefecture, consists of only two streets connected by four bridges over the Daxia. However, since curious onlookers gawked at Mannerheim a century ago, the town and lamasery have turned into a well-oiled tourist destination. Hoteliers, tour guides and taxis accosted me as I climbed off the bus. The main street is lined with souvenir shops, restaurants and small hotels. I booked a room at the Overseas Tibetan Hotel next to a concrete-encased gully full of trash that marks the border between the Tibetan and Chinese quarters. The hotel was overbooked so I was put up in the White Stupa Hotel across the street for one night. At 2,900 metres above sea level, the room was freezing. I went for a walk to warm up.

The street was abuzz with Tibetan pilgrims, herdsmen and monks in brilliant saffron- and magenta-coloured robes. Some young monks wore sneakers, talked on mobile phones and appeared to be window-shopping. The herdsmen still dress in traditional sheepskin-lined jackets tied with colourful sashes. They strutted down the sidewalks in cowboy boots, making me feel like I was in a lawless frontier town. Mannerheim admired this Tibetan machismo. "You see them striding about with heavy manly steps in their sheepskin coats edged with red and hitched up high," he wrote. "The furs are worn thrown off the right shoulder, so that their arms and breasts are bare." And these were just the women. Hui merchants, donning their signature skullcaps, still run many of the businesses. They cook steamed buns and spicy noodle dishes in local restaurants and run small grocery stores and tourist shops. As in Mannerheim's day, they are the commercial life of Labrang, although a few entrepreneurial Tibetans now run businesses too. The Overseas Tibetan Hotel is actually owned by Losang, a Nepalese Tibetan with an MBA from the United States.

"My room is freezing," I complained. "Would it be possible to turn the heat on?"

"There is no heat," Losang said.

"Perhaps I'll change hotels," I threatened.

"Actually, there's no heat in the entire town," he said with a smile. "The town's heating isn't turned on until the beginning of November."

I ate hot and sour soup in the hotel's Everest Café to warm up. That night I slept fully clothed shivering under the blankets. My breath formed into a light fog. To keep my head warm, I donned an *astrakhan* hat that I'd bought in Bukhara.

The next morning, I toured the monastery, a warren of lama residences, gleaming white stupas, monastic halls and towering temples. Labrang is the largest monastery in Amdo and one of the most sacred for Tibetan Buddhism. Its Living Buddha, or *gegen,* is called "Jamyang Zhepa" and is the third-most powerful cleric—behind the Panchen Lama, who is second, and the supreme pontiff, the Dalai Lama. Founded in 1709 by a Mongolian prince, Labrang is located in the Sino-Tibetan border region far from Lhasa and thus in a power vacuum. The Dalai Lama historically had little political authority here. "The monastery is held in great respect and is said to be very wealthy thanks to the generous gifts of Buddhist pilgrims," Mannerheim wrote. He had heard that when the Dalai Lama fled

Lhasa in 1904 after the British invasion, Labrang's Living Buddha sent a message to His Holiness at the monastery in Xining, a few days' journey from Labrang: "The Saviour at Labrang invites the Saviour at Lhasa to visit him and his monastery." Insulted, the Dalai Lama sent a curt reply via messenger: "Tell your master at Labrang that there is only one Saviour—the Saviour at Lhasa."

A century ago, three thousand lamas, including Tibetans, Mongols, Kalmyks and Buryats, worshipped in eighteen large and forty small temples at Labrang. In the summer of 1958, Tibetans rebelled against Communist land reforms and collectivization. The anti-Chinese revolt was brutally crushed, and Communist authorities began to dismantle Labrang: senior lamas were sent to labour camps or imprisoned, monks were scattered and temples and relics destroyed. A second wave of destruction occurred during the Cultural Revolution. All the temples were torn down except a few—one of which was used as a slaughterhouse, the others as offices of state-owned enterprises. In 1979, monks and Living Buddhas were released from prisons and labour camps. The Labrang monastery reopened in 1980 after being closed for a decade. Over the next twenty years, exact replicas of the razed temples, stupas and halls were rebuilt. About twenty-three hundred monks currently live and study at the monastery, although a state-controlled Monastery Management Committee tries to limit the number to eleven hundred.[4]

Xiahe's main road splits the lamasery in two. The lower quarter is tucked along the river and is dominated by the Gongtang Pagoda. With swooping emerald and gold tiled roofs, the five-storey temple is crowned by a gilded, decorative stupa. The rest of the monastery crawls up to the foot of a bleak mountain range, where the most spectacular temples overlook the river valley. Around the temples are prayer halls, administrative buildings and a tangle of courtyard residences. I took a guided tour of the monastery with a ruby-cheeked monk whose halting English was hard to comprehend.

In the Lion Buddha Hall, built originally in 1809, a golden statue of Tsongkhapa, the founder of the Gelugpa, or Yellow Hat Sect, of Tibetan Buddhism, stands two storeys tall in a candlelit room festooned in colourful banners. Another temple houses a room of painted sculptures made of rancid-smelling yak butter. Next door is the lamasery's museum showcasing old relics and gifts. I saw none of Mannerheim's offerings to the *gegen*, including "a watch in an enamelled case representing an adorable woman, whose rather pronounced charms were, perhaps, none too suitable for a monastery." We ended the tour at the Philosophy College's prayer hall. (The monastery has colleges dedicated to medicine, astronomy, art, philosophy and tantric studies.) The cold, gloomy hall was packed with youngsters crouched on cushions, murmuring tantric verses. A few had nodded off, giving up nirvana for napping.

I was amazed by the piety of the Tibetans. Pilgrims by the thousands walked clockwise around the three-kilometre perimeter, spinning thousands of prayer wheels in galleries and prostrating themselves. I saw an old woman clasp her hands together as if she were praying, and then dive into the dirt with arms outstretched. As the sun set behind a ridge, a heavy shadow swept over the monastery. Below a small pagoda in a sacred square, I found hundreds of monks performing their evening prayer. They huddled for warmth like penguins on bone-chilling cobblestones.

I made my way back to the Everest Café for piping-hot tea and to meet Dorje Lhundrub, a Tibetan doctoral student at Helsinki University. We had met earlier in the day at the lamasery's souvenir kiosk. Dorje spoke excellent English and knew Juha Janhunen. The Finnish linguistics professor had been coming to the Amdo borderland for years to study obscure Mongol dialects. Dorje had been a teacher of Tibetan grammar, Buddhist logic and poetry at a college in Xining, the provincial capital of Qinghai. Janhunen recruited him to Helsinki, where Dorje taught Tibetan for one year and then began a doctorate in comparative religion. He was in Labrang researching how the daily life of monks at Labrang has changed over the years. He himself had spent two years in the Ditsha Monastery about a hundred kilometres southeast of Xining.

"It's getting harder for the monastery to recruit monks," Dorje explained. "Tibetans are only allowed to have two children, which means parents are more reluctant to send one of their sons to a monastery." The austere lifestyle isn't for everyone either. "Many monks say that learning Buddhism is very hard," he said.

Still, modernity and China's boom times have softened the edges of monastic life. As China has become wealthier, families have been sending more money to their sons at monasteries. "Nowadays, the monks have become a little bit rich," Dorje said. "They don't have to worry about money or food." Authorities have also forced monasteries to become financially independent. Labrang generates revenue through restaurants, guesthouses, souvenir shops, guided tours and Tibetan pharmacies. Labrang is so prosperous that it relies very little on pilgrims who donate food as part of their religious observance. "You cannot find many poor monks," Dorje said.

Monks receive a bit of money after daily meals or at the end of the year. Some splurge on personal technology. "Mobile phones and computers used to be expensive," Dorje said. "Very few people used them. Later, lay people started to use them when they became cheaper. And now monks use them too, although they are prohibited in some monasteries." Monks even began to use the Internet, until senior lamas realized what type of pictures can be viewed online.

"In the past, the old monks would beat the little monks very severely when the little monks would be very, very naughty," Dorje said. Such corporal punishment, he explained, no longer occurs. Violence didn't quite fit my stereotype of a Buddhist monk—until I read about Mannerheim's reception at Labrang.

THE DAY AFTER his arrival, Mannerheim discovered that Godfather Ma had set the town against him. When he stepped out of his room, Tibetans began hooting and hissing. "The population seemed to be anything but friendly," he wrote. The two Hui soldiers who escorted him from Linxia "seemed to stand in great awe of everything Tangut." He ordered them to saddle their horses to ride to the monastery, but they refused. They said they would not accompany him unless the Godfather came along.

"We risked being stoned," wrote Mannerheim. "It was only when they realised that I was determined to ride there by myself, if necessary, that they obeyed my orders."

He called on two senior lamas to receive permission to visit the temples and to meet the *gegen*. The clerics were surprisingly amiable. "They simply dissolved in smiles and slight bows," Mannerheim wrote. He was overjoyed by the "elegant manners" of one lama; his "engaging smile" reminded him "of a famous courtier at the court of the Emperor Alexander III." Despite the pleasantries and gift exchange, Mannerheim was denied an audience with the *gegen*, who was said to be unwell. However, a lama would guide him around the monastery.

The next day the lama took Mannerheim down to the river and across a bridge to take panoramic photographs from the hillside. (This spot is still favoured by photographers who flock to Labrang.) The road along the river was alive with commerce. Tibetans sold food, Buddhist images, statues and "other objects belonging to their cult." The young men in particular, he wrote, "looked picturesque, draped theatrically in their furs, with a broad, red hem, one sleeve trailing in the dust." Their caps were cocked back and they wore large swords made of Damascus steel tucked in their sashes. The colourful merchants, however, refused to sell him anything or charged exorbitant prices. "The crowd was far from passive," Mannerheim wrote. "No sooner did we leave a group behind us than we heard hissing, whistling, loud laughter and clapping of hands, and suddenly a stone, surreptitiously thrown from behind, would whistle past our ears."

They sought refuge in a temple he called "Tungkö." An enormous gilt statue of Buddha sat in the centre of the two-storey temple, and a wooden column was decorated "with monstrous, heraldic bronze lions." The next temple was closed, but he visited two more before another door was slammed in his face and "all blandishments proved unavailing."

By this time, a large crowd of lamas had gathered and "showed their hostility in various ways." The monastic mob pursued the Baron as his escort desperately led him through various passages. As they crossed a square, more monks flooded out of an adjacent temple and began hooting, jeering and hurling stones. His anxious escort found Mannerheim refuge in a nearby temple. When they came out, the mob was waiting and followed "on our heels." Luckily, they soon reached the door of a Russian-speaking lama whom Mannerheim had promised to visit. They slipped inside to safety.

The Baron sent a message to a senior lama requesting permission to continue his tour. The cleric's reply, the Baron noted, "was as polite and non-committal as his whole personality." Enough was enough. "I lost my temper and decided to leave Labrang the next day."

I WAS VIOLENTLY attacked in Labrang too. I ordered braised beef with potatoes and sweet and sour pork—one of my favourites—for lunch in the Everest Café. I made it halfway down the street, perusing souvenir shops for Buddhist curios, before I felt intestinal gurgling. I ran frantically back to the hotel. By evening, the attack of food poisoning was in full swing. It took me two days to recover.

Eventually I returned to the monastery carrying a bound photocopy of the 1940 edition of Mannerheim's published journal. One of his photographs left me stumped. It showed a towering temple some dozen storeys high. A caption described it as the "Matsua sy temple at Labrang, from the east." I couldn't find this monastic high-rise anywhere. Most monks simply shrugged when I showed them the photo. Perhaps it had never been rebuilt, although this seemed unlikely since the restoration of Labrang had been methodical. I wandered into the Tibetan residential quarter west of the lamasery in search of this elusive tower. Immediately, a dozen curious Tibetans gathered around me. A red-robed nun grabbed my map and an old man with a chipped tooth snatched the diary.

"Don't mind them," said a young Tibetan in an odd English accent. "They are uneducated and don't know any better."

Tenzin was twenty-two years old. He wore blue jeans, a black belt studded with silver, a grey long-sleeved shirt and a black leather jacket. An amber pendant hung around his neck. His face was pockmarked by acne and his hair was so thick that it was naturally spiky. He was born in Labrang but, he said, had spent the last fifteen years in India at a school run by the Dalai Lama.

"Do you know of His Holiness the Dalai Lama?" he asked.

"Yes, of course," I said, surprised by his candour. "Would you like to go to a restaurant for some tea?"

"Perhaps my mom's home might be more private," he suggested.

A bell chimed as he pushed open a large wooden door to a courtyard home. It was located off a quiet alleyway. His grandfather, a stooped, wiry man, was doing some handiwork in the inner courtyard and his teenaged brother watched TV. A photograph of the Potala Palace in Lhasa hung on the living room wall. Tenzin poured some green tea into a beer glass for me. I could hear his grandfather singing a Tibetan folksong outside.

"How did you get to India when you were young?" I asked.

"We just escaped from here," he said nonchalantly. "My mother put me in a caravan of refugees when I was seven years old. Here, it is very difficult to get an education. It's all Chinese. My mother wanted me to have a proper Tibetan education." Every year, parents secretly send hundreds of Tibetan children to India for schooling. She also thought the Dalai Lama could discipline her mischievous child. "I was too naughty," Tenzin admitted. He went to a school in Gopalpur about thirty kilometres from Dharamsala, India, the capital of the Tibetan government-in-exile. This so-called Tibetan Children's Village has some fifteen hundred students.

He had returned to Labrang only three months ago. "I hadn't seen my home for fifteen years," he said. "I missed my mom and she needed my help." It took him one week to cross the massive Himalayan Range that separates India and Tibet. He hired a Nepalese human smuggler for ten thousand rupees (about $145). They slept during the day and travelled at night, avoiding border checkpoints and police stations. They trekked through snowdrifts and dangerous alpine passes. Fresh water from glacial runoff was, he said, "too cold to drink." They slept in caves and under plastic sheets to keep dry. "After the rains," he said, "there are earthworms that eat your blood."

Blood-sucking worms were the least of his worries. A few days before meeting Tenzin, a group of seventy Tibetans tried to escape to Nepal over the mountainous border. A Chinese border guard shot a nun in the back and a teenaged refugee, killing them both. Chinese authorities initially said the Tibetans had threatened the soldiers, but a Romanian TV producer on a mountaineering expedition caught the killings on video. "They're shooting them like, like dogs," an incredulous voice says on the video. The Tibetans are shown struggling through deep snow as a Chinese sharpshooter picks them off one by one.[5] About thirty-two refugees were captured. "About two to three thousands Tibetans, many of them children, escape every year," Tenzin told me. "Another thousand are captured by the Chinese."

In India, Tenzin had received a traditional Tibetan education and was thoroughly versed in the intricate details of Tibet's long struggle against its powerful neighbour. "In 1949, the Chinese started to occupy our country," he said, "and we rebelled against Chinese rule." At 10 AM on March 10, 1959, he added with precision, Chinese troops stormed into Lhasa and the Dalai Lama escaped to India. "Everyone knows about Tibet and our situation," he said confidently. "We have lots and lots of sponsors and friends around the world. The Chinese say Tibet is a part of China, but actually it's not part of China."

His homeland was at least beginning to look like China, however. "When I was a kid, there weren't many Chinese houses in Labrang," he said. "Now there are many." The Han Chinese population had swelled, causing ethnic tensions. "The Dalai Lama says the Chinese are not bad," Tenzin said. "Once we get our freedom, we'll be friends."

He caught me looking at a portrait of a six-year-old boy on the wall. He had rosy cheeks, protruding ears and a perplexed expression. After a search of candidates by senior Tibetan clerics, the Dalai Lama chose this boy as the Eleventh Panchen Lama in 1995. Chinese authorities immediately detained the child and his parents, and appointed their own sycophant as spiritual leader. Nobody has seen them since. "The Panchen Lama is in prison," Tenzin explained. "He's the youngest political prisoner in the world."

We made our way back to the monastery. Pilgrims were throwing cypress branches on a bonfire near the river, offering, as Tenzin explained, "food to the gods." Pungent smoke hung over the lamasery. We scurried along the narrow passageways toward the Jokhang temple, one of the few that Mannerheim actually visited. "The lamas better not find you trespassing," Tenzin warned, half-joking. "The temple is sacred. No foreigner visitors are allowed." We found a gateway and slipped quietly out of the monastery and began to climb the mountainside. The precipitous slope was covered in loose gravel, outcroppings and prickly shrubs. The hooves of sheep and mountain goats had cut narrow paths that crisscrossed the ridge. Tenzin deftly scampered up the mountain like an ibex, offering his hand to help hoist me up.

At the top, the view was spectacular. The Labrang Monastery is a vast honeycomb of tightly packed courtyard homes. The monks in their bright togas rushed about like bumblebees. Here and there, a golden roof or gleaming stupa poked up. The silvery Daxia River wound past the town and into verdant grasslands freckled with the black tents of Tibetan herdsmen. We walked along the ridge. It was blanketed in grass, lavender wildflowers and thousands of bits of paper. Each had an ink drawing of the Tibetan mystical Wind Horse carrying a wish-fulfilling jewel. Tibetans throw these into the wind as an offering to the gods, explained Tenzin. "The higher they fly, the better."

We descended the back side of the ridge into a dark ravine, where we came across a spot smothered with ashes and torn flags atop poles. It was apparently the site of a funeral pyre. "In the old days," Tenzin said, "Tibetans would cut the meat off the bones of dead bodies with a knife and axe, and feed it to vultures. The brain would be mixed with *tsampa* [roasted barley flour] and fed to the vultures too. At one temple in Lhasa, they have a stone that bodies would be butchered on. It is all oily and black." Mannerheim described this ritual of "sky burial" in his diary, explaining how vultures became "gravediggers" because Tibetans lacked firewood for pyres and were unable to dig graves in rocky, alpine terrain. In Labrang, this practice had long since ended. "There used to be a lot of vultures here," Tenzin said, "but not anymore."

The ravine led into the concrete gully that divides Xiahe and Labrang. We tucked into a small Tibetan café jerry-built with a rusted steel frame, clapboard and canvas roof. A Chinese soap opera blared on the TV. We ordered noodles with mutton. I was surprised to see a photograph of His Holiness mounted high on the wall. "It's very strict in Lhasa," Tenzin said. "If you put up a picture of the Dalai Lama the police will come. Here in Labrang it's not so strict."

Outside, street vendors began gathering up their goods as darkness set in. "Be careful of robbers and cheaters," Tenzin warned as we were about to part.

"But this is a town of Buddhist monks. What could possibly happen?"

Tenzin shook his head disapprovingly. "I heard that a rich foreign lady with many rings had her fingers cut off by Tibetan bandits," he said gravely. "My sisters were attacked one night too. I now carry a sword when I go out at night."

"A sword?"

He held up his hands a half-metre apart to show me its length. "Be careful walking alone at night," he said ominously. "There are a lot of robbers here."

THANKS TO THE Dalai Lama—Nobel Peace Prize laureate and global spiritual envoy—Tibetans enjoy worldwide repute as peace-loving mountaintop mystics. That hasn't always been the case. Tibetans were, historically, a fierce warrior race. You can see it in their temple architecture. The structures look like massive fortresses, with towering exterior walls and embrasure-like windows. The temples are often defensively situated on ridges and mountain slopes.

"The Tibetans are a lawless race," wrote one traveller to Labrang in 1912, "possibly 90 percent are robbers; they are continually at war amongst themselves, and this enables the Chinese to exercise some sort of authority over them."[6] It was marginal authority at best.

In Linxia, Mannerheim took on two armed Hui soldiers to protect him during his ride to Labrang. He was constantly warned that the area had "a bad reputation for robberies." He was even unable to find Tibetan guides because the road south of Labrang was too dangerous. "The country was wild and desolate for long stretches," he wrote, "and the bandits kept a lookout from a hill and ambushed travellers." One gang, it was said, even possessed modern rifles. "It sounded unbelievable," the Baron admitted, "but thinking it wiser to be prepared, I armed my men with all the arms in my stores and in my ethnographical collections." He handed out antique rifles and even old swords "to make the men feel more confident."

The Baron left Labrang in a foul mood. Ma-laoye had thwarted his every move. The Baron left his Chinese interpreter Zhao behind to make some ethnographical purchases and then set off. After a long ride, he commandeered the house of a leper, making the outcast sleep outside. He continued the next day along a tributary of the Daxia. It led into a beautiful valley dotted with Tibetan villages and several small lamaseries perched on the hillsides. Snow-capped peaks shone in the distance. By day's end, he had reached a sharp, narrow bend in the valley. Here, the Kajia lamasery was tucked into an amphitheatre in the side of a mountain. His small caravan installed itself in a nearby inn. Almost immediately "a few dozen indescribably importunate lamas" filled the courtyard.

Mannerheim begged them to "leave me in peace," to no avail. Annoyed, he ordered the inn's gate slammed shut. But the hillside around the inn, he wrote, "was soon swarming with red-clad lamas who welcomed me, as I came out into the yard, with some well aimed big stones." Infuriated, the Baron pulled out his shotgun and fired into the air. The lamas continued to rain rocks on him. "I fired another shot at the ground close to a venerable lama who had just hit me on the leg with a stone," he wrote. The blast dispersed the mob. Mannerheim sent a terse message to the head of the lamasery. A prelate visited him and promised "to cut the throat of the miscreant who had hit me with a stone," he wrote. "Pacified by this assurance that the authors of the disturbance would receive just punishment, I fell asleep."

AT THE URUMQI symposium, Juha Janhunen presented a paper on Mannerheim's diplomatic shortcomings at Labrang. Janhunen postulated that the Baron failed to understand "the intricate network of economic and cultural interdependency that existed, and probably still exists, between the four principle ethnic groups of the region: Han Chinese, Chinese Moslems, nomadic Tibetans and settled Tibetans." Hui merchants effectively controlled access to the monastery.[7] If he had known this information, Janhunen explained, Mannerheim might have been more diplomatic in his dealings with Godfather Ma. I didn't find this explanation entirely convincing.

Not long after Mannerheim left Labrang, a second expedition, led by the French army major Henri D'Ollone, arrived. On his way to the monastery, Tibetan brigands attacked one night, stealing two cameras, a rifle, cartridges and other items. D'Ollone sent two scouts ahead, who arrived hungry at Labrang after an eighteen-hour ride. A gang of young lamas met the Frenchman "with volleys of stones."[8] They shot one Tibetan before Godfather Ma intervened. In this case, the Muslim merchant did not instruct the lamas to attack the foreigners and, in fact, helped to save them. What had provoked these murderous monks? I went back to the monastery to find out.

It was a sunny, crisp autumn morning. Patches of ice glinted on Xiahe's main street. Leaves were turning saffron and red, matching the colours of the monk's robes. I took another tour, hoping to ask a few questions of our guide. The lama was exceptionally handsome with an athletic build, chiselled jaw and prickly stubble on his shaved head. He was studying Tibetan medicine and spoke with a slight Indian accent, although he denied ever visiting India. I waited until the end of the tour to ask my question, but a randy Australian woman jumped in first. "You are very good looking," she told the monk. "Are all the monks as good looking as you?" (An official government guidebook actually instructs visitors to "avoid flirting with monks.") The dumbstruck monk blushed, and I quickly filled the awkward silence with a question of my own.

"Under what circumstances can a monk resort to violence?" I asked. "Can he defend himself against an attacker? What would make a monk violent?"

"Monks don't fight," he replied firmly. "We argue."

"But—"

He cut me off with a scolding look before I could get to my story of the stone-throwing lamas. There would be, at least in this case, no arguing either.

I met Tenzin for lunch at a Tibetan restaurant next to the hotel. Fleetwood Mac and Bollywood pop music played on the stereo. The owner, apparently, had also spent time in India. Tenzin called a friend, who came by in a Chinese-made pickup truck. I threw my packsack in the back and we set off in search of the Kajia lamasery.

I had hired a taxi a few days earlier to take me to Kajia, but it ended in disaster. The Chinese taxi driver couldn't find the monastery. I grew frustrated and got into a screaming match about his payment: he wanted extra for a toll road. I finally acquiesced when he pulled into a police station and threatened to take me inside. Afterward, reflecting on what had happened, I felt slightly ashamed of my stubborn behaviour. Was I turning into Mannerheim?

In Tenzin's friend's truck, we drove along the Daxia River and then veered south along a tributary called the Luolang. The river valley was beautifully awash in golden sunlight illuminating the autumn foliage. Several small lamaseries hugged the mountainsides, their whitewashed stupas glowing. At the end of the valley, we climbed a pass into an adjacent valley, whose gently rolling hills were terraced with farming plots. At the entrance to the town of Hezuo, I spotted the towering fourteen-storey temple that matched the temple in Mannerheim's photograph. I rented a squalid room in an inn for three dollars. Tenzin took the key from the Chinese landlady and locked the door. "We must be very careful," he whispered. "There are robbers."

At the local bus depot, a chubby monk wearing sneakers and oversized Elton John-style sunglasses gave us directions to Kajia. We hired a taxi with a Chinese driver and backtracked about ten kilometres to where the Luolang makes a sharp bend into a dog-legged ravine. A small Chinese hamlet stood at the mouth of the ravine. In a portable sawmill by the river, Chinese workers were hewing thick beams. We crossed a decrepit bridge and climbed the hill toward Kajia's whitewashed walls and a gallery of prayer wheels. Three-wheeled motorized carts belching plumes of black smoke hauled slabs of stone up to the monastery. We paid the driver and wandered to a ridge above the monastery where a monstrous stone temple was under construction. We were shadowed all the way by curious kids, adorable in their burgundy togas. Back down in the residential quarter, we found a wrinkled old monk sitting on a chair in a doorway sunning himself. I posed a few questions that Tenzin translated.

"He says he doesn't know much about the monastery's history," Tenzin said after a short conversation. "I think he knows the history; he just doesn't want to tell us about it."

I brought out Mannerheim's diary. It had the desired effect: a dozen young boys and teenagers crowded around. They flipped through the journal and showed the old monk who feigned indifference. He handed it back to me and raised his face to the sun, catching the last rays before it slipped behind the ridge. A clerk at a nearby kiosk was more helpful, directing us to a residence up a dirt alleyway.

Jamyang Gyaltso invited us in. A glass atrium enclosed the home's veranda, providing a sweeping vista of the valley below. The unvarnished wooden interior produced a radiant patina. The monk invited us to sit at a rickety table. Jamyang had short black hair, sideburns and slits for eyes. Rosary beads were looped around his left wrist. He had very thin, pursed lips that hardly moved when he spoke. He said he became a monk at seventeen and had been at Kajia for fifteen years. He cleaned out some white cups with his bare hands and dug into a small bag for tea leaves.

Kajia was home to a hundred monks, he said, of which twenty were teenagers or children. It had three temples and 250 prayer wheels. As elsewhere, everything was destroyed in 1958 and the monks were now slowly rebuilding, piecing the temples back together stone by stone, timber by timber. The new temple had been under construction since 2002 and would be completed in 2011.

"What other buildings were rebuilt?" I asked.

"All of the monastery is rebuilt," he said. "The monks even rebuilt their homes themselves."

The water boiled, and Jamyang brought out a dented tin kettle. I asked him why Mannerheim would have received such a dastardly reception from the monks. "I don't know," he said. "We are glad to meet foreigners."

Tenzin, however, had his own theory. "The British had invaded Tibet at the time," he explained. "The monks couldn't understand what language [Mannerheim] was speaking. Perhaps they thought he was British."

"That sounds right," the monk said.

Tenzin then reiterated details and dates of the second invasion of Lhasa. In 1950, the People's Liberation Army invaded Tibet and forced the country to sign a seventeen-point peace agreement. Communist land reforms were delayed in Central Tibet, but were aggressively pushed in the Tibetan territories of Amdo and Kham, which became part of the Chinese provinces of Qinghai, Gansu and Sichuan. Armed resistance broke out there first. In the summer of 1958, the anti-Chinese and anti-Communist rebellion reached Labrang. The Chinese brutally crushed the uprising, destroying the monastery and disbanding the monks, who were seen as the hub of the guerrilla network.[9] On March 10, 1959, a full-scale rebellion exploded in Lhasa. The Chinese shelled the summer palace of the Dalai Lama, who escaped to India.

In 2008, I was reminded of Tenzin's history lesson and of the stone-throwing lamas. On the anniversary of the 1959 uprising, shortly before the Beijing Olympics, hundreds of monks protested in Lhasa against Chinese repression. The demonstration quickly turned violent. Days later, some four thousand protesters descended on the streets of Labrang. Back in Vancouver, I watched the protest on YouTube. Chinese shops were smashed, the monastery was barricaded and stones were hurled at riot police, who fought back with tear gas. The monks were at it again.

NORTHERN CHINA

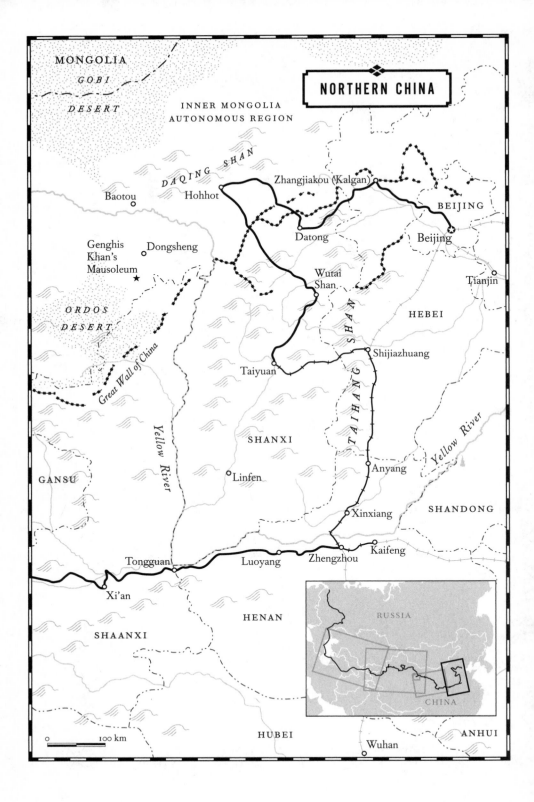

FOURTEEN

XI'AN

Capitalism with Chinese Characteristics

In a nutshell, it is my idea to make capitalism
create socialism in China.—DR. SUN YAT-SEN (1922)[1]

LONELINESS FOLLOWED ME throughout my journey. The ease with which I befriended strangers only seemed to reinforce how desperate I was for camaraderie. In Baku, my best friend was Ahmed, the young Pakistani trader and devout Muslim whose doctrinaire views on women—and most other issues—I found repugnant. He, in turn, must have privately recoiled at my wine drinking and liberal views on drugs, sex and marriage. Yet we became chummy, creating the illusion, at least for a few days, that we weren't both alone in a foreign land.

Ahmed complained to me bitterly about how other Pashtun merchants—free of the strict tribal customs that ruled their lives back home—were constantly swilling vodka and screwing whores in Baku. At Irkeshtam Pass, the border crossing to China, I was struck by the fraternity between Uzbek and Kyrgyz truck drivers as well. All ethnic tensions dissolved in glasses of vodka as the men bonded over a discussion about the price of prostitutes. Loneliness makes for strange bedfellows.

I had hoped that Mannerheim would become my travelling companion. By reading his journal and following in his footsteps, I hoped to share common experiences and perhaps bond with the Baron. Yet from his youth, Mannerheim was obsessively private. In St. Petersburg, fellow cadets failed to pry any salacious tidbits from the reticent young Finn. "The amours of most officers were public property in the regiment," remembered one Chevalier Guard, "but Gustaf Mannerheim withstood the whimsical mockery of friends and answered the most probing questions with a bland smile."[2] His biographers are also conspicuously silent about the alleged love affairs chronicled in Leonid Vlasov's *Women in the Life of Mannerheim*. Mannerheim himself dedicates only one terse sentence to his private life in his memoirs, saying that he was married in 1892.[3] The dearth of details about his personal life only adds to his mystique.

At the Urumqi conference, I heard gossip about one bond the Baron may have made. "I heard a story that Mannerheim took a Mongolian boy as a lover during his Asia trek," a Finnish scholar told me. This wouldn't have been altogether uncommon. Travelling merchants and soldiers dominated oases on the Silk Road, where female companionship was difficult to come by. Mannerheim even mentioned in his military report how "unnatural inclinations" were "common" among the predominantly Chinese male settlers in Xinjiang.[4]

I had heard all this before. "Facts about Mannerheim's homosexuality are nowhere to be found in black and white, just interpretations of texts and interviews with old folks," a Finnish friend told me. "There's lots of talk in [online] chat forums, but the topic is still very touchy among the elderly. The young people don't really care." In 2008, Katariina Lillqvist, a Finnish puppet animator, even produced an award-winning marionette animation called "Butterfly from the Urals." It depicts Mannerheim as a corset-wearing homosexual who brings home a beautiful Kyrgyz boy named Butterfly to be his valet and lover.

This speculation around the Baron's sexuality seems to be driven by a need to humanize (and perhaps modernize) our heroes, especially an aloof aristocrat whose stature has only grown more mythic and distant with time. Lillqvist sees Mannerheim as a symbol of loneliness, disconnected from his family and, at times, his country. "Mannerheim was a complex character who from his earliest years was seeking his place in a very strange and turbulent world," Lillqvist told a Helsinki newspaper. "He was the prisoner of his own legend."[5]

Mannerheim's Asian journal—one of only two personal diaries he kept—provides an unusually detailed glimpse into the daily life of the world's most famous Finn. Yet there are no passages about longing for friendship and certainly no Mongol lovers. More often than not, the Baron complains about his companions: his capricious translator, bad cook or lazy Cossack. A stiff unreality characterizes parts of his diary. Expressions of feelings, sexual or otherwise, are almost completely absent.

For two days, travelling by bus and then train through southern Gansu from Labrang to Xi'an, I read and re-read his daily jottings for this leg of the journey. In great detail, he described a monotony of "grey villages" and terraced mountainsides. "A tree is a rarity," he wrote.[6] He painstakingly listed the number of houses, crops, cows, horses, mules, donkeys and sheep in 188 villages. Yet in fifty pages there's hardly a single adjective describing how he was feeling. Then, finally, I came across this passage: "The greatest pleasure I enjoyed in this place was the sight of two delightful, rosy-cheeked Nordic girls, who spoke Swedish." He wrote it upon meeting Swedish-American missionaries in Liquan, a day's ride from Xi'an. The sentence appeared like one of those rare trees in Gansu's barren landscape. I desperately tried to read between the lines, but my speculations, like a mirage in a desert, often seemed more imagined than real.

XI'AN IS A buzzing metropolis. At the train station, just north of the ancient wall surrounding the downtown, I stepped into a crush of humanity, a torrent of bobbing black heads that spewed forth into car-clogged streets, flashy shopping malls and flagship stores selling Prada, Nike, Hermès, Versace and Gucci. The night air seemed electric. "I had the feeling that I had come to one of the hothouses in which the newly awakened China was being nurtured," Mannerheim wrote about Xi'an. I felt that same euphoria.

I hunkered down in a cheap hostel by the train station. For the first few days I called and emailed dozens of officials to arrange tours of universities, high-tech and export processing zones, industrial parks and suburban developments in this city of 8 million. On Friday night, I took a break, venturing into the city's nightlife, something I hadn't yet done in China. Searching online, I was surprised to find a gay club among a listing of bars, lounges and clubs in Xi'an. It was a kind of openness that I wasn't expecting in China. The club was nearby and offered evening "cabaret shows."

In the same way, I was surprised to find two passages in the Baron's diary suggesting he enjoyed drag shows. In Samarkand, Mannerheim watched three boys, age eleven to fourteen, "with long hair, masses of silver ornaments and dressed just like girls" dance to the music of tambourines and a clarinet-like instrument. Each boy dancer, or *bacha*, fluttered his arms and made long, graceful leaps reminiscent of European ballet. "From time to time the dance was interrupted by a spectator, with an expression of admiration and desire in his eyes, who treated the bacha to a cup of tea," the Baron observed. The spectator clutched his waist, while the boy sipped tea and stroked the "attentive cavalier's neck and shoulder." The "cries of delight from the crowd" and "wild yells" seemed to indicate, wrote the Baron, "that less innocent refreshment had been consumed earlier." In Xinjiang, a Uyghur cross-dresser also caught the Baron's eye. He tried to photograph the transvestite, but "he dropped a veil over his beautiful features and in reply to my entreaties only pressed a fan against them in an access of maidenly modesty."

Studio 21 was a dimly lit lounge in a basement located just off a main boulevard. The mostly male clientele sat at small tables around a stage hung with spotlights and glittering disco balls. Everyone drank Tsingtao beer and spat sunflower seeds onto the floor. The place was packed. The underground club felt rather homely and understated. I took a seat at the bar, ordered a beer and waited for the cabaret to begin.

The first performance featured four lithe young men in jeans and tank-tops gyrating with accompanying drag queens. The latter wore purple sequined tube-tops, low-cut bell-bottomed slacks and heavy streaks of blue eye shadow and blush. Only the nub of an Adam's apple betrayed their gender. The chubby, effeminate host, who had a large peacock plume pinned to his shirt, introduced the next performance, a fashion show inspired by *The Price Is Right*. A dozen drag queens in colourful silk gowns, feather boas and flowing wigs strutted on stage. One by one, they showed off merchandise wrapped in plastic: gentlemen's magazines, condoms, cigarettes, liquor, deodorant. The audience was subdued.

Next, the bartender hit the stage. He was a strapping, athletic lad with striking facial features: a slim nose, high cheekbones and a fake Hitler moustache. He wore army fatigues and a white bandana adorned with Japan's Rising Sun. He also carried a samurai's sword. When a gaggle of Chinese drag queens in dazzling cheongsams and stilettos fluttered onto the stage, I knew there would be trouble.

From my first night in Kashgar and almost every other night in China, I would flip through the TV channels in my hotel room and invariably come across movies—and even a few animated cartoons—about the "Anti-Japanese War" from 1931 to 1945. In the films, Japanese soldiers are typically depicted as automatons, devoid of pity, humour or any other sign of humanity. The Chinese, by contrast, are always poorly armed peasants who, through cunning and courage, miraculously overcome their vastly superior foe. The Chinese Communist Party's legitimacy is largely built upon its victory over the Japanese. With the decline of its ideology since the 1980s, the Party has been stoking nationalist fires to reinvigorate its rule. For more than a week during the previous year, tens of thousands of students and other citizens across China rose in violent demonstrations against Japan for approving a history textbook that glossed over its wartime atrocities. On the streets of Xi'an, I saw old people handing out pamphlets emblazoned with the slogan "Don't forget the war."

The bartender-cum-Japanese soldier swung his sword in mock battle, knocking down a Chinese transvestite. Ominous music blared as the pudgy host narrated the atrocity. The Japanese soldier pushed the others to the floor. He pretended to beat and stomp on the squealing divas with chunky army boots. But soon the tables turned. The courageous Chinese cross-dressers counterattacked with their pointed stilettos. It was a campy re-enactment of the Rape of Nanking—or, as I have come to remember this cabaret, the "Rape of Nanqueen"—in which Japanese soldiers beheaded, mutilated, raped and murdered tens of thousands of Chinese civilians in 1937. The audience cheered as the Chinese trannies prevailed.

It was a queer display of chauvinism, in more ways than one. China's deep-seated animosity toward its island neighbour belies the two nations' close economic ties and interdependence. About 100,000 Chinese study in Japan, more than in any other country. In 2005, the Japanese invested $6.5 billion in China—twice as much as the United States invested, and more than all European countries combined.[7] At $100 billion, Japan exported twice as much to China as the United States did,[8] including mechanical and electrical machinery that is modernizing Chinese industries. The country runs a trade *surplus* with China. In Xi'an, four of the top ten foreign investors are Japanese. And just as Japan built up its export economy in the 1970s—and drained manufacturing jobs from the United States—China appears to be following suit.

During intermission, a college student came up to me. Tommy, twenty-two, was short and bespectacled, with permed hair. He spoke a surprisingly breezy English, having picked up colloquialisms from bootlegged DVDs of *Queer Eye for the Straight Guy.*

"What do you think of China?" he asked.

"I'm surprised at the level of commercialism in Xi'an and all of China," I replied. "There isn't a building facade without an advertisement plastered on it. Everyone has something to sell. I wasn't expecting to find a Louis Vuitton flagship store in the interior of China either."

"The government says they are building 'socialism with Chinese characteristics,'" Tommy said, referring to the reformist vision of Deng Xiaoping, who succeeded Mao and launched the country's modernization campaign in 1978. "But everyone knows this is actually capitalism. Why doesn't the government just call it what it is?"

Words like "socialism" have lost their gist in the New China, while others have taken on strange twists. For example, the word for "comrade," Tommy later explained to me, is *tongzhi* (同志), literally meaning a person with "the same will." Its Communist meaning has fallen largely out of use, except among Party apparatchiks.

"So what does *tongzhi* mean now?" I asked.

"It means 'gay,'" Tommy replied with a smile.

IN XI'AN, THE capital of Shaanxi province, Mannerheim discovered that officials here were attempting to seed a market economy modelled on Japan's. "The Japanese were the governor's closest collaborators on technical issues,"[9] he wrote, and were playing "a significant role" in almost all aspects of Shaanxi's economic life:[10] Japanese engineers, whom Mannerheim suspected were "military men,"[11] had surveyed the railway extension west from Zhengzhou, the capital of neighbouring Henan province, to the provincial border; three Japanese were managing oil wells north of Xi'an that had opened the previous year; and eight Japanese instructors, whom Mannerheim also suspected could be "secret advisors of higher provincial officials," worked in the local school system, which itself was modelled on Japan. And of seventy-four overseas students from Shaanxi province, all but three were studying in Japan.[12]

Japan was China's model for modernization. In 1868, the ruling military shoguns were defeated and the Meiji Emperor was restored. A modern bureaucracy and constitution, patterned on Germany, centralized power in Tokyo. New factories employing Western technology and methods were sprouting up all over the country. Japan began to gain, according to one American observer at the time, "absolute commercial and maritime supremacy in the regions of Eastern Asia."[13] From 1872 to 1906, the country's foreign trade skyrocketed from 43 million to 843 million yen.[14] Japan became China's second-largest trading partner and suddenly emerged as an industrial and military power. That status was cemented when they crushed the Russian military in Manchuria in 1905. Impressed, the Chinese began to emulate Japanese reforms, drawing on their experts and enterprises. By 1907, 55 percent of all foreign firms and 65 percent of foreign nationals in China were Japanese.[15]

Despite close economic ties, the Chinese resented the island nation, having been defeated by Japan in 1895 in Korea and Formosa (now Taiwan). "[T]here is a tangible dislike and distrust in the highest layers of the Chinese society towards [Japan] which only increased as I approached the Pacific coast," the Baron wrote in his military report. "They failed to gain the admiration of the Chinese after their astounding military victories; on the contrary, there is a feeling of anxiety and distrust due to their insatiable political appetite and incredible arrogance."[16] Japanese agents were even suspected of advocating internal rebellion against the Qing Dynasty and smuggling arms to Canton.[17]

At a hot spring outside Xi'an, Mannerheim met a local military commander and his three wives. The Chinese general had visited Japan twice for a total of seven months. "He, too, spoke of the Japanese with anything but friendliness," the Baron wrote. "Their duplicity, cunning, selfishness and deceitfulness are qualities that strike every Chinese who comes into contact with them."

WHILE IN XI'AN, Mannerheim visited many new schools, including the lower military college. It had 270 students and taught Chinese classics, of course, along with Japanese, mathematics, military education, geography, physics and gymnastics. He occasionally saw cadets in black uniforms with white facings march through Xi'an in columns. The Baron took photographs of these military exercises, and thought the troops' gymnastics and marching were even "praiseworthy." Target practice was another matter: rifles were ancient and soldiers scored only thirty-three hits out of ninety-five shots.

Photographing and recording military exercises in China is nowadays fraught with peril, lest one be accused of espionage. After a weekend of sightseeing, including the famed Qin Terra Cotta Warriors, I decided to visit the Xi'an Aviation Museum at Northwest Polytechnical University near the city's high-tech park. Looking at dusty old warplanes was the closest I'd get to investigating China's highly secretive military machine.

In torrential rainfall, I strolled the university's leafy campus looking for the museum. Passing students just shrugged when I asked about the location of the *bowuguan*. An American teacher eventually pointed me toward the museum, which was closed. I then went to the Foreign Cooperation Office to ask about arranging a tour. A young receptionist offered me a seat while she conferred with an official in a glass office.

"The university is top secret," she said after her short consultation. "Do you have an invitation from someone?"

I hesitated. Top secret? Had I trespassed unwittingly on a military facility? Was I in trouble? Should I lie? "Nobody invited me," I said truthfully, "but officials in the Municipal Bureau of Foreign Trade and Economic Cooperation have invited me on a tour of Xi'an tomorrow."

She went back into the office. I flipped through a slick brochure on the table. The university was like the MIT of China, with schools of aeronautics, astronautics, material science, engineering, electronics, automation, computer science.

"There is a problem," she said upon her return. "You need an invitation from a vice-president of the university or a senior government official in order to visit the university. The university is affiliated with the military. You shouldn't be here."

Before slipping out of the office, I tucked the brochure into my satchel. It featured glossy spreads of jetfighters, rockets, drones, satellites and warships. It looked like an edition of *Jane's Defence Weekly*. For the past fifteen years, China's military budget had experienced double-digit growth, reaching an estimated $65 billion, second only to the United States at a mind-numbing $500 billion. The Chinese military was pouring vast sums into R&D and undergoing a rapid modernization. In the state-controlled *China Daily*, I read about the launch of a sleek, swept-wing fighter-bomber and news that the Chinese were building their own homegrown nuclear attack submarine, reconnaissance aircraft, frigates, destroyers, cruise missiles and advanced computerized warfare systems.

Deng Xiaoping once told his generals that "the army should subordinate itself to the general interest, which is to develop the country." By becoming economically strong first, he said "it will not be too difficult for us to produce a few more atom bombs, missiles and other pieces of modern equipment."[18] China's military is now reaping the rewards of two decades of unprecedented economic growth. Reading *The Selected Writings of Deng Xiaoping* aboard the train to Xi'an, I was reminded of a reform slogan of Qing-era officials: "Become strong by becoming rich first."

MANNERHEIM WELL UNDERSTOOD the reasoning behind this slogan. In the modern era, military power depended on not just well trained officers and soldiers, but on industries that could manufacture the armaments of mechanized warfare. Mannerheim saw this first-hand in the Russo-Japanese war. It was the world's first industrial war, fought on a scale never seen before and with modern equipment such as machine guns, iron juggernauts, troop trains and camouflage uniforms. The war, Mannerheim wrote, "had made it more clear than any previous armed conflict that war was no longer an affair of armies, but involved the whole nation."[19]

In this way, China was still incredibly weak. The Industrial Revolution was only just beginning in China, more than 150 years after it had begun in England. Most Chinese-owned enterprises were directly tied to government officials. Starting in the 1870s, mandarins such as Viceroy Li Hongzhang launched various "machine" or "manufacturing" companies, mostly in Eastern China. Only two dozen enterprises were running by the 1890s. There were even fewer in the vast western region: Mannerheim noted an armaments factory, a mint and a cotton mill in Xinjiang; another cotton mill and mines in Gansu; and oil wells in Shaanxi. The businesses usually had private money and management but were under strict government supervision and protection through monopolies, subsidies and other special privileges.[20] It was the birth of Chinese bureaucratic capitalism.

Foreigners were particularly bullish about China's economic future. Foreign trade almost quadrupled from 1878 to 1908, a period in which China experienced two wars, several famines and two rebellions.[21] Western observers predicted that by mid-century China's total foreign trade would equal Britain's.[22] And the Chinese were developing a taste for foreign goods.[23] The Chinese market, at more than 400 million people, was potentially the biggest in the world. Others dreamed about tapping Chinese labour, which cost only six to eight dollars per month, less than workers in British India.[24] One Westerner figured whole industries would eventually be "transplanted" to China. "The people themselves may lack the initiative," he wrote, "but foreign capital will utilize the opportunity for flooding the markets of the world with the products of cheap Chinese labour."[25]

The rewards could be huge, but so were the risks. Western businessmen complained that the Chinese had no "commercial morality."[26] A lack of contract law meant that the Chinese did business mostly "with men of known character and untainted connections." (This principle called *guanxi*, or "relationships," continues to underpin business in China today.) There were other risks too. "Special management boards," Mannerheim wrote, guided fledgling industries but were staffed with "mostly ignorant mandarins"[27] who were appallingly corrupt. "All is well so long as the business experiences trouble," he noted wryly, "but once it . . . begins to yield a profit, the mandarins are soon on the scene and lay hands on it on some pretext or other." Mannerheim worried that emerging industries would become "a new source for the insatiable greed of the ruling class."[28]

Railways were a primary example. Mannerheim noted that Peking had made building a "grandiose network" of railways its first priority.[29] British, French, German, Belgian, American and Russian syndicates either financed or directly controlled most railway construction since the 1870s. But by 1908, Mannerheim observed, Peking had forged an "absolutely new direction" in its policy. It ended the use of foreign concessions, which violated China's sovereignty. "The golden age for foreign railway builders seems to be over," Mannerheim wrote.

Chinese officials, often with no technical training, now headed construction. "These men," Mannerheim wrote, "usually copy the plans of the work they have seen being carried out very carefully [by foreign engineers] and make use of them, when they think the circumstances are more or less similar, but calculations are ignored entirely." To supplant foreign capital, officials also urged common people to become shareholders in new railroads called *minye*, or "popular enterprises." But there were few takers. "It is enough to mention that mandarins will supervise the construction to discredit all matters in the eyes of the population," Mannerheim wrote in his military report.[30] For example, 20 percent of the money raised to build the line from Zhengzhou to Tongguan on Shaanxi's border went missing. The son of the powerful Viceroy Yuan Shikai was rumoured to have embezzled the funds. Peking's nationalistic economic policy was proving disastrous: in 1908, only 256 kilometres of new railway lines were opened, compared to a peak of 2,646 kilometres in 1902 under foreign concessions.[31] "Nevertheless," wrote Mannerheim, "their motto is: no foreign undertakings and no foreign capital."

"Unfortunately at present," Mannerheim went on, "Mandarins carrying out activities were guided by their own interests. Will the old guard be replaced by new persons with a more honest outlook and a greater awareness of their duties? Will the awaking public opinion be able to make the ruling class put the interests of the nation higher than its own interests?"[32]

A century later, those same troubling questions about corruption—this time within the ruling Communist Party—are at the heart of China's economic reform.

HENRY YIN OPENED the door to the minivan and introduced himself. He had an exuberant smile and a full handshake. His hair was slicked back and he wore oversized glasses. He had so many titles that his business card unfolded like an accordion: founder and president of two companies, USA-China-Link and Giant Y, Inc.; president of the Fremont Rotary Club; an economic development commissioner for the City of Fremont; and past chairman of the Fremont Chamber of Commerce. He was in the business of schmoozing.

Yin was originally from Sichuan, but his family fled to Taiwan when he was two. He went to the United States for college, and ended up staying and raising his family in Fremont, a city located in Silicon Valley. For twenty years, he was in the import-export business and was now trying to cash in on his *guanxi* by organizing trade missions to China.

The delegation with him now included his wife, Maria; a lawyer; an accountant; a real estate agent; and two quiet Chinese businesswomen. Two officials from the Xi'an Municipal Bureau of Foreign

Trade and Economic Cooperation accompanied us for the three days.

The delegation had started its tour the previous week in Shenzhen, a booming city next to Hong Kong. It was one of Deng Xiaoping's first "special economic zones," Communist China's first experiment in market reform and opening up to the outside world. In the 1980s, Beijing established a series of these SEZs in coastal cities to encourage overseas investment and private enterprise. (In this way, SEZs served the same purpose as the treaty ports a century earlier, although the latter were forced upon China by belligerent foreign powers.) Shenzhen had gone from being a hilly fishing village in the Pearl River Delta in 1979 to a metropolis of 12 million, a roaring, neon-lit powerhouse of China's export economy.

"There's a saying that Xi'an represents thirty-five hundred years of Chinese history, Beijing a thousand years, Shanghai a hundred years and Shenzhen twenty years," Henry said. "It's more than just the age, though. It's the mentality of the people. It's how they think. It's how they do business." That was his polite way of saying that Xi'an, once China's ancient capital and the terminus of the Silk Road, had fallen behind the dizzying development of coastal metropolises.

"I can put you in contact with some people in Shenzhen. I don't want to say it in front of them," Henry whispered, nodding to the two Xi'an officials in the front of the van. There is, he explained, intense rivalry for foreign investment within China.

"I've noticed a lot more competition between provinces and districts in the past few years," said Bob, an accountant and California bank director, who was scouting outsourcing locations for clients.

"The Chinese tend to exaggerate," Henry agreed. "They are being too competitive."

We spent the morning visiting tourist sites—the Big Wild Goose Pagoda, ancient city wall and Bell Tower—and then the delegation went back to their rooms to change into business attire. I waited in the hotel lobby reading a story in *China Daily* about the Industrial and Commercial Bank of China launching one of the largest initial public offerings in history, at about $19 billion. While waiting for everyone, I also chatted with Joe, a sharp-dressed young lawyer from San Francisco. At six foot six, he towered over everyone in the lobby. He specialized in intellectual property, or IP.

"I guess you are in enemy territory," I joked.

"IP in China is a lost cause right now," he agreed. His strategy was to drum up business with Chinese companies who want to protect their IP in the United States. Once the Chinese get hooked on protecting their trademarks, patents and copyrights abroad, he reckoned, they would want the same protection at home. But at a banquet the previous night, Xi'an's mayor seemed "uncomfortable," according to Joe, talking about protecting intellectual property rights.

"What the mayor really wanted to talk about," Henry piped in, "was BPO."

"What's that?"

"Business Process Outsourcing."

"It's basically the keys to the kingdom," Joe said. "'Teach us everything you know so that we can run the business ourselves.'" BPO largely involves outsourcing internal business functions such as finance, accounting, records management and customer service. Joe's own advice to anyone wanting to do business in China is to keep intellectual property—particularly sophisticated components or processes—offshore as much as possible and simply do the assembly here.

Our tour of Xi'an was dominated by visits to "administrative committees" that ran the city's fledgling real estate developments and high-tech and industrial zones. From what I could tell, they operated like the "special management boards" that Mannerheim wrote about.

Our first stop that afternoon was the Xi'an Hi-tech Industrial Development Zone, a sprawling district southwest of downtown with wide boulevards, flawless landscaping and sleek modern architecture. "That's the biggest mall in Xi'an," Joe said, pointing to the curved glass facade of the Century Ginwa Shopping Centre. "It's very expensive."

We piled out of the van at the towering new headquarters of the high-tech zone's Administrative Committee. In a boardroom on the twenty-seventh floor, we met Jing Junhai, who holds several senior Communist Party positions and is Director of the Administrative Committee. In his mid-fifties, Jing wore a pinstriped charcoal suit, a pink tie and silver-rimmed glasses. He sat across from us with five similarly attired officials and spoke through a translator.

"The Xi'an Hi-tech Zone is one of the best areas to invest in technology in China," he said, beginning his pitch. It is the third most important high-tech zone in China. Labour is highly skilled, stable and cheap—far cheaper, he pointed out, than in Beijing, Shanghai, Shenzhen, Wuhan and Chengdu. Housing is half the price of Beijing's, and land is much more affordable. Some 300,000 people are employed in the zone, which is set to double in five years. "We are imitating the start-up years of Silicon Valley," he said. "We call Xi'an the new Silicon Valley."

Jing actually wrote a book on Silicon Valley's success. "In the book," he said, "I conclude that Xi'an is the city most like Silicon Valley in China and has all the characteristics of Silicon Valley." These, he explained, include a warm climate, an inland valley location and a cluster of universities, defence industries, aerospace and tech companies that will produce miraculous synergies and propel Xi'an into the future.

"How well have the Chinese done at copying Silicon Valley?" I asked Joe as we left for a tour of the forty-eight-square-kilometre zone.

"Well, they've invested a ton of money here. It's scary."

"Why is it scary?"

"Because they are sucking up all our companies."

The zone certainly looked like California. Tree-lined boulevards led past high-rise condos, verdant parks with sculpted hedges
and auto malls selling BMWs and Nissans. The sun was a dull orange
ball, emitting a soft warm glow that reminded me of a hazy day in
Los Angeles.

"Could we be in California right now?" I ask Maria, Henry's
wife.

"It's very modern," she said.

And suburban, I thought, as we pulled into the parking lot of
System Sensor. "As you can see," said Hong Baosen, the company's
managing director, "the layout is very American, a low building."
Baosen gave us a tour of the factory, a joint venture with Honeywell
Group. System Sensor is the biggest supplier of smoke detectors in
China, producing 3 million units per year. More than three hundred
workers in blue lab coats sat at long tables soldering circuit boards
and assembling the devices. The workers were all young and mostly
women.

"I wonder how much they get paid," I mused.

"They get a thousand yuan per month, about two thousand dollars per year," Joe said. "We can never compete. It's shocking."

Yet despite the supposed similarities to Silicon Valley, one key
ingredient seemed missing: home-grown innovation. The next
company we visited was the only one during the entire tour that had
actually invented something. Huaxun Microelectronics Inc. developed a computer chip for global positioning systems. Coincidentally,
its general manager, Peter Zhou, had spent several years living in
Fremont and working in Silicon Valley. The company, only two
years old, had already applied for ten patents. "Keep my business
card," Joe told him.

Our next stop was the Xi'an Software Park, located in a crescent-
shaped modern complex with a sky-lit atrium adorned with palm
trees. Here, twenty-four hours a day, employees of CompuPacific
International, a Michigan-based firm that is a leader in business

process outsourcing, digitized documents: county property records, birth and death certificates, medical insurance records, loan applications, consumer rebates.

"This is exactly what the mayor mentioned last night that they want to focus on," Henry said.

I could see the appeal. Xi'an's universities were churning out graduates in unprecedented numbers. This sort of business was relatively pollution free, labour-intensive and nominally white-collar. The chief operating officer, Chian Zhikui, who coincidentally had lived in Fremont for two years, took us downstairs to a room in which hundreds of youths in white lab coats tapped away at computer terminals. One woman was inputting a rebate from a Circuit City store in Schererville, Indiana. "I know that town," Joe said, peering over her shoulder.

"Can you imagine when they start outsourcing the banking sector how many jobs that will be?" he added in disbelief. Joe's father had lost his job at Hewlett-Packard and his sister had recently lost a job doing the sort of data entry that CompuPacific does. "It's troubling," Joe said. "We used to go to bed at night thinking that manufacturing is going overseas, but at least we have the service sector." Now, he sighed, even that is disappearing.

It rained the next day. We toured another technological development zone to the north. Joe plugged his law firm, and Henry plugged himself. "It's not how many people you know," he told officials. "It's who you know. I have friends in Xi'an and Silicon Valley." In a tax-free export processing zone, Bob and Joe grilled an official about possible lucrative tax loopholes before we toured a TV screen manufacturer and then a joint venture with Mitsubishi that produced industrial-sized electrical switches. Officials hosted a sixteen-course gourmet lunch and then we drove more than an hour east to the China Aviation Industry Base in the town of Yanling.

Entering China's aviation city was a bit spooky. Its new four-lane boulevards, cut through farmland, were empty. Smothered in a thick fog, the place looked ghostly. We pulled up to a brand new glass building that was the showroom for the massive development. The marble-clad foyer had a wooden bridge over a fountain that led to a huge model of the fledgling aviation city, which will eventually cover forty square kilometres.

"We are changing from an agricultural country to an industrial one," said Jin Qiansheng, director of the aviation base. "You can actually see this change taking place in Xi'an. Last year the land here was growing wheat and corn. Next year the land will be producing aviation parts and components."

In a boardroom that looked like an SAS airport lounge decked out in birchwood, he gave a PowerPoint presentation, rattling off impressive statistics: a third of China's aerospace manufacturing happens in Shaanxi province employing 130,000 people. Construction of the base had just begun the previous year and will eventually include residential neighbourhoods, a museum, an R&D centre, manufacturing facilities and a massive runway.

"We have a humble task to help the local farmers transform to an industrial society. Until I was eleven years old, I lived in a village," Jin said. "If it wasn't for Deng Xiaoping and his reform and opening-up policy, I would still be living in a farming village...If China does not transform itself from an agricultural to industrial society, we won't be able to feed ourselves. The earnings from our forty square kilometres will be hundreds of times greater than the two hundred square kilometres of surrounding farmland. Because of this type of development, we can have a stable society in China."

But developments like this are actually the leading cause of instability in China. Authorities had expropriated the land and resettled the farmers, probably with little or no compensation. By rezoning the land for industrial use, Jin explained, its profit potential went up a hundredfold. Authorities now leveraged loans from state banks based on this new land value that, in turn, financed the development's start-up. Such land seizures, however, were causing riots throughout China as peasant ire exploded in the face of corrupt and arbitrary local officials.

In this way, little has changed in a century. Qing-era officials did not seize land to finance their reform program, but rather taxed it, often exorbitantly. In Xi'an, the finance minister levied a heavy land tax along the proposed railway route to connect Shaanxi's eastern town of Tongguan to the railhead at Zhengzhou. The railway tax, Mannerheim wrote, "provoked protests and disturbances" among the peasants. "People who usually submitted to the traditional abuses of the authorities became indignant," he added in his military report. "The echo of their protests reached Peking and the new taxes have been cancelled."[33] Peking fired the corrupt minister, but not before "both he and many of his charming colleagues had managed to secure a decent income out of the transaction."

Whereas Qing officials forbade foreign capital in railway projects in 1907, Beijing had recently eased restrictions on foreign investment in aerospace. The aviation base director was now trying to raise $2.5 billion in overseas investment—largely equity since foreign banks were prohibited at the time from lending in China. Jin spent more than an hour describing convoluted and rather murky schemes to funnel cash into his development. The strategy involved, as far as I could tell, interconnected land leases, leasebacks, joint ventures, construction subsidiaries and venture capital funds.

"It's a shell game," Bob concluded, as we left. "If you did this in the United States, you'd have another Enron."

"Someone would be going to jail," added Joe.

"The Chinese mentality is *qin, li, fa*—friendship, truth, legality," Henry explained back in the van. "In the United States, it's the exact opposite. In the United States, your first concern is about legality and in China it's the last."

The next day we toured an even bigger development. The Chan-Ba Rivers Ecological District covers 129 square kilometres west of the city. The fertile farmland, explained an official with its

Administrative Committee, was being converted into "a very modern and fashionable district." The basin, at the confluence of two rivers, was about to sprout business parks, condominium towers, hotel resorts and an international exhibition centre. The area was a vast construction site. Workers were putting the finishing touches to its infrastructure: a concrete bridge, roads, levees and riverbank piers.

Later that day, at the end of our tour, Joe took me to the Century Ginwa Shopping Centre. It was shockingly empty. Where were all the shoppers? We sat in a stylish café, sipped cappuccinos and talked about China's spectacular rise. I mentioned how in three days we had toured some two hundred square kilometres of industrial and residential developments but not seen one chart about market demand or one statistic on the financial feasibility of any of the proposed developments.

"The government's philosophy," I said, "seems to be 'If you build it, they will come.'"

"It's a false economy," Joe said. He had seen grand real estate schemes in almost every city that he visited in China. On the outskirts of one industrial metropolis in Southern China, he had stayed at a five-star resort that was entirely empty. In an overheated economy experiencing double-digit growth, he explained, such poorly planned developments could survive, but an economic slowdown could be devastating. "I remember seeing on TV this guy driving a snowmobile. He was going really fast and actually drove across a lake," Joe said. "I thought 'Maybe that's China. If they slow down, they are going to sink.'"

"I'VE NEVER SLEPT with a woman," Tommy said. His grimace suggested he never wanted to either.

I had contacted Tommy to see if he'd accompany an American businessman and me to a KTV bar—the K stands for "karaoke"—on my last night in Xi'an. These establishments are all over China.

They are hard to miss, usually lit up like Las Vegas casinos. While singing seems innocent enough, KTV bars are often fronts for prostitution. Their clientele are mostly businessmen, bureaucrats and Party officials. They are the latest iteration of a storied trade on the Silk Road.

In southern Xinjiang, Mannerheim noted "whole streets of light women who offer the travelling merchant the joy and consolation he may require during his sojourn, of several weeks, in a strange town... In Khotan, a whole class of these consolers is said to be available for travellers under the name of 'merchants' wives.'" The Baron even photographed a Uyghur prostitute sitting in a carpeted room. She looks to be in her twenties and wears large decorative earrings, braided hair and a loose, flowing gown. An opium pipe is cupped in her hands and her expression is as mystifying as the Mona Lisa's. At a missionary hospital, Mannerheim also noted a negative consequence of the sex trade on the Silk Road: "Venereal diseases are far and away the most prevalent... [and] occur in a very severe form."

"Don't worry," I assured Tommy. "We aren't going to have sex with any girls, only singing."

We met the businessman in front of the Languifang KTV bar across from the Sheraton Hotel. He was married and originally from the Midwest. He was so clean-cut, all-American and wholesome looking that I could have mistaken him for a missionary. He invited me to join him on the condition that I not use his name. So let's call him Darrell. We walked up a flight of stairs. I was expecting a bar or cocktail lounge, but found myself at a hotel-style check-in desk. A clerk wore a white shirt, black slacks and bowtie. He escorted us to a small room with a black leather sectional sofa, coffee table and TV. A divider provided intimate space at the back. The room cost about five dollars an hour and each girl another twenty-five dollars. A few minutes later, a host came back with a dozen girls who lined up like livestock at a county fair.

"Pick one," Darrell said. "You're my guest. You get to pick first."

I felt awkward, embarrassed, ashamed. I hesitated. Darrell looked at me. "Pick one. Go on."

I pointed to a funky-looking girl with crimped, frizzy hair. She wore red boots, low-cut jeans and a skimpy tank top that revealed her belly button. She was the prettiest of the bunch, but had an empty, sulking stare. She didn't seem to be enjoying herself. That we had in common. Tommy picked a homely girl in an elegant, black evening gown. Her hair was pulled back in a tight bun. Darrell pointed at one girl, but the host shook his head.

"She doesn't sing," he said.

"I think she must have other talents, " I suggested.

Darrell gave me a knowing smile and then pointed to a tall girl with dyed red hair, jeans and a torn T-shirt. She looked like a rock star.

We ordered some Tsingtao beers and turned on the TV. A menu of Chinese and Western pop songs came up. Tommy and the girls sang catchy pop tunes from Hong Kong, Taiwan and Singapore. Darrell tried to convince me to sing, but I demurred. "The Chinese are terrible singers," he said, "but that doesn't stop them." After a few more beers, I caved in to the B52s' "Love Shack," a fitting song given the venue.

Darrell had an arm wrapped around his girl. Tommy's girl appeared to have her hands full too. "She's touching my crotch," Tommy complained, squirming toward me on the sofa. My girl, Anli, was acting like a wallflower—living up to her name, which means "Peace Lily." She sat, arms crossed, aloof and pouting. Darrell said something to her in Chinese. She reluctantly put her hand on my knee. An hour passed with more songs and more beer. The clerk then came back with a proposition: "Do you want a stripper?"

"Sure," Darrell said.

A few minutes later, a young dancer came in. She turned on a Chinese pop song and started to flail her arms above her head and shake her ass. She pulled off her top and awkwardly tugged off her tight-fitting jeans. By the second song, she had flung her bra and panties across the room. She was a busty girl with a voluptuous figure and pretty face. She jumped atop the coffee table and pulled Darrell up for a dance. He held her hips as she gyrated. She then hauled Tommy out of his seat. She pressed her large breasts against his chest. Tommy just giggled. I too was hauled up at the end. The entire performance lasted ten minutes. As she put on her clothes, Darrell slipped her twenty-five dollars.

"She's fat," Darrell's girl said after the dancer left.

"Yes, very fat," Anli agreed.

"These girls think she's fat," Darrell said, "but they're just jealous because of all the money she makes dancing. Most of these girls work during the day and KTV is moonlighting for them. Sex and dancing make the quick money. Sitting around and singing into the late night is tiring."

By midnight, we had exhausted our talents and the girls' enthusiasm, since no invitations back to hotel rooms would be forthcoming. Darrell slipped the maître d' a hundred yuan banknote and we exited back into the technicoloured glow of an electric night.

FIFTEEN

HENAN

The Harmonious Countryside

He who rules a state should worry, not about the poverty
of the people, but about the inequality in distribution. For with
equitable distribution, there is no poverty.—CONFUCIUS

"I'VE REALLY GOT a problem with Henan people," Tommy told me. "They scare me."

We were waiting in a cavernous departure hall for the night train from Xi'an to Zhengzhou, the capital of Henan province. Earlier in the week, Tommy had cautiously agreed to travel to Henan to be my translator for the weekend. "The Henanese are liars and cheaters," he warned.

Tommy surveyed the dim departure hall, crowded with the sun-blackened faces of *nongmin* (peasants), soldiers and migrant workers. He looked uneasy, his eyes darting suspiciously from face to face. It would be Tommy's first visit to Henan. My plan was to wander that province's countryside to gauge the *vox populi*.

Ever since the Qin Dynasty unified China in 221 BC, marking the start of imperial rule, the plight of peasants has determined the fate of China. The deranged and extravagant rule of the Qin

Emperor, who built the Terra Cotta Warriors outside Xi'an, instigated a peasant rebellion a few years after his death. This seminal dynasty lasted only fifteen years but set a pattern for the next two thousand. "There's a saying in China," Tommy told me, "that if you solve the problems of the farmer then you won't have any problems."

The most problematic place in China happens to be Henan. *China Daily* describes the province as "a major repository of the nation's rural poverty, workplace hazards, environmental degradation and disease."[1] Henan became infamous in 2000 when a gruesome story broke about desperately poor farmers being infected with AIDS from illegally selling their blood. By 2005, the United Nations estimated that fifty-five thousand blood donors were infected.[2] In some Henan villages, that accounted for up to 40 percent of the population. A more recent scandal involved peasants, including children as young as eight, being kidnapped and literally enslaved in brick-making factories.[3] In China, entire books have been written deriding and mocking the Henanese, who are usually portrayed as fraudsters, hooligans, bumpkins and bloodsuckers.

A month before I arrived in Zhengzhou, I read in *China Daily* about a drunken Henanese migrant worker who jumped into the panda enclosure at the Beijing Zoo. Zhang Xinyan, age thirty-five, guzzled four jugs of beer at a nearby restaurant and then climbed into the pen to pet cuddly Gugu, a sleeping panda. Frightened, Gugu bit a chunk out of his leg. Zhang retaliated by kicking and biting back. Newspapers around the world jumped on the bizarre story. "Man Bites Panda," read the headlines.

"The sad tale of panda-biting Zhang Xinyan is a metaphor for the modern Henanese experience," wrote one commentator, whose grandparents hail from Henan, in a Beijing magazine. "We come here to do a little drinking, and to express our earnest love for the nation's mascot, and what do we get? Scorn, derision, and a big hunk bitten out of each leg, that's what ... It's not easy being Henanese."[4]

EVEN IN MANNERHEIM'S day, Henan was understood to be the lair of notorious gangs that roamed the countryside robbing travellers. The province was widely known as "bandit-ridden Henan."[5]

It took Mannerheim two weeks to trek from Xi'an to Zhengzhou. At the town of Tongguan, near the boundaries of Shanxi, Shaanxi and Henan provinces, he rejoined the Yellow River. He was venturing into the heart of China, a countryside of rolling fields, terraced hills and yellow earth—as soft as "a block of butter," Mannerheim described—that silts the river and gives it its name. Caravans had cut such a deep grove in the soft soil that Mannerheim felt "imprisoned in a sunken road" for much of the trip. Trade caravans, he wrote, "raised clouds of dust that remained motionless for a long time and shrouded the road in yellow darkness."

The area was desperately poor. At 520 people per square mile, Henan was more than four times as densely populated as neighbouring provinces.[6] "The land was cultivated everywhere, the villages thickly dotted about and shady," he wrote. The road was "full of beggars, squatting on their knees in the dust or running after us and begging for alms in high voices."

Historically, peasants in China were ruled under a form of "bureaucratic feudalism."[7] They were subject to various land rents, trade tax, customary dues and corvée from the gentry. All-powerful mandarins dominated their lives. The symbol of state power was the *yamen*, the office and residence of local officials that also acted as the law court, prison, barracks, granary and treasury. Fortress-style walls often protected the *yamen*'s greedy and corrupt officials from peasant fury. Droughts, floods and infestations compounded the indescribable suffering. "Terrible tales are told of the last famine," the Baron wrote. "For instance, the fact there are now comparatively few beggars is said to be due to their all having perished. The avarice of the mandarins, I was told, did not give way an inch even in such circumstances." Relief funds from the United States were used to pay taxes instead of buying food. Freight prices were so high that the starving couldn't afford the rice shipped from the south anyway. "While people were dying of hunger in the streets and on the roads," he wrote, "the rice lay rotting." Missionaries in Central China reported terrible instances of cannibalism. "Children were slain and women were sold for a song," Mannerheim wrote.

Natural disasters were often seen as a sign that the gods disapproved of the emperor. According to one Han Dynasty scholar, "When a state is on the verge of ruin, Heaven will cause catastrophes to befall earth as warnings to the ruler."[8] Provoked by nature's wrath, peasant uprisings were often a bitter concoction of political revolt, banditry and religious superstition.

A series of major rebellions in the late nineteenth century almost unseated the Qing Dynasty. The Nian, Taiping and Muslim rebellions from 1851 to 1877 were followed by smaller uprisings by secret societies, dubbed *chiaofei*, or "religiously inspired bandits," by Qing officials. In Henan, secret society uprisings occurred in 1891, 1911 and throughout the 1920s. Their members were deeply impregnated with a sense of Daoist salvation, Buddhist millenarianism, superstition and anti-foreign fanaticism.

A confluence of factors spawned these societies. The last decades of the nineteenth century saw a rise in the number of marginal and displaced people as a result of population growth, demobilized soldiers, industrialization and new modes of transportation, including rail and river steamboat. At the same time, Confucianism, the orthodoxy of the ruling class, had outlived its usefulness. Its legitimacy had been severely sapped by widespread corruption, Christian evangelism, foreign imperialism and the rise of a new merchant class. Secret societies and large-scale rebellions blew apart the myth of Confucian harmony. The Qing court desperately tried to ban the *chiaofei* by outlawing gatherings of more than twenty male and able-bodied people.[9] By 1893, one viceroy called the secret societies, with names such as the Ko-lao Hui (Elder Brothers Society) and Hungchiang Hui (Red Spears),[10] "a hidden disease in all the provinces."[11]

With the exception of new schools in the countryside, Mannerheim saw little support for reforms in Henan. In Luoyang, one of three ancient capitals in Henan, the Baron saw lampposts overturned by superstitious peasants. "The population of the district," he wrote, "is reported to be inimical to Europeans and to everything that is foreign."

Mannerheim was overjoyed when he heard "the melodious whistle of a railway engine" in Zhengzhou, where north–south and east–west trunk lines intersected. Soldiers wore modern khaki uniforms, some Chinese spoke "broken French" and others donned European clothes. After twenty-two months of travelling, Mannerheim felt that he had finally "reached the civilized zone of China."

I WOKE AT 6:30 AM. The train had slowed. I pushed the curtain aside and saw a massive coal-fired power plant. Clouds of vapour rose from its cooling tower. It looked like a gigantic steaming cup of coffee, a morning pleasure that was a rarity in rural China. We soon arrived at the Zhengzhou railway station. Tommy and I crossed an expansive concrete plaza to a cheap hotel adjoining the bus station. We napped for an hour and then got ready for our trip to the countryside.

Tommy had a shower. He came out and dressed in black Adidas sneakers, blue jeans and a rainbow-striped sweater. He had bought most of his clothes at discount factory stores during a recent school trip to the United States. "I can't believe how cheap things are in the U.S.," he said without irony. He had picked up Calvin Klein dress shirts for only twenty-three dollars, Nike runners for nineteen dollars and twenty cheap ties. "They are four times the price in Xi'an," he said. His bouffant hairdo also cost him about three hundred yuan, more than some farmers make in a month. Donning a dazzling pendant on a silver necklace, Tommy looked like a courtier from the Bling Dynasty.

The Henan countryside seemed as alien to him as it was to me. Tommy grew up as a single child in an upper-middle-class family in Changchun, a sprawling industrial city in the northeast. For his parents, no sacrifice was too great. They paid seven thousand dollars in bribes to get Tommy into one of the best private high schools in the city. He performed poorly on his matriculation exam and thus failed to qualify for entrance into one of China's top-tier universities. A relative knew someone in the education ministry in Beijing, so for 150,000 yuan—about a year's salary for his father, who was a manager at an automobile factory—they bought him entrance to an elite university in Xi'an. His mother came back from the bank with the money stuffed in large plastic bags. "Look at what we are doing for you!" she screamed, waving it in his face. Tommy's eyes welled up with tears. They also financed his trip to the United States (four thousand dollars) and provided him with a thousand-yuan monthly allowance, equal to a quarter of his father's salary. Yet it still wasn't enough. Tommy borrowed from friends to pay for his shopping sprees, bar hopping and designer hairdos. "I'm a Little Emperor," he admitted with a smirk. "You think I'm high maintenance, don't you?"

"Is that a rhetorical question?" I replied.

"I seem spoiled, but I'm actually very tough," he said, searching his overnight bag for facial cream.

I wanted to visit a village called Shijiahe. Two years earlier, locals had risen up in protest against officials seizing farmland for industrial development. Several hundred marched on Zhengzhou, disrupting traffic. When they threatened another protest, a thousand police officers in a caravan of fifty armoured vehicles swooped into the town in the middle of the night. The police fired rubber bullets and beat residents. "They tried to push us back, but more and more villagers fought their way out," one farmer told the *Washington Post*. "Villagers were yelling at the police, telling them to arrest the real criminals, not the good people."[12] It was one of the rare rural protests reported by the foreign press. In the previous year, an estimated eighty-seven thousand incidents of "public order disturbances" had taken place in China, up from thirty-two thousand in 1990.[13] Illegal land seizures had instigated much of the mayhem.

In a province of 100 million people, locating a village of six thousand on a map was not easy. After two hours of searching maps and the Internet, we gave up. Nobody seemed to know where it was. Instead, we found a village Mannerheim had visited along the south bank of the Yellow River. Its name is Sishui.

Outside the hotel, we negotiated with a taxi driver, but he wanted thirty dollars for the eighty-kilometre journey. "Those guys are cheaters," another driver warned us. "They will drive you halfway and then demand more money or threaten to drop you in the middle of nowhere." We took the bus for two dollars instead.

It was a muggy, dull afternoon. The bus was so packed that a dozen people crouched in the aisle to hide from the view of the police, who stop overcrowded buses. As the bus trundled along, Tommy told me about a debate he'd had in his English class about ending the *hukou* system of residency permits that traditionally restricted peasants' mobility. His teacher pitted him and two others from the city against eighteen students from the countryside. "The farmers are poorly educated and crowd the cities," Tommy argued. "Their low education and poverty lead to criminality." Farmers are also uncouth, he explained: they spit, drink and lack manners. In 2003, Zhengzhou had actually loosened qualifications for residency. But in just three months, 150,000 migrants flooded the city, creating chaos and forcing authorities to restrict the flow.[14]

Authorities now planned to "perform major cardio-vascular surgery on the Chinese heartland."[15] Earlier in the year, the governor of Henan had announced an ambitious urbanization program to move one and a half million farmers into a cross-shaped cluster of cities with Zhengzhou at its centre. Just outside the city, I could see new roadways with streetlamps cutting across barren farmland, primed for suburban development. Factories and apartment blocks were under construction, and paving equipment lined the highway. Everything was blanketed by thick smog.

We changed buses in the town of Xingyang, hopping on a minibus that took us to Sishui. It was an unremarkable village with one commercial street of low, dirty brick buildings. I hired a three-wheeled taxi to take us to a hamlet next to the Yellow River. The road ended at a short embankment running along the river's edge.

"We are in the middle of nowhere," Tommy said, looking at the muddy river and a field of winter wheat wedged between two loess hills topped with small pagodas.

"Actually," I said, "we're in the middle of China."

Mannerheim didn't write much about Sishui. He arrived here by travelling along the river. "Some junks were sailing on it in a fresh breeze," the Baron recalled. "Their square sails, of grey cloth with a broad blue band stiffened by numerous parallel ribs, have rather a medieval appearance." The landscape was bleak. Sishui, Mannerheim wrote, was still suffering the effects of a flood that had killed several thousand villagers forty-two years earlier.

The Yellow River I saw was at its lowest level in recorded history, the result of drought and poor water conservation. What water remained was heavily polluted. We found some rusting riverboats moored along the bank. One was a restaurant selling wild turtle dishes. Some men tried to convince us to pay for a tour of the river, but there was little to see. Everything was tinged a dirty yellow, like an old photograph. We walked back to Sishui along a paved country road lined by vibrant green fields and humdrum houses. Along the way, we met seventeen-year-old Zhang Jiangbie, a high-school student studying in Zhengzhou. He had just returned home for the weekend.

"Why don't you study in the village?" I asked.

"I want to go to the big city," he said. In fact, nearly everyone already lived in the city. His father worked in Kashgar selling farm equipment. "Sometimes he comes home often, but other times only once a year. It depends how much money he makes," he said. During the Chinese New Year, he explained, the village is flooded with cars with licence plates from all over China.

"Are there any full-time farmers here?" I asked.

"Not as far as I know," he said. "The seeding and harvesting are done with machines, so women can do it. Husbands don't even need to come home to help." The village of two hundred, which is part of Sishui township, was eerily quiet. We saw mostly old people, women and children, and one mangy dog. "Farming is over for the season so many people go work in the factories," he said. Despite its desolate appearance—the local school had even closed due to a lack of students—the village was growing rich: they had farm equipment, the road was recently paved and new two-storey brick abodes clad in shiny white tiles had replaced earthen bungalows. By peasant standards, it was prosperous.

"In the past," said an elderly woman running a kiosk, "even with the harvest there wasn't enough to feed your family." She had four children, but they had all moved away. They've given up farming too. "He only farms for fun," she said of her seventy-year-old husband, who sat on a stool smoking cigarettes.

Down the road, we passed a large billboard, some ten metres long. "Worship science. Care for your family. Cherish your life. Oppose evil religions," read its bold characters. The billboard was illustrated with stories of wickedness. "Evil religions beguile and deceive people, growing and controlling their membership to the endangerment of society," the billboard stated. Cartoonish images depicted all sorts of evildoing: people cheated of money, swindled for sex, even raped. In one story, a woman joins a cult, sells her family's orchard and is "disappeared." "Her husband," the story goes, "was left to be both father and mother to their child, lost his livelihood, fell to the enormous stress of it all and abandoned his child by hanging himself to death." An ominous warning followed: "Many people who join evil religions break the law without being aware, yet the law is without feeling; violators will be prosecuted." A large fist is shown smashing an evildoer.

"What is the evil religion?" I asked.

"Everyone knows it's Falun Gong," Tommy said. "The government just doesn't say it."

The Chinese government bans this sect, which blends *qigong* exercises, Buddhism, Daoism and the eclectic philosophy of its master, Li Hongzhi. The decline of Communist ideology—as with Confucianism a century ago—has created a vacuum filled by not just Falun Gong but all sorts of strange sects and charlatans. Henan has become fertile soil for underground churches and wild evangelism. The sects have queer-sounding names like the Oriental Lighting, Crying Faction All Sphere Church and Three Grades of Servants. Many are led by Henanese bumpkins claiming to be the second coming of Christ or to cure illness by exorcising demons. Beijing bans and actively persecutes their followers, worried that these unorthodox spiritual movements might grow into political threats, just as the Boxer and Taiping rebellions threatened Qing rule.

Before leaving Vancouver, I interviewed one of these supposed "evildoers." Jiang Zhiwei was a frail, timid woman in her seventies. She was born in Lanzhou and began practising Falun Gong after she became ill with an incurable respiratory disease. Her doctor recommended *qigong*, which involves slow physical movements and regulated breathing. "Falun Gong is a really good type of *qigong*," Jiang told me. "Many people who practise it experience a miracle." Indeed, her health improved immensely; she began breathing easily again and found an inner peace from its teachings.

Falun Gong's rapid growth—some 70 million practitioners by 1998—frightened the Communist Party, which banned it as a "cult" in 1999. Jiang went to Beijing as part of a now infamous peaceful protest: ten thousand worshippers surrounded the Communist Party's compound, which startled authorities. The movement was immediately crushed. Jiang ended up imprisoned in a labour camp at age seventy-one. "Some practitioners were beaten to death," she said, her eyes welling up with tears. She eventually fled to Canada.

What I found fascinating about Jiang's story was how a complex series of interconnected factors led her unwittingly into revolt against China's Communist leaders. She became ill at a time when the state ended free, universal health care. The poor turned to cheap alternatives, leading tens of millions into the *qigong* movement. With Marxism largely discredited, they were also ripe for Falun Gong's spiritual salvation. However, it was an ecological collapse that began Jiang's harrowing journey from *qigong* to chain gang. Her respiratory ailment was brought about by Lanzhou's air pollution, the worst in the world. It was a systematic breakdown—a cascade of ecological and social problems—that, in the end, led this grandma to revolt. A cautionary tale, it seemed to me, about the complex challenges and unexpected dangers that lie ahead for China and its rulers.

The next day, Tommy and I took the bus to Cuimiao, an hour southwest of Zhengzhou. The teenager in Sishui had said it was a poor village where the kids went hungry. The countryside—gentle hills terraced with farming plots—was dotted with coal storage pits, power plants and factories. Starving children, however, were nowhere to be found. We chatted with one farmer who even seemed rather optimistic about the future.

Li Ershui, age fifty, had grey gums and yellow teeth. He invited us into his spacious, newly built house along a country road lined with fields of wheat and corn. He sat on a small stool picking his toenails. "The amount of money farmers earn depends on how well industry is doing in the countryside. I really don't care about the land," he said, puffing on a cigarette. "If I don't want to work on it, my neighbours will work my farmland. If there are foreign investors, they can also use the land."

Both his sons worked in a truck factory in Xingyang, a nearby township. He himself earned money hauling goods in a motorized cart. He had saved enough money to build this seventeen-hundred-square-foot house with a large central foyer and four rooms. It was solidly made of brick, cement and stucco. He was participating in a new subsidized health plan too, paying ten yuan a year to access discounted medical services.

"Reform takes time," he said. "Everyone is greedy. When you reach a certain level of happiness, people want more."

I asked about a large portrait of Mao in the living room, wondering how this squared with his obvious support for market reform. "Everyone's house looks the same," he complained. "Most people hang Chinese watercolour paintings on their living-room walls. I wanted something different, so I picked Mao. Nobody hangs up his portrait anymore."

When we got back to the Zhengzhou bus station, Tommy and I jumped in a taxi whose inquisitive driver asked what we were doing. "Interviewing farmers," Tommy said.

"I'm a farmer," he said. "The government turned my land into a high-tech development zone and paid me forty thousand yuan per *mou*, but the land was really worth 100,000 yuan." Without farmland, he explained, he was forced to drive a taxi in the city. "I really don't like the corruption," he went on. "A lot of officials are corrupt and we lack any controls over them. If there was less corruption, China would be in much better shape."

Even Beijing seemed unable to control the local officials. Recently, the Communist Party chief in Zhengzhou and one of his lieutenants were punished for illegally seizing land to expand a college. Beijing was making an example of these Henan officials in order to cool down the overheating property market. In China, investment in so-called "fixed assets" such as buildings, factories, roads and bridges was growing by 30 percent per year and represented 42 percent of GDP.[16] (Zhengzhou had an audacious $35-billion plan to triple the size of the city.) Beijing seemed at a loss to stop the rampant land seizures and curb the growth: higher interest rates, development fees, new restrictions on leasing farmland,

official investigations into corruption and illegal expropriation—
nothing seemed to work. Beijing even resorted to using satellites to
spy on unauthorized development in rogue provinces.

A century ago it was even more difficult for the central government to curb malfeasance. Throughout China, Mannerheim noted
stories of tax revolts and complaints about greedy mandarins. He
recorded mandarins' "abuse of power" and "extortions" in Yarkand,
and troops killing and wounding a dozen protesters when an angry
mob besieged a prince's palace in Hami. He heard of more revolts in
Gansu province as well. During the republican revolution in 1911, a
peasant revolt broke out in Henan against excessive taxation, which
was being used to finance the Qing reform program. The very
reforms that were meant to strengthen Qing rule were beginning
to unravel it. Thousands inscribed on their banners the slogan "Kill
the rich and help the poor!"[17]

The central government still worries that local corruption and
growing inequality will create social unrest and destabilize the
country—and Communist Party rule. In response, Beijing abolished the agricultural tax in 2006 after 2,600 years, promised to
boost spending on rural social services and agreed to safeguard
farmers' land-use rights. In a nod to Confucius, President Hu Jintao
packaged these reforms under the banner of a "harmonious society."

As an insurance policy, Beijing also opened thirty thousand new
rural police stations, instructing security forces to pay special attention to "mafia-like evil forces."[18] A century ago, Qing officials took
similar precautions. Mannerheim noted that Henan's security forces
were organized differently than other provinces'. There were more
police, and a ragtag militia of opium smokers, cripples and ras-
cals had been disbanded. These *qubing*, or "district soldiers," had
proved unreliable in taking up arms against fellow peasants. They
were replaced by new *lujun*, or "land forces," modelled on German
troops. "Their intention is self-explanatory," Mannerheim wrote.
"They are intended for 'fighting internal enemies.'"[19]

TOMMY LEFT ON the night train back to Xi'an. The next morning, I visited the Henan Provincial Museum. Henan is considered "the cradle of Chinese civilization." It is one of the few places, along with the "fertile crescent" in the Middle East and Indus River Valley, where civilization emerged with the development of agriculture, animal domestication and settlements. Some of China's earliest cultural relics, including the famed oracle bones, were dug up from the soft soil of the Yellow River basin in Henan. The museum, a massive pyramid structure clad in dark granite, was full of Henan's contributions to the world: the first ploughs, defensive walls, astronomical observatory, compass, movable type for printing, gunpowder. Henan was also the home of three ancient capitals—Luoyang, Kaifeng and Anyang—that ruled China for nearly three thousand years. Yet none of this seemed to matter today.

"Civilization left Henan a long time ago," an African-American teacher in Zhengzhou named A.J. told me, "and has yet to come back."

Tommy had put me in touch with A.J., who taught at a local technical university. He offered one of his students to be my translator for a few days. The student's English name was Jerry. He was twenty-one, rail-thin and wore black slacks, a beige jacket and a blue sweater over a red turtleneck. He had an acne-pocked face. From my hotel room, we spent a morning calling various government bureaus, universities, associations and institutes to set up interviews about agricultural and rural reform. Invariably, we got the brush-off.

"People won't cooperate with you unless they know they'll benefit from it," Jerry said. "Otherwise, it is not their responsibility. You need connections—*guanxi*."

"It's not my responsibility" was a common response. Finally, one official said she'd call us back. "This means no," Jerry explained. "The Chinese don't like saying no directly so they will make up a small excuse."

After an hour, however, the hotel room phone rang. I looked at Jerry. He picked up the receiver, listened in silence, then hung up. "The front desk asked if they could send up a girl to give us a massage."

A dozen officials gave us the runaround. "You should just leave this city," Jerry said despondently.

"Let's forget about bureaucrats," I said. "Perhaps you could help me talk to more farmers in the countryside."

"My parents were farmers," he said, "but they sold our farm because you can't make any money. They moved to Chongqing. My dad is a truck driver and my mom is a housekeeper and also a gatekeeper at a factory." Together, he said, they make about fourteen hundred yuan or two hundred dollars per month. They also grow their own vegetables on a small plot back in their home village.

"I hate farm work," Jerry said. "I had to work when it was very hot outside, about thirty-eight degrees Celsius. I'm very afraid of that. That's why I look black, very dark. My dad said, 'If you want to succeed you must go to school. That's the only way to success.'"

Both he and his older sister were enrolled in college until his father lost his job. He was working as a truck driver at a coal mine in Shanxi, the province directly to the north. "My dad almost lost his life," Jerry said. His truck veered off a mountain road and down a forty-metre cliff. He survived but was badly scarred. "From then on," Jerry said, "I loved my dad even more. He just suffered so much." When he lost his job, the family couldn't afford tuition for both children. So his sister dropped out, got married and had a child. "We always feel guilty about this," Jerry said.

"That year was very difficult. I don't want to talk about it," he added brushing tears from his face with the back of his sleeve. "I just hope that in the future I can get a good job and help my parents. I'm afraid of the future. I don't know what to do. I'm scared I'll let my parents down."

The phone rang. I looked into Jerry's bloodshot eyes and smiled optimistically. He reached for the receiver.

"Do you want some service?" asked the voice.

"Like what?" Jerry replied.

"A girl?"

"No," Jerry said, slamming down the receiver.

We took a lunch break, eating beef noodle soup at a nearby restaurant. "Most officials only care about their job and money. That's why it's so hard to meet with them," Jerry said. "Government officials are the biggest problem. There's no people or media to watch them."

We weren't back in my hotel room five minutes before the phone rang again. "Can we send a girl?" the hotel clerk asked. This went on all afternoon and into the evening. I finally pulled the cord out of the wall and went to bed.

The next day, Jerry kindly offered to take me to his home village. We took a bus two hours north of Zhengzhou, whose suburbs ended in rice paddies and wheat fields. The highway, parts of which were still under construction, crossed a new steel bridge over the murky Yellow River. The fresh asphalt glistened. We passed small factories, farmsteads and billboards advertising real estate projects. One boasted of a "Splendid Cosmopolitan City" that would soon sprout up from surrounding fields. We transferred to a local minibus at the industrial town of Xinxiang. Zaipo, his home village, lay seven kilometres to the southwest. The bus was crowded with farmers and migrant workers humping big bundles. A young man talked on a cell phone. "That's my local dialect," Jerry said. "People from other provinces can't understand it."

The Henan countryside was dotted with thousands of faceless little hamlets and villages. I didn't see a square inch that wasn't cultivated, inhabited or industrialized. We passed a power plant, a paper mill and small factories with brick chimneys. The bus dropped us at the start of a new four-lane street with lampposts. It looked out of place, next to verdant wheat fields. Jerry's brother-in-law was waiting for us and we both climbed onto the back of a Suzuki motorcycle for the short ride to the home of Jerry's sister. This hamlet—Jerry didn't even know its name—was nothing more than a couple hundred brick houses clustered around an intersection. His sister, Qinghua, lived with her in-laws in a spacious two-storey house. She was a short, pretty woman dressed in a tangerine turtleneck and jeans.

"You look healthy," she told Jerry. "Your skin has really lightened."

We sat down to eat lunch with her father-in-law, who was clad in a dark brown jacket and blue pants. He had the swarthy complexion of a *nongmin*.

"They say that China is a rich country," Qinghua said, bringing in a plate of steaming meat dumplings to go along with roasted garlic cloves, apples and boiled water, "but most people are poor. The gaps between the rich and poor are getting wider and wider."

"In my opinion, we have realized the reforms," her father-in-law said. "There are lights, telephones, TVs. We pay ten yuan for each person to get medical care. To be honest, you cannot make money just relying on farming. Take this area, for example. There are cotton textile mills, machine factories, paper mills and other factories. Some factories have closed down because of pollution, but we are still prosperous."

His own family made only a third of its income from farming. Since 1995, he and his son had been doing interior and home renovations. "Since the opening up and reform policy, you can earn money based on your ability," he said. "There's a lot of freedom. You can do anything you want, just as Deng Xiaoping said."

After lunch, Jerry and I climbed on a scooter and puttered through the dirt alleyways of the village. Old men played mahjong at the main intersection. "Even if their children move to the city, the old men won't leave," Jerry said. "They are very happy. They don't want to be isolated in the city."

We left the village and drove a few kilometres to an intersection where a street market is held three days a week. The bazaar serves fifteen nearby villages. People were selling bread, noodles, vegetables and secondhand items: pots, pans, clothes, books. It was a rummage sale. Jerry's sister had just opened the Sunshine Curtain Shop in a building on the corner. Its interior was festooned in colourful curtains with floral patterns, pink lace and golden hearts. A large bed piled with pillows and quilts sat in the middle. She had a foot-powered Crown sewing machine and an electric one too. She had spent three years learning to sew at a technical school in Zhengzhou. She sold bedding and curtains, and mended old clothes. Jerry slipped off his pants to be repaired.

"There are always holes in the pockets of his pants," Qinghua complained. "Do you have the same problem with Western clothes?"

"Actually, most of our clothes are made in China," I said.

"We seldom see foreign people here," she said, giggling self-consciously at her question. "It's like you're from another planet."

For all the hype about Beijing's new celebrity architecture, the sleek software parks of Xi'an, Shenzhen's roaring Special Economic Zone and Shanghai's futuristic Pudong district, the genesis and foundation of China's fantastic rise to global economic superpower status lies in Qinghua's little curtain shop.

At the beginning of the Great Leap Forward in 1958, Mao replaced the family with the people's commune as the basic social unit for farmers. Peasants were subject to strict grain rationing, production quotas and the *hukou* system, which basically tied them like serfs to the land. In three years, grain yields declined by almost 30 percent. Tens of millions starved. This district in Henan was one of the worst ravaged by famine.[20] Quietly, however, local cadres and farmers began assigning individual plots to families to alleviate their suffering. Each was responsible for a grain quota but could retain surplus production. The so-called "contracting responsibility to each household" system soon spread from initial experiments in Anhui and Henan provinces, unleashing the productive force of hundreds of millions of farmers across China. The new system created surpluses of both rural labour and income that became the stimulus for rural industry. Ten years after Deng Xiaoping launched his reform, 100 million peasants worked for township and village enterprises that, in the words of one Chinese economist, "sprang up like mushrooms."[21] Since the mid-1990s, rural industry has accounted for a third of China's industrial output.[22]

Each year, tens of millions of peasants flee the countryside for service, construction or manufacturing jobs in urban areas. The average farmer's income is about four thousand yuan ($585) a year. Jerry's sister, by opening her shop, was now earning up to eight thousand yuan. Since 1978, some 235 million people have been lifted out of rural poverty in this way. The migration from farm to city that has taken place in China in the past two decades took Europeans two centuries. The farmers' defiance against collectivization set off a chain of events that has transformed China and shaken the world. Think of it as an industrial revolution on steroids.

Jerry and I jumped back on the scooter and travelled a kilometre to Zaipo, the village where he grew up. "These people are rich," he said, pointing to a large, white-tiled three-storey house. "They own a factory." We turned down a dirt alleyway to the northeast corner of the village. "We call this neighbourhood Little Taiwan," he said, "because they are so rich." At the very edge of the village next to a field we came to his parents' home. The small, brown brick bungalow had tiny windows and a flat roof. It looked like a jailhouse. It became clear to me that not everyone is benefiting equally from China's boom.

"My friends in high school wanted to visit, but I didn't allow it because I was embarrassed that our house was so poor," Jerry said. "When they built this house they were poor and they are still poor. It's a heartbreaking story. When I say things haven't changed a lot, maybe I'm wrong. Maybe just my world hasn't changed."

WITH THE LOOSENING of the *hukou* system, a massive rural reservoir of 150 million migrant workers is flooding Chinese cities in "the world's largest ever peacetime migration."[23] Of these migrants, the Henanese make up the largest group. "We have a saying that the Henan people in China are like the Chinese people in the world," Tommy told me. "They are everywhere." The Henanese are often looked down upon. City kids have many rhymes to describe them:

> Henan hick carried a pile of shit,
> When I tried to help him,
> He said I beat him.
> When I gave him a bowl of fried rice,
> He said it was full of shit.[24]

The Henanese are to the Chinese what the Okies were to Californians in the Dirty Thirties. They have long suffered the wrath of their countrymen. And like the Okies, the Henanese, periodically uprooted by drought and floods, often migrated West only to find lands—desert, steppe and mountains—as hostile as those they left behind.

No matter where Mannerheim travelled, he kept coming across people from Henan. His Chinese teacher in Kashgar was Henanese and a top mandarin in Yarkand was from Henan, as was "almost the whole administration of Kashgaria." Nearing Dunhuang, the Baron met a dozen settlers from Henan riding in two carts. The next day he met another dozen. "This time two extraordinary ugly old women tripped along with the unnatural gait on their atrophied tiny feet among the men," he wrote. Two days later he met more Henanese migrants, and the next day yet another dozen "intrepid settlers." At Jiayuguan, Mannerheim looked at the records of all those passing through the Great Pass Under Heaven. "Settlers, large numbers of whom travel westward every year, have to pay 1 ch'ien [copper coin] per head for such registration or for obtaining a permit. A party of 500 Honanese recently manifested their objections to this unjust imposition by giving the collector of this bloodmoney a sound thrashing and going on their way without paying anything."

When Mannerheim arrived in Zhengzhou, the city was rapidly evolving into a railway hub. It would one day become the crossroads for China's two main trunk lines. The Peking–Hankow Railway, running north–south, opened in 1906 and a Franco-Belgian Syndicate had just completed a line between Kaifeng and Zhengzhou, the first leg of the Longhai Railway that would eventually stretch from the coastal city of Lianyungang to Urumqi. The railway radically realigned Henan, as villages and towns flourished along the trunk lines and withered along the bygone caravan routes and waterways. Nowadays, the Zhengzhou Railway Station has become a major way station for migrant workers travelling throughout China.

Jerry and I spent my final afternoon in Zhengzhou talking with several of them. Thousands of dark-clad men and some women huddled in groups on the station's cold stone concourse. Many slept there, under the eerie glow of halogen street lights. Six months before, Jerry had accompanied his father here to say goodbye before he went to Chongqing.

"A lot of people looked down at us. My dad's clothes were very poor and he had many bags," he said. "That's why I desire success. That's why. If you are a peasant in China, a farmer, it's very sad, very sorrowful."

The first migrant we spoke to was named Zhen Qitao. He was in his forties and wore a crewcut, dirty orange shirt and camouflage pants. He came from the coastal province of Shandong and worked in construction. He had been roaming China for the past thirteen years. "There's no factory in my hometown," he said. "Most of the young people move away." He made about eighteen hundred yuan per month. A Henanese migrant, Zhi Bin, wasn't so lucky: he too had been on the road for fifteen years, but earned a meagre eight hundred yuan a month. He had a wife and son at home. "It's very difficult to find work around my hometown," he said.

"I'm happy. I don't miss home at all," said another Henanese migrant named Zhang Zhonghuan, age fifty, squatting on old newspapers and eating sunflower seeds. "I have to work hard to make money for my family. If I stayed at home, who would make money? I don't want to work on the farm. I can get more money working outside the farm." He said he doubled his income by working in construction. By borrowing money from neighbours and relatives, he was able to send both his kids to university in Zhengzhou. Jerry and I spent two hours talking to more than a dozen migrants. All of them seemed more than happy to escape rural poverty. I had to admire their stoicism.

That night, I took Jerry to Toscana, an Italian Restaurant in downtown Zhengzhou. He had never eaten at a Western restaurant. I figured it would be a good experience, since he would need to learn about Western food and etiquette if he was going to become a successful interpreter. We ordered lasagne and Caesar salad.

"I think this is the first and last time I'll eat a Caesar salad," he said.

"Why? Don't you like it?"

"No, I don't think I'll have another opportunity," he said.

"Don't think like that. You'll have other opportunities to eat a Caesar salad. I'm sure of it," I said encouragingly. "Have big dreams, not small ones."

"I've had many, many dreams over the years," Jerry said. "They've all been broken or I have failed."

"Be persistent," I said.

"Can I ask you a question?"

"Sure."

"Is life fair or unfair?"

I knew where the conversation was going.

"Unfair," I had to admit.

"In school," Jerry said, "I began my studies at 5 AM every morning and worked until the late evening. I wanted to go to a famous university and to go to a military academy, but I failed. Many friends failed to go to famous universities too. Some now work in factories and only get three hundred yuan per month." The conditions were horrendous: sweltering heat, low pay, noxious air, long hours. "Other students just played soccer or basketball in school, but went to famous universities because of an uncle or relationship—*guanxi*. Is that fair? I don't think so. Many friends in the factories look very old. I'm afraid of the future. I'm afraid I'll be like my friends who work twelve hours a day in the factories."

He paused. "I just feel my way in the darkness."

He cut a square of lasagne. "I'll never forget this dinner for the rest of my life," he said. He awkwardly held his knife like a chopstick, squeezed between his index finger and thumb. "I saw people eating food in a movie once using a fork and knife. It looked easy, but it isn't," he said. He cut into the layers of pasta, cheese, tomato sauce and meat with the precision of a surgeon.

"From elementary school to university," Jerry went on, "my dad said, 'Work hard, work hard, work hard. We don't have money or relatives with power so you will only succeed by working hard.' That's why many students from the countryside work harder than students from the city." Initially, his parents wanted him to move back home, but they know it's a dead end. "They are going to let me go," he said. After university graduation, he too would head to the Zhengzhou Railway Station and set out, wandering China for a better future.

SIXTEEN

TAIYUAN

Opium of the People

*Why don't these missionaries stay in their own country and
be useful to their own people?*—EMPRESS DOWAGER CIXI[1]

THE SMOG WAS thick and blue as cotton candy. I could barely see
the aerated sewage ponds along the south bank of the Yellow
River. It was early morning. I was on the T58 train crossing a
steel bridge over the murky "mother river" on my way from Zhengzhou to Taiyuan, the capital of Shanxi province to the north.

I was travelling on the historic Peking–Hankow Railway, the
first major trunk line in China, connecting Peking (now Beijing)
with the populous Central Plains and Hankow (now Wuhan) in the
southern Yangtze River basin. Built in 1905, it is 1,212 kilometres
long. A three-kilometre steel bridge traversed the Yellow River and,
according to Mannerheim, was the "most remarkable part" of an
otherwise monotonous journey. Mannerheim mentioned that the
scenery was "slightly enlivened" by a rugged granite range running
"at a considerable distance" to the west, but these mountains never
materialized during my morning ride. I could barely see beyond a
half-kilometre of cotton and wheat fields. The sooty haze was just
too thick. I was heading deep into coal country.

The Chinese have been mining coal for centuries. Up until the twentieth century, their technology was shockingly primitive. They usually dug shallow pits, working coal outcrops near towns or waterways for ease of transport. By 1895, the Chinese began to grant widespread concessions to the French, Russians, Belgians, British and Germans to build modern railways and mines. One of the most lavish foreign concessions awarded coal, iron ore, petroleum and other mineral rights on 21,000 square kilometres of northern Henan and Shanxi provinces in 1898. It went to the British-owned Peking Syndicate. Peasant unrest and lack of railways delayed operations for several years, but eventually the syndicate dug bore holes and constructed two branch lines off the railway eighty kilometres north of Zhengzhou.[2] Across Northern China, coal mines began popping up like molehills. Within a decade, China's coal production had climbed threefold, reaching nearly 3 million tons in 1908.[3]

After eight hours, I arrived in Shijiazhuang, the capital of Hebei province, where, like Mannerheim, I changed lines, heading west across the Taihang Shan range into Shanxi province. In 1908, this east–west railway to Taiyuan had just been completed. Mannerheim enjoyed the "beautiful and wild scenery" from the private caboose of the train's second engineer, Mr. J. de Lapeyrière, who recounted in great detail the engineering feat to construct the line. The railway had been built to transport coal and iron from Shanxi to the Peking–Hankow line, but transport proved so expensive that the coal could not compete against coastal mines. Instead, the railway company jacked up the price of passenger tickets. A first-class ticket for the three-hundred-kilometre journey from Shijiazhuang to Taiyuan cost fifteen dollars—an "unusual" fare, according to Mannerheim. A century later, I paid five dollars and twenty cents.

The Taihang mountains are the Great Smokies of China, separating the loess plateau of Shanxi from the delta river region of the coast. Whereas the name of America's famed massif is taken from a natural haze rising from lush forests, Taihang gets its smokiness from burning coal. "The supply of coal and iron is said to be very considerable," Mannerheim wrote of Shanxi, "and the coal is supposed to be of excellent quality." In 1908, Shanxi's nascent steel industry produced only kettles, wagon wheels and ploughshares. Still, the iron ore and coal reserves of Shanxi seemed vast. From the train, Mannerheim could see "small black mounds" on mountain slopes near the town of Pingding, halfway to Taiyuan. Later, he studied maps produced by the Peking Syndicate that showed coal and iron deposits throughout the province. "In the future," Mannerheim wrote in his military report, "its material riches will be an inexhaustible source for the state treasury."[4]

Our train passed numerous rail wagons heaped with coal. I sat in a compartment with two Chinese businessmen and stared out at the bleak landscape. The autumn foliage had disappeared. Dark granite peaks loomed over barren farm plots and soot-stained villages trapped in deep gorges. Everything looked blackened. The train creaked and groaned as it rumbled along the serpentine line. Winter was nearing—it was October 30—and Shanxi's coal would soon be stoking furnaces across China. It is the largest coal-producing province in the country, with 270 billion tons in proven reserves. As a result, Shanxi has the ignominy of having sixteen cities on the State Environmental Protection Administration's "black list" for air quality below grade 3, meaning they suffer serious pollution.[5]

I arrived in Taiyuan at 10 PM and stayed at a business hotel across from the train station. I went for a stroll the next morning. Taiyuan is the most blighted city that I have ever visited. Like Lanzhou, it at one time claimed the title of the world's most polluted city. (That dubious distinction, according to a recent World Bank report, now belongs to Linfen, about two hundred kilometres away.) South of the train station, I came across a temple complex with twin soaring pagodas, then wandered along a river the colour of bile. Garbage was everywhere. Heaps smouldered on the streets. So many torn bits of plastic hung in trees that they looked like fall foliage. The roads were horrendously dusty, potholed and cracked. I saw a teenage boy crawling on the sidewalk, dragging his deformed legs behind him and begging for change. A sooty film covered everything.

By day three, I was ill with a sore throat and plugged nose. I felt so lethargic I could barely get out of bed. I lay wheezing the entire morning and only mustered enough energy to call the State Key Lab of Coal Conversion, the Taiyuan Iron and Steel Company and the Institute for Coal Chemistry to arrange interviews. Of course, everyone refused to talk to me. Finally, I reached an accommodating official at Taiyuan's municipal Foreign Investment Promotion Office who spoke a little English.

"Charlie," as his business card read, was waiting for me at the curb when my taxi arrived. In his mid-fifties, he had a nicotine-stained smile and was dressed in a dark blue jacket and black slacks. His office was in a building that looked like a Soviet ghetto: concrete floors; dim, deserted hallways; dirty yellow paint that was chipped and peeling. It was nothing like the sparkling municipal towers of Xi'an or even Zhengzhou. Charlie had a middle-aged, bespectacled female deputy and a young assistant who was sorting receipts in their small, cluttered office. In the course of an hour, the phones never rang. An economic hot zone Taiyuan was not.

Charlie sat me down, offered me tea and handed me an investment guide in which Taiyuan's vice mayor, Rong Tang, extended prospective investors a "worm hearted welcome."

"There are 213 projects that need investment," Charlie said, getting down to business.

"What about investing in the coal and steel industries?" I asked.

"If you want to invest in mining and coal, it is limited."

"Why?"

"Environment. This area we limit," he said, lighting a cigarette. "Steel is limited. You can make products out of steels. That okay.

But just make steel—this not okay." He took a long drag on his cigarette and leaned toward me. "So," he said frowning, "how much can you invest?"

"Well," I began in an apologetic tone, "I'm actually researching a book on China's modernization. I'm not investing myself, but perhaps someone who reads my book will be inspired to invest in Taiyuan."

Bemused by my response, Charlie picked up the phone and dialled a number. As he chatted in Mandarin, I flipped through Taiyuan's investment guide. It was arranged like a Chinese restaurant menu, divided into broad categories—agriculture, forestry, manufacturing and so on—with each investment project assigned a number to facilitate easy selection. Some investments sounded strangely intriguing: Project No. 23 was titled "Eco-friendly, Non-residual-toxin Pure Chinese Medicine Pesticide Damp Powder Preparation" and No. 16 was "Grandparent-generation Beijing Duck Breeder Duck Ranch." I could even invest US$9.88 million to help restore a sixty-metre-tall ancient Buddha statue and historic site. If you were crazy enough to invest in this squalid backwater, a $1.25-million investment in a new addition to the Taiyuan Mental Hospital (Project No. 12) might nicely cap your portfolio.

Charlie reached over and handed me the phone.

"Charlie said he can only offer you the brochures," a voice said in English, with a faint Chinese accent.

"What about setting up a tour of the Taiyuan Iron and Steel Company's mill?" I asked.

"Charlie said he has no contacts at TISCO," the man replied.

The state-owned enterprise has sixty-five thousand employees and $10 billion in annual revenues—greater than the GDP of Kyrgyzstan. It's the province's biggest employer, covering a vast swath of land just north of downtown Taiyuan. A new production line had just opened, making it the world's largest producer of stainless steel. It seemed highly unlikely that Charlie didn't know someone, anyone, at TISCO. This was just a polite way of saying he was unwilling to help me.

"What company do you work for?" I asked the mysterious English speaker on the phone, hoping to establish *guanxi*.

"Evergreen."

"You mean the Taiwanese transportation conglomerate?"

"No, we're a nonprofit organization."

"Oh, the Toronto-based environmental group? What sort of green development and environmental projects are you working on in Taiyuan?"

"Actually, we aren't an environmental group. We are named after a Norwegian missionary," he said.

"Evergreen doesn't sound Norwegian," I said somewhat baffled. "Are you a Christian organization?"

"We are an organization made up of people with Christian values," he said evasively.

"What do you do?"

The man, who never gave me his name, said Evergreen provides educational, medical and agriculture assistance to local communities and has about thirty employees including "many foreigners." He gave me the telephone number of Evergreen's director in Taiyuan, Andrew Kaiser. It appeared as though I had stumbled upon another foreign missionary.

TAIYUAN HASN'T ALWAYS been a blighted industrial town. Mannerheim was charmed by its old temples, medieval city wall, macadamized streets, public garden and pond, and shops decorated with beautiful, brightly coloured designs. Taiyuan, he wrote, had "an unusually attractive appearance" and looked "pretty in its verdant surroundings against the grey background of the mountains." The town sparkled in the sunshine.

But Shanxi and its capital had since fallen on hard times.

The province had once been one of the most prosperous in China. Its loess plateau was a trade corridor between Central China and the Mongolian steppe. Shanxi merchants controlled the lucrative tea and silk trade flowing to Russia on this overland route. Many merchants also became money exchangers, establishing China's first banks, or *piaohao*—literally "ticket store." Shanxi bankers grew rich, but other factors conspired to cripple the province. In the eighteenth century, sea trade began to supplant the overland route to Europe, and in 1875, the province was beset by a series of catastrophic droughts. No rain fell at all in 1877, leading to complete crop failure. The scene was gruesome. "Dogs eat the dead, and the starving eat the dogs," reported one Western missionary who brought relief to Shanxi.[6] People ate tree bark, pencils, clothing, even each other. In a letter from Linfen, another missionary wrote: "Five women were burned alive, hands and feet tied, for killing and eating children they had kidnapped from the streets."[7]

The drought may have destroyed crops, but it did bear "spiritual fruit."[8] In 1878, Timothy Richard, an Englishman, established the first mission in Taiyuan to provide famine relief. Thankful locals erected a sign over the entrance: "Save the World Church." Richard had been a missionary in Shandong, working closely with China's leading reformers, and recognized the ineffectiveness of open-air preaching on the Chinese. He took a practical—though highly controversial—approach to proselytizing. In order to sweeten the appeal of the Gospel, he established orphanages, shelters, elementary schools, a hospital and opium refuges. He also lectured on Christianity and modern science, and conducted a geographical survey to help prevent flooding. Soon, other Protestant sects began to arrive: the China Inland Mission, Scandinavian Alliance Mission, Baptist Mission Society, American Board Mission.[9]

By the late 1890s, medieval China and newly emerging modern China had begun to clash. The Boxer Movement spread quickly from village to village, igniting passions. It drew its members from the poor and dispossessed of Northern China. They were suspicious of Western technology—trains, steamboats and telegraph wires—believing it displaced Chinese labourers and upset the feng shui of the land. Boxers particularly despised "rice Christians," fellow Chinese the Boxers thought had sold their souls for the square meals provided by missionaries during the famine.

In 1898, the Yellow River—"China's Sorrow"—flooded, destroying fifteen hundred villages. Plagues of locusts and drought followed. Many Christian converts became aggressive and abusive to their non-Christian neighbours. Foreign missionaries, particularly Roman Catholics, often interfered in litigation and other local affairs on their behalf.[10] Suspicion of Christianity grew. Foreigners were even blamed for the drought.[11]

On the last day of 1899, the Boxers murdered their first missionary in Shandong, whose governor, Yu Xian, was consequently demoted to Shanxi. On January 11, Taiyuan missionaries cabled the foreign legation in Peking: "Outlook very black... secret orders from the Throne to encourage [Boxers]."[12] This warning went unheeded. By May, Chinese Christians were being attacked and murdered, their homes ransacked and burned. Then the Boxers laid siege to the foreign legations in Peking.

The fanatical sect initially frightened the Empress Dowager. "The Court appears to be in a dilemma," wrote Sir Robert Hart, an Englishman appointed Inspector General of China's Imperial Maritime Customs Service and the most knowledgeable foreigner on Court intrigues. "If the Boxers are not suppressed, the Legations threaten to take action—if the attempt to suppress them is made, this intensely patriotic organization will be converted into an anti-dynastic movement!"[13] Prince Tuan and his brother Duke Lan convinced the Empress Dowager that "the Boxers were sent by Heaven to enable China to get rid of all the undesirable and hated foreigners."[14] The Empress Dowager reluctantly declared war on the Western powers, seeing it as the lesser of two evils.

In Shanxi, Governor Yu arrested all the missionaries, including their wives and children, and brought them to the courtyard of his *yamen* in central Taiyuan. "There is much in town to remind one of

the terrible tragedy that took place about a month before the combined troops of the European powers and Japan put an end to the
licence of the Boxers' instincts by the occupation of Peking," Mannerheim wrote. "Treacherously lured into a trap by the promise of
protection by the governor of that time, 35 Protestant missionaries,
male and female, and 12 Roman Catholic nuns and monks, including two bishops, were put to death in a single day after horrifying
tortures in the governor's own lawcourt."

After fifty-five days, foreign troops invaded Peking and ended
the siege. The Empress Dowager fled first to Taiyuan and then to
Xi'an, where she negotiated a peace treaty. China was forced to pay
an indemnity to the Western powers. Governor Yu committed suicide and many other Boxer leaders were executed. Despite calls for
their execution, Prince Tuan and Duke Lan were (as we have seen)
exiled to Xinjiang.

In Taiyuan, the Protestant missionaries requested monuments
to the "martyrs" erected at various spots around the city, as well
as a half-million *taels* in reparations to establish Shanxi University. Mannerheim reported in 1908 that 250 Chinese students were
being "given a thoroughly western education."

"It seems as though the seed of this innocent blood had borne
fruit," he wrote, "for from the ashes of the victims' houses schools,
hospitals and churches have arisen, to contribute, each in its own
way, to remove the hatred of foreigners, the result of superstition
and ignorance, of which there was such a terrible outburst during
the Boxer rising."[15]

I COULD NOT find any physical reminder of past missionary work in
Taiyuan. Their "fruit" had apparently withered over the course of
a century. Mannerheim had mentioned a new building that housed
Shanxi University, but the university's campus had since relocated
to a southern suburb. I couldn't find the original hall in the jumble
of densely packed buildings downtown. However, I did happen

upon a Western-style café, where I enjoyed drinking Illy-brand Americanos, reading old copies of the *Shanghai Daily* and feasting on tuna melts, cheesecake and chocolate chip cookies. The Maya Café had a green-tiled bar and posters of Che Guevara, Hollywood movies and jazz singers on the wall. The owner had a penchant for the music of Diana Krall. I felt like I was in San Francisco.

One morning, an American walked into the café. He was boyishly handsome, the spitting image of a young Ron Howard, the Hollywood director. He wore a baseball cap, cargo pants, a grey sweater and an outdoor jacket tied around his waist. He looked to be in his early thirties. I immediately pegged him as an evangelical, for he had in tow two young children with wickedly curly hair. Only a missionary, I figured, would raise a family in such a godforsaken place.

He sat at a nearby table doing paperwork. Soon enough I heard him talking on his cellphone about revamping Evergreen's website. I had found the website the previous night and read about the organization's unusual genesis. In 1939, Peter Torjesen, whose Chinese name was Ye Yongqing (meaning "Leaf Evergreen"), was a Norwegian missionary in Hequ, a town not far from Taiyuan. He'd been church-planting and proselytizing in Shanxi for nearly twenty years. At the time, Shanxi was headquarters to Mao's ragtag army as they fought the Japanese invasion. Torjesen was harbouring a thousand Chinese refugees in his church compound when he was killed in a Japanese bombing raid.

Fifty years later, a reform-minded official in Hequ decided to erect a monument dedicated to Torjesen, whom the local Communist Party designated a "people's martyr." Torjesen's children and grandchildren were invited to Shanxi for the memorial's unveiling. The marble monument included a biblical inscription, in Chinese, from Jeremiah 17:7–8:

> Blessed is the man who trusts in the Lord ...
> He is like a tree planted by the water,
> That sends out its roots by the stream,

And does not fear heat when it comes,
For its leaves remain green,
And is not anxious in the year of drought,
For it does not cease to bear fruit.

Half a century after the tragic bombing, the vice-governor of Shanxi made an extraordinary proposal. He invited Torjesen's grandson Finn and his wife, Sandy, who were working as missionaries in Indonesia at the time, "to come back and continue the spirit of Peter Torjesen."

It was a clever, though highly unorthodox, move by the Communist Party boss to recruit a Western missionary to help attract foreign expertise and perhaps even investment to this underdeveloped region. In 1993, Finn returned to establish Shanxi Evergreen Service. Remarkably, in a country where proselytizing by foreigners is illegal, the missionaries were allowed to work openly as Christians. Evergreen's mission is to continue "the good works of Ye Yongqing, acknowledging God's gracious calling in our lives and reflecting the credibility of Christ." However, like the pragmatic Timothy Richards a century ago, Evergreen has taken a low-key, professional approach to proselytizing. The Torjesens set up agricultural, educational, medical and economic development programs and services. They would simply convince prospective converts that their helping hand was in fact the hand of God.

Their online newsletter was full of such testimonials. In one case, Evergreen sponsored a young woman to study medicine. "I am very grateful God gave me the opportunity to study and work at Evergreen and even gave me a new life," wrote Xin Lihua. "He did not forsake me." Another convert worked as a driver for Evergreen and was impressed by the foreigners' kindness. "Their actions," Zhou Bing wrote, "inspired me to want to know God."

I wanted to know more myself so I introduced myself to the young missionary in the Maya Café. His name is Mike Stern. The thirty-six-year-old has three kids altogether and a wife, Ashley.

Originally from Decatur, Illinois, Stern earned a degree in political science and history at Bob Jones University, a Christian college in Greenville, South Carolina. He went on to complete a master's in public policy from the Korean Development Institute in Seoul, where he met his wife. He spent two years teaching English in Taiyuan in the mid-1990s and came back in 2004 with his family. For the past two years in Taiyuan, he had been focusing his studies exclusively on Chinese. "If you want to get ideas and concepts across, you've got to be able to speak the language," he told me.

I explained to Stern that I had set up a meeting with Andrew Kaiser, Evergreen's Taiyuan director, for the next day. Over the phone, Kaiser had given me directions to the original Shanxi University building, but I was unable to locate it using my poor tourist map. I asked Stern for assistance. He said it was nearby and agreed to take me there in a taxi. Colin, his five-year-old son, came along while his daughter, Cora, stayed in the café.

We found the old university hall a block from Taiyuan's central square, hidden behind a high, protective barrier of Romanesque columns. The building looked like a castle, with a large central tower, parapets lining the roof and corner embrasures. Apparently the missionaries had designed it as a defensive fortress, lest they fall victim to further anti-foreign sieges.

Inside, large marble tablets were set into the walls on each side of a twin staircase. Inscriptions told the tragic tale that led to the university's founding. The plaques were enclosed in glass and chrome cases. Stern said that they had been plastered over during the Cultural Revolution, which likely saved them from destruction. Another plaque near the gate said that Shanxi University Hall had been built in 1902 by a missionary named Li Timotai, which is the Chinese name of Timothy Richard. It was one of three early modern universities established in China, stated the plaque, and was now the Taiyuan Teachers Technical College.

A mob of students in blue and white polyester tracksuits flooded past us into the school. We walked back to the street, where a gust of wind sent autumn leaves raining down on us. "In the spring, there are rolling clouds of dust that pick up junk and that move at thirty or forty miles an hour," Stern said. "Big, gigantic dust storms roll over the city." He pointed to fine yellow dust caking a parked car. During his two-year stay in the 1990s, the city was so dirty and polluted that after a day outside his blond hair turned black. He came down with asthma. "I couldn't hack it—the dirt and all," he said. Now, a decade later, he always wore a hat and carried wraparound sunglasses that, like goggles, kept airborne grit out of his eyes.

"Here it is," Stern said, slipping on his sunglasses and putting a hoodie over his son's head. He pointed down the street. I turned and saw a massive yellow dustball rolling over the tops of buildings. It started barrelling down the narrow street toward us. Stern quickly hailed a taxi. We dove into the car just as the dustball descended upon us. I got some grit in my mouth and had difficulty breathing.

"China is on the verge of an ecological disaster," said Stern, back in the café. He had read that in the Han Dynasty, two millennia ago, there was on average one dust storm every two hundred years. In the 1950s, it was one every two or three years. "It's been downhill ever since," he said. That summer Beijing had a record ten. "Look!" Stern yelled, pointing out the window. "It looks like we are having another one right now." On the street, people frantically dashed about searching for shelter as a fierce wind blasted a barrage of dirt, twigs, newspapers and garbage down the street.

In Stern's mind, China was also suffering from a spiritual disaster. The violent repression of religion during the Cultural Revolution, he explained, had left many Chinese feeling spiritually void. "These people have no values," he told me. "They've been wiped out." He said many students talk about *kongxu,* or their "emptiness." Students tell him, "I have nothing inside me."

"They are trying to fill that emptiness," Stern said.

"Is that why you came to Taiyuan, to help fill that emptiness?" I asked.

"Jesus Christ hung out with the down and out, not with the movers and shakers," he said. Evergreen is not overt about its evangelism, but, he said, "if people ask me what my motivation is, I tell them."

As the young missionary continued to talk, I began hacking uncontrollably. I could barely breath. I frantically gulped a glass of water to soothe my dry, irritated throat. "Taiyuan is getting to you," Stern said.

"RELIGION," KARL MARX famously wrote, "is the sigh of the oppressed creature, the heart of a heartless world, and the soul of soulless conditions. It is the opium of the people."

That certainly seemed true in Taiyuan a century ago. Missionaries brought food for the famished, medicine for the ill, education for the illiterate, hope for the hopeless. Yet to me, evangelicals also seemed cynically opportunistic, riding into town on the coattails of the Four Horsemen of the Apocalypse. They exploited famine, pestilence, death and war—particularly the Opium Wars—to push Christian teachings on Shanxi's vulnerable population.

In fact, missionaries were only able to return to China's interior (they had been banned in 1724) thanks to a treaty settling the Second Opium War in 1860. The British were so concerned about their trade deficit from importing silk, porcelain and tea—and the drain of silver from their treasury—that the British East India Company began illegally smuggling opium into China. Imperial edicts on prohibition and stricter enforcement ultimately led to clashes with Britain in the Opium War (1839–42) and the Second Opium War (1856–1860). Addiction grew, along with domestic opium production, which bedevilled the empire, especially Shanxi's rich bankers.

The Chinese actually associated Western religion with opium, in part because many Protestant missionaries arrived on opium clippers.[16] In 1890, however, missionaries, including a Baptist from Taiyuan, founded the Permanent Committee for the Promotion of Anti-Opium Societies, recognizing that widespread addiction was corroding civil society and their ability to spread Christianity. Missionaries lobbied the British Parliament to ban the opium trade and began drug rehabilitation work in the Chinese countryside. In 1908, China and Britain signed an agreement to steadily reduce opium imports from India as well as domestic cultivation.

Throughout China, Mannerheim saw the ravages of opium upon the people. It was grown everywhere, from the margins of the Taklimakan Desert to the banks of the Yellow River in Central China. He met an addicted army general with a tired gait, officers with emaciated faces, and entire garrisons "physically quite ruined by opium smoking." The viceroy of Gansu was himself addicted. "Europeans make fun of us," one mandarin explained to Mannerheim, "because we are weakened and become effeminate by opium smoking." Opium had enfeebled the empire so badly that Mannerheim wrote a section about its devastating effect in his military report to the Russian General Staff.[17] In Gansu, 50 percent of the province's exports was opium or tobacco. One missionary in Gansu told him that 6 to 8 million people—half the male population— were addicted to opium.

Shanxi was by far the most wasted region in the Empire. By 1900, almost 60 percent of the province was stoned.[18] "The present governor does not appear to be keen on the reform, but even if he were filled with the best intentions, the suppression of opium growing and its abuse in this province has to face some unusual obstacles," Mannerheim wrote. "The opium of Shansi has the reputation of being the best in China and is in great demand." The province's rich bankers were "known throughout the entire Empire for their admiration of opium as a means to pass on their fortunes to their heirs, who live idle lives and drink alcohol as well. Each of them considers it a personal duty to develop an opium smoking habit in their sons."[19]

The Chinese were trying to follow the example of Japan, which used "systematic draconian measures," according to Mannerheim, to eradicate opium smoking on the island of Formosa (now Taiwan). In 1906, an Imperial Edict was issued to limit the further spread of opium farming, processing and smoking, but local officials often ignored the directive.

"Instruments for smoking were sold openly and there were no restrictions on opium trading," Mannerheim wrote in his military intelligence report. "The orders to reduce the area of poppy fields introduced in some localities were abolished, and it was only the population's lack of certainty [about enforcement] that prevented them from enlarging poppy plantations."[20]

For their part, the missionaries lobbied officials and opened opium refuges. The missionary hospital in Taiyuan was one of the first in China—and perhaps even the world—to begin experimenting with the use of morphine to break opium addictions.[21] Morphine, administered hypodermically, was substituted for opium and over a month the addict was weaned off the narcotic. One missionary reported that the "treatment was so successful that the gentry presented the hospital with a plaque that proclaimed 'The wonderful needle is like that of old,' as if the hypodermic was a miraculous new kind of acupuncture."[22] Since missionaries dispensed the morphine, the Chinese in Taiyuan began to refer to it as "Jesus opium."[23]

"WE ARE NOT pastors," Andrew Kaiser told me the next day in Evergreen's new sixteenth-floor headquarters in downtown Taiyuan. The offices still smelled like fresh paint and off-gassing furniture. "We are professionals who are Christians." He usually introduces himself as a "Christian professional" *(jidu tu)* or a "Christian worker" *(jidu gongzouren)*.

Kaiser, age thirty-five, didn't look like a pastor. He had slicked-back hair and wore a blue checkered polo shirt. He looked—and talked—more like a management consultant. He had studied Chinese and political economy at Carleton College in Minnesota, but also held a master's in theology from a seminary. He came to

Taiyuan in 1997 to work for Evergreen. The independent, non-denominational Protestant mission is made up of about twenty-five Christian professionals and their families from the United States, Canada, Europe and Australia. Like Mike Stern, each recruit spends two years gaining professional fluency in Chinese and usually makes a long-term commitment to Evergreen (at least ten years). "One of the phrases that people use to describe us is that we are a 'boutique mission,'" Kaiser said. "It's an odd phrase."

But Evergreen is an odd mission. "We are Christians and the government knows we are Christians," he said. "We even partner with the government." Kaiser once even organized a community-based policing workshop for the Public Security Bureau, the very agency that many Christians accuse of persecution. "In the past, missionaries have been quite destabilizing, working outside the mainstream," Kaiser explained. Evergreen's strategy, however, is to work within the system, establishing *guanxi* with powerful officials and bringing about incremental change. This approach isn't without its critics, especially among other evangelicals. "I've been called a Communist sympathizer in print," Kaiser said. In this way, Evergreen is continuing the legacy of Timothy Richards, whose unconventional approach irked many mainstream missionaries a century ago.

Kaiser believes that there's more rule of law in China today and that by working above board Evergreen has gained the trust of local officials. "There's a lot more freedom than twenty-five years ago," Kaiser explained. "Western Christians see the regulations [on religion] as persecution, but it's actually progress." In any case, it wasn't the law that historically restricted religion in China so much as societal norms. "In the 1970s, socially acceptable religious practice was very limited," he said. That has changed. "There's virtually no stigma in social circles to say you are Christian." Indeed, a decade ago distributing Bibles—even those legally printed in China—made local police nervous. Nowadays, Kaiser said, nobody cares.

What really worries Kaiser isn't religious persecution, but China's rising nationalism. "That's the thousand-pound gorilla that all the old China Hands are watching," he said. I hadn't experienced any anti-foreign hostility myself, but Kaiser assured me it's lurking below the surface. "It's shocking," he said. "It's not a pervasive attitude. It's not the constant mood, but it's there." He saw this anti-foreign sentiment first-hand during violent protests in 1999 after the United States bombed the Chinese embassy in Belgrade. The government, Kaiser said, bused students to the protest.

With its ideology waning, the Communist Party uses nationalism to legitimize its rule. After the Tiananmen Square massacre, authorities launched a "patriotic education campaign" in schools and the mass media.[24] School kids are taught of China's "century of humiliation" at the hands of foreigners. Beijing occasionally whips up popular rage against American military misadventures, Taiwanese independence or Japan's wartime atrocities. Beijing must never be seen to be "toadying to the United States or other foreigners," Kaiser explained. "That was what the Boxer Rebellion was about: 'We have no pride in our country.'"

As its "heavenly mandate" crumbled, the Qing Dynasty began stoking nationalistic passions too. The Imperial Court encouraged the patriotic Boxers and the "rights recovery" movement against foreign concessions. Workers, students and merchants held protests and signed petitions against foreign-controlled companies. In his diary, Mannerheim noted that "the population's hostility and the obstacles made by the authorities" forced the Peking Syndicate to sell its mining and railway rights in Shanxi and Henan.[25]

In reality, the Qing Dynasty depended on foreigners to maintain their rule. Throughout China, Mannerheim noted how foreign machinery, armaments and military advisers helped strengthen Imperial forces against internal rebellion. A European officer corps even trained and led the Imperial army that defeated the Taiping Rebellion.

The Communist Party finds itself in a similar catch-22, explained Kaiser. Beijing needs foreigners to create the very wealth that is legitimizing its rule. All over the country, I saw foreign experts, technology and capital building the New China. Slumping growth, however, could seriously weaken the Communist regime's grip on power. Beijing may then "press the nationalistic button," Kaiser explained, to distract its citizenry from domestic woes. But the strategy could backfire if Beijing finds it impossible to placate patriotic calls for military intervention, boycotts or trade wars against foreign countries, particularly Japan, Taiwan and the United States. These would only exacerbate China's economic problems. "To maintain economic growth, they must keep the nation open," Kaiser said. "They need a place to sell their plastic widgets." Virulent patriotism could seriously undermine the Communist regime just as Han nationalism, inflamed by Qing officials, eventually engulfed and destroyed that dynasty.

For missionaries, however, China's problems come down to one fundamental. "There is a crisis of faith," Kaiser told me. "There was a value system and it had a shiny head and red star. It collapsed and the emperor wore no clothes." The Chinese are now groping to fill that void. "There's an emptiness in people's hearts," Kaiser said. "After 1989 [and the Tiananmen Square massacre], people said 'You can't put faith in the Party anymore.'"

In business-speak, Evergreen is exploiting this gap in the spiritual marketplace. Its product—a blending of commerce and Christianity—is gaining loyal customers. Evergreen offers a two-for-one deal: the promise of a better life and a better afterlife. In one rural county, Kaiser has seen Christian converts go from ten to five hundred in a decade. He estimates churchgoers in Taiyuan have doubled in the same period.

And what's the return on investment for Kaiser? "At the end of the day, if there wasn't some kind of faith driving our lives we probably wouldn't be here," he said. "It's too hard. The setbacks and frustrations are enormous . . . Without faith, there'd be no reason to do it. There'd be no joy."

TAIYUAN CERTAINLY FELT like purgatory. After four days in the city, a gloom overcame me. I fell ill with the flu: aching bones, sinus problems, sore throat, fatigue, a nagging cough. My spirits lifted only when I stepped aboard a bus to leave.

The bus was old and filthy, its windows smeared with dirt. I sat one row from the very back—a safe seat, I figured, in case of a head-on collision with a coal truck, a common occurrence in Shanxi. A peasant sat across the row and spat on the floor. Three other swarthy *nongmin* sat behind me and began smoking nonstop. I waved my arms angrily to clear the smoke and cracked open the window. I had hoped the bus ride would be a reprieve from Taiyuan's horrendous air quality. Yet no matter where I was in Shanxi, coal dust, grit and cigarette smoke followed.

Mannerheim actually saw smoking as a positive sign of China's modernization. Jesuit missionaries first introduced tobacco to China four hundred years ago, but it only became popular in the 1890s. Reportedly, the first words uttered by James B. Duke, the founder of British American Tobacco (BAT), on hearing of the invention of the cigarette machine were "Bring me the atlas." He turned over the pages until he saw a map of China, population 430 million. "That," he said, "is where we are going to sell cigarettes."[26] And he did. In China, BAT established a "monopoly that seemed unshakeable," writes one historian, and a mass advertising campaign that "left no region of China untouched."[27]

In Taiyuan, Mannerheim found thousands of posters and advertisements for BAT pasted on walls, houses, gates, temples and "every conceivable place." These advertisements, Mannerheim wrote, "prove that the town has already attained a high degree of civilisation." Mannerheim described how the local BAT representative, Mr. Widler, even printed ads on beautiful silk and gave them to mandarins who hung them in their residences. "The posters of the Tobacco Company must surely mark the frontiers of civilisation in China at present," the Baron wrote, "although we may soon expect to see them pasted up on the most inhospitable temple walls of Tibet." By 1930, BAT was selling 100 billion cigarettes each year in China. Mao nationalized the tobacco industry, but BAT is now back. About 1.7 trillion cancer sticks are consumed in China each year, accounting for 30 percent of the world market. Smoking, particularly among poor, less-educated males, has increased more than threefold since the 1970s. Sixty percent of men smoke tobacco, coincidentally the same percentage for opium addiction a century ago.

The bus quickly filled with a blue haze as the smokers fell into nicotine bliss. My spirits sank, although I knew that salvation lay just ahead for me. I was leaving polluted Taiyuan for one of Buddhism's holiest mountains. I imagined dramatic vistas, whimsical golden temples and invigorating alpine air. Paradise. I could almost smell it.

WUTAI SHAN

The Wanderer

Dalai Lama Won't Go Home. Proves an Embarrassing Guest for Official China.—WASHINGTON POST (July 12, 1908)

FROM TAIYUAN, Mannerheim travelled on horseback to Wutai Shan, a holy site set among five *(wu)* terraced *(tai)* mountains *(shan)* in northeast Shanxi. It is the most sacred of four Buddhist mountains in China. The Baron travelled lightly, having auctioned off most of his horses, rifles, cartridges and other gear in Taiyuan. Lukanin had developed pains in his stomach and diarrhea. As a result, Mannerheim dispatched the Cossack and most of his baggage, by train, to Peking. With only two barometers, a few books, clothes, blanket, soap and tins of food, he set off.

Outside Taiyuan, his small company, which consisted of his interpreter Zhao and a new Chinese cook whom he hired in Lanzhou,[1] walked and rode on a sunken road. A light rain dampened the dust. Shabby villages and poppy fields still in bloom dotted the landscape. By the third day of riding, they reached a valley in the Taihang Shan range. They proceeded into the dark massif along stony riverbeds and through gorges scattered with rugged villages, small Buddhist temples and burial mounds in the shape of stone stupas. The mountains grew higher, their ragged peaks veiled in heavy clouds and lower slopes terraced with fields of wheat, millet, maize, peas and poppies. After a long day's journey, they sought shelter in a "little, decayed temple," where they spent "a cold and uncomfortable evening."

The next day, Mannerheim came across Wang Fanglin, a Chinese army captain who spoke some English.[2] He was on his way back to Taiyuan from Wutai Shan. "He tried to pump me in regard to my intentions during my stay at Wut'ai Shan," wrote the Baron, who told Wang that he had "no settled intentions." Mannerheim continued on his way but soon realized that his cagey answer had failed to satisfy the suspicious Chinese officer. "I saw him following in my footsteps up the gorge, borne in his chair by mules."

The twisting gorge grew wilder. Rocky spurs thrust out of the loess slopes of the mountains. The road made a wide curve around a mountain and then clusters of temples came into view. Mannerheim had arrived at the main village of Wutai Shan.

He rode through a foul-smelling bazaar street. The small village lay in the bottom of a gorge, surrounded by grass ridges, colourful temples and mountain peaks. The village square was crowded with Chinese, Tibetan and Mongol pilgrims, the latter decoratively attired with silver ornaments, ribbons and coral insets. A white marble staircase led up to a dense complex of temples perched on a nearby hilltop. "The sun had broken through the clouds," Mannerheim wrote, "and the yellowish-golden and turquoise-blue tiled roofs of the mound sparkled in its rays." This hilltop temple complex was, he added, "the object of a new arrival's thoughts as much as of his gaze, for it is the present abode, not to say prison, of the Buddhists' pope, the Dalai Lama."

MY ARRIVAL IN Wutai Shan was as dark and gloomy as Mannerheim's was bright and sunshiny. I spent eight smoke-filled hours in the squalor of the overcrowded bus from Taiyuan. We crawled along serpentine roads behind overloaded coal trucks. The bus seemed to stop at every village, where tendrils of smoke slithered out of chimneys like apparitions in the night. It was dark by the time we reached Taihuai, the central village around which Wutai Shan's temples are clustered. Large tourist hotels, built of dark grey brick with swooping Chinese-styled roofs, lined the road into town. Most appeared closed for the winter. They reminded me of the desolate hotel in *The Shining*. This place of spiritual enlightenment—the "holy of holies," as Mannerheim described it—actually felt haunted.

I stepped off the bus into a blustery, freezing wind. I was in a nasty mood—cold, ill, hungry and exhausted. With my heavy pack, I trekked down the gloomy, deserted street and crossed a stone bridge to one of the few open hotels. It had comfortable, warm rooms, but I barely slept. My throat was swollen and my bones ached. I coughed and hacked all night. In the morning, I lay in bed listening to blasts of wind rattle the room's window and a rambunctious mouse squeak and scurry behind a heating grate in the wall.

Hunger set in around noon, forcing me out of my refuge. I donned my long johns, long-sleeved undershirt, dress shirt, sweater, Gore-Tex jacket, gloves, scarf and woolen tuque. Drawing in my arms and bowing my head, I pushed through the piercing wind in search of a steaming bowl of hot and sour soup. It was a cold, steely day. The leafless trees, grey temple walls, brown slopes and lifeless streets gave Wutai Shan a very uninviting air. It was Sunday afternoon and most shops were closed and dark, the weekend pilgrims having already left. After lunch, I bought some orange juice, oranges and instant noodle soup and scurried back to the sanctuary of my hotel room.

In Dunhuang, I had bought a seventy-five-page booklet on the Fourteenth Dalai Lama published by the Chinese government. The cover depicts Tibet's supreme pontiff wearing tinted glasses and jabbing a finger in the air. His Holiness looked like a cast member from *The Sopranos*. The booklet is a clumsy tirade against Tibetan independence. I found it entertaining in its utter absurdity.

Its three chapters are titled "Promoting Buddhism or Making a Mess of It," "Benefiting Tibetans or Doing Them Harm," and "Driving Tibet to Paradise or Hell." It condemns the Dalai Lama for secretly supporting the "sect empire" of Aum Shinrikyo, the Japanese cult whose leader was convicted of the poison gas attack in Tokyo's subway in 1995. The authors accuse His Holiness of being a CIA-backed "ringleader" of a separatist group, of "encouraging religious fanaticism," of being "a slave owner," of manipulating the selection process of the Panchen Lama, of defending "feudal serfdom," and of using the skulls and leg bones of "live persons" as religious objects. "It is really disgusting to see him, as the general representative of the feudal serfdom in Tibet, have the cheek to talk profusely about democracy, freedom and human rights," write the authors.

There are morsels, however measly, of truth in the booklet. The next day I went to a *wangba* (Internet café) to do some fact checking. The *wangba* was located in a crowded, windowless hovel in an alleyway off the main street. It was choked with cigarette smoke. I searched various news sources and journals via the Vancouver Public Library's electronic catalogue. This portal acted as a chink in the Great Firewall of China, allowing me to read information that would normally be censored. Here's what I learned: The Dalai Lama did meet and initially endorse the Japanese cult leader, an embarrassing episode that His Holiness later regretted; the Tibetan government-in-exile had received training from the CIA, but that was in the 1960s; His Holiness had softened his stance on Tibetan independence, calling for a "middle way" that grants Tibet special autonomous status similar to that of Hong Kong and Macau; and the Dalai Lama did involve himself in the selection of the Panchen Lama, as decreed by Tibetan tradition.

That summer Beijing had hardened its line against His Holiness, recognizing that the Dalai Lama was beginning a worldwide tour prior to the 2008 Beijing Olympics. His six-month itinerary included Peru, Chile, Brazil, Argentina, Belgium, Jordan, Canada (where he was awarded honorary Canadian citizenship) and Mongolia, as well as a month-long tour of the United States. A few weeks before I arrived in Wutai Shan, the Dalai Lama also visited Finland.

Juha Janhunen, the linguistics professor, had returned to Helsinki after the Urumqi symposium to co-host the Dalai Lama's visit. Janhunen is president of the Finnish-Tibetan Cultural Association and introduced His Holiness to a packed auditorium in Helsinki's Finlandia Hall. "[The Dalai Lama] seems to have a very realistic picture of the situation, and would seem to be ready to make a deal with the Chinese," Janhunen told me via email. "But the Chinese seem to be waiting for his death, rather than . . . a deal." Growing frail with age and beset by health issues, the Dalai Lama certainly doesn't have time on his side.

Speculation, in fact, was brewing that the next Dalai Lama could come from outside Tibet. It has happened before. According to Tibetan beliefs, the Fourth Dalai Lama was reincarnated in Mongolia in 1589 as the great-grandson of Altan Khan, the Western Mongol ruler who converted his tribesmen to Lamaism.[3] "If I would die now, it would be logical for my reincarnation to come from outside Tibet," the Fourteenth Dalai Lama told journalists at a press conference in Helsinki. There is nothing "logical" about the mystical process by which the Dalai Lama's reincarnation is chosen: it involves high lamas looking for visions shimmering on the azure waters of the holy lake Lhamo La-tso and a series of curious tests to affirm the rebirth. In reality, the current Dalai Lama just wants to keep the selection process out of the meddling hands of the Chinese Communist Party. "My successor could even be found in Finland," His Holiness joked.[4]

THE LINEAGE OF the Dalai Lama extends back more than six hundred years. Fourteen men have held the title, but only two Dalai Lamas have set themselves apart and been called "Great": the

Fifth Dalai Lama, builder of the Potala Palace; and the Thirteenth, Thubten Gyatso.

Gyatso was born in southern Tibet in 1876, when the prestige of the Dalai Lama was very low. Just a boy when he became Dalai Lama, Gyatso found himself alone and at the mercy of crafty, even regicidal, officials. His predecessors had all died young. The future didn't look good for the child pontiff. Yet Gyatso managed not merely to survive but to succeed in this precarious era. In 1894, the Dalai Lama, age eighteen, imprisoned the corrupt regent, seized the Tibetan state seal and forbade the Chinese *amban*, Peking's senior official in Lhasa, to interfere in Tibetan affairs. Through hard work and unflinching determination, he modernized government, the judiciary and Tibet's tiny army. He also launched Tibet's modern independence movement.

At the time, Chinese "suzerainty" over Tibet was nominal at best. In 1890, the Chinese government made a border and commercial treaty with British India, which the Tibetans refused to respect. Lord Curzon, the viceroy of India, sent an envoy to Lhasa. The *amban* told the British envoy that if Britain persisted in its treaty demands Tibet might seek assistance from Russia. Tibet now found itself a pawn at the centre of the Great Game.

The British believed that the Russians were conspiring with the alpine kingdom, possibly as a staging point from which to launch an attack on India. The Tsar and the Dalai Lama also had a mutual interest in Buryat Mongols, who lived in Russia's borderlands but who were followers of Tibetan Buddhism. In 1899, Agvan Dorjieff, a Buryat lama, became one of the Dalai Lama's teachers and eventually his trusted political adviser. Dorjieff convinced the young, inexperienced pontiff to seek help from the Russian Tsar against the British. In 1900, Dorjieff went to St. Petersburg with a letter to Nicholas II seeking an alliance. That same year Lord Curzon sent two letters to the Dalai Lama that were returned unopened. Curzon became paranoid and annoyed by Russian intrigues and secret Tibetan envoys to the Tsar's court. In 1904, as a pre-emptive strike against Russian scheming, Curzon sent a military expedition, headed by Sir Francis Younghusband, to Lhasa. The Dalai Lama fled to Urga (now Ulaanbaatar, the capital of the Republic of Mongolia), hoping to solicit Russia's help.

However, after its defeat in Manchuria and riven by internal rebellions, Russia could not afford a showdown with Britain in Asia. On August 31, 1907, while Mannerheim was trekking north of Urumqi, the Anglo-Russian Convention was signed. (There's no evidence that Mannerheim, whose orders were to collect intelligence on the Dalai Lama and the Tibetan independence movement, knew of the treaty at the time.) It formally ended the Great Game and recognized "the suzerain rights of China over Tibet."

The treaty effectively gave China a free hand over Tibet. In 1908, following a bloody uprising against the Han Chinese incursion into Tibet's traditional lands, Chao Erfeng, nicknamed "The Butcher," was appointed Manchu Resident in Lhasa. His goal was to convert Tibet into a full-blown Chinese province. Writing about his journeys in Tibet the next year, Sven Hedin lambasted the Dalai Lama as "an ambitious intriguer, who by his incautious policy provoked the offensive measures of Lord Curzon" and allowed China to seize "Tibet more tightly than ever in its dragon's claws."[5]

At the same time, the Chinese *amban* in Urga was pressuring the Dalai Lama to leave Mongolia and return to Tibet. Initially, a Chinese detachment escorted him to the Kumbum Monastery in Qinghai province.[6] His Holiness then turned east with his retinue of Tibetan bodyguards, lamas and a caravan of eight hundred camels. He defiantly trekked away from his troubled homeland and settled in Wutai Shan, only three hundred kilometres from Peking.[7]

In the handbook of the Urumqi symposium on Mannerheim, Dr. Sun Hongnian, a Chinese scholar with the state-run Borderland Research Centre, published an essay about Mannerheim's visit to Wutai Shan. At this holy mountain, Sun writes, the Dalai Lama met many foreign envoys to expand "his international political influence so as to fight against English aggressors." Sun's claim, like much of official Chinese scholarship on Tibet, is preposterous. By 1908, British troops had long left Lhasa. In reality, the Dalai Lama was orchestrating a nascent international campaign to free Tibet from Chinese rule. His Holiness was heartened by the arrival of a Russian military officer, believing Mannerheim held a secret message from Tsar Nicholas II.

ON MY THIRD day in Wutai Shan, the sky turned a brilliant blue that I hadn't seen since trekking in Kyrgyzstan. From my room, I could also hear the faint chiming of bells dangling from temple eaves. There are 108 temples in Wutai Shan. The highest, at just over three thousand metres, sits atop the north peak. About twenty were within walking distance of my hotel.

In the late afternoon, I mustered enough energy to climb the long, steep path to the Dailuoding Temple, atop a nearby mountain ridge. A lone, bedraggled beggar sat in the cold at the foot of the staircase. The zigzagging stairs were icy and whipped by sudden gusts of wind. I stopped several times to catch my breath. At the top, the wind became fierce. An old woman, wrapped in a sweater and scarves and selling rosary beads, constantly wiped tears from her eyes. I went to a terrace to take in the panorama. The sun had just dipped below Wutai Shan's western peak. A soft pink and orange glow fringed distant ridges as a heavy shadow spilled over Taihuai. With smoke rising from kitchen chimneys, the darkening gorge resembled a smouldering cauldron.

The next day was sunny and warm, which had a miraculous effect on my disposition. I took off my gloves and wool hat and unbuttoned my coat. I explored Taihuai's few streets and alleys, lined with picturesque shops selling Buddha statues, rosary beads, books, icons, canes, wooden swords and incense. The shops and streets were still eerily quiet. I spotted a few small groups of Chinese tourists and the occasional monk in vermilion robes.

I visited several temples tucked along the cobblestone streets. The Guangren Temple's gateway and three halls where laid out on a north–south axis and formed two courtyards that had been torn up to install new water and sewer pipes. Unfortunately, all the halls were locked.

Guangren is the temple where pilgrims from Tibet and Mongolia are usually received. However, a century ago the Dalai Lama stayed at Pusading Temple, a massive complex atop a nearby hill. I made my way along a sloping street and climbed the steep marble staircase lined with gleaming white birch trees. An elaborate Chinese gate stood at the top. In its Grand Hall, a dozen monks in yellow robes chanted in front of large statues of the Buddha. A passageway led me to a second courtyard and more prayer halls and pavilions. A plaque informed me that emperors Kangxi (1661–1722) and Qianlong (1736–1795) had stayed in the temple, thus bestowing on it "extra honor and privilege." In the courtyard, I found a large two-storey temple, which a guidebook told me was the centre of Tibetan Buddhism in Wutai Shan. Its high red walls and golden roof evoke the majesty of Lhasa's Potala Palace on a miniature scale, and so it is often called Lama Gong (palace). My guidebook said the roof's yellow colour symbolizes the Imperial family. No wonder the Thirteenth Dalai Lama installed himself here. Pusading was a veritable Imperial throne.

On my way back to the hotel, I followed a doglegged passageway at the bottom of the hill past a fortress tower to the gate of the Tayuan Temple. This was Mannerheim's temporary residence in Wutai Shan. An abbot's courtyard contained living quarters, meditation halls and workstations filled with scrolls and calligraphy brushes. I noticed an arched gateway at the far end of the courtyard. I paid two yuan to a caretaker and navigated around the entrance screen to find three small halls. They housed an exhibition on the Red Army, which was headquartered here for a period during the war against Japan. One displayed army maps and photos of military training exercises and of Dr. Norman Bethune, the legendary

Canadian doctor who died of blood poisoning caused by a cut he received while performing surgery on a wounded soldier at Wutai Shan in November 1939.

In the central building, I was startled by a white marble statue reverently placed in the foyer. At first glance, I thought it was the Buddha, but then realized it was a plump-cheeked Mao Zedong. The bust was surrounded by pink, red and orange plastic flowers. In an adjacent chamber, pilgrims slipped offerings of coins, banknotes and cigarettes through a screen onto a bed where, apparently, the deity of Chinese Communism had once slept.

"THE CHINESE AUTHORITIES seem to guard the Dalai Lama closely," Mannerheim wrote.

Wang, the Chinese army captain, told Mannerheim that "a cordon of soldiers" guarded the approaches to Wutai Shan. In the event of an attempt to escape, Wang explained, the Dalai Lama "would be stopped, by armed force if necessary." In his wanderings around Wutai Shan, Mannerheim saw no such cordon. "I could not help noticing, however, that [Wang] watched my movements with the greatest interest." Wang urged Mannerheim to take him as his interpreter during his audience with the Dalai Lama. But a Tibetan prince had already secretly informed Mannerheim that Wang was not welcome. The Tibetans despised Wang, whom they considered a spy, and prohibited him and his troops from the inner precincts of the temple.[8]

Wutai Shan was more podium than prison for the Dalai Lama. Upon arriving here, he sent messages to the Peking Legations inviting envoys to visit. William Woodville Rockhill, the American Minister in Peking, was the first. He pulled on his walking boots and set out for Wutai Shan on foot, a five-day trek from Peking. Rockhill was a scholar and diplomat who had explored Inner Asia in the 1890s and spoke Tibetan. He had left Wutai Shan only a day before Mannerheim's arrival.

"The Talé Lama seems to me a man of undoubted intelligence, open-minded . . . a very agreeable, kindly, thoughtful host, and a personage of great dignity," Rockhill reported back to President Theodore Roosevelt.[9] The Dalai Lama told Rockhill about his struggles against the Chinese and how his country's remoteness meant Tibet had "no friends abroad." Rockhill assured His Holiness that he was mistaken: Tibet had many foreign well-wishers who hoped to see Tibetans "prosper and happy." Later, during the Dalai Lama's visit to Peking, Rockhill became a confidant to the Tibetan leader, quietly pushing a rapprochement with the Chinese.[10]

That summer the Dalai Lama received a parade of envoys: a German doctor from the Peking Legation;[11] an English explorer named Christopher Irving;[12] R.F. Johnson, a British diplomat from the Colonial Service;[13] and Henri D'Ollone, the French army major and viscount. The Dalai Lama hoped to patch up his relations with Britain and bolster his international standing. These first audiences with the mysterious Buddhist pontiff were much anticipated.

On his second day in Wutai Shan, a messenger ran into Mannerheim's room in the Tayuan Temple and gestured that the Dalai Lama was ready to receive him. Mannerheim duly prepared himself. While he was shaving and changing his clothes, another frantic messenger arrived to express the Dalai Lama's impatience. "I was just as impatient," he wrote, "but could not possibly dress any faster." A few minutes later, an anxious Tibetan prince appeared to ask what Mannerheim meant by keeping His Holiness waiting. At a swift pace, the Baron and prince climbed the steep staircase to Pusading Temple.

Wang, in full dress uniform, was waiting at the top with a Chinese honour guard. By this time, Mannerheim's Russian identity was well known. Indeed, outside Xi'an a Chinese brass band welcomed him with the Russian Imperial anthem. The Chinese had reason to worry about Mannerheim's visit. Chinese authorities had just arrested two Russian military officers who were inciting the

Mongols to break from China and become a Russian protector-ate.[14] During his stay in Urga, the Dalai Lama sent messages to the Tsar through various envoys. His Holiness told one Russian military intelligence officer that both Tibet and Mongolia should "irrevocably secede from China to form an independent allied state, accomplishing this operation with Russia's patronage and support, avoiding bloodshed."[15] If Russia wouldn't help, the Dalai Lama insisted, he would even ask Britain—his former foe—for help. After his visit with the Dalai Lama, Mannerheim, in fact, trekked to Hohhot, the regional capital of Inner Mongolia, to gauge the rebellious mood of the Mongols.

Wang could barely hide his wrath when Mannerheim told him that he could not attend his audience with the Tibetan pontiff. The Chinese captain argued with two of the Dalai Lama's assistants. As the Baron slipped into a small reception hall, he caught sight of Wang "making vain efforts to force his way in behind me." Later, as he left the Dalai Lama's inner sanctum, Mannerheim wrote, "I was pounced upon immediately by [Wang], who tried to pump me as to what we had talked about during such a long audience."

The Dalai Lama sat on a gilded armchair placed on a dais along the back wall of the small room. Two old Tibetans, unarmed, with beards and hair speckled with grey stood behind him. The Dalai Lama was frocked in "imperial yellow with light-blue linings" and a "traditional red toga." The thirty-three-year-old pontiff had a dark brown face, shaved head, moustache and a tuft of hair under his lower lip. His eyes were large and his teeth gleamed.[16] Mannerheim noticed "slight hollows in the skin of his face, which are supposed to be pockmarks." He appeared a bit nervous, "which he seems anxious to hide." Otherwise, Mannerheim thought he was "a lively man in full possession of his mental and physical faculties."

Mannerheim made a "profound bow," which the Dalai Lama acknowledged with a slight nod. They exchanged silk scarves. An old lama acted as translator from Tibetan to Chinese, and then Zhao translated from Chinese for Mannerheim. His Holiness began with small talk, asking Mannerheim about his nationality, age and journey. The Dalai Lama then paused and, twitching nervously, asked if the Tsar had sent a secret message for him. "He awaited the translation of my reply with obvious interest," wrote Mannerheim, who informed him that he hadn't the opportunity to personally speak with Nicholas II before his departure. The Dalai Lama then gestured, and a beautiful piece of white silk with Tibetan letters was brought out. It was a gift that Mannerheim was to deliver personally to Nicholas II. Mannerheim asked if he could also convey a message to the Tsar.

"What is your rank?" asked the Dalai Lama.

"Baron," came the reply.

Satisfied, His Holiness asked him to stay another day to give him time to write the letter to the Tsar, but later changed his mind.

The Dalai Lama told Mannerheim he had been enjoying his journeys in Mongolia and China, but "his heart was in Tibet." Many Tibetans were urging him to return. His officials claimed up to twenty thousand pilgrims visited the Dalai Lama each month, but Mannerheim thought it was "an undoubted exaggeration." The Tibetan pontiff was in the midst of a showdown with Empress Dowager Cixi, who wanted him to come to Peking to perform the kowtow. The Dalai Lama, Mannerheim wrote, "does not look like a man resigned to play the part the Chinese Government wishes him to, but rather like one who is only waiting for an opportunity of confusing his adversary." The wily Tibetan pontiff had postponed his journey so many times that a joke was circulating in Peking referring to him as the "Delay Lama."[17]

Mannerheim spoke encouragingly about Russia's sympathies for Tibet's struggles against the Chinese. Russia's troubles were over, the Baron assured him, and "the Russian Army was stronger than ever." Now, all Russians watched His Holiness's footsteps with great interest, he added. The Dalai Lama, Mannerheim recalled, "listened to my polite speeches with unconcealed satisfaction."

Twice the Dalai Lama ordered his bodyguards to check if Wang was eavesdropping on their conversation. It was a dangerous time for the Dalai Lama, who knew his life may be in danger if he returned to Lhasa.[18] The Chinese were tightening their grip on Tibet. Lamas were being assassinated, monasteries plundered and Tibetans evicted from their nomadic pastures. Peking needed the Dalai Lama to be a compliant vassal who could calm his restless followers and ease Tibet's incorporation into the Chinese Empire.

But the Dalai Lama proved defiant. He visited Peking that September and immediately fell out with the Imperial Court, which issued a decree demoting him to "a loyal and submissive Vicegerent bound by the laws of the sovereign state."[19] A prominent Imperial censor also openly denounced him as "a proud and ignorant man."[20] Rumours spread in Tibet that he had been assassinated. Outraged at various reforms, lamas threatened a "holy war" against the Chinese.[21] By the end of the year, a rebellion broke out, leading to the defeat of Chinese troops.[22] The Dalai Lama eventually returned to Lhasa in 1909 and sent telegrams to Britain and all European countries attacking Peking's claim over Tibet.

In February 1910, Chinese troops invaded Lhasa. The Dalai Lama fled to India. An Imperial decree denounced His Holiness as "an ungrateful, irreligious obstreperous profligate who is tyrannical and so unacceptable to the Tibetans, and accordingly an unsuitable leader of Lamas."[23] After the fall of the Qing Dynasty, His Holiness returned to Tibet in 1913, declaring the country independent. He died in 1933, leaving a prophetic last testament for the next Dalai Lama:

> We must guard ourselves against the barbaric red communists... the worst of the worst. It will not be long before we find the red onslaught at our own front door... and when it happens we must be ready to defend ourselves. Otherwise our spiritual and cultural traditions will be completely eradicated... and the days and nights will pass slowly and with great suffering and terror.[24]

Recognizing the clear and present danger, Mannerheim offered the Dalai Lama an unusual, though practical, gift: a Browning revolver. The Baron apologized that he didn't have a better offering, but explained that after two years' journey he had no other items of value. The Dalai Lama laughed, "showing all his teeth," as Mannerheim showed His Holiness how to quickly reload seven cartridges into the revolver. The Dalai Lama relished the demonstration. "The times were such," Mannerheim wrote, "that a revolver might at times be of greater use, even to a holy man like himself, than a praying mill."

EIGHTEEN

INNER MONGOLIA

The Soot Road

*If my body dies, let my body die, but do not let
my country die.*—GENGHIS KHAN[1]

UN YAT-SEN, nationalist revolutionary and founding president
of the Republic of China, had some very modern ideas that still
live on in China. He figured that "waste Chinese labor and foreign machinery," along with disbanded soldiers from overpopulated
provinces, should be sent to China's fertile hinterlands. Colonization, of course, had been going on since the Qin Dynasty established farming garrisons to expand its frontiers in the third century
BC. But Sun added a modern twist to this ancient stratagem: he
wanted to adopt "scientific methods" for colonization borrowed
from the West.[2]

Railways could help, Sun reckoned, and become "a greatly prof-
itable undertaking." Han Chinese colonists should be sent beyond
the Great Wall, where they could farm, mine and build modern
industries—all linked to markets by rail. Sun had travelled to
Canada and the United States and knew that the railway was key
to their westward expansions. Sun had even seen first-hand how

migrant Chinese workers had helped build the railways across the Rocky Mountains to the Pacific Coast. All along the track, pioneers homesteaded on native Indian land and brought civilization to the so-called "savages." Sun thought the colonization of Inner Mongolia and Xinjiang—lands primarily inhabited by "barbarians"—was "the most urgent need of the first magnitude."

Today, the main boulevard of Hohhot, the capital of the Inner Mongolia Autonomous Region, is named in honour of Sun Yat-sen. It is called Zhongshan, which is the Mandarin form of his Cantonese first name. If you look down Zhongshan Road—past the scooter shops blaring Chinese pop music, the mall full of Clarks shoes and Satchi attaché cases, the glitzy KTV bar, the Chinese-language bookstore, KFC, McDonald's, Pizza Hut, Holiday Inn and even farther on past the Chinese billboards advertising new condo developments to a promenade called Frontier Old Street, where Chinese merchants hawk Mongolian tourist trinkets—you can see the future of Tibet.

Over the past century, Han Chinese colonization has been so overwhelming that Inner Mongolia—once the base of Genghis Khan's Mongol empire, which covered 33 million square kilometres and stretched as far west as the Baltic Sea—seems hardly Mongolian at all. Only 4 million people, about 17 percent of the region's population, are ethnic Mongols. In Hohhot, it's even less, about 10 percent. The rest, by and large, are Han Chinese. The dramatic influx of Chinese began a century ago, the final conquest of a settled, agrarian civilization over pastoral nomads. In 1908, Mannerheim noted the rapid invasion of Han Chinese onto the Mongolian steppe. When the railway was extended to Hohhot in 1919, writes one historian, "Han settlers immigrated by the millions, scattering Mongols from their most fertile grazing pasture."[3] Inner Mongolia proved that with perseverance—and a railway—the Chinese could colonize and secure even a hostile region.

Colonization of Tibet, however, proved far more trying. "Tibet is a poor and barren country which produces nothing worth exporting," wrote a Chinese newspaper in 1904. "Its sole products are incense and images of Buddha. The roads thither are dangerous and almost impassable. The coldness of the climate renders life unendurable."[4] And the Tibetans themselves—ungovernable nomads, stone-throwing lamas and xenophobic bandits with a propensity to murder—made "the roof of the world" dangerously inhospitable to outsiders. In 1908, Peking proposed building a railway[5] to Tibet to "open and civilize" the country,[6] but violent unrest against the Chinese was sweeping the land. Tibetan militancy largely stymied wide-scale Han migration until 1959, when the People's Liberation Army suppressed an uprising in Lhasa that sent the Dalai Lama into exile.

While the official 2000 census puts Tibet's Han Chinese population at a mere 6 percent, it is by most independent accounts much higher. Counting army garrisons and migrant workers, some scholars and Tibet activists estimate that two-thirds of Lhasa is Han Chinese. They fear the Han population will rise further thanks to the completion of a new railway a hundred years after its construction was first purposed. As I set out from St. Petersburg in July, the first passenger train arrived in Lhasa. In a massive display of military control, soldiers of the PLA dotted the 1,118-kilometre route—the highest railway in the world, at 4,500 metres above sea level—to guard against saboteurs.

Human-rights activists see the railway as a demographic death blow precipitating the "cultural genocide of Tibet." It was a point made by the Dalai Lama during his trip to Helsinki. "I remember well his comment on the Peking-Lhasa railway," Juha Janhunen told me in an email. "[The Dalai Lama] said that every day 6,000 people go to Tibet by this railway, and of them 2,000 remain." The Dalai Lama then pointed to the colonization of Inner Mongolia as "a warning example" for the fate of Tibet.

FROM WUTAI SHAN, I took a bus to Datong, a dreary city just inside the Great Wall, near the Inner Mongolia border. It turned out to be the coal capital of China and has been singled out for having the fourth-worst air pollution in the world. On some days, Datong's smog is reportedly so thick that motorists must turn on their head-lights in the middle of the day. Mannerheim found it to be a sleepy town with meagre trade. "The women, who are famed for their beauty, form an important and valuable article of export," he wrote. Many mandarins and wealthy merchants came to the town to buy a wife.

"Beautiful" isn't exactly how I would describe the young woman who was sitting in my seat when I boarded the night train from Datong to Hohhot. A purple burn scar disfigured her face and she was missing several fingers. She was clutching a baby and verbally heaped scorn on me when I showed her my ticket. A policeman con-vinced her to shift over one seat. Her baby then spat up the remnants of an orange on my lap. As we departed Datong, other screaming matches broke out as passengers wrestled for seats. The clatter and squabbling went on for an hour until everyone settled down and the stuffy wagon went silent with sleep.

As the train rumbled into a suburb of Hohhot, I awoke to find masses of grey concrete mid-rise apartment blocks under construc-tion, lit by the eerie glow of floodlights. This went on for a kilo-metre or two. The economy wasn't just booming in Inner Mongolia, it was exploding at an annual rate of 24 percent, more than twice as fast as any other province in China. No matter what Beijing did, including punishing the regional governor and two vice-governors for flouting decrees, the central government couldn't rein in Inner Mongolia's overheated economy.[7]

"This is *jiu chengshi*—the 'old city'—but now it's a new city," said Sechenbaatar, a linguistics professor at Inner Mongolia Normal University in Hohhot. "Twenty years ago there was a narrow street here. Now it's wide."

Sechenbaatar was stocky, with a round face and large, droopy earlobes that made him look like the Buddha. He wore a double-breasted grey blazer, polo shirt and blue slacks. He had studied and taught Mongolian in Helsinki and toured Yugur communities in Gansu province with Juha Janhunen, who kindly put me in contact with the affable scholar. Sechenbaatar agreed to show me Hohhot's old walled city, or what was left of it. We met the morning after my arrival.

Our taxi crawled down a car-clogged boulevard lined by the bland modernism of the New China: stucco, gleaming tiles and mirrored glass adorned facades. A huge billboard advertised new residential condos: "Victoria Town—Vogue England, Enjoy Gentlemen Life." We passed through the city's Muslim quarter too, which consisted of more spanking new mid-rises in pastel yellow with Ottoman arches and gilded domes. I spotted a KFC, by far the most popular Western fast food outlet in China. The taxi dropped us off in the middle of Hohhot's cluster of Buddhist temples, which played a pivotal role in the colonization of Inner Mongolia.

Hohhot has a long settlement history, but its modern foundation was laid by Altan Khan. The Mongol prince, who converted his people to Lamaism, built a walled garrison and two Buddhist temples here in 1557.[8] The Chinese later gained control of the city, renaming it Guihua.[9] But it was the Qing Dynasty's Manchu rulers who truly yoked the city and Inner Mongolia to the Chinese Empire. The Manchus broke up the Mongols' tribal system by granting Mongol chiefs aristocratic ranks, and incorporated them into "banners," the Manchu military system. This effectively divided the Mongols, ensuring loyalty to Peking. The rise and spread of the "yellow church" (that is, Tibetan Buddhism), and a centralized monastery system in Inner Mongolia under Imperial patronage also increased Manchu authority. Peking subsidized the construction of temples and installed their own local primate. By the time Mannerheim rode beyond the Great Wall, the number of monasteries in Inner Mongolia under Peking's authority exceeded one thousand.[10]

The growth of monasteries had two added advantages in controlling the warlike Mongols: first, at least one son per family took monastic vows, which sapped the Mongols' martial spirit. And second, as Mongols flooded into Hohhot to worship, Chinese merchants followed, setting up lively markets outside monastery walls. A Chinese merchant class grew steadily in Inner Mongolia during the nineteenth century as Mongols and monks acquired a taste for Chinese goods.

Trade was so bustling that Mannerheim could find only "two microscopic rooms" in the shed of a caravanserai for accommodation. The inn was run by three elderly men from Tianjin and catered chiefly to merchants travelling with camel caravans along a route skirting the southern fringes of the Gobi Desert. Hohhot's suburbs of shops, homes and inns were so dense that Mannerheim barely even noticed the town's defensive wall. He estimated ten thousand households in Hohhot, of which 30 percent were Chinese Muslim.

"Even a hundred years ago, Hohhot was a Chinese city," Sechenbaatar said, "but there were some Mongols." Indeed, Mannerheim called it a "Chinese town."

The taxi dropped us at an expansive concrete plaza that fronted the famed Da Zhao Monastery. It was built by Altan Khan. We strolled into the complex, whose lavish exterior ornamentation looked Chinese but whose interior was distinctly Tibetan. Its spacious prayer hall was decorated with *thangka* art, hanging cylindrical silk banners and prayer wheels. In a rear chamber stained with the soot of burnt incense sat a four-hundred-year-old silver Buddha.

"Before the Cultural Revolution, there were many, many temples in Inner Mongolia, maybe more than one thousand," Sechenbaatar told me. Most were destroyed or gutted by Red Guards in the late 1960s.[11] As in Tibet, those that survived are now being restored or completely rebuilt. Da Zhao's exterior paint was surprisingly vibrant, not soot-stained or dulled. A new pavilion was under construction too. Across the street, we found workmen applying gleaming red lacquer to the swooping eaves of a pavilion in the Xilitu Zhao temple complex, which was, according to the Baron, "the most magnificent temple group in the town." Its main prayer hall, built "in pure Tibetan style," was adorned with glazed turquoise tiles that sparkled in the morning sun. It sat next to a freshly demolished residential block.

"When I came to Hohhot twenty-eight years ago, it was a country seat, a small town," Sechenbaatar said. "Since the 1980s, it has become much more developed." Residential towers now loom over the quaint Buddhist temples. To the west sits what's left of Old Hohhot. A monumental Chinese gate led us onto Frontier Old Street and a warren of mud-brick homes and decrepit alleyways. The shabby tourist promenade was hung with red lanterns and lined with dusty souvenir and antique shops. "Twenty-eight years ago, all the streets were like this in the Old Town," Sechenbaatar said.

We went for an early dinner at a Mongolian restaurant on a bustling downtown street. As we nibbled sweet yellow biscuits with yak butter and heavy cream, Sechenbaatar told me about the unusual cultural connection between Finns and Mongols. As it turns out, a Finn is the founder of Mongolic dialectology and Altaic linguistics. The latter field includes Turkic, Mongol and Manchu.

In 1898, Dr. G.J. Ramstedt travelled to Outer Mongolia (now the Republic of Mongolia) at the request of Otto Donner, president of the Finno-Ugrian Society. Donner cofounded the society in 1883 to study Uralic languages (Finnish, Estonian, Hungarian and Saami) with the hope of discovering their ancient roots. The origins of Finnish, which is neither a Romanic nor Germanic language, had baffled scholars for centuries. A number of uncanny similarities in vocabulary and grammar hinted that Finns might be a lost tribe of Mongols. Ramstedt's research quickly made him a leading expert in Mongolian linguistics. A decade later, Donner hoped that Mannerheim's ethnographic research could shed further light on this mystery. Mannerheim corresponded with Ramstedt, who identified and dated Uyghur and Mongolian script fragments that the Baron collected. Mannerheim also gave Ramstedt his linguistic notes on the Eastern Yugur, who speak an obscure Mongol dialect.

"Most European scholars now don't believe there is a relationship between the two language families," explained Sechenbaatar, who earned a PhD in Mongolian linguistics at Helsinki University. The research of early Finnish scholars did spark an abiding interest in Altaic languages among Finns, though. Janhunen, for example, is a world leader in Altaic linguistics, especially the process by which dialects spread and change.[12]

Nowhere has the language changed more rapidly than in Hohhot. Sechenbaatar told me that most of the ethnic Mongols live in a district around the city's universities. "I don't think you'll recognize the Mongols," he said. "Many look just like the Chinese. I can't even recognize them unless they speak Mongolian." The problem is that a growing number don't sound Mongolian either. "Many children have forgotten their mother tongue," he said. He estimates that of the region's four million Mongols, more than a quarter can't speak their mother tongue. That's especially true, he said, in the cities. I asked him why the language was dying, but the scholar brushed the topic aside. "I don't know," he said.

I picked up our conversation on this politically sensitive subject two days later, aboard a bus on our way to the grasslands north of Hohhot. I was bundled up in four layers of clothes, a scarf, gloves and wool hat. The packed bus was so cold that the windows fogged up from our breath.

"In recent years, many people have moved into the cities," Sechenbaatar said. Now, he estimates, up to 30 percent of Mongols are city dwellers, and the proportion is growing. Most come for better jobs, education and other opportunities. Some Mongol herders, he explained, were also being resettled from the steppe due to environmental problems. In the cities, Mongols mix with the dominant Han population and send their children to Chinese school. As a result, native Mongol speakers are dwindling and the number of Chinese loan words in Mongol has surpassed one thousand.

Our bus wound its way into the rugged Daqing Shan range, which forms a ramp to the great Mongolian plateau to the north.

The mountains mark the transition zone between the agrarian civilization of Central China and the nomadic peoples of the steppe. After twenty kilometres, we reached Wucheng county and the Mongols' legendary steppe.

I peered out at the undulating landscape. Below a pale blue sky, I did not see native grasslands. Instead, long brown and yellow strips of tilled fields, in a checkerboard pattern, lined the highway toward the horizon. There was nothing wild about the land's strict geometry. Rather, it looked like the endless farmland of Central China. "There are no Mongols here," Sechenbaatar said. Han Chinese had colonized these grasslands.

IN 1908, HOHHOT consisted of two walled towns: Guihua, the Chinese town; and Suiyuan, a Manchu fortress about two kilometres to the northeast. Built in 1737, Suiyuan was surrounded by a fifteen-metre-high wall with corner turrets and gun embrasures. It was the political and administrative centre of Inner Mongolia, a forlorn outpost of the Chinese Empire. "The buildings are small and neglected and there are a few poor shops," Mannerheim wrote. "The inhabitants look poor."

The only thing left of the Manchu fortress, which today sits under swooping highway viaducts lit up in neon at night, is the *jiangjun yashu,* the headquarters of the military governor of Inner Mongolia. The grey, Chinese-style pavilions once housed government offices, grand halls and living quarters for the general and his family. They are now a museum displaying official Qing seals, historical photographs, weapons and a mandarin's office. The general's former residence houses an exhibit on Empress Dowager Cixi, who apparently lived in Hohhot in her late teens.

At the time of Mannerheim's visit, Cixi was most unhappy with General Yi. The military governor of Inner Mongolia was, in fact, awaiting sentencing on corruption. His misconduct was so egregious that the Mongols were on the verge of open rebellion. Under the general's ruthless settlement policy, Mongols were losing vast areas of land to Chinese newcomers without compensation. Local noblemen complained to Peking, which sent an inspector to investigate. General Yi was found to be enriching himself through land scams. He was immediately dismissed and put on trial.

According to Mannerheim, Chinese migration had been "going on for more than a thousand years, gradually conquering the lands of adjacent Mongolian tribes and driving them to the north."[13] By the 1850s, vast swaths of pastureland had already fallen into the hands of Chinese merchants. As a result of heavy taxes and usurious moneylenders, indebtedness grew among the Mongols, who relinquished land titles to pay their debts. Slowly, the Chinese displaced Mongol herdsmen and their nomadic traditions.[14]

Thanks to General Yi and Peking's new policy lifting restrictions on colonization, Han migration peaked at the time of Mannerheim's visit to Hohhot. "Swarms of Chinese," in the words of a British diplomat at the time, began to overrun Inner Mongolia.[15] The "speed of invasion," he reported, was startling. Between 1899 and 1902, he saw Chinese settlers "ploughing the virgin turf" and pushing north by more than five kilometres a year. Around this time, Peking established a special management board to control the unprecedented migration. Mannerheim called the board "Könn wu tu" or *kenwutu* in pinyin, meaning "reclaim weedy earth." It was basically a department to convert wild grasslands into cultivated farmland for Han Chinese colonists. A board was established initially in Hohhot, and soon six other branches within an eighty-kilometre radius came into being.

General Yi was, Mannerheim wrote in his military intelligence report, as ambitious as he was greedy in implementing Peking's colonization policy:

> Plots of land are taken away from the Mongols by falsifying decrees of [the Emperor, and] are sold for a small price to Chinese colonists... Needless to say all money is transferred not to Mongol landowners but to the General and his associates. To frighten

the Mongols and put an end to the increasing disturbances among them severe measures are being undertaken, which included execution of an official in Djungar [a district in Ordos]. The result was the opposite to the desired one: public unrest is increasing rapidly.[16]

General Yi was so worried about a revolt that he called for cavalries from Lanzhou, Xi'an and Taiyuan to amass on the borders of Ordos. Mannerheim arrived soon after General Yi's dismissal and canvassed local Mongols. "Though reserved in nature they expressed their indignation and described the violence of the authorities," he wrote. "They said that the danger had passed for the present, but that the situation was nearing a state of armed clashes with the Chinese." Peking was able "to cool down the Mongols," according to Mannerheim, by suspending any further selling of land until the completion of Yi's sentencing.

Most Chinese and Manchu officials were reticent to talk to Mannerheim, who had difficulty confirming statistics about the number of Chinese settlers. He heard that the *kenwutu* controlled 50 million *mou* of land, or thirty-three thousand hectares, divided into a half-million plots. Most of the Han settlers came from Zhili, Shandong and Shanxi, provinces suffering from devastating floods, drought and social unrest. Some Mongols, he reported, "abandoned their nomadic lifestyle and became farmers" too.

Mannerheim understood the "clearly political goal" behind the intense colonization. It was part of China's plan to consolidate its ethnic borderlands "and destroy the semi-independent and uncertain position of present Mongolia . . . and lead to the end of independent Mongolia."

"NOW, IT'S VERY good," Buhchulu said, referring to Han-Mongol relations. A fit, good-looking forty-eight-year-old, Buhchulu is a Mongolian folklore researcher at the Inner Mongolia Academy of Social Sciences in Hohhot. He had taught Mongolian in Helsinki for a year and knew Juha Janhunen. We met at my hotel shortly after my tour of the wintry, wind-swept steppe with Sechenbaatar. I was surprised, at first, by Buhchulu's conciliatory tone.

"A century ago, the Mongols seemed in a rebellious mood, according to Mannerheim's diary," I said.

"At that time, among the Mongols many were angry with the central government in Beijing," Buhchulu admitted. "It's now a very good relationship between the Han Chinese and Mongols." I pressed him on China's language policies toward minorities. "We have good policies," he insisted. "We have national minorities schools. If you want to learn your traditional language you can learn it."

Buhchulu then pointed to the Saami, the indigenous reindeer herders of Northern Europe, as an example of the West's historically poor treatment of indigenous peoples. He had done research in Norway and was well versed on the Saami's grievances. It is certainly true that as the Chinese were colonizing the southern Mongolian steppe, the Scandinavians were pushing the Saami high above the Arctic Circle and had begun an aggressive program to exterminate their culture. But at least the Scandinavians are today attempting to right historic wrongs. The Saami are even experiencing a cultural reawakening, which I witnessed first-hand during a trip to the Norwegian Arctic in 2000. That certainly can't be said of the Mongols in China.

"We teach the [Mongol] language in the university, but the language among the population, day after day, is getting smaller," Buhchulu conceded.

"Why?"

"I don't know. We have good policies but the language is shrinking."

"But why?" I insisted.

"I haven't thought about that," Buhchulu said. "I just think about folklore."

"Really?"

"I'm not a politician or social linguist," he said. "I don't know about these things."

Buchulu then quickly changed topics, telling me that he'd seen a large Mongolian knife on display at the Mannerheim Museum in Helsinki.

I wanted to press him further about the decline of the Mongolian language, but knew such probing was unwise and, in fact, unfair: ethnic minorities know better than to openly criticize Beijing's human rights record.

We continued our conversation at a Mongolian restaurant near the former residence of General Yi. The young waitress wore a traditional pink dress with green trim and pewter embroidery. A matching cone-shaped hat studded with a ruby sat cocked atop her head. She spoke Chinese to Buchulu, who replied in Mongolian. We drank milky tea with millet and ate a lamb hotpot with spicy Chinese sauces.

Buchulu was part of a team of twenty researchers creating an online digital database of Mongol culture. He had just returned from sixty days of fieldwork, travelling in the countryside collecting Mongol folklore, superstitions and proverbs, many of which were first uttered by Genghis Khan. "Genghis Khan was my great-great-grandfather," said Buchulu, who comes from the same clan, called Borjigin, as the world conqueror. Mongols, in fact, were celebrating the eight hundredth anniversary of Genghis Khan's inauguration as Mongol ruler in 1206.

"Genghis Khan didn't like to drink so much," Buchulu said, pouring me another glass of "Great Wall" brand red wine. "He said a man should drink only three times a month."

"How do you know he said that?" I asked.

"Folklore. We have a lot of oral stories. If you travel in the Inner Mongolia countryside you can hear a lot of stories of Genghis Khan," Buchulu said. "Mongols remember very clearly about Genghis Khan just like it was yesterday. It was eight hundred years ago, though. The tales aren't necessarily true, but they are oral stories." A book titled *Genghis Khan's Word*, he said, was still wildly popular among Mongols. It is a compendium of sayings that have been passed down from generation to generation.

"For example," Buhchulu said. "'Don't wash clothes in rivers and lakes.' That's a rule of Genghis Khan."

The folklorist then paused and leaned back pensively.

"'Don't cut the trees freely. It's not good.' That's another saying of Genghis Khan."

"He sounds like an environmentalist," I said.

That prompted Buhchulu to quote yet another saying of this medieval eco-crusader: "'Don't freely dig up the earth!'"

FREELY DIGGING UP the earth is exactly what I saw during a long, numbingly cold bus ride the next day to Genghis Khan's mausoleum in the heart of the Ordos prefecture.

From Hohhot, the bus drove along the southern foot of the Daqing mountain range. Fallow farmland and fields of broken corn stocks lined the highway. After an hour, the cornfields gave way to rammed-earth greenhouses with coal-burning stoves and retractable reed roofs to keep crops from freezing during the bone-chilling nights. In the steely morning light, I saw Chinese farmers rolling back the reed mats as the sun climbed into the sooty sky. Despite water shortages, poor soil and a severe climate, the Chinese had already begun to dig up this area at the time of Mannerheim's journey. In his military intelligence report, the Baron noted Chinese colonists all the way to the modern city of Baotou, where the highway swings south across the Yellow River into Ordos. As we drove south along Route 210, farmland became scarcer, replaced by sand and prickly shrubs. After 125 kilometres, the bus arrived in Dongsheng, the capital of the prefecture.

Ordos covers some 87,000 square kilometres. It is bounded on three sides by the Yellow River, which makes a dramatic elbow-shaped detour into Inner Mongolia from Central China. Almost

50 percent of the prefecture is desert, which deposits 100 million tons of yellow sand into the river each year. The rest of Ordos is a wilderness of mangy pasture. These lands had once been home to powerful Mongol clans, but by 1908 Mannerheim reported that up to thirty thousand Chinese had colonized the area.

The prefecture, with a population of 1.5 million, is now 88 percent Han Chinese. So many Chinese farmers dig up so much of Inner Mongolia that most sandstorms in Beijing, some six hundred kilometres to the east, occur during March and April, when farmers till their chalky fields for the spring planting. Vicious windstorms blow away the topsoil, leading to horrendous erosion and gritty squalls throughout Northern China. In Ordos, deserts have been growing at an alarming rate. Excessive cultivation, over-grazing and drought have degraded the natural grassland. As a result, the Chinese government has relocated 400,000 farmers from the margins of Ordos's two deserts into the city and surrounding townships.

I switched buses in Dongsheng and continued south. The terrain grew even bleaker. In places, huge sand dunes rose out of the grassland. A river we passed was bone dry. What few farms I saw had tiny plots hemmed in by stones and shrubbery—measly protection against the encroaching sand. It was hard to believe Genghis Khan, once the most powerful figure in the world, would choose this niggardly landscape as his final resting place.

However, it hadn't always been this desolate. Tang Dynasty records described Ordos as a "beautiful area with vast pasture and clear streams." One legend tells how Genghis Khan, upon spotting a forested ridge, declared it "a desirable resting-place for an old man." Nobody truly knows where the great Khan is buried. (He died in Gansu province.) For a time, his memorial shrine wandered across the Gobi Desert and Altai Mountains, but eventually came to rest on a ridge in Ordos, which means "tent-palaces" in Mongolian.

The parking lot of the Genghis Khan Mausoleum was almost deserted. I saw only a handful of visitors, including an SUV full of Chinese army officers. A large marble Chinese gate led me up a stairway to an equestrian statue of Genghis Khan. The warm afternoon sunlight glinted off the white marble steps, which gently climbed a ridge forested with small pines and cypresses. The soil was so sandy that all the trees were secured with wooden crutches to protect them from being uprooted by gales.

At the top of the ridge sits the mausoleum, consisting of three round pavilions connected by corridors. These are supposed to resemble Mongolian yurts, but their whitewashed walls, colourful blue domes and swooping eaves made them look like flying saucers. In the foyer, I was met by a marble statue of the great Khan below a frieze of gilt dragons and a mural of his conquered territories. His empire stretched as far south as Egypt and Greece, and as far north as Russia. Behind the entrance, I entered a mourning hall containing three *ger* (yurts) for Genghis Khan and two of his many wives. Various personal items were on display: his bow, milk bucket, clothing, yak-tail standards. His saddle—apparently eight hundred years old—looked immaculate.

The entire mausoleum smacked of fakery. In fact, most of the "relics" were apparently reproduced in the 1970s.[17] The pavilion had been built in 1954 and felt more like a kitschy Chinese tourist attraction than a sacred site. It had been completely renovated the previous year. About a kilometre away, atop another sandy ridge, stood two towering white marble plinths crowned with statues of galloping horses. Its dramatic scale bore the indelible stamp of Soviet monumentalism.

Despite their historical rivalry against the Mongols, the Chinese claim Genghis Khan as one of their own. The Mongol ruler did not conquer China, according to official histories, but rather "unified" it in 1206. His conquests paved the way for his grandson, Kublai Khan, to found the Yuan Dynasty (1271–1368). "The Chinese say Genghis Khan is their master," Sechenbaatar told me. "The Mongolians say 'No, no, no! Genghis Khan is ours!'" Having conquered their lands, the Chinese are now resolved to absorb the Mongol mythology.

The bus meandered back to Dongsheng along a country road paved in fresh asphalt. We passed Han settlements clustered around factories on the arid steppe. The streets were neatly laid out with cement curbs and streetlights that forked at the top like yak horns. New suburbs sprawled up a sloping ridge on the city's outskirts. Despite its declining agricultural land base, the prefecture was experiencing phenomenal growth: GDP had skyrocketed 40 percent this year, the sixth-fastest-growing city in China.[18] As it turns out, the Chinese have found an even more lucrative way to dig up the earth than tilling the soil.

The previous year, Ordos had overtaken Datong as the country's coal capital, producing 150 million tons. The prefecture's proven coal reserves of 168 billion tons account for one-sixth of China's total. On the outskirts of town, I spotted a massive coal pit. Oily black mountains soared four or five storeys. Leaving Ordos the next day aboard another bus, I watched hundreds and hundreds of coal trucks streaming north. The convoy of orange, green and purple trucks—and even three-wheeled motorized carts heaped with coal—stretched almost a hundred kilometres. It ended at the Shulinzhao power plant just south of Baotou. Dozens of cranes were completing what looked like a massive expansion. Clouds of steam rose from a half-dozen cooling towers. New smokestacks painted with red and white stripes looked like gigantic candy canes.

A century ago, Peking reined in the corrupt General Yi for his greed and ambition. Inner Mongolia is again under the control of rogue officials. The construction of illegal coal-burning power plants was largely driving Inner Mongolia's excessive growth. Unlicensed power plants worth some US$5 billion were under construction, despite repeated orders from Beijing to stop. The previous year, six workers died and eight others were injured at one illegal construction site. The scandal provoked Beijing to send an investigative team to Inner Mongolia. The regional Party Chairman was forced to hand in a "self-criticism." Seven other officials were disciplined, and two more faced prosecution.

China burns 42 percent of the world's coal and is adding the equivalent of nearly the entire U.K. power grid each year in new coal-fired plants.[19] Northern China's smokestacks spew a noxious cloud so gargantuan that satellites have tracked it floating over the Pacific. Mountaintop sensors in Washington, Oregon and California have detected sulphur compounds, carbon and other toxic by-products from China's smokestacks.[20] The country's coal plants have become the main cause of the rapid increase in greenhouse gas emissions that cause global warming. Coal will remain king in the foreseeable future too: it represents 60 percent of the world's remaining recoverable hydrocarbon reserves.[21]

As I watched carbon streaming from the towering funnels, I realized that the route I had trekked was a veritable "Soot Road," the newest iteration of that storied trade route of yore. A World Bank environmental report on China later confirmed my suspicion: Mannerheim's route traversed what are now the most polluted areas of China, perhaps even the world.

The Soot Road is the greatest energy corridor on Earth in terms of the production, distribution and consumption of fossil fuels. The region holds 33 percent of the world's proven gas reserves and 36 percent of the world's coal, plus almost 9 percent of the world's oil.[22] One hundred and eight thousand kilometres of pipeline in Central Asia and China now replace the old caravan routes. From the oil-soaked autocracy that is the New Russia, I flew to the boom-town of Baku and followed these new pipelines across the deserts and steppes of Inner Asia. In Xinjiang, I saw oil refineries on the edge of the Taklimakan, coal mines cut into the Tian Shans, coal-fired power plants in every oasis and massive petrochemical plants on the outskirts of Urumqi. I then shadowed the pipeline route to the steel mills of Jiayuguan and choked on the photochemical smog belching from Lanzhou's vast oil refineries. Heading east to Henan and then north into Shanxi and Inner Mongolia, I soon found myself in coal country and in the most polluted cities in the world. Yet it wasn't until I arrived in Ordos, China's fledgling new coal capital, that I came to a brutal realization about the sooty trail that I had been trekking.

What happens on the Soot Road will likely determine the future of the world, especially as a rising China extends its influence in Central Asia through new energy and security alliances, such as the Shanghai Cooperation Organization. Yet this New Great Game is already nearing its endgame. China is depleting its mammoth coal reserves faster than any other country, and peak oil, according to some analysts, is already upon us. As the region's hydrocarbon reserves are drained, the rivalry for their remaining riches may grow more intense. At the same time, global warming is likely to produce severe environmental shifts that could prove deadly to this dusty region already suffering from drought, desertification and pollution. Energy conflicts, increased social and environmental stresses on an already vulnerable population and growing Islamic radicalization caused by ruthless regimes could further rock the region—and the world.

In this new rivalry, China is no hapless pawn. In 2009, for example, China completed its first direct oil pipeline (some 2,200 kilometres) to the Caspian Sea through Kazakhstan and opened an eighteen-hundred-kilometre gas pipeline to Turkmenistan that undermined Russia's long-standing dominance over Central Asia's natural gas.[23] Beijing is profoundly changing the rules of the game.

I was now dying—in more ways than one—to get to Beijing, the terminus of my journey. I had been travelling the Soot Road for nearly five months, covering more than fifteen thousand kilometres by train, plane, ferry, car, horse and camel. In that time, I had slept in forty-seven different hostels, hotels, inns, private homes, yurts, tents, train sleepers and even a converted tractor-trailer at the Irkeshtam Pass. On November 16 in Dongsheng, I woke late and wrote in my journal:

> I don't feel well this morning—low energy and a sore throat from the dry climate and dust and pollution. I don't even feel like getting out of bed. What is there to see? I'm in a provincial industrial town. I must have passed through a hundred just like it.

Leaving Ordos by bus later that day, the weather bitterly cold, my mind became gripped by an apocalyptic vision from the past. Peering out at the endless caravan of coal trucks thundering down the highway in clouds of black dust, I was reminded how the world must have trembled at the sight of the dust storms kicked up by the hooves of advancing Mongol armies. Eight hundred years later, we still have much to fear from the land of Genghis Khan.

BEIJING

Reawakening

China is the theatre of the greatest movement
now taking place on the face of the globe.
—W.A.P. MARTIN, *The Awakening of China* (1907)

TURN-OF-THE-CENTURY Peking overwhelmed the senses. The capital—now known as Beijing—was both exotic and toxic. Its urban design, dating back to the 1400s, evoked ancient Chinese theories of cosmology. Streets, buildings and walls followed principles of feng shui, ensuring that man-made aesthetics did not conflict with supernatural forces. Emphasis was placed on symmetry, proportion, balance and common-sense building techniques for ventilation, plumbing and solar heating.

At Peking's centre stood the Forbidden City—"the Great Within"—the secret heart of the most introverted empire the world has ever known. Sunlight reflected off the yellow-tiled roofs of its grand palaces, radiating a golden halo over the city. Peking grew out from this gilded core in concentric walled districts like the rings of a tree. Around the Forbidden City stood the Imperial City, a complex of palaces, temples, administrative bureaus and gardens for the mandarins, who managed the day-to-day affairs of the Empire. This quarter was, in turn, protected by the Tartar City, reserved for garrisons of Imperial guards and Manchu bannermen charged with defence of the capital. Its massive clay walls, more than twelve metres high and some twenty metres thick at the base, featured parapets, watchtowers and projecting square bastions.[1] To the south lay the sprawling Chinese City, a residential and commercial quarter for commoners.

In 1908, Peking was home to more than a million people. Residents lived in intimate courtyard homes hidden in *hutongs* (alleyways) and strolled wide bazaar streets framed by intricate memorial arches. A cacophony of languages—Mongol, Manchu, Mandarin, Cantonese, Tibetan, Turkic—could be heard in its bustling markets. Endless camel caravans brought the riches of Eurasia across the Gobi. Foreigners were invariably awed by the city's Oriental verve, architectural splendour and great antiquity. Lord Curzon called Peking a fabulous Babylon "without parallel in the modern world."[2]

Yet if this exoticism was Peking's yin, its filth and stench were its yang. In diaries and letters home, foreigners railed bitterly about "the sickening odour" and "dusty and malodorous streets."[3] Sanitation and cleanliness were in a deplorable state. The "infragrant population," complained one visitor at the time, was ignorant of the most basic standards of hygiene.

On July 25, 1908, Mannerheim arrived from Kalgan, a town in the mountains north of Peking. He stayed in the Legation Quarter, which was tucked inside the southeastern corner of the Tartar City. This district for foreigners, badly damaged during the Boxers' siege in 1900, had been rebuilt to rival the grand architecture of Europe.

Mannerheim took a room in Hôtel des Wagons-lits, a luxurious abode built in 1905 in Flemish-Gothic style. The hotel overlooked the Jade Canal, a euphemism for a trickle of green sludge that ran between brick parapets into a moat surrounding the Imperial City. The hotel was conveniently kitty-corner to the Russian Legation. Along this tree-lined street also stood many other Western embassies. The quarter housed all the amenities of European high society: foreign banks, post offices, gentlemen's clubs, churches, grand hotels and shops stocked with the latest European delicacies, including Monopole champagne. Manchu princes, with their beautiful concubines in tow, enthusiastically patronized the district's stores.

"It was with feelings of indescribable pleasure that I took possession of my quarters in Hôtel des Wagons-lits,"[4] Mannerheim later recalled. Rooms featured English beds with silk eiderdowns, lace curtains, electric lights, hot and cold running water and comfortable easy chairs. Its haughty airs and showy guests reminded one Dutch traveller of the "snobbishness and vulgarity of Monte Carlo."[5] After the 1911 revolution, the hotel became the posh refuge of Peking's vanquished aristocracy.[6] It seemed like "an earthly paradise" to the Baron.[7]

For six weeks, Mannerheim worked in a pavilion in the Russian Legation's beautiful garden, writing his intelligence report to the General Staff, redrawing route maps and organizing his meteorological and scientific data. He also renewed acquaintances with foreigners who had previously served in embassies in St. Petersburg, and got to know the legation's military attaché, Colonel Lavr Kornilov, a Cossack whom he had met in Tashkent. Mannerheim even left his "faithful" horse Philip with Kornilov.[8] (In 1917, Kornilov became the Commander-in-Chief of the Russian army and led a failed counter-revolutionary coup. He was eventually killed by the Bolsheviks after leading his White Guards on a legendary "ice march" across Russia's frozen steppe.)

Mannerheim made no notes describing Peking. His last entry in his diary is from Kalgan. In his military report, he wrote that he didn't want to bore readers about things that were "all too familiar." His letters home also reveal little. This despite the fact that a week after his arrival the German barracks, just down the street, burned to the ground, its munitions magazine exploding, killing several soldiers and shattering nearby windows.[9]

This deadly inferno aside, Mannerheim likely found Peking a tamed bastion of modernity. After all, he had just spent two years trekking through the restless outer reaches of the Chinese Empire. He had faced untold hardships and hostility: wintry blizzards, scorching deserts, treacherous alpine passes, excruciating bouts of rheumatism, stone-throwing lamas, a deceitful companion, endless nights in smoky mud hovels and flea-infested yurts. He travelled among some of the world's most obscure peoples—Yugur, Torgut, Tibetan, Sart, Abdal, Xibo—whose way of life hadn't changed in centuries.

In contrast, change was rampant throughout the Legation Quarter and beyond. Peking was sprouting European architecture, grandiose railway stations, swish hotels, tennis courts, polo grounds, a racetrack, Western-style schools and universities, telegraph lines, street lights, modern banks. The Dutch traveller Henri Borel complained at the time that a "vile conventional modern style" was obliterating Peking's ancient beauty.[10] He was bewildered by the incessant construction, "as if the Modern had conquered, and were triumphantly erecting a new, vulgar, cosmopolitan town in the ancient holy fortress."[11] The only modern building showing any "character and distinction," he observed, was built by a Dutch architect. "It is," he wrote, "solid yet characteristic, sumptuous yet sober."[12]

Mannerheim found himself in the epicentre of a New China whose reform edicts were only beginning to reverberate in the far-flung corners of the Empire. In Peking, more than anywhere else, he witnessed, as he put it, the "remarkable awakening of the 'Middle Kingdom' from its centuries of slumber."

THE NIGHT TRAIN from Hohhot slowed as we drew into Beijing's sprawling suburbs the next morning. Pulling open the curtain, I saw an insipid mass of residential towers—a Great Wall of Condos. Its putty-coloured stucco walls stretched for well over a kilometre. I waded through a crush of migrant workers and commuters in the arrivals hall of Beijing's Western Railway Station. It's one of the largest in Asia. The station's postmodern architecture, which includes a massive central archway and whimsical roofs, is supposed to evoke the grandiose pagoda gates of Old Peking.

After queuing for forty minutes, I climbed into a taxi that crawled up a clogged ramp onto Beijing's elevated Third Ring Road, only to get caught in the morning rush hour. The jammed expressway—there are 3.5 million cars in Beijing and the number is growing by one thousand every day—was framed by imposing modern bank towers, hotels, residential blocks, concrete overpasses and billboards galore. It took forty minutes to travel ten kilometres to Wudaokou, the heart of Beijing's university district in the city's northwest corner.

After a week in Wudaokou, I relocated across town to the Central Business District, where I took Mandarin lessons at a private school in Jianwai Soho, an ultra-modern commercial and residential complex. A Japanese architect designed its eighteen white towers, which gleam like paper lanterns at night. Across the street stood Beijing's World Trade Centre, the heart of the district and a vast construction zone. The city's tallest skyscraper, at 330 metres, was under construction. Meanwhile, up the road from Soho, Beijing's most awe-inspiring structure was also taking form. It is a radical reinvention of the skyscraper and is now arguably Beijing's most recognizable building. Dutch architect Rem Koolhaas designed the eerie edifice to house the headquarters of China Central Television. It is a monumental, looping glass and steel structure. Two towers dramatically lean toward each other, connected by a horizontal, elbow-shaped section cantilevered thirty-six storeys above the street. It has been compared to a futuristic archway, a "twisted doughnut" and, ominously, the Ministry of Truth in Orwell's novel *1984*.

I rented a room in a spacious twenty-sixth floor penthouse a kilometre to the south. A young professional couple owned the flat: Jesse Liu was a graduate student at the Foreign Affairs University and her husband, Champson, was a post-doctoral scholar at the

University of Zurich in Switzerland and an editor at the *People's Daily*. My roommates included an engineer working for Siemens and a Chinese lawyer who earned his degree from the University of Liverpool. Everyone spoke English, rose early and worked late. I rarely saw them.

The day I arrived at the Soho complex for Mandarin lessons, crews were erecting a ten-metre Christmas tree in its central plaza. My local supermarket was festooned with Christmas decorations: Santa portraits, red and green banners, ornaments, fake Christmas trees, tinsel. I strolled the well-stocked aisles listening to "Jingle Bells" and "Santa Claus Is Coming to Town." Cashiers wore velvety elf hats.

"Christmas is quite popular now in Beijing, and in order not to feel lonely, I suggest you pay a visit to the Wangfujing Church or the famous Dongjiaominxiang Church... where the Boxer Uprising Tragedy happened," Champson wrote me in an email from Zurich a few days before Christmas. "Perhaps you can get a first-hand experience about the evolving role of Westernization and religion in China."

I asked Champson why the Yuletide spirit seemed to infect so many Beijingers—or at least its shopkeepers. Its "strange popularity," he wrote back, is "a result of the gradual Westernization of China. The Chinese are generally open to foreign influence in terms of culture, and are ready to accept anything that is cool, fun-making and with a modern connotation. Actually, since the late Qing Dynasty, the history of China has been a process of adaptation and assimilation of Western cultures and ideas—Marxism itself is a German school of philosophy."

Beijing certainly seemed to have fallen victim to the worst excesses of both Soviet central planning and American-style consumerism. Its ring roads, Tiananmen Square, Mao mausoleum and Soviet-inspired government buildings reminded me of Moscow, and the gridlocked traffic, poor public transit, suburban sprawl and ubiquitous billboards screamed Los Angeles. Autocrats and auto-mobiles rule this city. Old Peking—the clay walls, pagoda gates, temples and *hutongs*—is fast disappearing under mountains of con-crete and steel.

"The national bird of China is the crane," quipped Hu Xinyu, managing director of the Beijing Cultural Heritage Protection Cen-tre. Construction cranes are indeed everywhere in China, and so is this joke. I heard it in Lanzhou, Xi'an, Taiyuan and even far-flung Kashgar. The country was gobbling up 40 percent of the world's concrete and a third of its steel. The scale of construction easily dwarfs the Ming Dynasty's expansion of the Great Wall.

Hu's office was located in a tony tenth-floor apartment in a residential high-rise called Park Avenue. It overlooked the Second Ring Road, which roughly traces the old city wall and moat. Dur-ing the Great Leap Forward, Mao ordered the wall, gates and pago-das razed. "In such a politically fanatical period," Hu explained to me, "the wall was considered part of feudal society." Old Peking's walled quarters and strict geometry were bulldozed to make way for a network of ring roads and broad thoroughfares as wide as football fields, ideal for military parades. The destruction intensified during the Cultural Revolution. Hôtel des Wagons-lits, a symbol of bour-geois extravagance, was demolished. A charmless modern hotel now stands in its place. The Legation Quarter became a playground for senior Party cadres, its stately embassies and mansions now pri-vate guesthouses and hotels run by the State Council.

However, rampant development since the 1990s is actually responsible for "more destruction of heritage than the Cultural Revolution," explained Hu. This exhaustive makeover was meant to transform Beijing into a sleek, twenty-first-century metropolis for the 2008 Summer Olympics—the symbol of New China.

As for Old China, it hasn't been entirely forgotten. In 2002, the Beijing municipal government published a conservation plan of twenty-five protected historic areas. However, the heritage designations cover only 1,038 hectares, or 17 percent, of Old Peking. "Courtyard by courtyard, *hutong* by *hutong,* the city has been mapped in detail," Hu said, showing me the conservation plan, a thick tome with dozens of intricate maps. "The problem is that nobody is using this book." He explained that private home-owners and developers simply ignore the rules when renovating historic buildings and *hutongs.* Through publicity, neighbourhood vigilance and litigation, the Heritage Protection Centre aims to stop this death by a thousand cranes. "The old flavour of Beijing is being lost," Hu lamented.

Like Mannerheim, I felt my arrival in Beijing was more denoue-ment than climax. The city appeared "all too familiar" to me too: McDonald's, Pizza Hut, KFC and Starbucks outlets, glitzy malls, Carrefour hypermarkets, shiny bank towers, Japanese restau-rants, pizzerias. "To me, going to Beijing is like going to America," Andrew Kaiser, the Taiyuan missionary, complained to me. "You can't spit without hitting [a foreigner]."

Yet a strange, shadowy aura seemed to hang over the capital. And it was more than just the thick, unhealthy haze that shrouds the streets. Beijing is still a secretive city, with many buildings and entire blocks walled off or fenced in from the world. A century ago, few foreigners or Chinese were aware of the intrigues occurring behind the vermilion walls of the Forbidden City. Nowadays, the private Imperial palaces and temple halls are must-see tourist attrac-tions. But other precincts remain off limits: China's Communist rul-ers have installed themselves next door in a palatial compound with two tranquil lakes, ornate pavilions and private residences. Zhong-nanhai, or the "Sea Palaces," is the secretive nerve centre of the world's newest rising power. Its main entrance, built by Yuan Shikai in 1911, is called Xinhuamen, or the "Gate of New China."

Visiting this walled and heavily guarded world would be impos-sible. It is home to the highest-ranking members of the Communist Party, and houses offices of the Party's Central Committee, the State

Council, the Central People's Government and the Party's Military Commission. But accessing Zhongnanhai wasn't that important: I knew the future of "New China" rests as much with the masses living outside that gate as with the powerful few sequestered within.

MANNERHEIM'S INTELLIGENCE report covers almost every facet of China's development. It is 177 pages long, with sections on railway construction, troops, schools, the opium trade, industry and mining, Japan's influence on reform and the colonization of ethnic borderlands. The most detailed section—some forty-seven pages—is on military improvements, which were of obvious importance to the Russian General Staff at the time.

At the end, Mannerheim offered his own take on China's most pressing challenges. Reform initiatives, he observed, were being implemented inconsistently from province to province. "All that is a natural consequence of the great independence enjoyed by China's provincial officials in executing various edicts..." he wrote. "Their activities are often just paper work, their reports are not always truthful, the reforms and novelties begun by one official are neglected by his successor, etc. But each day enhances a group of progressively minded players. The time is not far off when proponents of progress will occupy most of the important posts in the provinces." In this way, China's march toward modernity—however unsteady and haphazard—seemed unstoppable. "Even now," he went on, "one can safely say that the reforms have put down roots so deep that the roots cannot be taken out any longer."

As the Baron saw it, only two "serious obstacles" stood on China's "road to progress." First, the empire lacked enough personnel trained in Western science and methods. Overseas students and school reform, he figured, would eventually fill this gap. The second obstacle was more pressing: the central government lacked the finances to carry out many reforms. China's entire financial system was a throwback to medieval times.

Mannerheim described a financial system so grotesquely unscrupulous that tax revolts were common throughout the Empire. At the root of the problem was a curious farrago of tax collecting practices known as "squeeze." Underpaid officials at every level would squeeze revenue from subordinates who, in turn, levied onerous taxes on impoverished peasants. At each level, tax revenue would be siphoned off to finance officials' salaries and extravagant lifestyles. Each mandarin would attempt to hide the true amount of taxes collected, thereby reducing the squeeze from above. Only about a tenth of provincial revenues actually trickled up into Peking's coffers.[13]

Yet the country's ambitious reform program required enormous amounts of cash to build schools, armaments factories and railways, and to pay the salaries of troops, teachers and foreign advisers. New taxes were thus introduced, which offered unprecedented opportunities for sticky-fingered provincial officials to enrich themselves. The Imperial Court was outraged. *Chinese Public Opinion*, the Empire's first official foreign-language newspaper founded in 1908 by Grand Councillor Yuan Shikai, condemned the "huge cancerous growth of dishonesty throughout the whole official world." It recommended that the new Board of Finance in Peking be tasked with centralizing tax collection and abolishing corrupt provincial practices.[14]

Mannerheim read *Chinese Public Opinion*, echoing its views in his intelligence report.[15] "China's riches are so great," he wrote, "that as long as the financial management of the country doesn't disintegrate and get used for enrichment of innumerable greedy administrative officials . . . the influx of money to the central government treasury would undoubtedly be enough to breathe a new accelerated tempo into implementation of reforms."[16] Yet the system of squeeze was so entrenched that he worried Peking would "not dare to launch drastic reforms in the field of finance" lest Han officials turn against the ruling Manchus. Cash-strapped, Peking did, in fact, continue to turn to consortia of foreign financiers to fund new railways, piling on 126 million British pounds in foreign debt by 1907.[17]

China's monetary system was in even worse shape. Peking found it impossible to shut down provincial mints in order to standardize coinage throughout the Empire. In Urumqi, Mannerheim visited a mint that was producing "dollar" coins of varying sizes with a dragon design inscribed in Chinese and Turki. These were supposed to replace worn-out banknotes. "Such large notes, rather like oilcloth, are hard to fold and in every respect disagreeable to handle," the Baron complained. The *tael*—a weight of silver that was supposed to be the foundation of the monetary system—was also not uniform.

In 1904, the United States sent Professor Jeremiah Jenks of Cornell University to China to study currency reform. He advised Peking to introduce a new gold standard, which would integrate China into the global financial system. Initially, Peking seemed receptive to the idea, but after consideration the powerful Grand Councillors Yuan Shikai and Zhang Zhidong balked. They argued that the value of silver—the foundation of Chinese currency—was declining compared to gold and that a devalued currency could boost China's exports and reduce its massive trade deficit (imports exceeded exports by 74 percent).[18] The country also had no gold reserve to speak of, and would thus have to borrow from foreign banks to buy bullion. These new gold reserves would, in turn, quickly be drained to pay for the country's massive trade deficit. In the end, an edict was issued instituting a new standardized silver coin weighing one *tael*.[19]

Monetary disagreements aside, Peking welcomed closer ties to the United States, which returned $14 million of its Boxer indemnity. The money helped to finance the tuition of Chinese students overseas, a generous gesture given the Great Powers' harsh treatment of China. Peking hoped a Sino-American alliance could thwart Japanese aggression in Manchuria. Washington's support fell short of an outright military alliance, but the United States—a rising global power at the time—saw a commercially and militarily strong China as a stabilizing force in the Far East.

As part of a public relations campaign, Wu Tingfang, the Chinese Minister to the United States, spoke to a packed audience at Carnegie Hall in New York on May 5, 1908. Wu propounded on China's peaceful rise—a mantra that China's Communist leaders would enthusiastically take up a century later. Wu's speech, titled "The Awakening of China," was reprinted in *Chinese Public Opinion* a few months later. "What does this awakening of China mean to the world?" Wu asked. "To my mind, it means in the first place true and lasting peace in the Far East." This peace would be founded, he reasoned, on the strengthening of China militarily against aggressors—particularly Japan—and its integration into the global economy, especially trade with the United States. "Again the awakening of China means the development of commerce, and the day is not distant when the Pacific Ocean will rival the Atlantic with the number of ships that sail on its surface," he said. "The world will then witness an expansion of trade never before known in its history and this trade will also be a safeguard in the interests of universal peace."[20]

At this time, the world was experiencing its first "gilded age" of globalization. Railways, steamers and the Panama Canal had drastically reduced the time and cost of transportation. The telegraph, transoceanic cables and newspapers connected people like never before. By 1900, more than a million people were migrating in great waves to the New World. Tariffs were declining and global trade was exploding.[21] Most countries had adopted the gold standard, creating a global financial system. Capital gushed to developing countries in search of higher profits. It was an era of "haute finance," of unprecedented financial innovations: new private debt and equity instruments, bills of exchange, bond finance, derivative securities, foreign direct investment. By 1914, foreign assets represented 20 percent of global GDP, a level that wasn't reached again until 1985.[22]

In this context, it's understandable that finance preoccupied Mannerheim. The Empire, he figured, could be given "new life" and be turned "into a powerful state only if financial reform is given first priority." By 1907, however, there were indications that the global financial system itself was unstable. That year the United States faced a banking crisis that caused its stock exchange to lose more than a third of its value. A backlash was also brewing worldwide. In China, globalization—although no one used this term at the time—was seen as colonial exploitation. Opposition to foreign domination manifested itself in slogans such as "China for the Chinese" and protests against usurious foreign loans, opium smuggling, unfair treaties and railway and mining concessions. The ruling Manchus found themselves the target of Han nationalist ire. A few years later, a wave of nationalistic bloodshed swept the world in the first truly global war. Mannerheim ended up commanding a Tsarist regiment on the Eastern Front. The last age of globalization did not end happily.

THROUGHOUT MY TRIP, I read article after article in *China Daily* about the banking system and monetary reform. Yet the financial climate couldn't have been more different than a century ago. Far from running trade deficits, China carried enormous surpluses—$178 billion in 2006, soaring to $295 billion by 2008. As a result, China was amassing a sensational foreign currency reserve. It topped $1 trillion—the largest in the world—while I was in Beijing. Two years later it doubled. The Chinese were, in turn, loaning great gobs of cash to the United States. In an odd twist of fate, some of the world's poorest citizens were financing the extravagant lifestyles of its richest. It was—and continues to be—a strangely synergistic arrangement that financial historian Niall Ferguson has termed "Chimerica." Compared to the Manchus, Beijing has also done a phenomenal job centralizing tax collection: in 1978, it controlled only 16 percent of all government revenue; the proportion is over 54 percent today.[23]

In other ways, contemporary China would be uncannily familiar to Mannerheim. During my six months there, the State Council (the equivalent of the Qing Dynasty's Grand Council) was attempting to curb official corruption in the hopes of placating peasants outraged by land seizures and exorbitant taxes. Beijing still struggles to control its provincial underlings. "The heavens are high and the Emperor is far away" is an old proverb I heard several times in reference to the attitudes of local officials toward Beijing. As they were a century ago, the Americans are still lecturing the Chinese about reforming their currency, accusing Beijing of suppressing the value of the renminbi—China's unit of currency—in order to boost exports. The financial system was also undergoing significant changes. While I was in China, three state-owned banks went public, listing themselves on the stock exchange and raising tens of billions of dollars in private equity. China's financial sector was preparing to open itself to foreign rivals under new World Trade Organization rules.

Before departing Vancouver, I saw China as a mighty coal-fired dragon set to devour the world—or at least its scarce resources. It was hard not to be awed by the superlatives: it is the fastest growing and biggest country in the world, with the second-largest economy. Yet after my trek through its far reaches, I did not fear China, but grew to fear *for* China. Since the reform movement was launched in 1978, the country has made incredible progress. Hundreds of millions of people have been lifted out of dire poverty. But China remains beset by problems: violent ethnic unrest sporadically flares up among the Uyghur and Tibetans; the population is aging at a troubling rate thanks to the one-child policy; selective abortion has created a dangerous imbalance of young men in parts of the country; corruption is rife; an angry nationalism is percolating among the disenfranchised; vast areas appear on the verge of ecological collapse; climate change could seriously undermine food security; the stock exchange, according to one economist I met, is "a gaming casino;" there aren't enough good jobs for millions of graduates; many state-owned enterprises remain stubbornly inefficient; easy credit, politicized lending and murky balance sheets threaten the stability of the banking system. Many of these problems are interconnected so that a crisis in one area could spill over into others, potentially leading to widespread social breakdown. The Communist Party thus maintains a seemingly iron grip, recognizing that it faces stresses unimaginable to the Manchus a century ago.

"We need a New Deal with Chinese characteristics," Dr. Hu Angang, a renowned economist at Tsinghua University, told me. Hu explained that a modern safety net could allay anxiety throughout Chinese society, from rural farmers, who hoard more than 40 percent of their household income in savings, to the Communist Party elite, who remain fixated on anything that threatens social stability.

Logan Wright, a young American financial analyst whom I met in Beijing, figured the first domino might fall on December 11, 2006. Early that morning, I walked a kilometre north from my apartment along the undulating viaduct of the Third Ring Road, already clogged with buses and cars. I stepped carefully around gobs of yellow spit on the sidewalk. Hacking up half a lung is a morning ritual for Beijingers. I went to the China World Trade Centre and wandered through its ritzy three-level shopping mall. It was empty and quiet except for the clip-clopping of my shoes on its polished marble floors. I found what I was looking for on the ground floor of one of the trade centre's modernist towers.

It was a branch of HSBC, the London-based bank that was founded in 1865 as the Hongkong and Shanghai Banking Corporation. This morning WTO rules kicked in that forced China to open its $5.1 trillion financial industry to foreign competition.

HSBC was one of eight foreign banks that would be allowed to take domestic deposits in renminbi. Given the dubious balance sheets of state-owned Chinese banks, which are often used as ATMs to finance every pet project of local officials, no matter their economic viability, Wright figured Chinese depositors—at least the savvy ones—would immediately rush to place their savings in more secure foreign banks. I came to witness the massive line-ups of panicked depositors pushing and shoving—the harbinger, perhaps, of impending financial doom. Yet I found the sidewalk deserted, the bank dim. For forty minutes, I waited out front in the calm pewter light of dawn. The branch opened, uneventfully, later that morning.

Wright wasn't entirely wrong. A financial crisis eventually rattled China. About a year after my stroll around the China World Trade Centre, HSBC wrote down $10.5 billion in toxic sub-prime mortgages. That was the beginning of a global financial meltdown and the Great Recession that would force many Western countries into de facto nationalization of their banks through astounding billion-dollar bailouts. Surprisingly, China weathered this storm better than most countries. "I don't think the smart man would bet against these people," Ralph W. Huenemann, a business professor at Peking University, told me. "[The Chinese] take it on the chin and then come fighting back."

ONE GLARING OMISSION stands out in Mannerheim's otherwise comprehensive intelligence report. It is missing from his personal diary as well. Nowhere does he mention—even in passing—political reform. The oversight probably says more about Mannerheim, who was deeply skeptical of democracy,[24] than it does about the sorry state of political reform in China at the time.

The Imperial Court had come to the uncomfortable truth that the empire's "backward condition" was due, at least in part, to its system of rule.[25] The Boxer Rebellion, foreign invasion, mass uprisings, attempted revolutions, rice riots and widespread calls for reform left them little choice. In 1905, the Empress Dowager ordered a five-member commission to study the political systems of foreign governments. If China wanted to be strong, the reasoning went, it needed a constitution.[26] The commission travelled to Japan, Great Britain, France, Belgium, Germany, Russia, Austria and the United States. A year later, the Empress Dowager accepted its recommendation for a constitution modelled after Japan's.[27] "All are agreed," an Imperial edict announced, "that the lack of prosperity in the state is due to the separation between the officials and the people and the lack of cooperation between the capital and the provinces." The Empire would grow stronger if "public questions are determined by consultation with the people."[28] A Bureau of Constitutional Affairs, a National Assembly and provincial deliberative assemblies were soon established. By the time Mannerheim arrived in Peking, the pages of *Chinese Public Opinion* overflowed with edicts on political reform and constitutional regulations.

On September 1, 1908, while Mannerheim was still in Peking, an edict laid out a cautious timeline to establish a parliament in nine years. However, the Emperor would retain absolute power, relegating the prospective parliament to an advisory role. "China's best plan for reform," stated *Chinese Public Opinion*, "is undoubtedly to adopt the motto 'Festina Lente' [make haste slowly] and with assurance made doubly sure by repeated trial each forward step should be made secure before it is finally adopted."[29] (In 1978, Chinese President Deng Xiaoping took this same cautious approach to reform, summarized by his slogan "crossing the river by feeling for stones.") The newspaper warned against following Russia's rash example: "The hurried institution of the Duma in Russia is a horrible example of what absolute fools a body of men, untrained in the ways of statecraft, can make of themselves." (Again, a century later, China's Communist leaders came to the same conclusion while watching the Soviet Union disintegrate in 1991 from glasnost's speedy pace).

Yet the Imperial Court found itself criticized for grandiloquent decrees that were nothing more than "paper reforms," cynical attempts to thwart real change and maintain privileged Manchu rule.

In the early days of the Self-Strengthening Movement, a few progressive governors pushed reforms on a reluctant, suspicious peasantry. Peking too was slow to embrace change. But by 1908, reforms had caused widespread social and economic transformation. "Now the whole spirit of the people is changed," Wu Tingfang told the audience at Carnegie Hall.[30] A torrent of new social forces—republican revolutionaries, Han nationalists, student radicals, Christian sects, industrialists, Chinese-language newspapers—was fast eroding the antiquated political structures of the Qing Dynasty. Confucian orthodoxy too was in ripe decay.

The Manchu rulers viewed public opinion as "a stream which if obstructed in its course will cause the water to overflow the banks and cause much damage."[31] By slowly introducing limited political reforms, including a watered-down parliament and deliberative pro-vincial assemblies, the Manchus hoped to crack open the floodgates slightly to dilute popular discontent. Their intent was not to follow public opinion but to control it and even repress it if need be.

That was especially true of the nascent Chinese press. The first modern newspapers, modelled on those in the West, were estab-lished in the 1870s. They were seen as the conduit of the *vox populi*. Many were titled *Public Opinion*, or *yulun* in Chinese. Their pop-ularity rose with growing literacy and a technological and com-munications revolution that was sweeping the country. In the first decade of the twentieth century, the length of railways in China increased almost seven-fold[32] and the volume of mail soared more than thirty-fold to 355 million items.[33] Some 126,000 kilometres of telegraph lines—described by one historian as the "Victorian Internet"—also stretched as far as Kashgar and linked China to a global transoceanic cable network.[34] Thriving coastal newspapers used the rail and the post to spread news into the interior of China.

From 1905 to 1908, the number of newspapers and printed material distributed by the post rose from ten million to seventy million.[35] Officials grew fearful of these newspapers, which were often run by reformers and subversives. Journalists were despised as "ruffians in scholars' robes," who incited disturbances and fostered dissent.[36] Yuan Shikai even thought journalists fabricated much of the social unrest.

The first edicts on censorship, in 1898, proved ineffective. But in 1907, authorities began enacting stricter regulations. Early the next year, a new law forced all copy to be submitted for censorship before publication.[37] The press laws also prohibited unfavourable mentions of the Imperial Court. Although the laws were largely ignored, the repressive atmosphere instilled a degree of self-censorship, and newspapers were occasionally shut down for sedition. Peking also issued a circular order to all post offices "to look for and open suspicious looking letters."[38]

Of course, if censorship failed—which was indeed the case—Peking could always call on its newly modernized army to repress public opinion and disband rabble-rousing newspapers. "It is already conceded, even by the most pessimistic critics in China," wrote one Western observer in 1908, "that the new troops are sufficiently numerous and sufficiently well organized to crush any rebellion, no matter how many provinces might be involved."[39]

By this time, however, the stream of public opinion had become a raging river. China had changed, but its rulers—and system of rule—had not. Even the army proved ineffective. In 1911, reform was swept away by revolution.

LIKE MANNERHEIM, I heard little talk of political reform during my trek through Northern China. Many Chinese groused about local corruption, land seizures, horrendous pollution, shoddy schools, unemployment, low wages and a lack of health care. People called for better environmental protection, greater religious freedom and an end to corruption. Yet these remedies were never framed around fundamental political reform. No one—not even privately—whispered about national elections or unseating China's Communist rulers. Prosperity, not politics, preoccupied everyone.

"Over the years, I've had my expectations for democracy in China lowered by the Chinese people around me," the missionary Andrew Kaiser told me. He did put some faith in the new middle class, those who can afford to have (and pay penalties for having) two kids and own a car, business and perhaps more than one apartment. They might put demands on the government to protect property rights, maintain the rule of law and ensure that their tax dollars aren't misspent. "These people are enfranchised. They have a certain standard of living and want to keep it," he said. "These are the people I put hope in." Still, the size of the burgeoning bourgeoisie was exaggerated, he figured. One estimate puts the proportion of the population that is middle-class or above at 62 percent.[40] "Don't believe the hype," Kaiser warned. The fate of China, he insisted, largely depends on whether Beijing can keep the country's 600 million "grumpy" peasants happy—a threat to rulers throughout China's long history. "The peasants can throw the Emperor out," Kaiser said. "There's no doubt about it."

The almost complete lack of political reform in China today belies the breathtaking transformation that I witnessed taking place. Thirty years of spectacular growth—unparalleled in human history—has produced whole new social classes: nouveau riche Party officials, billionaire tycoons, middle-class professionals, yuppies, rural shopkeepers, entrepreneurs. People have an unprecedented freedom to prosper. The Internet and mobile phones stream a mind-boggling volume of megabytes to increasingly tech-savvy citizens, whom authorities struggle to control. Some 180 million Chinese kids study English each year, creating a new breed of globalized, pop-culture-consuming youth. Millions of new converts are flooding cathedrals and underground house-churches. Buddhist temples are being restored. Confucianism is back in vogue. The one-child policy has eroded traditional family structures. Gays and lesbians are openly gathering in nightclubs. Chinese artists and musicians have eked out surprising freedoms. And most tellingly, I did not meet a single Communist Party official who mouthed Marxist bafflegab.

Champson, my Beijing landlord, put me in contact with Dr. Ni Yuping, a thirty-one-year-old scholar and a member of a national research project on the Qing Dynasty. Ni lived in Huilongguang, a sprawling new suburb of cookie-cutter condos, with his wife and newborn child. I wanted to talk to him about a book I was reading on late Qing history.

It was written by Hu Sheng, a Marxist theorist, senior Party cadre and former president of the Chinese Academy of Social Science. Hu died in 2000 at age eighty-two. The book, titled *From the Opium War to the May Fourth Movement*, describes how late-Qing officials grew rich from corrupt and inefficient state-owned enterprises and "effectively forestalled the free development of Chinese capitalism."[41] "Comprador bureaucrats," Hu points out, allowed foreign capitalists to exploit Chinese workers who laboured "under the worst possible conditions and with the lowest possible wages." Hu's doggedly Marxist critique of late-Qing rule, I thought, seemed uncannily applicable to China's current crop of Communist rulers, a paradox that I hoped to discuss with Ni.

Carrying his apple-cheeked newborn, the youthful scholar led me into his upstairs study. But he wasn't interested in discussing Marxist theory. In a country wracked by grotesque levels of inequality, dialectical materialism turns out to be bunk. Instead, Ni brought out *The Modernization of China* by Gilbert Rozman, a sociology professor at Princeton University. "This book is very influential in China," Ni said. He then pulled out a second tome titled *Xian Dai Hua*, or *Modernization Theory* in English, by Samuel P. Huntington. The Harvard professor became famous for *The Clash of Civilizations*, a controversial thesis about the cultural roots of global conflict, which pits East against West. "His books are very influential too," Ni said.

First published in 1968, *Modernization Theory* explains how scientific and technological revolutions transform societies from early industrialization to mass urbanization in successive, unstoppable waves. Economic transformation eventually leads to new social patterns, effectively undermining traditional sources of authority and loyalty.[42] As societies modernize, Huntington argues, they become more complex and disordered.[43] Corruption, growing inequality and new sources of wealth often emerge. If old political structures are incapable of channelling these new social forces and mediating conflict, instability and violence may result. "The primary problem of politics is the lag in the development of political institutions behind social and economic change," he writes.[44] Under certain conditions—the alignment of the bourgeois intelligentsia and peasants against a calcified, corrupt regime, for example—revolutions can ignite. In a country obsessed with social stability, Huntington's research resonates with many Chinese scholars and officials who are attempting to understand transformation in China, both past and present.

According to Ni, the Qing Dynasty tried "to preserve decadent and outworn institutions, at least in form, long after they should have been overhauled or abolished."[45] At the same time, new ideas from the West were galvanizing Chinese society. "Most of the revolutionaries were Western-educated," Ni explained. "They believed in democracy, not in absolute Manchu control."

"Take reform in China now," Ni went on, drawing a striking parallel between the Manchu Court and the Communist Party. "If we open our gates to the West, we can learn new technologies. At the same time, we have to face the new ideas of the West, like democracy. The Communist Party, especially [President] Hu Jintao, is very nervous about this. But they have no choice."

After the Cultural Revolution, China was in a wretched state: starving, terrorized, economically crippled. Deng Xiaoping had to instigate reforms to strengthen the country against internal unrest. Reform began in the economic sphere among rural farmers, then spread throughout China. Political reform also began with the election of rural village governments. "I think, step by step, reform will eventually reach the central government." Ni insisted.

"Democracy is unavoidable," agreed Li Fan, one of China's leading democracy activists. "It will come." Li is president of a think tank called the World and China Institute. I visited him in his office, not far from the Olympic Bird's Nest Stadium—the defining symbol of the New China. A table was piled high with titles, many of them probably banned in China: *China Since Tiananmen*, *Electoral Authoritarianism* and *The River Runs Black: The Environmental Challenge to China's Future*. He bought the books during a recent trip to the United States.

Since founding the World and China Institute in 1993, Li has been quietly pushing political reform at the local level. In the 1980s, disgruntled farmers, enraged by graft and illegal taxes, fought for the election of local village leaders and committees. About a million villages now hold elections. While many elections suffer from rigged nomination processes, gerrymandering and other irregularities, they nonetheless represent genuine progress in terms of political reform. Li's strategy is to cultivate this grassroots democracy without threatening the Communist Party's authority—at least not yet. "If nobody wants democracy from top to bottom," Li explained, "then I have no choice but to work from the bottom up." In 1998, Li helped to orchestrate an election in a Sichuan township, a step up from the village level. Township elections have since spread to a few other provinces. And many cities, including Beijing, are now experimenting with *hutong* power through elected neighbourhood committees.

Li believes that democracy can play a constructive role by peacefully resolving social conflicts in China. Elections are like release valves, preventing popular anger from boiling over into outright unrest. But Li worries that these valves may not be in place when

China really needs them. A faltering economy, for instance, could quickly erode the Communist Party's legitimacy and spark sudden turmoil. "If China has a financial crisis, the whole world will have a political crisis," said Li. Still, he is hopeful that democracy will grow organically in China, from villages to townships, prefectures and provinces and eventually to those ruling from within the walls of Zhongnanhai. "In 2020, we should have national elections," Li told me. "I'm optimistic about that date."

I heard this same view from many other observers, both Chinese and foreign, in Beijing. "There are disputes over timing (will it take ten years or fifty years?) and mechanisms (will it be elite-led or mass-led, violent or peaceful?), but the large bulk of China observers, including leaders of the Communist Party, seem to believe that democratic opening is almost inevitable," writes Daniel Bell, a forty-two-year-old Canadian philosophy professor at Tsinghua University, in *Beyond Liberal Democracy: Political Thinking for an East Asian Context.*[46]

I attended a reading that Bell gave from his just-released book at an English-language bookstore in Beijing's Chaoyang District, home to many foreign embassies and expat bars. In the book, he proposes the development of a "modern Confucius democracy" with an elite upper house selected through examination. This chamber of cerebral second thought, called Xianshiyuan, or "House of Virtue and Talent," would temper the populist impulses of a lower house selected through elections. "It would be Chinese-style democracy: rule by the people, with Confucian characteristics," he writes.[47] Not long after his reading, however, government censors forbade Bell to publish his ideas on political reform in a Chinese academic journal. So far, Communist Party leaders, like crafty Qing officials of a century before, have embraced only the most incremental and timid political reforms.

While Beijing's political institutions—including the Party's Central Committee, Politburo, People's Congress, State Council and Presidency—haven't changed much, the behaviour of their leaders has. Public opinion is a growing force in Chinese politics, at least in certain spheres. Communist leaders are increasingly heeding the warnings of the ancient Chinese statesman who said, "To stop the voice of the people is more dangerous than to dam the flow of a river."[48]

Victor Yuan charts the turbulent currents of Chinese public opinion. As chairman of Horizon Research Consultancy Group he is one of China's leading pollsters. "We are doing more and more work for the government," Yuan told me in his swish seventh-floor corner office in the Chaoyang District.

Public opinion is a rather new social force in China. It awoke about a century ago as a result of growing literacy, the telegraph and the founding of native Chinese newspapers. Nowadays, the explosion of news sources and new information technologies such as the Internet and mobile phones has created a current that is stronger, wilder and more difficult to control. Authorities have gone to incredible lengths to both monitor and manipulate public opinion. While I was in the country, Beijing erected the Great Firewall of China, and Google.cn went live with a censored version of its popular search engine. This widespread surveillance and censorship has generated outrage in the West. Lesser known, however, is the fact that authorities are also listening to the *vox populi*. Officials monitor feedback on government websites, listen to chatter in the blogosphere and use polling and focus groups to gauge public opinion.

Yuan insisted this sensitivity isn't rooted in altruism; rather, he explained, the Party is simply trying to find "technical solutions" to maintain and strengthen its rule. I've come to think of this as "technotarianism": technology becomes the primary tool to destroy or weaken civil society. Like dredging and constructing dykes to tame the flow of a river, the government's approach is to use information technology and quantitative research methods to control and, on occasion, brutally contain public opinion. But the task seems impossible: in 2009, there were almost 400 million Internet users in China, and the country's 850 million mobile phone subscribers sent a staggering 900 billion text messages. Cunning youths are constantly finding new ways to encrypt messages, communicate in code and get around the firewall. Beijing's attempts at censorship may prove as effective as Qing officials trying to comb through more than 250 million pieces of mail to intercept subversive messages a century ago.

According to Yuan's forecast, Chinese public opinion will only grow more assertive and irreverent. In the traditional Chinese family, he explained, children were subservient to their parents and older siblings. Confucianism dictated filial piety, with the father as god and ruler over the household. But the one-child policy means the child now reigns supreme—the sole heir whose education and success may determine a family's future prosperity. That's a position of power that no youngster—barring perhaps child emperors—has ever had in Chinese history. According to Yuan, about 40 percent of China's 300 million families are part of this "single-kid generation."

China has become a country of Little Emperors: the generation is self-interested, fun-seeking, opportunistic, aggressive and "de-ideological," Yuan said. The problem, at least for the Communist Party, is that this generation also has an anti-authoritarian streak. "Politically," Yuan said, "they don't believe that a president is someone you can't criticize."

Bill Liu believes this deep generational divide is key to China's future. He is a balding, bespectacled and soft-spoken man in his late fifties. He is the father of Maylee, a classmate of mine at the Mandarin-language school in Beijing. I visited them and Bill's elderly, regal-looking mother in a well-appointed condominium close to the Central Business District. Bill's story is typical: his father was a Guomindang soldier in Central China, and the family escaped to Taiwan in 1949, when Bill was only four. He spent his youth in

Taipei and at nineteen, moved to Kirksville, Missouri, to earn an MBA. He opened three successful Chinese restaurants in Palo Alto, California, before going into the mortgage business and then the import-export business in the 1990s. Then, in 2003, Bill's life took an unusual turn: he abandoned business and moved to Beijing.

Here, Bill began working for a nonprofit organization placing Chinese students in high schools in small-town America. He takes about forty kids a year. Many are the children of senior Party cadres or high-ranking brass in the military. When one teenager arrived in the United States, Maylee discovered the girl had "huge bricks of cash" amounting to $40,000. Another time, Bill went to Wuhan to interview a prospective student.

"He drove up in a Rolls Royce," Bill said.

"How can a teenager in China drive a Rolls Royce?" I asked incredulously.

"He wasn't driving. He had a chauffeur."

The teenagers spend a year in the United States with host families. "When they arrive," Maylee said, "we take a group photo, and they are expressionless." To illustrate the transformative effect of studying abroad, Bill showed me a blurry photograph of himself and four Chinese teenagers in an airport departure hall, ready to return to China after their year abroad. Donning a white jacket, baseball cap and big smile, Bill looked like a doting grandfather. The kids were beaming. After that year, a spell was lifted: the kids became more open-minded, independent and assertive. "They are going to cause a headache for the government," Bill said, grinning mischievously.

He knows his history: a century ago, foreign-educated students didn't just create a headache for China's rulers—they brought about a fatal aneurism. Bill is confident and hopeful that China will become a superpower as long as education reform continues. "And if the education system is reformed," he said, "then the political system will have to be reformed too." His biggest worry is the

Communist Party's reluctance to embrace this change. If political reform lags too far behind rising expectations, or if a sudden confluence of economic, social and environmental crises overwhelms outdated institutions, there could be trouble.

"The next century is China's century," Bill went on proudly. "It will take two generations—sixty years—to rebuild the country." He picked up the blurry photo of himself and the four lanky teens. "I'm putting my faith in my generation."

"The young generation is our hope," agreed Xu Youyu, a well-known liberal scholar, outspoken critic and researcher at the Institute of Philosophy at the Chinese Academy of Social Sciences. Xu's life couldn't be more different from Bill Liu's. Born at the start of the Communist Revolution, he graduated middle school and quickly became a fanatical Red Guard in Mao's Cultural Revolution. He moved to the countryside for several years before working in a factory. He began university, at age thirty-one, in 1978, the year Deng Xiaoping launched his modernization program. He has been a visiting scholar at Oxford, Harvard and Stanford, and is China's leading proponent of John Rawls, an American philosopher whose theory of justice balances freedom with equality of opportunity.

"In China, the problem is very simple," Xu told me in his Beijing apartment. "Almost every single rich person has earned their income illegally." Wealth is entirely determined by the power of *guanxi*. Corruption is endemic. "Almost everyone in China recognizes that political reform is necessary," he explained. "If political reform is not carried out, continued economic reform won't happen. But political reform is just empty words from the authorities."

About two years after my visit, Xu and some three hundred activists, lawyers and academics signed Charter o8, a manifesto calling for constitutional democracy and the rule of law in China. As one of the highest profile signatories, Xu has been interrogated and harassed by police, and has defied demands to withdraw his signature. Some senior Party officials consider Charter o8 a movement to overthrow the Communist government. "Such an interpretation of the Charter and the allegations of criminality are absurd," Xu told a London newspaper, "but that is not new in China."[49]

Charter 08 states that the Communist Party's "approach to 'modernization' has proven disastrous. It has stripped people of their rights, destroyed their dignity, and corrupted normal human intercourse." What little political reform there has been in China has "extended no further than the paper on which it is written." The Charter goes on:

> The stultifying results are endemic official corruption, an undermining of the rule of law, weak human rights, decay in public ethics, crony capitalism, growing inequality between the wealthy and the poor, pillage of the natural environment as well as of the human and historical environments, and the exacerbation of a long list of social conflicts, especially, in recent times, a sharpening animosity between officials and ordinary people.
>
> As these conflicts and crises grow ever more intense, and as the ruling elite continues with impunity to crush and to strip away the rights of citizens to freedom, to property, and to the pursuit of happiness, we see the powerless in our society—the vulnerable groups, the people who have been suppressed and monitored, who have suffered cruelty and even torture, and who have had no adequate avenues for their protests, no courts to hear their pleas— becoming more militant and raising the possibility of a violent conflict of disastrous proportions. The decline of the current system has reached the point where change is no longer optional.[50]

The Charter's signatories call for sweeping political reform: a new constitution, the separation of powers, legislative democracy, an independent judiciary, greater freedoms, protection of human rights and private property, and much more.

The outrage and attacks against China's ruling regime—and the call for genuine political reform—echo similar demands in the dying days of the Qing Dynasty. The timing of the manifesto wasn't lost on its authors. Charter 08's opening line reads: "A hundred years have passed since the writing of China's first constitution."

IT IS FAR too simplistic to suggest that history is just going to repeat itself, that Communist rule, like the Emperor's Mandate of Heaven, is going to dissolve suddenly in a revolutionary cauldron. Few Chinese see this as even desirable, given China's bloody twentieth century. "Nobody likes revolutions," Ni Yuping, the Qing-era scholar, told me.

A century ago, China was much smaller. It had a population of 460 million compared to 1.3 billion today. Its connections to the global economy were tangential. Mannerheim counted only a handful of modern factories throughout Northern China. A simple, medieval social structure of mandarins and peasants still governed daily life. Radical changes were surely afoot, but China was transforming at a snail's pace compared to today. Even still, China experts and foreign travellers back then were overwhelmed by the phenomenal speed and scale of change. In his memoirs, Mannerheim quotes an unidentified Englishman with thirty years' service in the Chinese administration (probably Sir Robert Hart, Inspector General of the Imperial Maritime Custom Service) who said: "After three weeks in China one is prepared to write a book about her, after three years an article, but when one has been there thirty years one realizes that one knows nothing."[51]

The country's dizzying transformation left the Chinese themselves perplexed. "The exchanges taking place are so kaleidoscopic in rapidity and mysterious in character," said Wu Tingfang, the Chinese Minister to the United States, in 1908, "that even a native of the land, unless he is a keen observer, gets bewildered and is left behind in the swiftly moving onward progress of his country." As a result, most books about China published at the time—and there were many—had, according to Wu, "only historical value."

I felt equally bewildered by what I saw taking place in China. How to make sense of it all? The more I travelled, and the more

I saw and learned about China, the more complex and confused became my understanding. It is a country, as one Finnish journalist has written, of "a million truths."[52] Perhaps the sage Lao Tzu, circa 550 BC, said it best: "The further one goes, the less one knows."

In the world's oldest civilization, books about the past—even those written more than a century ago—aren't just of "historical value." The most sacred of China's classics, *The Book of Changes,* or *I Ching,* which dates back two thousand years, says that hidden treasures lie buried in the "many sayings of antiquity and many deeds of the past" that, if discovered, can strengthen one's character. The past can make us wise to the future, or at least teach us humility.

After a long day's journey—riding on horseback across the rolling pastures of the Alai Mountains, barrelling down the desert highways of the Taklimakan or trekking through dirt poor villages along the Yellow River—I would collapse in the evening and read Mannerheim's journal before falling asleep. His daily entries gave me context and comfort, hints of what lay ahead on the road and, perhaps, in China's future. The Baron became a sort of oracle.

Mannerheim was hopeful about China. Huge advances had been made in the reform of schools, construction of railways and factories, modernization of the military. The Imperial Court appeared set to finally implement currency and financial reform. A constitution was in the works. The entire spirit of the people was beginning to stir in a national awakening. "All this led one to expect that the empire would have a new and great future," Mannerheim wrote, "and that it was growing into a power, with which other nations would some day have to reckon."

A century later, that day of reckoning is surely upon us.

EPILOGUE

To the Finland Station

*From the dearly bought experiences of earlier
generations, coming ones will learn to avoid their mistakes.*
—C. G. MANNERHEIM, *Memoirs*

MANNERHEIM HAD originally planned to return to St. Petersburg via Japan and the United States, or perhaps via India and the Suez Canal, but he could only finance such a trip—his first to North America or the subcontinent—if he earned an "extra premium" on his stock investments. That appeared not to be the case. The only option remaining, he grumbled in a letter to his brother, would be "the unpleasant railway trip across Siberia."[1]

He had enough money, however, to make an eight-day trip to Japan. The Baron departed Tianjin by steamship, visiting Shimonoseki and Kyoto. He made no notes of this trip, but commented years later in his memoirs that the Japanese "had succeeded so much better than the Chinese in the task of introducing modern methods and reforms."[2] He then sailed aboard the steamship *Yeiko Maru*[3] to Vladivostok, where he boarded the dreaded Trans-Siberian Railway.

The train lumbered across the continent at twenty miles per hour. The journey along the world's longest railway—some nine thousand kilometres—rolled through desolate steppe, taiga, rugged mountains and boreal forest. It was a trip of ugly monotony. "As far as the eye can see," wrote one traveller in 1908, "are the snow-covered wastes, treeless, houseless, lifeless."[4] After two weeks aboard the locomotive, Mannerheim was back in St. Petersburg, "the Russian cholera centre," as he described, "with all its misery, stink, filth and plague." The date was September 25, 1908.[5]

MY FINANCES WERE as badly depleted as Mannerheim's. Originally, I had planned to travel to Japan, following in the Baron's wake. The passenger ferry from Tianjin to Kyoto was cheap, but getting from Kyoto to Vladivostok proved far too expensive. So I opted for the Trans-Manchurian Railway instead. It runs north of Beijing for 2,300 kilometres and then connects to the Trans-Siberian.

"Take a lot of food," James Palmer, a young British writer, told me the night of my departure from Beijing. "The Russians love to share their food, and you don't want to be caught with nothing to share." He suggested chocolate bars, sausage, hunks of cheese, crackers and, of course, vodka.

Palmer, whom I met regularly at an expat bar in the Sanlitun entertainment district, had travelled extensively in Mongolia and Siberia. He was researching a book on Roman Ungern von Sternberg, a Baltic German nobleman and, coincidentally, a contemporary of Mannerheim. Indeed, Ungern's career followed an uncannily similar trajectory to Mannerheim's: both men were barons and officers in the Imperial Russian army; both fought in the Russo-Japanese War and in Galicia during the First World War; upon the collapse of Imperial Russia, both battled Bolsheviks to found independent, breakaway states. Mannerheim became Finland's first commander-in-chief and regent. Ungern's ascent to power was bloodier and far more flamboyant. Gripped by fanatical Buddhism, Ungern thought himself the reincarnation of Genghis Khan. During the Russian Revolution, his rogue army captured

Urga (now Ulaanbaatar) and he installed himself as the last khan of the kingdom of Mongolia. Paul Pelliot also resurfaces in our story. At the time, he was a secret agent for the French Army in China and Siberia and helped the "mad Baron," as he came to be known, organize the anti-Bolshevik resistance there.[6] Ungern turned out to be a lunatic and bloodthirsty ogre. His short reign was long on medieval barbarity. Palmer titled his book *The Bloody White Baron*.

I did as he advised, stocking up that night on Cadbury bars, water, toilet paper, snacks and a bottle of "AK-47" Russian vodka. I also bought a bottle of twelve-year-old Glenlivet Scotch. The journey would take six days. I hoped to make friends.

Train K19, the Trans-Manchurian Express, was painted in Russia's national colours: white, blue and red. A dour Russian conductor checked my ticket at Beijing's Central Railway Station. My first-class compartment had two beds and featured dark wood laminate, brown upholstery and copper-coloured curtains. It smelled musty and felt overheated. The wagon filled with Russians and Buryat Mongols from Russia's Transbaikal region. Chinese passengers travelled largely in second class, detraining before we reached the Russian border. We left shortly after 11 PM.

I awoke the next morning to Manchuria's bleak, wintry landscape. A dusting of snow covered deserted fields and grey villages of clay-tiled roofs. The air was thick with smoke from coal stoves, power plants and the factories of China's industrial rust belt. Leafless trees lined the track. Their wiry branches, blackened with soot, stood out sharply against the milky landscape like an intricate Chinese papercut. The train passed through the gritty industrial centres of Changchun and Harbin, but I saw only their silhouettes in the smog.

At the Russian border town of Zabaykalsk, passengers left the train for several hours while the bogies' wheels were changed because of the different gauge of the Russian rails. It was a cold but brilliant morning. The streets and platform glistened with ice.

I met the only other foreigners on the train. Ben and Hugh were twenty-one-year-old students from Tasmania. We agreed to meet that night in the dining car. In halting English, the Russian waitress listed the menu: steak wrapped with bacon, pork cutlets, beef stew, meat soup. "Do you have any dishes with no meat?" asked Ben, a vegetarian. "Yes," came her stern reply. "We have chicken and fish." All the food was lathered in sour cream, cheese and gobs of grease. The dining car was sweltering, causing us to sweat profusely. I was soon as oily as the pork cutlet. For several hours, we guzzled beer, chewed the fat—in more ways than one—and eventually stumbled back to our compartments "off chops," as the Tasmanians say.

The next morning, Siberia looked as miserable as I felt. Forlorn villages rolled by. Rickety wooden houses, their unpainted siding blackened by age and the elements, huddled together like castaways on the frozen wastes. Teetering and collapsed dachas were evidence that Siberia's population was in steep decline—a stark contrast to the economic boom I had just witnessed in China's vast hinterland. People were dying, from alcoholism, violence, poverty, loneliness.

By the time we reached Irkutsk, the midpoint of the journey, the train was virtually deserted. Here, Ben and Hugh disembarked; their courageous plan was to experience a Siberian winter. A wagon occupied by two pot-bellied, bearded Russians separated me from the dining car. After four days aboard the train the men had grown rancid with body odour. To avoid the stench, I spent the rest of the trip in my compartment. I read, slept, ate instant noodles and drowned the hours of monotony in Glenlivet. I was utterly relieved to reach Moscow. It was unusually mild, some seven degrees Celsius. Moscow had yet to experience a major snowfall. The capital was remarkably quiet too, having just finished celebrating the Russian Orthodox New Year.

I stayed the night in a hostel and went on a guided tour of the Kremlin the next morning, during the year's first blizzard. Felix was my guide, an avuncular, hefty man with ruby cheeks. His caustic commentary on Russia's history was entertaining and insightful. In the Assumption Cathedral, where Mannerheim attended Nicholas II's coronation, Felix pointed out Russia's imperial insignia, a double-headed eagle representing the Tsar's supposed reign over Rome and Constantinople, the capitals of Western and Eastern Orthodoxy. "What happens if you have two heads looking in opposite directions?" he asked. "Schizophrenia. It was an unfortunate choice for a coat of arms and explains the violent swings in Russian history."

I was looking forward to visiting St. George's Hall in the Kremlin Palace next door. According to my guidebook, the enormous vaulted corridor, supported by twisting zinc pillars, stands as a monument to Russia's great military victories. Marble plaques, engraved with the Knights of the Order of St. George, cover its walls and columns. Mannerheim was awarded Russia's highest military honour for his gallantry during the First World War. I wanted to see his plaque, but unfortunately the palace was closed.

Instead, Felix took me to the Kremlin's Armoury Museum. The first thing we saw was a seventeenth-century velvety blue Dutch sailor's jacket. It had fitted sleeves and was hemmed above the knees. The jacket was far trimmer—and much more stylish—than the dowdy gown-like garments worn by boyars in medieval Moscovy. "Peter the Great wanted to modernize Russia in the mould of Western Europe," Felix explained. The Tsar forced boyars to shave their beards and encouraged European attire. "People changed their appearance, but not their mentality."

I was reminded of this irony later that day while lunching in the food court of Okhotny Ryad, a subterranean shopping mall next to the Kremlin. Its glitzy shops sold every international brand imaginable. Young Russians moped around with their ball caps askew and jeans pulled down exposing their underwear, like American hip-hoppers. Russians, I thought, certainly look like Westerners. I mentioned this to a Lebanese businessman staying at the hostel that night. But he dismissed any comparison between the West and Russia as preposterous. "Democracy in Russia?" he scoffed. "These people need a dictator."

IN ST. PETERSBURG, Mannerheim submitted his final report, which he had begun drafting in Peking. It amounted to 198 typewritten pages.[7] He was then summoned one Sunday afternoon to give an account of his expedition to Nicholas II, who rarely received first-hand reports on conditions in Asia. Such an audience was a great honour and Mannerheim faced it with "a certain excitement."[8] He asked how long his account should take and the Tsar told him twenty minutes would suffice. Nicholas II's questions and comments indicated that he was listening attentively. With outstretched hands, the Tsar accepted the Dalai Lama's gift of white silk.

"A glance at a clock showed me that what I had thought was a short account had taken an hour and twenty minutes, whereupon I humbly apologized for the length of my report," Mannerheim recalled. "The Emperor smilingly thanked me for an interesting account, and said that he, also, had failed to notice how time went."[9]

The Tsar asked Mannerheim what his plans were. Now that the journey was over, Mannerheim worried that his long absence would stymie his advancement. He expressed his concern that he might have missed promotion. He told the Tsar that he hoped that he might soon command a regiment. The Tsar reassured him and pointed out that few men had been privileged to undertake such an important mission. "I later realized how true this was," wrote Mannerheim.

The Baron's expedition certainly impressed the Tsar, who spoke about it with "keen interest and admiration" to Sven Hedin at an audience in January, 1909.[10] Nicholas II even advised Hedin to contact Mannerheim. It became clear to the Baron that his work was well received. After completing his military intelligence report in St. Petersburg—it was dated October 31, 1908—he was able to write with satisfaction that his superiors were pleased. He was offered command of a cavalry regiment in Poland. The Chief of the General Staff assured him of rapid advancement.

BACK IN ST. PETERSBURG, I found the streets damp and grey and the people sullen and sober—especially compared to the summertime revelry I had witnessed before my departure. I checked into the Nord Hostel next to the General Staff Building, then took a commuter train twenty-five kilometres west to Pushkin. The town was formerly called Tsarkoye Selo, or the "Tsar's Village." A summer retreat for the Tsar and Russian nobility, it consists of magnificent parks and palaces. In 1904, Nicholas II moved his family here to get away from the filth, disease and revolutionary violence of St. Petersburg.

I spent an hour immersed in the flamboyant rococo architecture of Catherine Palace. Its ostentation is obscene: the palace's Great Hall and corridors are an orgy of lavish sculptural design, inlaid parquetry, ceiling paintings and gilded mirrors and decorations; the Italian architect used more than two hundred pounds of gold on its interiors. The palace's Amber Room is bejewelled with mosaic amber panels. There's even a drawing room in chinoiserie style, its turquoise silk wallpaper embellished with Oriental scenes. China was all the rage in the mid-eighteenth century, when trade links began to develop with the Far East. Catherine the Great even built a "Chinese Village" of pavilions with decorative curved roofs, and a Dragon Bridge in the palace's park. (A new "Chinese Village," called the Baltic Pearl, was under construction in a southwest suburb of St. Petersburg. The $1.35-billion megaproject, financed by a Shanghai state-owned enterprise, covers two hundred hectares next to Constantine Palace.)

While skimming through a guidebook in the palace's souvenir shop, I realized Nicholas II never lived in Catherine Palace. The last Tsar of Russia had more homely tastes. Indeed, Mannerheim was "struck by his simplicity and lack of ostentation."[11] Nicholas and his family lived in Alexander Palace, a much smaller neoclassical residence just down the road. Unfortunately, I didn't have time to visit its dowdy studies or modest reception rooms, where Mannerheim likely debriefed the Tsar. I had to hurry back to St. Petersburg.

I found Alexey Shkvarov, the retired naval officer and Mannerheim aficionado, waiting for me in front of the hostel. He smiled, genuinely happy to see me after seven months. "Let's go for dinner," he said. We crossed the Palace Bridge and went to the Ivanhoe Restaurant on the embankment. It was located in a cellar with low, vaulted ceilings. Thick, rustic wooden tables were set with wrought iron candlesticks, giving it a medieval flair. We drank coffee, and Shkvarov smoked Kents non-stop. Over quail egg soup and mutton kebabs, I recounted my trip, especially the centennial celebration and conference on Mannerheim's Asia journey held in Urumqi.

"I don't know why there weren't any Russian scholars there," I said. "After all, Mannerheim was in the employ of the Russian Tsar."

"Finns don't like to talk about Mannerheim's journey in Asia because he was involved in intelligence gathering," Shkvarov said. "But it was so; he was a Russian spy."

That proved to be an intolerable truth for at least one drunken Finn whom Shkvarov met in the bar of a Helsinki hotel. "The Finn was angry that a Russian wrote about Mannerheim. He took my book and threw it on the floor," Shkvarov said. The irate drunkard then attacked Shkvarov, but hotel security quickly intervened. "There was a bit of fighting."

Later that night, I too found myself in a heated battle about Mannerheim with the desk clerk at the hostel. Vlad was a portly, bespectacled young Russian. His grandfather had fought in the Winter War against Finland, whose astonishing defence, Vlad explained, was because of "the heavily fortified Mannerheim Line."

"That's Soviet propaganda," I shot back. "It wasn't well fortified at all, just earth mounds, trenches and a few bunkers. The Finns barely had any heavy artillery either."

I shot down several of his dubious theories about why Russia wasn't able to easily overwhelm its remarkably smaller, weaker neighbour. Vlad then paused, seemingly out of ammunition in our war of words. "Well," he finally rejoined, "Mannerheim was one of the smartest generals in the Imperial army. In fact, he was probably the smartest general in Russia." Vlad, I had to admit, had a good point, however ironic: Soviet Russia's defeat was a result, in part, of the gallantry and strategic brilliance of a former Russian general.

Therein lies the perplexing paradox that is Gustaf Mannerheim, a man who seemed to defy history or, perhaps, a man orphaned by history, left behind by world events. He was, as one biographer notes, "a cosmopolite in the age of nationalism; an aristocrat in the age of democracy; a conservative in the age of revolution. These facts were at the same time his glory and his tragedy."[12] After the Russian Empire collapsed, and with it all the privileges of the nobility, the Baron returned to Finland like "a stranger from a sunken world." Late in Mannerheim's life, a Frenchman even compared him to a member of the court at Versailles who had survived into the middle of the twentieth century.[13]

Early the next morning, I went to the Finland Station to board a train for Helsinki. It was the same station where Mannerheim, on December 31, 1917, ultimately bid farewell to his "sunken world" of Imperial officers, courtiers, princesses and emperors. The old railway terminal, however, had been demolished, and a modern Soviet structure had replaced it. In a concourse out front, a soaring statue of Lenin commemorates his return to Russia to lead the October Revolution in 1917.

"Beer or juice?" asked the Russian conductor as our train rolled out of the Finland Station. "Juice," I responded. It was, after all, 8 AM and, at this northern latitude, pitch-black outside. The dead of winter was upon me. About two hours later, I saw the first rays of sunlight as we approached the Finnish frontier. Above the dark Karelian pine forest squatted deep purple clouds fringed in shimmering pink and silver. The dilapidated Russian dachas had disappeared, and just across the border I spotted the first Finnish farm: a trim, idyllic custard-coloured home and large red barn. A hundred years ago, travellers also immediately sensed they were entering a "country of rock and forest and clean, neat little villages so different to the untidy, unpainted villages of North Russia."[14] I had that same sense of leaving another world behind, of crossing a threshold from East to West.

THE STORY OF Mannerheim's journey across Asia didn't end in St. Petersburg, nor of course did his illustrious career as a military leader and statesman. In 1909, the Russian General Staff published Mannerheim's report in Volume 81 of its series on military intelligence on China.[15] Two years later, the Finno-Ugrian Society published Mannerheim's seventy-two-page article on the Yugur tribes of Gansu. Mannerheim's main journal, however, remained unpublished for decades.

Finally, in the autumn of 1936, encouraged by his friend Sven Hedin,[16] the Baron suggested that the Finno-Ugrian Society publish some of his Chinese materials. "For want of time I have had to postpone from year to year the fulfilment of my original intention of preparing the notes made on the journey for publication," he claimed. That's hard to believe, considering he held no public office and spent considerable time between 1919 and 1931 travelling, hunting and doing philanthropic work. Indeed, 1936 seemed an extraordinarily inopportune time for Mannerheim to be editing this long-forgotten Asia journal. The Baron, now age sixty-nine, had become the chairman of Finland's Defence Council. He was busy building up the armaments industry and army for an impending world war.

Nevertheless, Kaarlo Hildén, a professor of economic geography, became his editorial assistant. By June 1938, an English translation was ready, which Mannerheim corrected. Hildén was under the impression that the publication was "his foremost object of interest."[17] Mannerheim often called the editor at home and sent him hundreds of pages of memos and notes on the most trivial matters. He kept working on the journal even after the Soviets attacked in the fall of 1939, and despite having been appointed Finland's commander-in-chief once again. Mannerheim signed the preface to *Across Asia* at the General Headquarters of the Finnish army in February 1940—just as Soviet forces were unleashing an unprecedented onslaught and had breached the Mannerheim Line.

Why would the Field Marshal attend to such a trivial matter in the face of imminent doom? Perhaps memories of his exotic adventure along the Silk Road helped him escape, however briefly, from the daily horrors of war. Or perhaps the rabid anti-Bolshevik and aristocrat wanted to finish the journal—and establish his reputation as a famed explorer—before he was either imprisoned or executed by the Red Army. Whatever the reason, the book was published in April 1940, a month after a truce miraculously saved Finland from Soviet clutches.

He and Hedin kept up an effusive correspondence during the war years and right up to Mannerheim's death in January 1951. They often wrote about China. Hedin called his two-volume work "brilliant," and months before his death addressed a letter to "the magnate of Asian research."[18] Yet it wasn't until a half-century later, in the late 1990s, that Finnish, Chinese and Russian scholars began seriously and systematically studying Mannerheim's Chinese diaries, notebooks, photographs, intelligence reports and collections. With the reawakening and spectacular rise of China, his insights seem more relevant than ever.

I WAS ELATED to step out of the Helsinki Central Railway Station into a sun-splashed wintry morning. Despite being banned from China and twice arrested in Central Asia, I had, to my own amazement, completed my mission. Yet one of my goals remained stubbornly elusive. I had wanted to get to know Mannerheim himself. In his memoirs, personal letters and speeches, he revealed so few personal details or emotion. I had hoped that by retracing his route and reading his diary each day, I would discover a deeper, perhaps hidden, understanding of him. Yet his Asia journal is steely, stoic and, at times, caustic. One Finnish historian notes that, despite being charming, Mannerheim always kept his distance. "If someone tried to cross the line marked by Mannerheim," the historian writes, "he would show that person his place with an ironic comment or jab."[19] The Baron showed little camaraderie toward his Cossacks, Uyghur cooks or Chinese interpreters. He and his diary remained insufferably aloof.

"We Finnish people like to just see Gustaf Mannerheim as a very brave hero, but he also had his human character," said Ursula, a desk clerk at my Helsinki hostel, late one night. The sixty-year-old had read every book about Mannerheim—his memoir, Asian journal, numerous biographies, anthologies of personal letters, war histories, novels—but she too felt detached from the Baron. "There was an aura of mystery, of sadness and loneliness, to his personal life. He was an aristocrat, perhaps the last of his generation," she said sombrely. "He was very distant, somehow."

The next day, I went for a walk down Mannerheim Way, Helsinki's main boulevard. It was to be a fitting end to my long and exhausting journey. At the bronze equestrian statue of the Marshal in front of the city's contemporary art museum, I turned left down a side street and stopped at the Museum of Cultures, the final resting place of his Asian collections. Its Far East exhibit includes artefacts from Mannerheim and other Finnish explorers. There is a large selection from the Tibetan lamasery of Labrang: a conch shell, prayer beads, bronze statues, butter lamps, charm boxes, thunderbolt sceptres, ritual bells—all collected by Mannerheim's Chinese guide, of course, since the Baron himself was violently run out of town by stone-throwing monks. I then continued another kilometre to Hietaniemi, a large forested cemetery on a sandspit jutting into Helsinki's western harbour. It is the final resting place of the founder and saviour of free and independent Finland.

In the quietude of a late winter's day, I strolled along paths lined by silver birch, fir and pine, their boughs heavy with snow. The forest floor, a jumble of crosses, headstones and statues, was awash in a velvety Nordic light. Nearing the point of the sandspit, I came out of the forest. The path cuts diagonally across open fields of flat tombstones. These graves for ordinary soldiers who died in the Second World War are laid out with strict geometry, like a battalion awaiting a marshal's review. Indeed, the tomb of Marshal Mannerheim, a simple, pinkish slab of Finnish granite, commands a view over these fallen soldiers. I brushed away the snow atop the tomb to find Mannerheim's coat of arms and two crossed marshal batons cast in bronze.

I cracked open a bottle of Marskin Ryyppy, the aquavit flavoured with vermouth and gin favoured by Marshal Mannerheim. I frosted a schnapps glass in the snow and then delicately poured it right to the brim, as was the drinking custom of the Marshal himself. I drank the bitter schnapps in three gulps, without spilling. I then took a deep breath, my lungs expanding with alcohol vapour and arctic air. Despite the cold, I felt a warm, tingling sensation as my chest swelled.

I closed my eyes.

Hietaniemi is, by far, the most tranquil place in Helsinki. Here Mannerheim rests, reunited with his "sunken world" but not entirely in peace. I could still hear the faint rumble of traffic over a distant bridge and the mechanical drone of the towering Salmisaari thermal power plant across the water. The din of the modern world—incessant and inescapable—felt more chilling than the breathless winter air.

ACKNOWLEDGMENTS

THIS BOOK AROSE from a long and trying journey. It began in September 1999, when I received the call to adventure. Anssi Kullberg, a Finnish friend, suggested that we retrace Mannerheim's journey across Asia. We were supposed to meet in Osh, Kyrgyzstan, but world events intervened. In July 2006, Israel and Lebanon descended into war. As a Finnish diplomat in Damascus at the time, Anssi was unable to leave his post. I was on my own. However, I will forever be indebted to Anssi for initiating this Silk Road adventure. The book is a testament to our friendship and captures, I hope, his intrepid spirit.

Throughout this journey, Harry Halén, retired philologist from Helsinki University, has offered me candid insights, shared route maps, answered my many questions and helped me with translations. He also read and corrected the draft manuscript. All remaining mistakes, of course, are my own. I can't thank Harry enough for his scholarly generosity.

The list of individuals who helped me along the way is long. Many of them—guides, translators, scholars, officials and others—are mentioned in the narrative. However, I would like to recognize several people who aren't mentioned or who went out of their way to assist me. For travel advice and assistance, I thank writer Gary Geddes, Finnish documentary producer Vesa Saarinen,

Ben Carrdus with the Uyghur American Association, Tibetan activist T.C. Tethong, Fikrin Bektashi with Transparency Azerbaijan in Baku, Alison Gill with Human Rights Watch in Moscow, Aleksey Knizhnikov with Crude Accountability in Moscow, members of the Kyrgyzstan Community-based Tourism Association, Linda Jakobson with the Finnish Institute of International Affairs in Beijing and friends Lisa McIntosh Sundstrom and Greg Sundstrom in Vancouver. I must make special mention of Juha Janhunen, professor at Helsinki University, who shared contacts in Inner Mongolia, provided travel advice and helped me decipher the complicated history of the Yugur peoples. Thanks must also go to several friends who hosted me during research trips to Helsinki, Stockholm and London, including Anssi Kullberg, Estelle Taylor, Tanis Bestland Malminen and Johannes Malminen. Johannes also read an early draft of the manuscript and provided valuable feedback.

For helping to translate Swedish, Finnish, Chinese and Russian texts, I would like to thank Magnus Wittbjer, Johannes Malminen, Sampo Marjomaa, Arran Landry, Anatoli Koroteyev, Eric Walberg and Alexsey Shkvarov.

Several individuals and institutions were incredibly helpful in my archival and historical research, including Ildikó Lehtinen with the Finno-Ugrian Society in Helsinki, Pilvi Vainonen with the Museum of Cultures in Helsinki, Marja-Leena Hänninen with the National Board of Antiquities in Helsinki, Matti Karttunen with the Headquarters Museum in Mikkeli, Finland, Håkan Wahlquist with the Sven Hedin Foundation and Museum of Ethnography in Stockholm, Fredrik Fällman with the Mission Covenant Church of Sweden in Stockholm and Susan Whitfield with the International Dunhuang Project at the British Library in London. I also greatly appreciate the hardworking staff at the Vancouver Public Library who processed my many interlibrary loan requests.

I'm grateful to Scott Steedman, who signed me to Canada's top publisher of literary nonfiction. Douglas & McIntyre publisher

Scott McIntyre must be thanked not just for enthusiastically supporting this book but also for avidly promoting a group of emerging literary nonfiction writers on the West Coast.

John Burns, my editor at Douglas & McIntyre, has been a wonder to work with. His candidness, savvy and sharp editorial acumen helped to tighten the narrative, improve the book's pace and much else. John also wasn't afraid to provoke me at times, forcing me to rethink sections of the book, which led to new insights.

Thanks to the B.C. Arts Council and Canada Council for the Arts for grants that helped to finance the research and writing of this book, and to my literary agent, Amy Rennert, for her diligence and constant encouragement.

A heartfelt *xie xie* to Charlotte Lowe for bestowing on me a Chinese name and for her insights on Chinese culture and food.

My brother Victor and his wife Leslie have been pillars for me over the years, and I'll always be beholden to them for helping to launch my literary career.

My partner, of course, has heroically endured living with a writer, a fate I would not wish upon my worst enemy. The loving support that I received throughout the research and writing of this book constantly energized and amazed me.

ERIC ENNO TAMM
February 20, 2010
Ucluelet, British Columbia, Canada

A NOTE ON SOURCES

THE VAST MAJORITY of the research for this book comes from two primary sources: my first-hand account of events, people and places recorded from July 2006 until January 2007 as I travelled from St. Petersburg to Beijing, and Gustaf Mannerheim's own first-hand observations in his published travelogue, private letters and military intelligence report.

While travelling across Central Asia and China, I carried with me a bound photocopy of the 1960 reprint of Mannerheim's journal *Across Asia from West to East in 1906–1908* first published in two volumes in 1940 with fourteen folding maps. Harry Halén, retired secretary of the Asian and Africa Studies Department at the Helsinki University, subsequently edited a new edition of *Across Asia* published in 2008. Halén meticulously revised spellings to be more consistent with the Wade-Giles transcription system and corrected thousands of misprints and errors that were made when Mannerheim's diaries, originally handwritten in Swedish, were translated and edited into the published English volumes. Halén has also restored passages relating to Paul Pelliot and Mannerheim's health, which were omitted from the original published text. Throughout the book, all references to and quotations from Mannerheim's journal have been taken from Halén's 2008 edition.

Mannerheim's military intelligence report, published by the Russian General Staff as Volume 81 of its Collection of Geographical,

Topographical and Statistical Materials for Asia in 1909, has not yet been published in English. Eric Walberg and Anatoli Koroteyev, a native English speaker and native Russian speaker respectively, translated the report for me. The section dealing with the Chinese army, pages 87 to 134, was only partially translated due to limited financial resources. Mannerheim's incredibly detailed military descriptions were also of limited use to me, since I conducted no on-the-ground research on the strength of China's army.

Regarding personal interviews, I have included materials gathered before and after my trek across Asia, which I've made clear in the text. I should also mention that most of my guides, drivers and translators, whom I quote, were paid for their services. As mentioned in the "Note on Names and Spellings," I have disguised the identities of many of these individuals, given the precarious political conditions in Central Asia and China.

In the notes that follow, I have excluded, for the sake of brevity, references to personal interviews and to Halén's 2008 edition of Mannerheim's journal. I have cited other primary sources, including the journals of Paul Pelliot, Aurel Stein, Sven Hedin and several others who were travelling through Central Asia at the time of Mannerheim's journey, and materials gathered from the National Archives of Sweden, the archives of the Mission Covenant Church of Sweden in Stockholm, the Political and Secret Department files of the Indian Office Records at the British Library in London, Mannerheim's private records in the National Archives of Finland and Mannerheim's Asia photographs stored with the National Board of Antiquities in Helsinki. A multitude of secondary sources, which have helped me immensely in enriching the narrative with meaningful historical and contemporary context, have also been cited.

ENDNOTES

PROLOGUE

1. Rodzianko. *Mannerheim,* 223.
2. Quoted in Lehmusoksa, *Dining with Marshal Mannerheim,* 259.
3. Ibid., 259–263.
4. Mannerheim. *Memoirs,* 453.
5. Search "Mannerheim and Hitler" on YouTube to watch a Nazi propaganda film about Mannerheim's birthday party.
6. Trotter. *The Winter War,* 3.
7. "The Liberator of Finland Mobilizes Against Russia," *Life,* October 23, 1939, 22.
8. "Editorial: Finland Should Quit," *Globe and Mail,* Dec. 23, 1941.
9. "Editorial: Finns Seek Peace," *Globe and Mail,* Feb. 15, 1944.
10. Despite pressure from the Nazis, Mannerheim refused to deport Finnish-Jewish soldiers and even visited a Helsinki synagogue to commemorate their sacrifice.
11. Jägerskiöld. *Mannerheim: Marshal of Finland,* 162.
12. Hedin. *Germany and World Peace,* 350.
13. Hedin. Letter to Gustaf Mannerheim, dated June 24, 1940, Stockholm. National Archives of Finland.
14. Rintala. *Four Finns,* 37.
15. Halén. *An Analytical Index to C.G. Mannerheim's "Across Asia from West to East in 1906–1908,"* 7.
16. Colquhoun. *China in Transformation,* 58.
17. Gifford. *China Road,* xvii.
18. Fairbank. *China: A New History,* 218.
19. MacMillan. *The Uses and Abuses of History,* 16.
20. This popular, though apocryphal, aphorism of Confucius is likely a liberal rewording of a quotation from *The Analects:* "As to the past, reproof is useless; but the future may still be provided against."
21. Mannerheim. *Memoirs,* 216.

CHAPTER I

1. Conrad. *The Secret Agent*, 36.
2. Laqueur. *A History of Terrorism*, 12.
3. Ibid.
4. Ferguson. *The War of the World*, 73.
5. Laqueur. *A History of Terrorism*, 34.
6. Mannerheim. *Memoirs*, 22.
7. Marshall. "Russian Military Intelligence, 1905–1917," 394.
8. Quoted in Marshall, *The Russian General Staff and Asia, 1800–1917*, 102.
9. Halén. "Mannerheim and Military Intelligence in China 1906–1900," 72–73. Also Mannerheim. "Preliminary Report on the Trip Undertaken by Imperial Order Across Chinese Turkestan and the Northern Provinces of China to Peking in 1906–07 and 1908." In *Collection of Geographical, Topographical and Statistical Materials for Asia 81*. St. Petersburg: Military Publishing House, 1909, 1. (Original published in Russian and translated by Eric Walberg and Anatoli Koroteyev for author.)
10. Mannerheim. *Memoirs*, 27.
11. Ibid., 234.
12. Ibid., 6.
13. Lehmusoksa. *Dining with Marshal Mannerheim*, 89.
14. Jägerskiöld. *Den unge Mannerheim*, 64.
15. Rodzianko. *Mannerheim*, 31.
16. Ibid., 43.
17. Jägerskiöld. *Mannerheim: Marshal of Finland*, 7.
18. Ibid., 33.
19. Screen. *Mannerheim: Years of Preparation*, 33.
20. Figes. *A People's Tragedy*, 112.
21. Lincoln. *Sunlight at Midnight*, 189–192.
22. Figes. *A People's Tragedy*, 23.
23. Quoted in Rintala, *Four Finns*, 27.
24. Baker and Glasser. *Kremlin Rising*, 252.
25. Vihavainen, ed. *Mannerheim: An Officer of the Imperial Russian Army*, 4–5.
26. Quoted in Lehmusoksa, *Dining with Marshal Mannerheim*, 64.
27. Ibid., 89.
28. Figes. *A People's Tragedy*, 184 and 202.
29. Jägerskiöld. *Mannerheim: Marshal of Finland*, 12.
30. Quoted in Vihavainen, ed., *Mannerheim: An Officer of the Imperial Russian Army*, 59.
31. Mannerheim. Letter to his father, dated July 27, 1907, Urumqi. National Archives of Finland.
32. Mannerheim. *Memoirs*, 28.
33. Jägerskiöld. *Gustaf Mannerheim*

1906–1917, 22. See also Halén, "Mannerheim and the French Expedition of Paul Pelliot," 46.

34. Sandberg. "Mannerheim the Photographer," 5.

CHAPTER 2
1. Tolf. *The Russian Rocke-fellers*, 61.
2. Figes. *A People's Tragedy*, 223.
3. Henry. *Baku*, 3.
4. U.S. Department of Energy. *Azerbaijan: Country Analysis Briefs*. Washington, DC: U.S. Department of Energy, August 2006. http://eia.doe.gov.
5. Yergin. *The Prize*, 131.
6. Bey. *Blood and Oil in the Orient*, 42.
7. Reiss. *The Orientalist*, 14.
8. Henry. *Baku*, 3.
9. Villari. *The Fire and Sword in the Caucasus*, 181.
10. Tolf. *The Russian Rockefellers*, 100.
11. Marvin. *The Region of the Eternal Fire*, 283–307.
12. Ibid., 283.
13. Tolf. *The Russian Rocke-fellers*, 97.
14. Henry. *Oil Fuel and the Empire*, 6.
15. Mannerheim. *Memoirs*, 110.
16. Marvin. *The Region of the Eternal Fire*, 304.
17. Said. *Ali and Nino*, 208.
18. Ibid., 106.

CHAPTER 3
1. Global Witness. *It's A Gas*.
2. Steyn. "One-Man Stan."
3. Quoted in Hopkirk, *The Great Game*, 406–407.
4. Theroux. "The Golden Man," 54–65.
5. Indian Office Records, Political and Secret Department, British Library. "Memorandum of information received during the month of July 1906, regarding affairs on and beyond the North-West Frontier of India."
6. Indian Office Records, Political and Secret Department, British Library. "Memorandum of information received during the month of November 1906, regarding affairs on and beyond the North-West Frontier of India."
7. See Turkmenistan's country profile on the website of the Internal Displacement Monitoring Centre: http://www.internal-displacement.org.

CHAPTER 4
1. Kipling. *Kim*, 217.
2. Roy. *The New Central Asia*, viii.
3. The term Uzbek comes from Özbek, the name of a fifteenth-century dynasty that ruled Central Asia and spoke an eastern Kipchak dialect. See Roy, *The New Central Asia*, 16–17.

4. Duyvendak, J.J.L. "Paul Pelliot." In Walravens, *Paul Pelliot*, xi–xix.

5. Sinor, Denis. "Remembering Paul Pelliot, 1878–1945." In ibid., xxviii.

6. Translation of article in preface to Swedish edition of *Across Asia* written by Harry Halén. Information comes from Aleksandr Smirnov, "Археопогия и военная разведка." 1 / 2006, 75–79).

7. Hopkirk. *The Great Game*, 2–3.

8. See also Hopkirk, *Setting the East Ablaze*.

9. Mannerheim. *Memoirs*, 255–261.

10. Cadogan, Alexander, Foreign Office. Letter to F.M. Bailey, dated December 19, 1944. British Library.

11. See Halén, *An Analytical Index*, 111; and Jägerskiöld, *Gustaf Mannerheim*, 30.

12. Indian Office Records, Political and Secret Department, British Library. "Memorandum of information received during the month of December 1906, regarding affairs on and beyond the North-West Frontier of India."

13. Indian Office Records, Political and Secret Department, British Library. "Memorandum of information received during the month of November 1906, regarding affairs on and beyond

the North-West Frontier of India."

14. "Gen. Subbotich Disgraced," *New York Times*, December 26, 1906.

15. Hastings, Max. "Our Man in Trouble," *Sunday Times* (London), July 20, 2006.

16. Murray. *Murder in Samarkand*, 27.

17. Ibid., 132.

18. Ibid., 68.

19. Kamalova, Vitaliev and Shields. *Front Line Central Asia*, 99.

20. Pelliot. *Carnets de route*, 18.

21. Indian Office Records, Political and Secret Department, British Library. "Memorandum of information received during the month of July 1906, regarding affairs on and beyond the North-West Frontier of India."

22. See Halén, *An Analytical Index*. The Cossacks' names also appear in Mannerheim's "Preliminary Report," 1.

23. Halén. "Mannerheim and the French Expedition of Paul Pelliot," 31.

24. Forbes Manz. "Central Asian Uprisings in the Nineteenth Century," 267–281.

25. Indian Office Records, Political and Secret Department, British Library. "Memorandum of information received during the month of December 1906, regarding affairs on and beyond

the North-West Frontier of
India."

26. International Crisis Group.
Uzbekistan; and Akiner. *Violence
in Andijan, 13 May 2005.*

CHAPTER 5

1. Hedin. *The Silk Road,* 234.
2. Fraser. *The Marches of
Hindustan,* 262.
3. Ibid., 265.
4. Ibid., 266.
5. Hedin. *The Silk Road,* 230.
6. Spector, Regine A. "Who Owns
the Marketplace? Conflict over
Property in Contemporary
Kyrgyzstan." Prepared for the
Graduate Student Conference,
Department of Political Science,
University of California,
Berkeley, May 2, 2007.
7. International Crisis Group.
Kyrgyzstan, 4.
8. Abrams, Joshua. "The Big
Freeze," *Steppe Magazine* 4
(Summer 2008), 8.
9. "Go West Young Chinaman,"
Economist, January 4, 2007.
10. Mannerheim. *Memoirs,* 12.
11. Halén. "Mannerheim and the
French Expedition of Paul
Pelliot," 38. Originally quoted
in Jägerskiöld, *Gustaf Manner-
heim, 1906–1917,* 31.
12. Halén. "Mannerheim and the
French Expedition of Paul Pel-
liot," 32; and Jägerskiöld. *Gustaf
Mannerheim, 1906–1917,* 34–35.

13. Kurmanjan-Datka Charitable
Foundation. *Tsarina of the
Mountains,* 34.
14. Halén. "Mannerheim and the
French Expedition of Paul
Pelliot," 37.
15. Pelliot. *Carnets de route,* 36.

CHAPTER 6

1. Goldsack, W. "How to Reach
and Teach Illiterate Moslems,"
30. Paper presented at the First
Missionary Conference on
Behalf of the Mohammedan
World, Cairo, April 4–9, 1906.
In *Methods of Mission Work
Among Moslems.* New York:
Fleming H. Revell Company,
1906.
2. Quoted in Screen, *Mannerheim:
The Years of Preparation,* 60.
3. Jägerskiöld. *Gustaf Mannerheim,
1906–1917,* 21–22.
4. Pelliot. *Carnets,* 44.
5. Quoted in Screen, 63.
6. Hopkirk. *Foreign Devils on the
Silk Road,* 10.
7. For an early history of Xinjiang, see Millward and Perdue,
"Political and Cultural History of
the Xinjiang Region Through
the Late Nineteenth Century,"
27–62.
8. Skrine and Nightingale. *Macartney at Kashgar,* 20.
9. Government of India. *Military
Report on Kashgaria (Confidential),* 105. Indian Office Records,

Political and Secret Department, British Library.

10. *Scotsman,* Feb. 4, 1904.

11. Indian Office Records, Political and Secret Department, British Library. "Memorandum of information received during the month of November 1906, regarding affairs on and beyond the North-West Frontier of India."

12. *Methods of Mission Work Among Moslems.* Papers read at the First Missionary Conference on Behalf of the Mohammedan World held at Cairo, April 4–9, 1906. London: Fleming H. Revell, 1906, 169.

13. Ibid.

14. Avetaranian. *A Muslim Who Became a Christian,* 87.

15. *Methods of Mission Work Among Moslems,* 169 and 10.

16. Zwemer, Samuel M. "Editorial," *The Moslem World* III, no. 2 (April 1913), 113.

17. Hultvall. *Mission and Change in Eastern Turkestan,* 23–26.

18. Ibid., 21.

19. China Aid Association. "Two American Companies and Two Chinese Companies Ordered to Shutdown in Xinjiang for Alleged Religious Infiltration." Midland, TX: China Aid Association, October 10, 2007. http://www.chinaaid.org/2007/10/10/two-american-companies-and-two-chinese-companies-ordered-to-shutdown-in-xinjiang-for-alleged-religious-infiltration (accessed on May 11, 2008).

20. The number of Christians affiliated with state-recognized religious bodies is only 21 million. Estimates of unaffiliated Christians (members of so-called "house churches") range from 50 to 70 million. See "Religion in China on the Eve of the 2008 Beijing Olympics," The Pew Forum on Religion and Public Life: http://pewforum.org/importance-of-religion/religion-in-china-on-the-eve-of-the-2008-beijing-olympics.aspx.

21. Radio Free Asia. "Wild Pigeon: A Uyghur Fable." June 27, 2005. http://www.rfa.org/english/news/arts/uyghur_literature-20050627.html (accessed on April 30, 2008).

CHAPTER 7

1. Mannerheim. "Preliminary Report," 159.

2. Tyler. *Wild West China,* 19–20.

3. Fraser. *The Marches of Hindustan,* 194.

4. Screen. *Mannerheim: The Years of Preparation,* 67. Also Halén. "Mannerheim and Military Intelligence in China 1906–07," 7;

and Halén. *Sotilastiedustelijana Kiinassa*, 5–8.

5. Hopkirk. *Foreign Devils on the Silk Road*, 37.

6. Ibid., 44–46.

7. Jarring, Gunnar. "The Toponym Takla-makan," *Turkic Languages* 1:2, 1997, 227–241; and Jarring, Gunnar. "Central Asian Turkic place-names: Lop Nor and Tarim area," *Reports from the Scientific Expedition to the North-Western Provinces of China Under the Leadership of Dr. Sven Hedin.* The Sino-Swedish Expedition, publication 56. VIII. Ethnography, 11. Stockholm, 1997, 447.

8. Hopkirk. *Foreign Devils on the Silk Road*, 136.

9. Ibid., 68.

10. Ibid., 81.

11. Hedin. *Trans-Himalaya*, 65.

12. Indian Office Records, Political and Secret Department, British Library. "Abstract of News Reports received by the Special Assistant for Chinese Affairs to the Resident in Kashmir during the ten days ending on the 30th June 1908."

13. Hopkirk. *Foreign Devils on the Silk Road*, 137.

14. Stein. *Ruins of Desert Cathay.* Vol. 1, 116.

15. Screen. *Mannerheim: The Years of Preparation*, 60.

16. Jägerskiöld. *Gustaf Mannerheim, 1906–1917*, 38.

17. Tyler. *Wild West China*, 19–20.

18. Zhu, Zhe. "Terrorists killed in Xinjiang," *China Daily* (Beijing), January 9, 2007. http://www.chinadaily.com.cn/cndy/2007-01/09/content_777937.htm (accessed on May 25, 2008).

19. "China to tighten control over foreign surveying, mapping," *Xinhua*, August 31, 2006.

20. Between the oases of Yarkand and Muji, covering 160 kilometres, Mannerheim noted forty-two *paotai*, or one almost every four kilometres.

21. Halén. "Mannerheim and the French Expedition of Paul Pelliot," 39.

22. Miettinen. "Terracottas from Khotan in the Mannerheim collection," 115.

23. Wiemer. "The Economy of Xinjiang," 169.

24. Mannerheim. "Preliminary Report," 163.

25. Ibid.

26. Bovingdon. *Autonomy in Xinjiang*, 24.

CHAPTER 8

1. *Chinese Public Opinion*, July 7, 1908.

2. Mannerheim. *Memoirs*, 33. In his diary (p. 347), he translates it as "the horse that jumps through the clouds."

3. See Halén, *Analytical Index*, 113.

4. The spelling of Mannerheim's Chinese name in the 2008 edition of *Across Asia* is "Ma Ta-han." "Ma Dahan" is the proper pinyin form.

5. Screen. *Mannerheim: The Years of Preparation*, 63; and Jäger-skiöld, *Gustav Mannerheim, 1906–1917*, 21.

6. Mannerheim. *Memoirs*, 33.

7. Quoted in Wu, Aitchen K., *Turkisan Tumult*, 239.

8. Mannerheim. "Preliminary Report," 1.

9. Bovingdon. *Autonomy in Xinjiang*, 27.

10. Indian Office Records, Political and Secret Department, British Library. Abstract of News Reports received by the Special Assistant for Chinese Affairs to the Resident of Kashmir, September 10, 1907.

11. Tyler. *Wild West China*, 168–171.

12. Millward. *Violent Separatism in Xinjiang*, 2004.

13. Jägerskiöld. *Gustaf Mannerheim, 1906–1917*, 59.

14. Government of India. *Military Report on Kashgaria (Confidential)*, 89–90. Indian Office Records, Political and Secret Department, British Library.

15. Smith, Joanne N. "Making Culture Matter: Symbolic, Spatial and Social Boundaries between Uyghurs and Han Chinese," *Asian Ethnicity* 3, no. 2 (September 2002), 153–174.

CHAPTER 9

1. Fleming. *News from Tartary*, 235.

2. http://chinaheritage-newsletter.org/features. php?searchterm=003_ twomuseums.inc&issue=003.

3. Millward and Perdue. "Political and Cultural History of the Xinjiang Region through the Late Nineteenth Century," 48.

4. Mannerheim. *Memoirs*, 229.

5. Mannerheim. "Preliminary Report," 119.

6. Screen. *Mannerheim: The Years of Preparation*, 78–81.

7. Cole, ed. *Conflict, Terrorism and the Media in Asia*, 115; and "Chinese experts reject US human rights report," *China Daily* (Beijing), March 9, 2002. http://www.chinadaily.com.cn/en/doc/2002-03/09/content_110116.htm.

8. Quoted in Bovingdon, *Autonomy in Xinjiang*, 27–28.

9. Ibid.

10. Halén, ed. *Sotilastiedustelijana Kiinassa*, 18–19.

11. Quoted in Ruotsila, "The Churchill-Mannerheim Collaboration in the Russian Intervention, 1919–20," 7.

12. Mannerheim. *Memoirs*, 233.

13. Ibid., 236.

14. Mannerheim. Commander-in-Chief's Order of the Day, no. 34, March 14, 1940.

15. Mannerheim, Baroness Anastasie. "My Father Baron Mannerheim," *Daily Sketch* (London), February 26, 1940. Archives of the British Library.

16. Millward and Perdue. "Political and Cultural History of the Xinjiang Region through the Late Nineteenth Century," 68–71.

17. Wu, Aitchen K. *Turkistan Tumult*, 43–44.

18. Hedin. *Across the Gobi Desert*, 340.

19. Tyler. *Wild West China*, 94.

20. Wu, Aitchen K. *Turkistan Tumult*, 48–49.

21. Ibid., 52.

22. Gardner and Tursun. "Contested Histories," 357.

23. Ibid., 372.

CHAPTER 10

1. Macartney, George, M. Aurel Stein, L. D. Barnett, Lord Curzon, Henry Trotter, T. H. Holdich and Sven Hedin. "Explorations in Central Asia, 1906–8: Discussion," *The Geographical Journal*, 34, no. 3 (September 1909), 264–271.

2. Hopkirk. *Foreign Devils on the Silk Road*, 113.

3. Ibid., 169–170.

4. Stein, Aurel. "Sir Aurel Stein's Expedition in Central Asia," *The Geographical Journal*, 46, no. 4. (October 1915), 269–276.

5. Hopkirk. *Foreign Devils on the Silk Road*, 138–139.

6. Mirsky. *Sir Aurel Stein*, 231.

7. Ibid., 231.

8. Mannerheim. Letter to Pelliot, dated February 7, 1907, Maralbashi.

9. Mannerheim. Letter to Pelliot, dated March 4, 1907, Kucha.

10. Halén. "Baron Mannerheim's hunt for ancient Central Asian manuscripts," 48.

11. Halén. "Mannerheim and the French Expedition of Paul Pelliot," 60–61.

12. Huntington, Ellsworth. "The Depression of Turfan," *The Geographical Journal* 30, no. 3. (September 1907), 254–273.

13. Mannerheim. Letter to Otto Donner, dated February 17, 1908, Lanzhou. Quoted in Halén, *Mannerheim: An Officer of the Imperial Russian Army*, 86.

14. Stein. *Ruins of Desert Cathay*, 345.

15. Mannerheim. Letter to Otto Donner, dated February 17, 1908, Lanzhou. Quoted in Halén, *Mannerheim: An Officer of the Imperial Russian Army*, 86.

16. Wood. *The Silk Road*, 2002, 191.

17. Hopkirk. *Foreign Devils on the Silk Road*, 181–182.

18. Ibid., 182.

19. Stein. *Ruins of Desert Cathay*, 25.

20. Ibid., 28.

21. Ibid., 165.

22. Ibid., 164.

23. Ibid., 167.

24. Ibid., 171.

25. Hopkirk. *Foreign Devils on the Silk Road*, 184.

26. http://idp.bl.uk/pages/collections_ch.a4d#2.

27. Halén. "Baron Mannerheim's Hunt for Ancient Central Asian Manuscripts," 51.

CHAPTER 11

1. D'Ollone. *In Forbidden China*, 17.

2. Lovell. *The Great Wall*, 260.

3. Ibid., 21.

4. Wang, Jin. *The Great Pass Under Heaven*. Jiayuguan: Culture and TV Broadcasting Bureau of Jiayuguan City, 2003, 5.

5. Quoted in Lehtinen, "The Mannerheim Collection," 90.

6. Mannerheim. "A Visit to the Sarö and Shera Yögurs," 1.

7. Ibid.

8. Ibid., 12.

9. Lehtinen. "Plait pendants in the Marshal Mannerheim collection," in *C.G. Mannerheim in Central Asia 1906–1908*. Helsinki: National Board of Antiquities, 1999, 105.

10. Mannerheim. "A Visit to the Sarö and Shera Yögurs," 10.

11. Ibid., 12.

12. Ibid., 18.

13. Ibid., 10.

14. Ibid., 20.

15. Ibid., 21.

16. Ibid., 31.

17. Ibid., 32.

18. Ibid., 39.

19. Janhunen, Juha. "Sampling the Mongols of Gansu and Qinghai," *Journal de la Société Finno-Ougrienne*. Helsinki: Finno-Ugrian Society, 2004, 366.

20. Mannerheim. "Preliminary Report,"159.

21. Kafka, Franz, trans. Macolm Pasley. *The Great Wall of China*. London: Penguin Books, 1992, 6.

CHAPTER 12

1. Ayers. *Chang Chih-tung and Educational Reform in China*, 205.

2. http://idp.bl.uk/archives/news30/idpnews_30.a4d.

3. Leung, ed. *Political Leaders of Modern China*, 226.

4. Bailey. *Reform the People*, 19.

5. Chang Chih-tung. *China's Only Hope: An Appeal*, 105.

6. Ayers. *Chang Chih-tung and educational reform in China*.

7. Martin. *The Awakening of China*, 234.

8. "China At Last Awake to Western Progress," *New York Times*, Sept. 17, 1906.

9: Mannerheim. "Preliminary Report," 142. Statistics corroborating Mannerheim's estimates can also be found in Kuo, *The Chinese System of Public Education*.

10. Mannerheim. "Preliminary Report," 144.

11. Ibid., 135.

12. Martin. *The Awakening of China*, 219.

13. Ayers. *Chang Chih-tung and educational reform in China*, 248.

14. Yang, Shu. "The Academic Significance of C.G. Mannerheim's Exploration," *Handbook of Conference and Field Investigation*, Research Centre for China's Borderland History and Geography, Xinjiang Academy of Social Sciences, and Helsinki University, September 28, 2008, 134–136.

15. Chang and Halliday. *Mao: The Unknown Story*, 438.

16. China National Bureau of Statistics. *China Statistical Yearbook* 2006.

17. *China Brief* 6, no. 24 (December 6, 2006). Jamestown Foundation: Jamestown.org/china_brief/article.php?articleid=2373246 (accessed on November 6, 2008).

18. Qiu, Jane. "Obituary: Qian Xuesen (1911–2009), founder of China's missile and space programme," *Nature* 462 (December 10, 2009), 735.

19. Qiu, Jane. "Publish or Perish in China," *Nature* 463 (January 12, 2010), 142–143.

20. "Editorial: China's Challenges," *Nature* 454 (July 24, 2008), 367–368.

21. Halén and Pedersen. *C.G. Mannerheim's Chinese Pantheon*, 6.

22. *Gansu Cultural and Natural Heritage Protection and Development Project: Consolidated Environmental Assessment and Environmental Management Plan*. World Bank, August 29, 2007, 12.

23. Winchester. *The Man Who Loved China*, 266–277.

24. Hu. *The Chinese Renaissance*, 107.

25. Ibid., 82.

26. Ibid., 296 and 301.

27. Ibid., 32.

28. Ayers. *Chang Chih-tung and educational reform in China*, 253.

29. Cameron. *The Reform Movement in China 1898–1912*, 75.

30. "Education in China," *Chinese Public Opinion*, December 24, 1908.

31. Pott, F.L. Hawks. "China's Method of Revising Her Educational System," *Annuals of the American Academy of Political and Social Sciences* 39 (January 1912), 96.

32. Mannerheim. "Preliminary Report," 144.

33. Ibid.

34. Ibid., 171.

35. Fairbank. *China: A New History*, 217.
36. "Editorial: China's Challenges," *Nature* 454 (July 24 2008), 367–368.

CHAPTER 13

1. "Central Asian Exploration," *Nature*, January 7, 1904, 225.
2. Hedin. *My Life as an Explorer*, 376.
3. "Dr. Sven Hedin in Tibet: Important Discoveries," *The Times of London*, February 6, 1907.
4. Slobodník. "Destruction and Revival," 7–19.
5. Huggler, Justine. "Repression under China: Murder in the mountains," *The Independent*, London, October 26, 2006.
6. Pereira. "A Visit to Labrang Monastery," 418.
7. Janhunen. "Mannerheim at Labrang," 83.
8. D'Ollone. *In Forbidden China*, 275.
9. Slobodník. "Destruction and Revival," 7–19.

CHAPTER 14

1. Sun. *The International Development of China*, 168.
2. Rodzianko. *Mannerheim*, 35–36.
3. Mannerheim. *Memoirs*, 9–10.
4. Mannerheim. "Preliminary Report," 165.

5. Räikkä, Jyrki. "Katariina Lillqvist makes political art out of puppet animations," *Helsingin Sanomat*, March 1, 2008. http://www.hs.fi/english/article/Kata riina+Lillqvist+makes+political +art+out+of+puppet+animati ons+/1135234727191 (accessed on August 25, 2008).
6. Mannerheim. "Preliminary Report," 637.
7. China National Bureau of Statistics. *China Statistical Yearbook* 2006, 753.
8. Ibid., 740–743.
9. Mannerheim. "Preliminary Report," 154.
10. Ibid., 158.
11. Ibid., 157.
12. Ibid., 141.
13. Weale. *The Coming Struggle in Eastern Asia*, 330.
14. Ibid., 433.
15. See *The Foreign Trade of China*, 287 and 395.
16. Mannerheim. "Preliminary Report," 158.
17. "Boycotting the Japanese," *Chinese Public Opinion*, May 7, 1908.
18. Deng. *Selected Works*, 104.
19. Mannerheim. *Memoirs*, 23.
20. Hu. *From the Opium War to the May Fourth Movement*, 418.
21. See *The Foreign Trade of China*, 391–392.

22. Weale. *The Coming Struggle in Eastern Asia*, 589.
23. Colquhoun. *China in Transformation*, 149.
24. Ibid., 70.
25. Ibid., 58.
26. Ibid., 261.
27. Mannerheim. "Preliminary Report," 152.
28. Ibid., 156.
29. Ibid., 81.
30. Ibid.
31. Huenemann. *The Dragon and the Iron Horse*, 76.
32. Mannerheim. "Preliminary Report," 159.
33. Ibid., 82.

CHAPTER 15

1. Sun, Shangwu. "Cross holds the hope for Henan," *China Daily* (Beijing), February 15, 2006.
2. "Blood debts," *Economist*, January 18, 2007.
3. Wou. *Mobilizing the Masses*, 15.
4. Kuo, Kaiser. "Henan Bites Back," *That's Beijing*, November 2006, 160.
5. Wou. *Mobilizing the Masses*, 15.
6. Broomhall. *The Chinese Empire*, 149.
7. Chesneaux. *Peasant Revolts in China, 1840–1949*, 11.
8. Hu. *The Chinese Renaissance*, 397.
9. Davis. *Primitive Revolutionaries of China*, 12.

10. Chesneaux. *Peasant Revolts in China, 1840–1949*, 3.
11. Ibid., 9.
12. Pan, Philip P. "Farmers' Rising Anger Erupts in China Village, Land Seizures, Stagnation Fuel Unrest," *Washington Post*, August 7, 2004.
13. Bergsten, Gill, Lardy and Mitchell. *China's Rise*, 96.
14. Liu, Melinda. "Migrants' Rights: Opening up the system," *Newsweek*, January 31, 2005.
15. Sun, Shangwu. "Cross holds the hope for Henan," *China Daily* (Beijing), February 15, 2006.
16. Lardy, Nicholas R. "China: Toward A Consumption Driven Growth Path," *Policy Briefs in International Economics*, no. PB06-6, October 2006, Peterson Institute for International Economics, Washington, D.C., 2.
17. Chesneaux. *Peasant Revolts in China, 1840–1949*, 63.
18. Li, Lin. "China extends police presence in countryside," *Xinhua*, Nov. 7, 2006. http://en.ce.cn/National/Rural/200611/07/t20061107_9315408.shtml (accessed on Dec. 16, 2009).
19. Mannerheim. "Preliminary Report," 95.
20. Zhou. *How the Farmers Changed China*, 49.
21. Wu. *Understanding and Interpreting Chinese Economic Reform*, 65.

22. Ibid., 119.
23. Tuñón. *Internal Labour Migration in China*, 5.
24. Zhou. *How the Farmers Changed China*, xix.

CHAPTER 16

1. Preston. *The Boxer Rebellion*, 27.
2. Weale. *The Coming Struggle in Eastern Asia*, 577–580.
3. Wright. "Growth of the Modern Chinese Coal Industry: An Analysis of Supply and Demand, 1896–1936," 317–350.
4. Mannerheim. *"Preliminary Report,"* 155.
5. "Most polluted province steps up environmental efforts," *Xinhua*, September 12, 2006.
6. *China's Millions: The CIM*, mss 33, citing Francis James's "Scenes in the Famine Districts" article in the journal *China's Millions*, May 1878, 69–70. Unless stated otherwise, all references to the CIM journal *China's Millions* refer to the British edition of that publication.
7. Barber, W.T.A. *David Hill: Missionary and Saint*. Charles H. Kelly: London, 1899, 200.
8. Kaiser. *A History of Protestant Missions in Shanxi*, 11.
9. Edwards. *Fire and Sword in Shanxi*, 1903.
10. Hart. *The Peking Legations*, 7.

11. Quoted in Preston, *The Boxer Rebellion*, 29.
12. Seagrave. *Dragon Lady*, 301.
13. Ibid., 308.
14. Ibid., 301.
15. Ibid., 743–44.
16. Lodwick. *Crusaders Against Opium*, 33–35.
17. Mannerheim. "Preliminary Report," 145.
18. Williamson, H.R. *British Baptists in China: 1845–1952*. London: The Carey Kingsgate Press Ltd., 1957, 49.
19. Mannerheim. "Preliminary Report," 150.
20. Ibid., 150.
21. *China's Millions: The CIM*, mss 68–71.
22. Ibid., mss 13–14, as recorded in the journal *China's Millions*, February 1887, 28.
23. Ibid., mss 13–14; Seagrave. *The Soong Dynasty*, 334; and Spence. "Opium." In *Chinese Roundabout*, 250.
24. Shirk. *China: Fragile Superpower*, 62.
25. Lee. "China's Response to Foreign Investment in Her Mining Industry (1902–1911)," 70.
26. O'Sullivan B. and Chapman S. "Eyes on the Prize: Transnational Tobacco Companies in China 1976–1997," *Tobacco Control* 2000:9, 292.

27. Cochran. *Big business in China: Sino-foreign Rivalry in the Cigarette Industry, 1890–1930*, 19.

CHAPTER 17

1. Mannerheim mentions in a notebook that he hired Li Xuwen in Lanzhou (see Halén, ed., *Sotilastiedustelijana Kiinassa*, 37). In his military report, he referred to him as "an excellent cook." Mannerheim. "Preliminary Report," 77.
2. Mannerheim called him "Weng." An English visitor to Wutai Shan later that summer identified him as Wang Fanglin. See Irving, "Wu-t'ai-shan and the Dalai Lama," 151–163.
3. Laird. *The Story of Tibet*, 146.
4. "Dalai Lama says his successor 'could even be a Finnish woman'," *Helsingi Sanomat*, October 2, 2006.
5. Hedin. *Trans-Himalaya*, 229–230.
6. Shaumian. *Tibet: The Great Game and Tsarist Russia*, 125.
7. Irving. "Wu-t'ai-shan and the Dalai Lama," 154.
8. Ibid., 157.
9. Rockhill, W.W. Letter to President Theodore Roosevelt, dated Jun 30, 1908. Library of Congress, Washington, D.C.
10. Meyer and Brysac. *Tournament of Shadows*, 420–21.

11. Bell. *Portrait of a Dalai Lama*, 81.
12. Irving. "Wu-t'ai-shan and the Dalai Lama," 152.
13. Younghusband. *India and Tibet*, 381–84.
14. *Chinese Public Opinion*, July 21, 1908.
15. Shaumian. *Tibet: The Great Game and Tsarist Russia*, 114.
16. Rockhill, W.W. Letter to President Theodore Roosevelt, dated Jun 30, 1908. Library of Congress, Washington, D.C.
17. *Chinese Public Opinion*, September 29, 1908.
18. Bell. *Portrait of a Dalai Lama*, 79.
19. Shaumian. *Tibet: The Great Game and Tsarist Russia*, 148.
20. *Chinese Public Opinion*, October 22, 1908.
21. "The Political Condition of Tibet," *Chinese Public Opinion*, December 1, 1908.
22. "Government troops defeated," *Chinese Public Opinion*, November 12, 1908.
23. *New York Times*, February 25, 1910.
24. Laird. *The Story of Tibet*, 282.

CHAPTER 18

1. As with many of the sayings of Genghis Khan, the source of this quote isn't definitively known. However, it is widely quoted

among Mongols today. See Campi, Alicia, "Globalization's Impact on Mongolian Identity Issues." Burke, VA: U.S.-Mongolia Advisory Group, August 2005. http://usmongoliagroup. com/article_globalization.htm (accessed on December 20, 2009).

2. Sun. *The International Development of China*, 17–19.

3. Williams. *Beyond Great Walls*, 28; and Gaubatz. *Beyond the Great Wall*, 69.

4. Indian Office Records, British Library. Memo from Ernest Satown, British Legation, Peking, to Lord Curzon, dated February 18, 1904.

5. "Railway loan to be raised," *Chinese Public Opinion*, Nov. 24, 1908; and "Thibetan Affairs," *Chinese Public Opinion*, December 5, 1908.

6. "The Censorship of the Foreign Press," *Chinese Public Opinion*, November 14, 1908.

7. Nuo, You. "Wasteful loans a catalyst for rampant lending craze," *China Daily* (Beijing), *August 28, 2006.*

8. Gaubatz. *Beyond the Great Wall*, 62–70.

9. Lattimore. *The Desert Road to Turkestan*, 20.

10. Fairbank, John K., ed. *The Cambridge History of China: Volume 10, Late Ch'ing, 1800–1911,*

Part 1. Cambridge: Cambridge University Press, 1978, 52–54.

11. Hyer and Heaton. "The Cultural Revolution in Inner Mongolia," 114–28.

12. http://www.helsinki.fi/hub/ articles/?article=36.

13. Mannerheim. "Preliminary Report," 165.

14. Fairbank. *China: A New History*, 352–355.

15. Campbell. *Travels in Mongolia, 1902*, 35.

16. Mannerheim. "Preliminary Report," 166–167.

17. Man. *Genghis Khan*, 309.

18. Zhao, Shijun. "Ordos: A land of opportunity," *China Daily* (Beijing), August 25, 2008. http://www.chinadaily.com.cn/ bw/2008-08/25/content_ 6966939.htm.

19. Massachusetts Institute of Technology. *The Future of Coal*, 63.

20. Bradsher, Keith and David Barboza. "The Energy Challenge: Pollution from Chinese Coal Casts a Global Shadow," *New York Times*, June 11, 2006.

21. Hughes. "The Energy Issue: A More Urgent Problem than Climate Change," 86.

22. The countries I travelled through include Russia, Azerbaijan, Turkmenistan, Uzbekistan, Kyrgyzstan and China. I have included Kazakhstan, a country I did not visit, in my statistics as

well. Oil, gas and coal reserves and consumption statistics can be found on the website of the U.S. Energy Information Administration: http://www.eia.doe.gov.

23. "Kazakhstan expands China oil pipeline link," *China Daily* (Beijing), July 2, 2009. http://www.chinadaily.com. cn/china/2009-07/02/content_8348504.htm (accessed on December 21, 2009). And Wu Jiao and Zhang Jin. "Pipeline pulls region closer, *China Daily* (Beijing), December 15, 2009. http://www.chinadaily.com.cn/ bizchina/2009−12/15/content_ 9178513.htm (accessed on December 21, 2009).

CHAPTER 19

1. Borel. *The New China*, 29–30.
2. Preston. *The Boxer Rebellion*, 15.
3. Ibid., 13.
4. Mannerheim. *Memoirs*, 70.
5. Borel. *The New China*, 79.
6. Fairbank, Feuerwerker, and Twitchett. *The Cambridge History of China: Volume 12, Republican China, 1912–1949, Part 1*, 159.
7. Jägerskiöld. *Gustaf Mannerheim 1906–1917*, 79.
8. Ibid., 80.
9. "Great fire in Legation Quarter," *Chinese Public Opinion*, August 4, 1908.
10. Borel. *The New China*, 42.
11. Ibid., 35−36.

12. Ibid., 43.
13. One American observer estimated that China collected $212 million in revenue from all levels of government in 1907. Financial reform, he estimated, could bring that to $600 million or more without even raising tax rates. "Chinese Finance Run on a System called 'Squeeze,' " *New York Times*, July 5, 1908.
14. "Financial Reforms," *Chinese Public Opinion*, August 1, 1908.
15. Mannerheim clipped a short article that appeared in the August 20, 1908, edition of the newspaper, which stated: "A certain Russian, employing two Chinese as interpreters has been travelling through Shen King, Kansu, Shensi, Honan and Shansi and has taken surveys of many important places. Photographs and sketches have been made freely and he is now reported to be travelling southward." The small newspaper fragment can be found in Mannerheim's records in the National Archives of Finland in Helsinki.
16. Mannerheim. "Preliminary Report," 173.
17. In 1908, China paid £7 million in annual interest payments on foreign loans. "The Question of China's Currency," *Chinese Public Opinion*, October 8, 1908. One pound sterling was roughly

equal to six taels. The debt figure comes from Morse, *The Trade and Administration of the Chinese Empire*, 441.

18. "The Question of China's Currency," *Chinese Public Opinion*, October 8, 1908.

19. "Edict", *Chinese Public Opinion*, October 8, 1908.

20. Wu, Tangfang. "The Awakening of China," *Chinese Public Opinion*, July 9, 1908.

21. Ferguson. *The Ascent of Money*, 286.

22. Ibid., 295.

23. China National Bureau of Statistics. *China Statistical Yearbook* 2008, 263.

24. Rintala. *Four Finns*, 37.

25. Edict of September 1, 1906, quoted in Bell and Woodhead, *The China Year Book*, 353.

26. Cameron. *The Reform Movement in China 1898–1912*, 100.

27. Mackerras. *Modern China*, 214–219.

28. Cameron. *The Reform Movement in China 1898–191*, 103.

29. "Festina Lente," *Chinese Public Opinion*, August 22, 1908.

30. Wu, Tangfang. "The Awakening of China," *Chinese Public Opinion*, July 9, 1908.

31. "The Constitution Regulations," *Chinese Public Opinion*, July 30, 1908.

32. Huenemann. *The Dragon and the Iron Horse*, 76.

33. Statistics from Bell and Woodhead, *The China Year Book*, 199; and Morse, *The Trade and Administration of the Chinese Empire*, 388.

34. Montague and Woodhead. *The China Year Book*, 213.

35. Ibid., 198.

36. Judge. *Print and Politics*, 144.

37. Ibid., 145.

38. "Precautions against Rebellions," *Chinese Public Opinion*, October 20, 1908.

39. Weale. *The Coming Struggle in Eastern Asia*, 567.

40. http://economist.com/surveys/displaystory.cfm?story_id=13063298.

41. Hu. *From the Opium War to the May Fourth Movement*, 421.

42. Huntington. *Political Order in Changing Societies*, 37.

43. Ibid., 47.

44. Ibid., 5.

45. Ni. *The Sea Transport of Tribute Grain and Social Transformation in the Qing Dynasty*.

46. Bell. *Beyond Liberal Democracy*, 172.

47. Ibid., 175.

48. Quoted in Hu, *The Chinese Renaissance*, 311.

49. Spencer, Richard. "Leading Chinese dissident stands by call for freedom of speech," *Daily Telegraph* (London), January 11, 2009. http://www.telegraph.co.uk/

news/worldnews/asia/
china/4217917/Leading-Chi-
nese-dissident-stands-by-call-
for-freedom-of-speech.html.

50. Link, Perry, trans. "China's
Charter 08," *The New York
Review of Books* 56, no. 1
(January 15, 2009). http://
www.nybooks.com/
articles/22210.

51. Mannerheim. *Memoirs*, 74.

52. Jakobson. *A Million Truths*,
2000.

EPILOGUE

1. Mannerheim. Letter to Johan
Mannerheim, dated August
22, 1907, Urumqi. National
Archives of Finland.

2. Mannerheim. *Memoirs*, 71.

3. Jägerskiöld. *Gustaf Mannerheim,
1906–1917*, 80.

4. Manley, ed. *The Trans-Siberian
Railway*, 40.

5. Jägerskiöld. *Gustaf Mannerheim,
1906–1917*, 80.

6. Flandrin. *Les Sept Vies du
Mandarin Français*, 203–225.

7. Jägerskiöld. *Gustaf Mannerheim,
1906–1917*, 110.

8. Ibid., 108–109.

9. Mannerheim. *Memoirs*, 72.

10. Screen. *Mannerheim: The Years
of Preparation*, 83; and Jägerskiöld. *Gustaf Mannerheim,
1906–1917*, 109.

11. Mannerheim. *Memoirs*, 8.

12. Rintala. 22.

13. Ibid., 37.

14. Rodzianko. *Mannerheim*, 32.

15. Ten annexes, which Mannerheim
considered the main results of
his expedition, have yet to be
found in the Russian archives.
According to Harry Halén,
recent rumours suggest that "the
material may yet be [found] in
the Military Archives in Moscow." Halén. "Mannerheim and
Military Intelligence in China
1906–1908," 68–79.

16. Mannerheim. Letter to Sven
Hedin, dated June 12, 1937.
National Archives of Finland.

17. Halén. *Analytical Index*, 6.

18. Letters from Sven Hedin to
Gustaf Mannerheim, circa 1940
and May 27, 1950. National
Archives of Finland.

19. Selén. "Mannerheim's
Personality," 212.

SELECTED BIBLIOGRAPHY

Akiner, Shirin. *Violence in Andijan, 13 May 2005: An Independent Assessment.* Washington, DC/Stockholm: Central Asia-Caucasus Institute, 2005.

Avetaranian, John. *A Muslim Who Became A Christian: The Story of John Avetaranian, An Autobiography 1861–1919.* Completed after death by Richard Schäfer and translated from German by John Bechard. Hertford: Authors Online Ltd., 2002.

Ayers, William. *Chang Chih-tung and Educational Reform in China.* Cambridge, MA: Harvard University Press, 1971.

Bailey, Paul J. *Reform the People: Changing Attitudes Towards Popular Education in Early Twentieth-Century China.* Vancouver: University of British Columbia Press, 1990.

Baker, Peter and Susan Glasser. *Kremlin Rising: Vladimir Putin's Russia and the End of Revolution.* New York: Scribner, 2005.

Bell, Charles. *Portrait of a Dalai Lama: The Life and Times of the Great Thirteenth.* London: Wisdom, 1987.

Bell, Daniel A. *Beyond Liberal Democracy: Political Thinking for an East Asian Context.* Princeton, NJ: Princeton University Press, 2006.

Bell, H.T. Montague and H.G.W. Woodhead. *The China Year Book.* London: George Routledge & Sons, 1912.

Bergsten, C. Fred, Bates Gill, Nicholas R. Lardy and Derek J. Mitchell. *China's Rise: Challenges and Opportunities.* Washington, DC: Peterson Institute of International Economics, 2008.

Bey, Essad. *Blood and Oil in the Orient.* New York: Simon and Schuster, 1932.

Borel, Henri. *The New China: A Traveller's Impressions.* London: T. F. Unwin, 1912.

Bovingdon, Gardner. *Autonomy in Xinjiang: Han Nationalist Imperatives and Uyghur Discontent.* Washington, DC: East-West Center Washington, 2004.

———with Nabijan Tursun. "Contested Histories." In *Xinjiang: China's Muslim Borderland,* edited by S. Frederick Starr, 353–374. Armonk, NY: M.E. Sharpe, 2004.

Broomhall, Marshall. *The Chinese Empire: A General and Mission Survey.* London: Morgan & Scott, 1906.

Cameron, Meribeth E. *The Reform Movement in China 1898–1912.* New York: Octagon Books, 1963.

Campbell, C.W. *Travels in Mongolia, 1902.* London: Tim Coates, 2000.

Chang, Jung and Jon Halliday. *Mao: The Unknown Story.* New York: Knopf, 2005.

Chang Chih-tung. *China's Only Hope: An Appeal,* translated by Samuel I. Woodbridge. London: Oliphant, Anderson & Ferrier, 1901.

Chesneaux, Jean. *Peasant Revolts in China, 1840–1949.* London: Thames and Hudson, 1973.

China National Bureau of Statistics. *China Statistical Yearbook.* Beijing: China Statistics Press, 2006.

China National Bureau of Statistics. *China Statistical Yearbook.* Beijing: China Statistics Press, 2008.

Chinese Public Opinion. Peking, May 1908–Jan. 1909.

Cochran, Sherman. *Big Business in China: Sino-Foreign Rivalry in the Cigarette Industry, 1890–1930.* Cambridge, MA: Harvard University Press, 1980.

Cole, Benjamin, ed. *Conflict, Terrorism and the Media in Asia.* New York: Routledge, 2006.

Colquhoun, Archibald R. *China in Transformation.* New York: Harper & Brothers Publisher, 1899.

Conrad, Joseph. *The Secret Agent.* Hertfordshire, U.K.: Wordsworth Editions, 1993.

Davis, Fei-Ling. *Primitive Revolutionaries of China: A Study of Secret Societies of the Late Nineteenth Century.* Honolulu: University Press of Hawaii, 1977.

Deng, Xiaoping. *Selected Works of Deng Xiaoping: Volume II (1982–1992).* Beijing: Foreign Language Press, 1994.

D'Ollone, Henri. *In Forbidden China: The D'Ollone Mission 1906–1909,* translated by Bernard Miall. London: T. Fisher Unwin, 1912.

Edwards, F.H. *Fire and Sword in Shanxi: The Story of the Martyrdom of Foreigners and Chinese Christians.* London: Oliphant Anderson & Ferrier, 1903.

Fairbank, John King. *China: A New History*. Cambridge, MA: Harvard University Press, 1992.

———, Albert Feuerwerker and Denis Twitchett. *The Cambridge History of China: Volume 12, Republican China, 1912–1949, Part 1*. Cambridge, U.K.: Cambridge University Press, 1983.

Ferguson, Niall. *The Ascent of Money: A Financial History of the World*. New York: Penguin, 2008.

———. *The War of the World: Twentieth-Century Conflict and the Descent of the West*. New York: Penguin, 2006.

Figes, Orlando. *A People's Tragedy: The Russian Revolution 1891–1924*. London: Jonathan Cape, 1996.

Flandrin, Philippe. *Les Sept Vies du Mandarin Français: Paul Pelliot ou la Passion de l'Orient*. Paris: Rocher, 2008.

Fleming, Peter. *News from Tartary: A Journey from Peking to Kashmir*. New York: Marlboro Press, 1999. Originally published in 1936.

Forbes Manz, Beatrice. "Central Asian Uprisings in the Nineteenth Century: Ferghana Under the Russians." *Russian Review* 46 (1987), 267–281.

Fraser, David. *The Marches of Hindustan: The Record of a Journey in Thibet, Trans-Himalayan India, Chinese Turkestan, Russian Turkestan, and Persia*. London: William Blackwood and Sons, 1907.

Friedman, Thomas L. "The First Law of Petropolitics." *Foreign Policy*, May/June 2006, http://www.foreignpolicy.com/articles/2006/04/25/the_first_law_of_petropolitics (accessed on December 30, 2009).

Gaubatz, Piper Rae. *Beyond the Great Wall: Urban Form and Transformation on the Chinese Frontiers*. Palo Alto, CA: Stanford University Press, 1996.

Gifford, Rob. *China Road: A Journey Into the Future of a Rising Power*. Toronto: Random House, 2008.

Global Witness. *It's a Gas: Funny Business in the Turkmen-Ukraine Gas Trade*. London: Global Witness, 2006.

Government of India. *Military Report on Kashgaria (Confidential)*. Simla: Division of the Chief of the Staff, Intelligence Branch, 1907.

Halén, Harry. *An Analytical Index to C.G. Mannerheim's "Across Asia from West to East in 1906–1908."* Helsinki: Finno-Ugrian Society, 2004.

———. "Baron Mannerheim's Hunt for Ancient Central Asian Manuscripts." In *C.G. Mannerheim in Central Asia 1906–1908*, edited by Petteri Koskikallio and Asko Lehmuskallio, 47–52. Helsinki: National Board of Antiquities, 1999.

————. "Mannerheim and Military Intelligence in China 1906–1900." In *Mannerheim: An Officer of the Imperial Russian Army, Marshal of Independent Finland,* edited by Timo Vihavainen, 68–89. Helsinki: St. Petersburg Foundation of Finland, 2005.

————. "Mannerheim and the French Expedition of Paul Pelliot." In *Aspects of Research into Central Asian Buddhism: In Memoriam Kogi Kudara,* edited by Peter Zieme, 33–68. Turnhout: Brepols Publishers, 2008.

————, ed. *Sotilastiedustelijana Kiinassa, C.G. Mannerheimin muistiinpanoja 1906–08.* Helsinki: Unholan, 1994.

———— and Bent Lerbaek Pedersen. *C.G. Mannerheim's Chinese Pantheon.* Helsinki: Finno-Ugrian Society, 1993.

Hart, Robert. *The Peking Legations: A National Uprising and International Episode.* Shanghai: Kelly and Walsh, Limited, 1900.

Hedin, Sven. *Across the Gobi Desert.* New York: E.P. Dutton & Company, 1933.

————. *Germany and World Peace.* London: Hutchinson & Co., 1937.

————. *My Life as an Explorer.* New York: Kodansha International, 1996.

————. *The Silk Road.* New York: E.P. Dutton and Company, 1936.

————. *Trans-Himalaya: Discoveries and Adventures in Tibet.* London: Macmillan and Co., 1909.

Henry, J.D. *Baku: An Eventful History.* London: Archibald Constable & Co., 1906.

————. *Oil Fuel and the Empire.* London: Bradbury, Agnew, 1908.

Hopkirk, Peter. *Foreign Devils on the Silk Road.* Amherst, MA.: University of Massachusetts Press, 1980.

————. *The Great Game: The Struggle for Empire in Central Asia.* New York: Kodansha International, 1990.

————. *Setting the East Ablaze: On Secret Service in Bolshevik Asia.* Oxford: Oxford University Press, 1984.

Hsiao, Liang-lin. *China's Foreign Trade Statistics 1864–1949.* Cambridge, MA: Harvard University Press, 1974.

Hu, Sheng. *From the Opium War to the May Fourth Movement.* Beijing: Foreign Language Press, 1991.

Hu, Shih. *The Chinese Renaissance.* Beijing: Foreign Language Teaching and Research Press, 2000.

Huenemann, Ralph William. *The Dragon and the Iron Horse: The Economics of Railroads in China 1876–1937,* Cambridge, MA: Harvard University Press, 1984.

Hughes, J. David. "The Energy Issue: A More Urgent Problem than Climate Change." In *Carbon Shift: How the Twin Crises of Oil Depletion and Climate Change Will Define the Future,* edited by Thomas Homer-Dixon, 59–98. Toronto: Random House, 2009.

Hultvall, John. *Mission and Change in Eastern Turkestan.* An authorized translation of the original Swedish text, *Mission och revolution i Central-asien: Svenska Missionsförbundets mission i Ostturkestan 1892–1938.* Renfrewshire: Heart of Asia Ministries, 1987.

Huntington, Samuel P. *Political Order in Changing Societies.* New Haven, CT: Yale University Press, 1968.

Hyer, Paul and William Heaton. "The Cultural Revolution in Inner Mongolia." *China Quarterly* 36 (December 1968), 114–128.

International Crisis Group. *Kyrgyzstan: A Faltering State.* Asia Report 109 (December 16, 2005).

———. *Uzbekistan: The Andijon Uprising.* Asia Briefing 38 (May 25, 2005).

Irving, Christopher. "Wu-t'ai-shan and the Dalai Lama." *New China Review* 1, no. 2 (May 1919), 151–163.

Jägerskiöld, Stig. *Den unge Mannerheim.* Helsinki: H. Schildt, 1964.

———. *Gustaf Mannerheim, 1906–1917.* Helsinki: Albert Bonniers Förlag, 1965.

———. *Mannerheim: Marshal of Finland.* Minneapolis, MN: University of Minnesota Press, 1987.

Jakobson, Linda. *A Million Truths: A Decade in China.* New York: M. Evans and Company, Inc., 2000.

Janhunen, Juha. "Mannerheim at Labrang." In *Handbook of Conference & Field Investigation: The International Symposium for the Study of Mannerheim's Journey to Xinjiang & Field Investigation* hosted by the Research Centre for China's Borderland History and Geography and Helsinki University, September 28, 2006, 80–88.

Judge, Joan. *Print and Politics: "Shibao" and the Culture of Reform in Late Qing China.* Palo Alto, CA: Stanford University Press, 1996.

Kaiser, Andrew T. *A History of Protestant Missions in Shanxi.* An unpublished partial manuscript provided by the author, 2006.

Kamalova, Nozima, Vitali Vitaliev, and Acacia Shields, eds. *Front Line Central Asia: Threats, Attacks, Arrests and Harassment of Human Rights Defenders.* Dublin: Front Line, 2004.

Kipling, Rudyard. *Kim.* New York: Penguin Books, 2000.

Kuo, Ping Wen. *The Chinese System of Public Education.* New York: Columbia University, 1914.

Kurmanjan Datka Charitable Foundation. *Tsarina of the Mountains: Kurmanjan and Her Times.* Bishkek: Ilim, 2002.

Laird, Thomas. *The Story of Tibet: Conversations with the Dalai Lama.* New York: Grove Press, 2007.

Laqueur, Walter. *A History of Terrorism.* New York: Little, Brown, 1997.

Lattimore, Owen. *The Desert Road to Turkestan.* New York: Kodansha International, 1995.

Lee, En-Han. "China's Response to Foreign Investment in Her Mining Industry (1902–1911)." *Journal of Asian Studies* 28, no. 1. (November 1968), 55–76.

Lehmusoksa, Risto and Ritva Lehmusoksa. *Dining with Marshal Mannerheim.* Helsinki: Ajatus Kirjat, 2005.

Lehtinen, Ildikó. "The Mannerheim Collection of Central Asia Artefacts at the Museum of Cultures in Helsinki." In *Mannerheim: An Officer of the Imperial Russian Army, Marshal of Independent Finland,* edited by Timo Vihavainen, 90–95. Helsinki: St. Petersburg Foundation of Finland, 2005.

———. "Plait Pendants in the Marshal Mannerheim Collection." In *C.G. Mannerheim in Central Asia 1906–1908,* edited by Petteri Koskikallio and Asko Lehmuskallio, 95–112. Helsinki: National Board of Antiquities, 1999.

Leung, Edwin Pak-wah, ed. *Political Leaders of Modern China: A Biographical Dictionary.* London: Greenwood Press, 2002.

Lincoln, W. Bruce. *Sunlight at Midnight: St. Petersburg and the Rise of Modern Russia.* New York: Basic Books, 2000.

Lodwick, Kathleen L. *Crusaders Against Opium: Protestant Missionaries in China, 1874–1917.* Lexington, KY: University Press of Kentucky, 1996.

Lovell, Julia. *The Great Wall: China Against the World 1000 BC–AD 2000.* London: Atlantic Books, 2006.

Mackerras, Colin. *Modern China: A Chronology from 1842 to the Present.* London: Thames and Hudson, 1982.

MacMillan, Margaret. *The Uses and Abuses of History.* Toronto: Viking Canada, 2008.

Man, John. *Genghis Khan: Life, Death, and Resurrection.* New York: Macmillan, 2007.

Manley, Deborah, ed. *The Trans-Siberian Railway: A Traveller's Anthology.* Century: London, 1988.

Mannerheim, C.G. *Across Asia from West to East in 1906–1908.* Edited by Harry Halén. Helsinki: Otava, 2008.

———. *Memoirs of Marshal Mannerheim.* Translated by Count Eric Lewenhaupt. New York: E.P. Dutton and Co., 1954.

———. "Preliminary Report on the Journey Undertaken by Imperial Order Across Chinese Turkestan and the Northern Provinces of China to Peking in 1906–07 and 1908." In *Collection of Geographical, Topographical and Statistical Materials for Asia 81.* St. Petersburg: Military Publishing House, 1909. (Original published in Russian and translated by Eric Walberg and Anatoli Koroteyev for author).

———. "A Visit to the Sarö and Shera Yögurs." *Journal de la Société Finno-Ougrienne* 27 (1911).

Marshall, Alexey. *The Russian General Staff and Asia, 1800–1917.* London: Routledge, 2006.

———. "Russian Military Intelligence, 1905–1917: The Untold Story behind Tsarist Russia in the First World War." *War in History* 11, no. 4 (2004), 393–423.

Martin, W. P. *The Awakening of China.* 1906. http://www.gutenberg.org/etext/15125 (accessed December 30, 2009).

Marvin, Charles. *The Region of the Eternal Fire.* London: W.H. Allen and Co., 1884.

Massachusetts Institute of Technology. *The Future of Coal: Options for a Carbon-Constrained World.* 2007. http://web.mit.edu/coal.

Meyer, Karl E. and Shareen Blair Brysac. *Tournament of Shadows: The Great Game and the Race for Empire in Central Asia.* Washington, DC: Counterpoint, 1999.

Miettinen, Jukka O. "Terracottas from Khotan in the Mannerheim collection." In *C.G. Mannerheim in Central Asia 1906–1908*, edited by Petteri Koskikallio and Asko Lehmuskallio, 113–116. Helsinki: National Board of Antiquities, 1999.

Millward, James. *Violent Separatism in Xinjiang: A Critical Assessment.* Washington, DC: East-West Center Washington, 2004.

——— and Peter C. Perdue. "Political and Cultural History of the Xinjiang Region through the Late Nineteenth Century." In *Xinjiang: China's Muslim Borderland*, edited by S. Frederick Starr, 27–62. Armonk, NY: M.E. Sharpe, 2004.

Mirsky, Jeannette. *Sir Aurel Stein: Archaeological Explorer.* Chicago: University of Chicago Press, 1977.

Morse, Hosea Ballou. *The Trade and Administration of the Chinese Empire.* New York: Longmans, Green, and Co., 1908.

Murray, Craig. *Murder in Samarkand: A British Ambassador's Controversial Defiance of Tyranny in the War on Terror*. London: Mainstream, 2006.

Ni, Yuping. *The Sea Transport of Tribute Grain and Social Transformation in the Qing Dynasty*. PhD diss., Peking University, 2003.

Norrback, Märtha. *A Gentleman's Home: The Museum of Gustaf Mannerheim, Marshal of Finland*. Helsinki: Otava, 2001.

Pelliot, Paul. *Carnets de route, 1906–1908*. Paris: Les Indes savantes, 2008.

Pereira, George. "A Visit to Labrang Monastery, South-West Kan-su, North-West China." *Geographical Journal* 40, no. 4 (October 1912), 418.

Preston, Diana. *The Boxer Rebellion: The Dramatic Story of China's War on Foreigners That Shook the World in the Summer of 1900*. New York: Berkley Books, 1999.

Reiss, Tom. *The Orientalist: Solving the Mystery of a Strange and Dangerous Life*. New York: Random House, 2005.

Rintala, Marvin. *Four Finns: Political Profiles*. Berkeley: University of California Press, 1969.

Rodzianko, Paul. *Mannerheim: An Intimate Picture of a Great Soldier and Statesman*. London: Jarrolds, 1940.

Roy, Olivier. *The New Central Asia: The Creation of Nations*. New York: New York University Press, 2000.

Ruotsila, Markku. "The Churchill-Mannerheim Collaboration in the Russian Intervention, 1919–20." *Slavonic and Eastern European Review* 80, no. 1 (January 2002), 1–20.

Said, Kurban. *Ali and Nino*. New York: Vintage, 2000.

Sandberg, Peter. "Mannerheim the Photographer." In *Handbook of Conference & Field Investigation: The International Symposium for the Study of Mannerheim's Journey to Xinjiang & Field Investigation* hosted by the Research Centre for China's Borderland History and Geography and Helsinki University, September 28, 2006.

Screen, J.E.O. *Mannerheim: The Years of Preparation*. Vancouver: University of British Columbia Press, 1993.

Seagrave, Sterling. *Dragon Lady: The Life and Legend of the Last Empress of China*. New York: Vintage, 1993.

———. *The Soong Dynasty*. New York: Harper Perennial, 1986.

See, Chong Su. *The Foreign Trade of China*. New York: Columbia University, 1919.

Selén, Kari. "Mannerheim's Personality." In *Mannerheim: An Officer of the Imperial Russian Army, Marshal of Independent Finland,* edited by Timo Vihavainen, 208–213. Helsinki: St. Petersburg Foundation of Finland, 2005.

Shaumian, Tatiana. *Tibet: The Great Game and Tsarist Russia.* New York: Oxford University Press, 2000.

Shirk, Susan L. *China: Fragile Superpower.* Oxford: Oxford University Press, 2007.

Skrine, C. P. and Pamela Nightingale. *Macartney at Kashgar: New Light on British, Chinese and Russian Activities in Sinkiang, 1890–1918.* London: Methuen, 1973.

Slobodník, Martin. "Destruction and Revival: The Fate of the Tibetan Buddhist Monastery Labrang in the People's Republic of China." *Religion, State and Society* 32, no. 1 (March 2004), 7–19.

Spence, Jonathan D. *Chinese Roundabout: Essays in History and Culture.* New York: Norton, 1993.

Stein, Aurel. *Ruins of Desert Cathay: Personal Narrative of Explorations in Central Asia and Western Most China.* London: Benjamin Blom, 1968.

Steyn, Mark. "One-Man Stan: Saparmurat Niyazov (1940–2006)." *The Atlantic Monthly,* January 2007, http://www.theatlantic.com/magazine/archive/2007/03/one-man-stan/5631/ (accessed on December 30, 2009).

Sun, Yat-sen. *The International Development of China.* New York: G. P. Putnam's Sons, 1929. Originally published in 1922.

Theroux, Paul. "The Golden Man: Saparmurat Niyazov's Reign of Insanity." *The New Yorker,* May 28, 2007, 54–65.

Tolf, Robert W. *The Russian Rockefellers: The Saga of the Nobel Family and the Russian Oil Industry.* Stanford, CA: Hoover Institution Press, 1976.

Trotter, William R. *The Winter War: The Russo-Finnish War of 1939–40.* London: Aurum Press, 2002.

Tuñón, Max. *Internal Labour Migration in China: Features and Responses.* Beijing: International Labour Organization, 2006.

Tyler, Christian. *Wild West China: The Taming of Xinjiang.* London: John Murray, 2003.

Vihavainen, Timo, ed. *Mannerheim: An Officer of the Imperial Russian Army, Marshal of Independent Finland.* Helsinki: St. Petersburg Foundation of Finland, 2005.

Villari, Luigi. *The Fire and Sword in the Caucasus.* London: T.F. Unwin, 1906.

Wagel, Srinivas R. *Finance in China.* New York: Garland Publishing Inc., 1980.

Walravens, Hartmut, ed. *Paul Pelliot (1878–1945): His Life and Works—A Bibliography*. Bloomington, IN: Indiana University Research Institute for Inner Asian Studies, 2001.

Warner, Oliver. *Marshal Mannerheim and the Finns*. Helsinki: Otava, 1967.

Weale, B.L. Putnam. *The Coming Struggle in Eastern Asia*. London: Macmillan and Co. Ltd., 1908.

Wiemer, Calla. "The Economy of Xinjiang." In *Xinjiang: China's Muslim Borderland*, edited by S. Frederick Starr, 163–189. Armonk, NY: M.E. Sharpe, 2004.

Williams, Dee Mack. *Beyond Great Walls: Environment, Identity, and Development on the Chinese Grasslands of Inner Mongolia*. Palo Alto, CA: Stanford University Press, 2002.

Winchester, Simon. *The Man Who Loved China: The Fantastic Story of the Eccentric Scientist Who Unlocked the Mysteries of the Middle Kingdom*. New York: HarperCollins, 2008.

Wood, Frances. *The Silk Road: Two Thousand Years in the Heart of Asia*. Berkeley: University of California Press, 2002.

Wou, Odoric Y. *Mobilizing the Masses: Building Revolution in Henan*. Palo Alto, CA: Stanford University Press, 1994.

Wright, Tim. *Coal Mining in China's Economy and Society 1895–1937*. Cambridge, U.K.: Cambridge University Press, 1984.

———. "Growth of the Modern Chinese Coal Industry: An Analysis of Supply and Demand, 1896–1936." *Modern China* 7, no. 3 (July 1981), 317–350.

Wu, Aitchen K. *Turkisan Tumult*. London: Methuen & Co., 1940.

Wu, Jinglian. *Understanding and Interpreting Chinese Economic Reform*. Mason, OH: Thomson, 2005.

Yergin, Daniel. *The Prize: The Epic Quest for Oil, Money and Power*. New York: Simon & Schuster, 1991.

Younghusband, Francis. *India and Tibet*. London: Asia Educational Service, 1993.

Zhou, Kate Xiao. *How the Farmers Changed China: Power of the People*. Boulder, CO: Westview Press Inc., 1996.

INDEX